SINGAPORE'S ECONOMIC DEVELOPMENT

Retrospection and Reflections

World Scientific Series on Singapore's 50 Years of Nation-Building

The complete list of titles in the series can be found at
http://www.worldscientific.com/series/wss50ynb

World Scientific Series on
Singapore's 50 Years of Nation-Building

SINGAPORE'S ECONOMIC DEVELOPMENT

Retrospection and Reflections

Editor

Linda Y. C. Lim
University of Michigan, USA

World Scientific

NEW JERSEY · LONDON · SINGAPORE · BEIJING · SHANGHAI · HONG KONG · TAIPEI · CHENNAI · TOKYO

Published by

World Scientific Publishing Co. Pte. Ltd.
5 Toh Tuck Link, Singapore 596224
USA office: 27 Warren Street, Suite 401-402, Hackensack, NJ 07601
UK office: 57 Shelton Street, Covent Garden, London WC2H 9HE

Library of Congress Cataloging-in-Publication Data
Singapore's economic development : retrospection and reflections / edited by Linda Y.C. Lim (University of Michigan, USA).
    pages cm. -- (World Scientific series on Singapore's 50 years of nation-building)
  Includes bibliographical references.
  ISBN 978-9814723459 (hardcover) -- ISBN 978-9814723466 (pbk.)
  1. Economic development--Singapore. 2. Singapore--Economic policy. 3. Singapore--Economic conditions.
I. Lim, Linda, editor. II. Lee, Soo Ann, 1939–   Governance and economic change in Singapore. Container of (work):
  HC445.8.S575 2016
  338.95957--dc23

                2015034539

British Library Cataloguing-in-Publication Data
A catalogue record for this book is available from the British Library.

Cover image: Singapore Chinese Clan Associations Collection, Courtesy of National Archives of Singapore

In-house Editor: Li Hongyan

Typeset by Stallion Press
Email: enquiries@stallionpress.com

Printed in Singapore

Contents

CHAPTER 1

Fifty Years of Development in the Singapore Economy: An Introductory Review

Linda Y. C. Lim

The chapters in this volume provide a retrospective analysis of Singapore's economic development during the past 50 years, from the perspectives of different policy domains. This introductory review highlights common themes among the chapters, chiefly the primacy of economic growth in driving social as well as economic policies, the interconnection between different policy arenas, the persistence of a particular development model despite sharp changes in policy direction, and the dominant role of the state. The authors collectively conclude that economic policy was both innovative and effective in the first two to three decades of independence, particularly in simultaneously delivering on both rapid economic growth and improved social welfare. In more recent decades, economic growth and social welfare for a significant minority of residents have begun to diverge. Looking ahead, there appears to be a consensus that slower GDP growth, higher productivity, a relative shift from manufacturing to services and from a global to a regional market orientation, and more vibrant and innovative local private entrepreneurs, are necessary for continued economic development. There is also consensus that public policy must pay greater attention to directly meeting the growing social needs of the population, especially the poor, low-income, elderly and other vulnerable groups.

1. Introduction

Singapore's economic success has for decades attracted attention throughout the developed and developing world, from scholars, policy-makers and business practitioners alike. This Special Issue to commemorate 50 years of Singapore's existence as an independent political and economic entity aims to bring together the analyses of economists who have studied various dimensions of this success, many of us for decades. The goal of this introductory review essay is to holistically explore the linkages between the different chapters collected in this issue, with a view to gaining a deeper understanding of the development process Singapore's economy has undergone in the last half century. The essay is organized thematically — beginning with a statement of the economic policies and strategies deployed, turning next to an evaluation of the outcomes, and concluding with current challenges, and prospects for the future.

2. The Policies

Singapore's economy is often erroneously characterized in the popular international media as having developed from nothing — even "a malarial swamp" (Jacobson, 2010) or "a mosquito-infested seaside village" (Cohen, 2015) — at independence. On the contrary, Lee Soo Ann reminds us in his chapter on governance and economic change that Singapore well before independence was already an established commercial and financial hub for Southeast Asia and the British Empire, the second richest place in Asia after Japan, and one of the world's busiest seaports. Its policies of free trade, capital and labor flows had all been in place since the modern city's founding by Stamford Raffles in 1819, it had a convertible currency based on the British pound sterling, with a British legal system, modern transport and communications infrastructure and public services including education and healthcare, and English as the common language. Continuation of the colonial-era "openness" aspect of Singapore's economy after independence is explored in Chia Siow Yue's chapter on international trade and investment, and Tilak Abeysinghe's chapter on lessons from Singapore's experience for other developing economies. Even iconic Singapore social policies like Housing Development Board (HDB) public housing, discussed here by Sock-Yong Phang, and Central Provident Fund (CPF) savings for retirement, analyzed by Ngee-Choon Chia, and its unusual currency board system, reviewed by Peter Wilson, had their origins in colonial-era policies and institutions.

A second common mis-characterization is that Singapore's post-independence rapid growth was the result of "laissez-faire economics". In fact, it was only the laissez-passer policies of the British colonial era that were retained by the successors of Raffles, and these were pursued to their practical and logical extremes when Singapore began to enter into a proliferation of free trade agreements (FTAs) with its major trading partners in the 2000s (S. Y. Chia). By the early 1950s, laissez-faire economics had left the colonial port city with a multi-racial immigrant population growing too rapidly for the city's inadequate housing stock to shelter, and for its stagnant entrepot trade-based economy to absorb — resulting in 12% unemployment, and periodic labor and urban unrest, including race riots. As Lee notes, a governance change was required to empower a local government to deal with these problems. Following self-government in 1959, even before merger with Malaysia in 1963, the PAP-led legislative assembly established a statutory board, the HDB, to build high-rise flats in which city slum-dwellers could be relocated (Phang). The government also established the Economic Development Board (EDB) to develop industrial infrastructure and promote investment to create jobs (S. Y. Chia). There were early investments in education and in health, especially family planning to lower fertility and slow population growth, as Yap Mui Teng and Christopher Gee discuss in their chapter on demographics and population policy. Intervention in the economy was not, however, limited to the provision of public and merit goods, or to the earlier post-independence years. As Tan Kim Song and Manu Bhaskaran show, the role of government in modern Singapore has been both "more extensive and more intrusive" up to the present day.

Giving priority to the development of social infrastructure before attracting private investment was a hallmark of independent Singapore's early public policies, reflecting both the city's very obvious social needs at the time, and the PAP's own social democratic ideology, influenced by post-war Labor parties in the U.K. and western Europe. Where Singapore innovated was in how it funded social services and infrastructure construction.

This was done through expansion of the British-era CPF involving mandatory contributions by both employers and employees toward a retirement portfolio for employees (N. C. Chia). Singapore also innovated in allowing citizens to use their CPF retirement savings to purchase housing — initially just the "public housing" units built and managedby HDB, later extended to include private housing. The HDB is an unusual public-private hybrid model, with residents enabled to buy their flats, using their CPF savings to partially pay for mortgages. To ensure national security, which Abeysinghe considers one of the important noneconomic factors underlying Singapore's economic success, compulsory military service was introduced for males. Founding Prime Minister Lee Kuan Yew believed that national servicemen needed to have an ownership stake in their society, to motivate them to fight for the nation, hence the policy of encouraging near universal home-ownership.

Fiscal and monetary policies, the bedrock of most governments' economic policies, are also unusual, if not unique to Singapore. Mukul Asher, Azad Singh Bali and Chang Yee Kwan argue that the raison d'etre of public financial management is to serve Singapore's "location-based growth strategy" essentially through a low tax regime. The public sector has a much larger role in the economy than reflected in the budget, with extensive use of unconventional nontax revenues to fund off-budget economic activities, even while national spending on healthcare and pensions makes very limited use of social risk pooling. Persistently large budget surpluses over many decades, as well as high domestic savings due to the CPF and other factors, have resulted in large balance of payments surpluses, which have been continuously added to the foreign exchange reserves. As Wilson explains, Singapore's monetary policy since 1981 does not employ conventional interest rate management, given the extreme openness of the economy. Instead, it is aimed at managing the exchange rate against an undisclosed basket of currencies, with the primary aim of controlling inflation. Over time, this has resulted in currency appreciation, in both nominal and real terms. A portion of the income earned on the reserves, managed by the Government of Singapore Investment Corporation (GIC), is returned to the budget for public expenditure. Tan and Bhaskaran further argue that the accumulation of public surpluses has been a goal of government policy, and not merely a means to developmental ends.

Pang Eng Fong and Linda Lim's chapter on labor and productivity characterizes Singapore's development model as "state-driven, multinational-led, export-oriented and manufacturing-focused". Lacking a domestic market or natural resources, foreign companies have been attracted here after independence by investment incentives (S. Y. Chia), and by the liberal import of low-, middle- and high-skilled foreign labor. Where multinationals were hesitant to enter, the investment gaps have been filled by the state itself, which gave rise to the government-linked companies (GLCs) that have not only survived to the present day, but flourished. Tan and Bhaskaran further characterize the post-2000 phase of Singapore's economic growth as "foreign talent driven", in contrast to the earlier "foreign investment driven" phase.

Taken together, all these elements of public policy in Singapore are geared first, to facilitate economic growth through subsidies and a compliant workforce for foreign corporations (Tan and Bhaskaran; Pang and Lim), and second, to ensure social welfare in a manner consistent with an overarching philosophy of self-reliance for individuals and households, as argued by Irene Ng in her chapter on social welfare policy, both under the aegis of a highly interventionist state.

Several common themes link the chapters in this volume. First, nearly all the papers note the primacy of economic growth in government policy, not just in the early years of high unemployment, but throughout the republic's fifty-year history, with high growth rates targeted well beyond the income threshold at which GDP growth tends to slow down in developed countries. Besides industrial policy, social policy was also harnessed to this end. Thus, housing and industrial estates were well integrated as a matter of policy, the object being to ensure that affordable housing kept factory wages low (Lee; Pang and Lim), while employers' CPF contributions and rentals on state-owned industrial estates were reduced in economic recessions to lower business costs (N. C. Chia; S. Y. Chia; Pang and Lim; Tan and Bhaskaran). Concurrently, a liberal foreign worker policy lowered labor costs directly and increased employer flexibility (Pang and Lim), and acted as a buffer against local unemployment in downturns. Public finances were oriented toward providing incentives and subsidies to investors (Asher, Bali and Kwan; Tan and Bhaskaran), while also catalyzing the "efficiency infrastructure" and "development welfare" (Abeysinghe) so essential to long-term growth. "Productivist" social welfare policies focused on human capital development for economic growth (Ng), while the energy and environmental policies which Chang Youngho discusses were also motivated by growth — directly through investments in petroleum refineries and energy efficiency measures to improve competitiveness, and indirectly through creating a livable urban environment to attract foreign investment and talent.

A second and related theme is the interconnection between different policy arenas which increased the effectiveness of individual policies. The best known of these is the mobilization of individuals' CPF savings to finance their publicly-constructed housing, thus quickly solving a major housing problem while avoiding budget deficits, besides creating a home-ownership society, and motivating national service (N. C. Chia; Phang). The use of racial quotas in public housing estates also helped to create community among different races and religions, fostering national unity and preventing the formation of ethnic ghettoes and voting blocs. HDB, CPF and labor policy also served industrial policy conducted largely by the EDB. Housing, education and health policy — discrimination in the allocation of flats and school places, and pricing of healthcare — were used to promote family planning during the anti-natalist years of the 1960s and 1970s, while budget measures such as tax reliefs and child payments were employed during the pro-natalist decades that followed (Yap and Gee).

Third, as might be expected during a period as long as fifty years, there were sharp changes in policy direction, but within the same development model and institutional infrastructure. HDB's goals moved from dealing with a chronic housing shortage and providing affordable basic housing in the 1960s through the 1980s, to upgrading, market deregulation and asset enhancement after 1990, with some return to a focus on affordability in very recent years, especially for young couples and the elderly. CPF moved quickly from retirement savings to mortgage financing, later adding nonhousing investments, healthcare and education financing to its allowable expenditures. Investment incentives and industrial policy moved progressively up the technological ladder from labor- to capital- and skill-intensive, while foreign labor policy swung back and forth between heavy dependence and tightening. Perhaps most dramatically, population policy that was emphatically anti-natalist in the 1960s and 1970s was totally reversed in the 1980s to encourage higher fertility. There was also a switch from public provision to partial privatization of public and social services, reflecting an ideological shift from state to individual responsibility for social welfare that has recently begun to shift back.

Fourth, through all of Singapore's developmental stages, the dominant role of the state in the economy was maintained and even expanded, contrary to the standard economic policy prescription that validates state intervention only for developing countries and in the case of market failure such as externalities. Rather than the state retreating with the development of markets and institutions and rising incomes, state and state-linked entities have reached into ever more areas of public and even private life, including marriage and procreation, and the provision of commercial goods and services, including commercial property development, transportation, supermarkets,

insurance, and financial market activities, which in other developed market economies would be the purview of private enterprise. From a governance perspective, it is
likely that strong central executive control, an undivided legislature, and what
Abeysinghe calls "politicians with high opportunity cost" facilitated swift decision-
making and policy implementation by not just the civil service, but also statutory
boards, GLCs, the National Trades Union Congress (NTUC) and other state-linked
units and their numerous private sector subcontractors. Tan and Bhaskaran emphasize the importance of a pervasive multi-faceted state apparatus, under long-lasting
single-party political control, in enabling the rapid mass mobilization of resources for
economic growth during different developmental phases.

3. Policy Outcomes

There is no question that well-designed policies, and the governance system that
underlay them, succeeded in bringing about very quick results in almost every policy
domain, and in so doing took Singapore into the league of developed economies.
First, the overriding goal of high GDP growth, to which all policies were harnessed,
was achieved for a sustained period, with full employment and low inflation delivering rising real incomes; in the earlier phase of development, there is also evidence
that the distribution of income improved (Ng). This together with the provision of
welfare-enhancing public infrastructure and social services constituted the success of
the implicit "social contract" that the government hadwith voters (Tan and Bhaskaran).

Second, each policy achieved its multifaceted goals. Most strikingly, during the
Lee Kuan Yew era (1959–1990), housing policy succeeded not only in increasing the
quantity and quality of the national housing stock, but also lifted the savings rate and
home-ownership, while fostering racial integration, and distributing resources to
lower income groups (Phang). "Efficiency infrastructure", "development welfare"
(Abeysinghe), and tax incentives and subsidies for investors (S. Y. Chia) were funded
without budget deficits, thanks to extensive nontax revenue earned by state agencies
delivering such infrastructure and services (Asher, Bali and Kwan). Investments in
education increased human capital which contributed to both rising incomes and
industrial restructuring through skills and technology upgrading, while energy policy
facilitated both Singapore's industrialization and its later transition to a more services-
oriented economy (Chang). The anti-natalist policies of the 1960s and 1970s contributed to dramatically reduced fertility (Yap and Gee) while facilitating GDP
growth and industrialization through increased female labor force participation and
higher savings from reduced dependency ratios (Pang and Lim).

The admirable achievements in these policy arenas were greatly enabled and
enhanced by a favorable global market environment for export manufacturing (including multilateral trade liberalization and the spread of information, communication

and transportation technologies). Other developing economies also embarked on the same path, particularly the other "Asian NICs" (newly-industrialized countries) or "Asian Tigers" of South Korea, Taiwan and Hong Kong in the 1960s, followed by the so-called "Little Tigers" of Malaysia, Thailand and the Philippines in the 1970s, China in the 1980s, and Vietnam in the 1990s. Although these countries' export competitiveness derived primarily from factor-based comparative advantage in relatively labor-intensive industries, many also followed the same policies that Singapore did of openness to trade and foreign investment, fixed or tightly managed exchange rates, domestic market liberalization, infrastructure development and statist industrial policy, though most did so only selectively (for example, through segregated export processing, free trade or special economic zones). All grew GDP and incomes at rapid rates until progress was stalled by the Asian financial crisis of 1997–1998.

Due to its extremely small size and limited resources, Singapore's comparative advantage changed much more quickly than that of other countries, swinging from excess supply to excess demand for labor in just seven years, after which policy sought to shape comparative and competitive advantage in a much more dirigiste mode, going beyond openness and "tax holidays" to targeted sector-specific (fiscal, financial, human and in-frastructural) capital subsidies. These were complemented by an increasingly liberal policy of importing foreign labor and talent to prolong extensive growth through factor accumulation, which resulted in low and even negative productivity growth from the second decade of independence onward (Pang and Lim; Tan and Bhaskaran). The depression of both capital and labor costs preserved international competitiveness and Singapore's attractiveness to foreign investors, thus extending high GDP growth rates well beyond what very high per capita income combined with very low productivity growth would otherwise allow.

This trajectory ultimately proved to be economically unsustainable, given diminishing returns especially the extreme scarcity of land and its importance as an input into housing and transportation. As both public and private housing prices rose due to heightened scarcity values intensified by foreign demand (the result of open capital and labor markets) rather than generalized inflation (held low by very effective if unorthodox monetary policy), Singaporeans saved more of their income to spend on housing, with a corresponding fall in the share of income spent on consumption of other goods and services to a very low level by local historical and comparative international standards (Asher, Bali and Kwan; Tan and Bhaskaran). Becoming "asset-rich and cash-poor" (N. C. Chia; Phang) in a rapidly-ageing society (Yap and Gee), where most retirement savings lodged at the CPF (periodically diminished by cuts in employer contributions in downturns) have been devoted to housing (HDB), poses serious problems for retirement income adequacy. The integration of CPF savings with HDB housing policy, so perfect for a much younger, lower income, higher fertility society in a much lower cost, faster growth era, now presents difficult policy challenges in a much older, higher income, lower fertility society in a much higher cost, lower growth era. Higher land and property costs have also directly (e.g., through commercial rents) and indirectly (e.g., through higher wages required to compensate local and foreign workers for higher housing costs) reduced international competitiveness and hence the capacity for growth through foreign investment. An atypical failure to provide adequate housing, transportation and healthcare amenities for the large foreign labor and talent influx imported to propel economic growth in the 2000s ultimately proved to be the unraveling of the input-driven development model. Heightened social and political discontentment, coupled with declining welfare of the lower income resident population, finally forced a belated change in economic strategy.

While individual policies interacted to enhance their collective effectiveness, successful policy in one domain also had negative impacts on other policy domains. For example, during the labor-intensive era of development, low skilled manufacturing jobs were plentiful for lowly educated residents, for whom employment and wages rose rapidly, reducing poverty and inequality (as also happened in other East Asian countries) and increasing ability to pay for affordable public housing out of CPF savings (unique to Singapore). But as Singapore's comparative advantage shifted, returns to internationally mobile capital and skills increased while those to low skilled domestic labor decreased, as in other developed countries subject to the same forces of intensified global competition and skill-biased technological change, resulting in increased income inequality. In Singapore, however, this process was intensified by the massive import of low-skilled labor in the continued pursuit of high growth, which depressed wages at the lower end of the scale, as well as productivity growth by removing the incentive for firms to automate and innovate (e.g., Pang and Lim). At the same time, the policy to attract global talent, especially into the financial services sector, pushed salaries up dramatically at the high end of the labor force (e.g., Tan and Bhaskaran). Not surprisingly, earned income inequality in Singapore is now greater than in most other developed countries, and overall inequality is even greater if wealth inequality were also taken into account. Combined with the rising cost of living, this has introduced challenges of poverty and retirement adequacy for significant proportions of the population (Ng; N. C. Chia), unlike the situation in the earlier post-independence years.

While openness has always made Singapore vulnerable to external shocks from booms and busts in global markets, successful industrial upgrading through more recent statist policies has increased economic volatility (e.g., four recessions in the 2000s) given concentration in a few volatile and capital-intensive industries (Pang and Lim; Tan and Bhaskaran). Volatility not only reduces growth and productivity, it also makes macroeconomic stabilization more challenging, reducing the degrees of freedom which monetary (Wilson) and fiscal (Asher, Bali and Kwan) policy previously had to pursue other goals, more so for fiscal policy. Worse, increased volatility has arguably reduced welfare for the working class and forced them to shoulder higher risks, in the absence of an effective social safety net, at the same time as industrial upgrading increased the skill wage premium, worsening income inequality. The priority given to economic growth, in particular to heavily capital-intensive industries like petroleum refining and chemicals, may also conflict with environmental goals of reducing energy use and pollution, e.g., Singapore's per capita energy consumption rose to internationally high levels even as other policies increased energy efficiency and reduced carbon emissions (Chang). Growth based on large imports of foreign labor and talent has resulted in not just increased physical congestion, especially with respect to transportation, but has also increased the risk of social divisions between indigenous citizens and "new residents", exacerbated by ethnic and housing clustering.

One area in which policy has notably failed on its own terms is population policy (Yap and Gee). While other developed countries and especially their high income dense urban cities have also experienced sharp falls in fertility, Singapore's fertility rate is one of the world's lowest, despite three decades of policy attempts to raise it. Since Singapore also has much greater government intervention in citizens' lives than other developed countries, as many of these chapters detail, one might speculate on the ways in which the whole gamut of economic growth, education, housing, labor market, retirement, healthcare and other policies taken together could have influenced marital and fertility decisions, of which housing affordability has been the most obvious and much commented on. In addition, rapid population ageing, itself partly the consequence of past population policies, makes it difficult for an entire generation of now elderly Singaporeans with few children to simultaneously monetize the housing assets in which their retirement savings have been concentrated, without depressing asset values.

4. Challenges and Future Prospects

Collectively, the chapters in this volume broadly concur that economic policy in Singapore was both innovative and effective in the first two to three decades of independence, particularly in simultaneously delivering on both rapid economic growth and improved social welfare. The city state benefited from favorable initial conditions, including strategic location, institutions, infrastructure, an experienced entrepreneurial and skill base in commercial services (though not in manufacturing), and established business relationships with Southeast Asia and even the world. Like other Asian NICs, Singapore also benefited from technological and institutional developments that facilitated the globalization of multinational manufacturing supply chains and developed country markets that were open to exports from developing countries; and like them, it employed statist industrial policy to accelerate industrialization and technological upgrading in targeted sectors. The early developmental outcomes in terms of high growth, expanded employment, increased incomes and, for a time, improved income distribution, were also similar to those in the other Asian NICs, as are some of the current problems of slowing growth, increasing inequality, low fertility and, for some, a certain degree of de-industrialization.

But Singapore also differed from the other Asian NICs in a number of important ways. Most obviously, its much higher starting income level, lack of an agricultural sector, very small size, extreme economic openness, and elected government (which South Korea and Taiwan lacked before the late 1980s, and Hong Kong still lacks today) distinctively shaped many specific policy choices. The first and most notable feature of Singapore's unique political economy was the government's pro-activist social policy — particularly HDB and CPF, but also policies on health, education and family planning — as an integrated part of the overall development strategy and complement to industrial policy. But social services were not just provided as consumption goods which served to win votes for the PAP government from an electorate desperately in need of housing and jobs. They also contributed to cost competitiveness and the attraction of foreign investment. The need to fund such services led to the development of many off-budget funding sources for government development expenditures, including through statutory boards and GLCs, thus eschewing the need for deficit budget financing (Asher, Bali and Kwan; Tan and Bhaskaran).

Second, small size and extreme openness together led to the evolution of Singapore's unique and immensely successful exchange rate management-based monetary policy, whose chief goal was to mitigate imported inflation and preserve the purchasing power of Singapore households' savings. This, and the policy of attracting multinationals to set up production bases, required a stable (or, as it transpired, gradually appreciating) currency, given the high dependence of both consumption and production on imported inputs, and the need to minimize the uncertainty associated with currency fluctuations. Persistent budget and savings surpluses were reflected in large current account surpluses, and transformed into massive external reserves — both to ensure currency stability, and very likely, to give the vulnerable small, new and open nation a measure of national security, given the government's "siege mentality" at its birth (Tan and Bhaskaran). The strength of the currency in turn boosted the development of financial services, including foreign exchange trading and the wealth management business which has taken off since 2000 (Wilson).

A third distinctive difference between Singapore's development model and that of the other Asian NICs, which has been extensively written about, is the heavy reliance of the industrialization process on foreign investment (S. Y. Chia), as opposed to the nurturing of domestic industrial entrepreneurs which South Korea and Taiwan favored. Several contingent factors may explain this policy choice, which has proven to be very consequential and sheds light on the shrinking share of manufacturing in GDP in recent years. Lack of an industrial entrepreneurial class and Singapore's miniscule domestic market at the time of independence, made it difficult if not impractical to cultivate or protect national enterprises. While the other Asian NICs also mostly lacked experienced domestic industrial entrepreneurs (Hong Kong's transplanted-from-the-mainland garments industry excepted), Singapore's local entrepreneurial class of Chinese immigrants were traditionally oriented to trading and services, and lacked the technological know-how and global networks necessary to export manufactures to developed country markets. Once multinationals had established themselves, and as the state sector itself expanded, given Singapore's small size, local entrepreneurs might have been crowded out in factor markets (for land, labor and skills) or found it more lucrative and less risky to supply and service the state and multinational sectors, rather than compete with the latter. For its part, the government may have preferred a high foreign economic presence as a safeguard of sorts against the risk of regional aggression. Whatever the reasons, prolonged dependence on foreign enterprises has left the economy lacking the "inherent production capacity" and "core of strong vibrant local enterprise" necessary to propel its development into the future (Tan and Bhaskaran). At the same time, "an investment approach … putting bets on many new industries with the expectation that some would pay off handsomely even if others fail — limited the likelihood of developing sufficient depth and globally competitive scale in any of these industries, since all would be competing for already extremely scarce resources."[1]

Looking ahead to the nation's next 50 years, Singapore confronts two major economic challenges. The first is sustaining economic growth and continuously improving living standards, and the second, ensuring social security and basic needs are met for its population.

With respect to economic growth, a consensus has emerged among economists, policymakers and local business leaders that the Singapore development model of the past 50 years is no longer viable, or adequate to deliver improved living standards for the citizen population. Most of this reasoning has centered on domestic supply-side (i.e., resource) constraints, particularly land and labor, which have resulted in high costs and deteriorating competitiveness. But there are also external demand side constraints arising from demographic, macroeconomic, structural, technological and institutional changes in the world economy (Lim, 2015). As Finance Minister Tharman Shanmugaratnam noted in his Budget 2015 speech: "The current global

---

[1] Tan and Bhaskaran, in this volume, noting that in 2003 "The Economic Review Committee…identified bioscience, global banking and finance, wealth management, lifestyle industries, arts and culture, media and design, education and healthcare, among others" as examples of "creative and innovative" industries to be promoted. Added to this list would be the ongoing massive investments in petroleum refining and chemicals that they and Chang describe.

environment is not … just a temporary challenge. We may see prolonged sluggish growth in the advanced world, as well as continued consolidation in China's growth as it reforms and rebalances its economy. We should not count on significantly stronger global demand over the medium term."

Fortunately, there is also an emerging consensus on what can and should be done going forward, and government policy is slowly moving in that direction. First, as announced by Prime Minister Lee Hsien Loong in January 2015, is a reduction in the targeted and expected annual GDP growth rate to 2% to 3%, much more typical of and achievable by an already high-income developed economy, than the 3% to 5% proclaimed by the Economic Strategies Committee in 2010. Second is the continued and reinforced push to increase productivity (Pang and Lim; Wilson), the only means of ensuring rising living standards: this involves greater selectivity, though still an absolute increase, in foreign labor imports, as well as subsidies for business investment and skills training as domestic factor prices/resource costs realign themselves to market forces. Third, as part of this economic restructuring, heavily subsidized manufacturing's share of GDP is likely to shrink further, as its share of employment already has, while that of services, which are more aligned to Singapore's long-term comparative and competitive advantage, will continue to increase (Pang and Lim; Tan and Bhaskaran). Given Singapore's path dependence on large MNCs, and in stark contrast to Korea, Taiwan or even Germany, it is inconceivable that a small and medium-sized manufacturing sector supplying them will survive in its current state once these MNCs relocate to cheaper and spatially superior locations with larger markets. Fourth, and related to the previous point, recognition that a vibrant private entrepreneurial sector is necessary for innovation at the technology and income frontier is bringing renewed policy focus on local entrepreneurs and SMEs, though to date heavy state promotion of innovation has been noticeably inefficient (Tan and Bhaskaran). Fifth, as noted by UOB chief economist Jimmy Koh, "There's one thing that's become absolutely clear — we have become expensive, as a nation. We either increase scale, or increase productivity — and for the former, we have to get out of Singapore." (Ang, 2015) This too will bring Singapore closer to other developed countries, which have a much more balanced mix between inward and outward FDI (on which, for Singapore, see S. Y. Chia). Government policy here includes grants to encourage local SMEs to invest outside of Singapore, and there is increased recognition that the country's economic future lies less in continuing as a "global city" and more in closer linkages with Southeast Asia, its regional "hinterland" (Tan and Bhaskaran).

There is also growing consensus in the social policy arena on the need to rethink provision for social security and basic needs for a rapidly ageing population, given real wage stagnation or decline especially in lower wage occupations, income inequality (a Gini around 0.47 for labor income only) and relative poverty rates (20% to 22% of the population) which are high relative to other East Asian (and developed western) countries. Singapore's welfare policies have lagged the developed world, if not the Asian NICs, even as declining social mobility through the educational system (Ng), and a high (nearly 50%) rate of inadequate retirement savings (N.C. Chia) present new challenges. The government has responded vigorously in recent Budgets by increasing social transfers, particularly to the working poor (Workfare), the elderly (Pioneer Generation healthcare subsidies), the elderly poor (Silver Support scheme), and lower income HDB homeowners (with various schemes to help them "age in place") (Ng; N.C. Chia; Phang). But it appears to be still fundamentally averse to social risk pooling, universal entitlements and income redistribution in social policy, despite a long held willingness to provide ever-increasing performance-based subsidies to corporations under the state's industrial policy (Tan and Bhaskaran). Thus, recent CPF reforms of increasing the wage ceiling, contribution rates, interest rate and payment periods are still based on self-reliance and individual responsibility for retirement adequacy, while the new MediShield Life health insurance scheme remains largely based on commercial principles.

Asher, Bali and Kwan suggest that "the continued reluctance to introduce social insurance principles in pension and healthcare financing arrangements" reflect policy makers' "mindset ... wedded to the requirements of the location-based strategy" — a low tax regime with industrial policy subsidies, free capital repatriation and high foreign ownership. But they detect the beginnings of a "mindset shift" and note that large budget and off-budget surpluses indicate that policy reforms "will not be constrained by a shortage of fiscal resources, or by institutional and organizational capacities." As an example, the pension cost of the means-tested, noncontributory income support system targeted to needy elderly proposed by N.C. Chia will cost less than 1% of GDP even as the population ages and growth slows.

Budget 2015's increase in the top marginal income tax rate from 20% to 22% (still well below the 28% rate prevailing till 2002 when it was lowered to attract foreign talent), explicitly to provide funds for increased government social expenditures, may signal a gradual "mindset shift" in social policy. Finance Minister Shanmugaratnam confirmed that fiscal sustainability continues to be ensured by budgetary prudence, the constitutional requirement to balance budgets within each (average 5-year) term of government, and by the allowed use of 50% of "net investment returns" (NIR) on reserves managed by the Monetary Authority of Singapore (MAS) and the sovereign wealth funds GIC and Temasek Holdings.

Ng argues that dealing with poverty, inequality and social mobility requires more than a "mindset shift" in favor of more income transfers and social subsidies, necessary (and still inadequate) as these are. Publicly-funded housing (HDB), pension (CPF), healthcare, education and skills training policies are also important. So is "wage correction" which she notes may have to advance ahead of productivity growth, given the large gap that has developed over decades of wage suppression at the lower end of the labor market. This will mitigate poverty and inequality, but in the short to medium term will have an adverse impact on international competitiveness, particularly of SMEs, and hence economic growth. However, rising wages will also incentivize work and productivity, while adding to the currently low (40%) wage and consumption shares of GDP, helping the economy rebalance toward higher consumption of domestic services, and thus a less volatile and less unequal GDP.

Another policy domain where a "mindset shift" is required is the ultra-low fertility rate which, insofar as it may derive from the local economic environment, is likely to characterize new immigrants as well as native citizens. Policies to increase marriage and fertility have been in existence for three decades now and rely heavily on financial incentives, including cash bonuses, to encourage births, but have had a notable lack of success. Ho (2015) notes that other high income, low fertility developed countries in Europe have succeeded in reversing low birth rates, some to replacement level, through public policies which "promote work-life integration and gender equality within the family". However the Singapore government, though aware of these policies, seems unwilling to try them, either for ideological reasons (e.g., unwillingness to let go of patriarchal cultural norms, and fear that "welfare makes people lazy") or because long parental leaves (the essence of the European policies) will raise costs to employers and further jeopardize economic growth.

5. Conclusion

The prospect for the future, then, is that Singapore will make a delayed transition from the high growth but low productivity middle-income manufacturing-based economy led by multinationals serving the global market that it was from 40 years ago, to a low growth but higher productivity high income services-based economy led by local enterprises serving a domestic and regional (as well as global) market. To a large extent, this reflects a return to the city state's pre-independence role as a regional services hub for Southeast Asia (Lee). How this market-determined (comparative and competitive advantage-based) transition will actually take place is still uncertain. For example, S. Y. Chia believes that state industrial policy can have a role to play in nurturing domestic entrepreneurs and encouraging them to venture overseas, which will preserve a large state apparatus; whereas Tan and Bhaskaran, and Pang and Lim, prefer to rely on market forces and a downsized state. In social policy, there is more consensus on the need for a more activist state role utilizing multiple policy levers — except, curiously, on the part of the state itself which continues to promote individual self-reliance and now "collective responsibility" and philanthropy (Budget, 2015) to mitigate poverty and inequality.

Finance Minister Tharman Shanmugaratnam's Budget 2015 speech summarized the government's current philosophy as follows: "This Budget is focused on building Singapore's future. We must reach our next frontier as an economy, with firms driven by innovation, and higher incomes coming from deep skills and expertise in every job. We must ensure a society that is fair and just, where everyone has a chance to move up and do well regardless of where they start. And we must complement a culture of personal effort and responsibility with stronger collective responsibility, especially for our elderly." This statement clearly re-prioritizes social needs as a social (and hence governmental) responsibility. But the Budget policies on which it is predicated continue to focus on state-driven resource allocation, including the nurturing of private enterprise (not usually the competence or role of states in market economies), and a differentiated education and skills training model (which implies some degree of continued state targeting of specific skills, and which Ng notes could entrench existing inequalities). The boundaries between state and market, public and private, global and local, financial and social forces in Singapore's economy remain to be negotiated, if not contested, in the next 50 years.

Acknowledgment

I would like to thank Choy Keen Meng, who conceived of this project and helped at various stages in the process of coming up with this volume, including providing comments and suggestions on the essays.

References

Ang, P (2015). Time for S'pore firms "to venture out". *Business Times*, 6 March.
Cohen, M (2015). Lee Kuan Yew "doesn't trust" the nation he built. www.forbes.com March 30.
Ho, KP (2015). Europe's baby bump holds lessons for S'pore. *The Straits Times*, 5 March.
Jacobson, M (2010). The Singapore Solution. *National Geographic*, January.
Lim, LYC (2015). Beyond the "Global City" paradigm. In *Singapore Perspectives 2015: Choices*, S Hoe and C Soon (eds.). World Scientific and Institute of Policy Studies.

CHAPTER 2

Governance and Economic Change in Singapore

Lee Soo Ann

The Singapore economy went through several changes due to changes in its mode of governance from being a trading outpost of the East India Company (EIC) to being part of the colony of the Straits Settlements, and more recently to being a British colony by itself, then to being part of Malaysia and now an independent republic. These modes of governance enabled the economy to grow until Singapore became more important and also more closely linked to the outside world. British rule, British capital and the response of the people who came, enabled Singapore to integrate technological change so that it is now part of a global network. However a declining rate of births and a large foreign population now compel Singapore to make further changes.

1. Introduction

That the Singapore economy has grown and changed is without doubt. Critical to its change is the mode of governance of the economy and the characteristics of its people. These factors interacted with each other to bring about changes in the economy which enabled growth to take place. There were obviously other factors at work too, such as the growth in population, the inflow of capital from abroad, technological transfer and so on. But changes in the mode of governance and people characteristics were made possible by these factors.

Four modes of governance are identified in this essay. The first is the Singapore run by the East India Company (EIC) and the India Office of the British government up to 1867. Second is the Singapore run as part of the Straits Settlements colony of the British government from 1867 onwards. Third is the Singapore as a British colony from 1946, initially completely run by the British and then internally self-governing, ending with Singapore being part of Malaysia in 1963–1965.

The fourth mode is that of the Singapore governed as an independent republic from 1965. It is argued in this essay that major structural changes in the Singapore economy occurred under the first three modes of governance. There were undoubtedly other changes in the 50 years that Singapore has been an independent republic. But these were dependent on the economic structure changes which occurred before 1965, which also help determine what further changes are probable after 2015. Economic history lays the foundation roots of the spreading tree that is Singapore today. Without an adequate appreciation of such roots, it would not be wise to speculate on what further changes are possible or probable.

2. Singapore as Part of the EIC and the India Office

Stamford Raffles, an agent of the EIC, signed the agreement with the Sultan of Johor to setup a trading settlement in 1819, initially on a tenancy basis and then through a purchase of the island in 1824. In 1815, Malacca was returned to the Dutch: it had been occupied by the British from the start of the Napoleonic Wars in 1795 to prevent the French from occupying what were then Dutch possessions in Southeast Asia. Malacca was one of these, a strategic port obtained from the Portuguese by the Dutch in 1641.

After Malacca was returned to the Dutch, its maritime rivalry with the British increased. The Dutch were in a superior position because Malacca was located at the narrowest point of the Straits of Malacca which linked the Indian Ocean and the South China Sea. As noted by Wong (1991a, p. 20), "whoever possessed Malacca could choke the spice trade that passed through the Straits". Lord Hastings, then Governor-General of the EIC,[1] consequently revived an old scheme to secure the Straits of Malacca by "the establishment of a station beyond Malacca, such as may command the southern entrance of those Straits", while leaving implicitly to the Dutch the command of the Sunda Straits.[2]

Riau was a priority, but alternatively Raffles could try for another site in the then Johor-Riau sultanate. After finding the Kerimun islands (at the southern end of the Malacca Straits) and Siak (on the east coast of Sumatra) not suitable, Raffles landed in what was the island of Singapore in January 1819. The old name of Singapore was Temasek, and Raffles had read about it being previously an important sea-town (which was what Temasek means), from the Sejarah Melayu or Malay Annals in the years that he was governor of Java in 1812–1815 (when he learned Malay). Thus "the

---

[1] The EIC in a revision to its charter in the 1750s added political control to the original trading functions given to it by the Queen when it was formed in 1600.

[2] The Sunda Straits is between Java and Sumatra and this together with the Straits of Malacca and the Lombok Straits (between Java and Lombok) constituted three maritime gateways to the spice islands in the Moluccas which attracted the formation of not only the British EIC in 1600 but also the Dutch EIC in 1602.

choice of Singapore as a British settlement was more the outcome of circumstances than of design" (Wong, 1991a, p. 19).

Singapore was then a largely deserted island with only a few hundred *orang laut* (sea people), but Raffles envisaged it becoming as important a port as Temasek had been. He initiated an economic change, that of laying the framework for free trade, rather than that of mercantile trade[3] which had been the prevailing philosophy. Adam Smith had written about free trade[4] in *The Wealth of Nations* (1783), and Raffles adopted this new policy,[5] in contrast to the taxed trade practiced by neighboring ports which followed mercantilist philosophy.

As the island had hardly any people, Raffles also adopted a policy of the free movement in and out of people of any race, language or religion. Spice traders came in response to the incentive of being free of trade taxes; many were Chinese residing in other parts of Southeast Asia such as Malacca, who for centuries had been the carriers of trade between China and Southeast Asia. This people factor plus a change in the mode of governance of Singapore enabled the economic change of free trade to propel the growth of trade in spices. In an 1824 Anglo-Dutch treaty, Malacca became British and, together with Penang (obtained in 1784) and Singapore (founded in 1819), constituted the Straits Settlements as a presidency of the EIC.

In terms of governance, the Straits Settlements capital was moved in 1836 from Penang to Singapore, which emerged as the hub of the spice trade through its capacity to link Bugis and Chinese spice traders with the EIC and British independent traders. After governors of the Straits Settlements came to be located in Singapore, they emphasized its growth. For example, free trade meant that revenue in Singapore was always low, but Straits Settlement governors saw to the import of convict labor from India who built roads and important buildings in Singapore that still exist today.

Competition between the EIC and independent traders led to the 1833 loss of the EICs China trade monopoly. But the spice trade through Singapore grew, whether conducted by the EIC or independent traders. Sailing ships arrived in Singapore from November to March with the northeast monsoon and left Singapore from May to September with the southeast monsoon. There were also other places in the Riau

---

[3] When Western Europe opened up to what the voyages of discovery in the 16th century brought back in terms of spices, the propelling force was the idea that the wealth of a nation depended on its bullion, i.e., its stock of gold and silver, and this meant that exports must exceed imports which is the backbone of mercantilist philosophy.

[4] Adam Smith advocated the economic advantages of trade even if such trade did not result in an increase of bullion. To him, it was the level of economic activity that mattered, not the amount of gold, silver or other precious metals.

[5] Singapore had no agriculture or metal mining to produce crops or metals for export and so the concept of mercantile trade was to Raffles not valid for Singapore.

Table 1.   Early trade of Singapore.

Year	The West (%)	East Indies (%)	Southeast Asia (%)	India (%)	Others (%)	Total
1825	18	14	48	20	0	100
1845	22	22	34	21	1	100
1865	25	15	43	15	2	100

Source: Wong (1991b).

Archipelago and Sumatra where sailing ships could rest in between monsoons (which explains the rise of Palembang, for example, as a major port), but the attraction of Singapore lay in the fact that the EIC was British and had made Singapore the capital of the Straits Settlements.

Britain became the major world power in the 19th century, based largely on its navy, having defeated the French under Napoleon in 1814. In 1836 the EIC initiated efforts to eliminate pirates, the major threat to free trade, and by 1854, cooperation between the British, Dutch and Spanish (who controlled the Philippines) navies had eliminated this threat. The trade of Singapore in its first 50 years was largely with the rest of Southeast Asia (see Table 1).

An 1857 uprising of Indian sepoys (soldiers) led to a re-examination of British rule in India, and in 1858 the EIC was abolished by the British parliament and an India Office of the British government was setup to run India. As the Straits Settlements had been part of the EIC, it came under the purview of this office from 1858, but traders petitioned the government to transfer its governance to that of the Colonial Office. The Straits Settlements was just too far for the India Office officials to take into consideration its special needs now that its trade had become sizeable.

3. Singapore as Part of the British Straits Settlements Colony

A subsequent 1867 transfer of the Straits Settlements to the Colonial Office enabled the British to extend their influence over the nine Malay States in the peninsula when first tin and then rubber production became important. The Straits Settlements still comprised Penang, Malacca and Singapore, but now the governor was appointed by the Colonial Office rather than by the Governor-General of India. These governors came from outside India and brought with them Straits Settlements-centric, rather than India-centric policies.

Singapore experienced a new lease of activity after the spice trade died down with the advent of refrigeration. Rubber cultivation and tin mining led to unprecedented prosperity not only for the nine Malay States in the peninsula but also for Singapore, which by then had become not only the port of entry for immigrants to the Malay

States, but also the processing center for raw rubber and tin, and the port from which processed rubber and refined tin were exported.

To handle the export of rubber and tin, British shipping and insurance, British management of rubber estates and tin mines led to Singapore becoming a business rather than merely a spice trade center. Financial activity also expanded into the raising of capital for rubber and tin, rather than just financing entrepot trade in spices. Singapore became a Southeast Asian business center as Indonesian rubber and tin also made its way to Singapore.

By virtue of its geographical position, Singapore also became the center for British expansion into Sarawak and Sabah in the neighboring large island of Kalimantan or Borneo. The discovery of oil in Sarawak cemented the position of Singapore as the distribution hub for the three commodities of rubber, tin and oil. Sabah also had timber which was exported to Singapore (Table 2).

During this period, a major economic change was the issue of a new Straits dollar currency by a currency board setup by the Straits Settlements government in 1906. This currency replaced the previous use of multiple currencies, some based on gold and some on silver. The settlements of Penang, Malacca and Singapore had no single currency serving all three territories. Traders and immigrants brought their currency with them from their countries of origin. Those from India would bring in theirs based on the rupee, those from the Dutch East Indies that based on the Dutch guilder and those from China that based on Chinese silver or more commonly Spanish or Mexican dollars, so-called because the silver came from Mexico which was then ruled by the Spanish. Coins based on the rupee and guilder were in gold whereas those from China or Mexico were in silver. When the price between gold and silver became volatile, traders could be caught holding the weaker metal coins.

By the mid-1880s, notes had replaced coins and although this was convenient, it did not remove the instability caused by fluctuations in gold or silver prices as the notes would either be gold or silver-based. All trade required the use of money of some sort and the failure of some Asian banks which issued notes compounded the

Table 2. Major commodity exports of Straits Settlement Singapore.

Year	Total	Tin	Rubber	Petroleum	16 other important tropical commodities
$000					
1895	114,734	19,417	n.a.	1,386	34,423
1905	197,619	39,980	528	1,068	49,388
1915	303,860	55,000	54,642	1,206	49,994
1925	899,853	72,556	405,844	71,127	81,345

Source: Huff (1994, Appendix Table A.1).

insecurity of having multiple currencies. Hence traders in Singapore (which by then had overtaken Penang and Malacca in the volume and value of trade) petitioned the Straits Settlements to take on the task of currency issue. Fortunately, the practice of currency boards issuing currency had been done elsewhere in the British Empire and the Straits Settlements government followed suit.

The new Straits dollar satisfied the needs of new immigrants and new Chinese banks arose which used the Straits dollar deposits of Chinese immigrants and companies formed by Chinese. These banks served the Chinese in both the Straits Settlements and the Malay states as Chinese immigrants usually knew only the Chinese language. They complemented the British banks which serviced the needs of the largely British-owned rubber plantations, shipping and insurance companies, and tin mines. The British banks did serve Chinese traders through the use of compradores who knew both English and a vernacular language, but their customers were largely British companies and individuals who knew mainly English.

The currency board system effectively made the economy of Malaya (both the Straits Settlements and the Malay States) part of the sterling area, a currency bloc comprising much of the then British Empire. Capital was free to move between the United Kingdom as the seat of that Empire and its colonies and protectorates at fixed exchange rates. Although the pound left the gold standard in the 1930s, that system of free capital movement made possible by the currency board issue of the Straits dollar benefitted the growth of finance and banking in Singapore, which was the headquarters of the board. The board invested its assets in the London capital market, all currency being fully backed at an exchange rate which was to remain unchanged for over 60 years from 1906.

Another important change was the integration of British direct rule over the Straits Settlements with British indirect rule over the nine Malay States which, state by state, accepted British advice in the administration of all matters except those in Malay religion and customs. On paper, the governor of the Straits Settlements ruled only Penang, Malacca and Singapore. The British advisers to the sultans (or rulers) of the Malay States were attached only to the appropriate sultan. However these British advisers being all members of the British Colonial Service came to report to the Straits Settlements governor because of his seniority and also because Singapore was the major city of the Straits Settlements.

This meant that there emerged a British policy for what came to be known as British Malaya, comprising the three British Straits Settlements and the nine Malay States. Singapore through this change became the hub of the Malayan economy based on export commodity production. The British through the Federated Malay States (an administrative federation of the four Malay States of Perak, Selangor, Pahang and Negri Sembilan) constructed a railway bringing tin and rubber down to Singapore whose port was expanded by deep water wharves in Tanjong Pagar to handle steam shipping. Previously the Singapore port was the only one that was around Singapore river which handled the spice trade.

Singapore is an island and goods from the peninsula had to be ferried by barges across the straits of Johor. But with the growth in the rubber trade, a causeway or land bridge was built in 1921 on which lorries, cars and trains could move people and goods to and from Singapore. This integration under British rule enabled people to move between the Straits Settlements and the nine Malay States in a way which would set the stage for further population and economic growth in Singapore.

The free movement of people from other parts of Southeast Asia to and from Singapore caused the population of Singapore to grow from a few hundred in 1819 to 10,000 in 1824 and 82,000 in 1860. Singapore was very much a frontier town made up of mainly single males. Those who were married came largely from Malacca which had a Chinese population from the time Cheng He, the Chinese admiral of the Ming Emperor, visited Malacca in the early 1400s.

Chinese immigration into Singapore accelerated after the Straits Settlements became a colony in 1867. The advent of tin mining and then rubber cultivation brought in large numbers of Chinese who were now allowed to leave China more freely after China lost the Second Opium War in 1858–1860. More treaty ports were given to not only Britain but also France, Japan and Germany, from which Chinese (mainly single men) could board ships for the Nanyang, or South Seas of which Singapore was the hub. The administrative change from 1867 integrating direct rule of the Strait Settlements with indirect rule of the Malay States led to a greater flow of people to Singapore over and above the needs of entrepot trade. Now people came to Singapore in order to go up to the peninsula where there was now rubber cultivation and tin mining; some stayed in Singapore (Table 3).

More importantly, there now emerged an increase in the number of females. At first only married women were allowed to leave with their husbands after 1860, but after the Chinese Empire was overthrown in 1911, single women were allowed to

Table 3. Components of Straits Settlement Singapore population increase.

Intercensal period	Population increase	Natural increase	Net migrational increase
1881–1891	43,900	−30,600	+74,500
1891–1901	45,200	−42,400	+87,600
1901–1911	76,500	−59,500	+136,000
1911–1921	115,000	−38,500	+153,000
1921–1931	139,000	+15,900	+123,500

Source: Saw (1991, Table 10.2).

leave as passports were then issued by the new Republic of China. With the immigration of single women, the demography of Singapore changed. Single women married the single men who were then dominant in the Singapore population profile, and from 1921, there was a positive natural increase (excess of births over deaths) in population, the number of deaths falling due to improvements in public health.

More single women left China after the Japanese invaded China in 1930, due to atrocities committed by the Japanese, and the world entered into the Great Depression which badly affected the tin and rubber industries. The Straits Settlements government cut the number of males who could enter Singapore since jobs would not be available for them. However they left intact the numbers of females who could be admitted and large numbers of Chinese females entered Singapore. They found jobs in food retailing, domestic service and tailoring. As a consequence, the sex ratio became more balanced. Marriages took place and a major demographic structure emerged which would change the nature of Singapore from being a transient to becoming a permanent society. During the 1930s, women and children made up the majority of immigrants entering Singapore (Table 4).

Estimates of gross domestic product from 1900 to 1939 show the volatile nature of the Singapore economy due to it being part of a Malayan economy dominated by tin, rubber and oil (Table 5). Foreign trade in rubber and tin acted both as an engine of growth and a source of economic instability (Choy and Sugimoto, 2013).

The major Asian nation of Japan was becoming more militaristic at the same time that she became industrialized. Anticipating the Japanese intention to obtain the rubber, tin and oil they needed from British Southeast Asia, the British set about building a naval base in Singapore in order to forestall the Japanese navy. However, this made Singapore even more of a target for the Japanese to aim at, when World War II broke out in 1939.

After the Japanese occupation of Singapore in 1942–1945, the British dismantled the Straits Settlements and separated Singapore out as a separate colony. This separation enabled a new administrative change, that of developing Singapore on its own, rather than as part of a greater Straits Settlements. However, links continued with the

Table 4.   Composition of Chinese immigrants examined.

	Total	Men (%)	Women (%)	Children (%)
1900–1903	201,801	88.8	6.4	4.8
1911–1913	254,159	82.6	9.1	8.3
1921–1923	160,983	73.0	14.3	12.7
1926–1929	324,181	69.7	16.2	14.1
1934–1938	147,101	45.4	36.1	18.5

Source: Huff (1994, Table 5.1).

Table 5. Singapore GDP and its composition in selected years from 1900–1939.

	Consumption	Govt.	Investment	Net exp.	GDP
$ million at current prices					
1900	33.7	2.2	4.3	−5.2	35.1
1910	46.7	3.8	12.8	−1.9	46.7
1920	137.7	11.3	49.1	−51.6	146.5
1927	174.4	14.5	43.8	−67.6	165.1
1928	184.0	14.7	72.4	−33.8	237.3
1929	183.7	15.9	71.1	10.6	281.3
1930	171.4	16.5	37.6	13.5	239.0
1931	131.1	16.5	27.8	−11.3	164.1
1932	119.0	14.5	20.1	−11.5	142.0
1935	144.5	12.7	33.7	13.2	204.1
1939	201.4	15.5	55.1	−5.7	266.3

Source: Sugimoto (2011, Table 3.1).

peninsula and to the British Borneo territories, as all of them shared the same currency, the Straits dollar, renamed as the Malayan dollar when the Malay States and the British Borneo territories joined the currency board agreement in 1938.

4. Singapore as Self-Governing Under British and Malaysian Rule

Rubber, tin and oil continued to be exported from Singapore after 1945. These industries were not drastically affected by the Japanese occupation and the Korean War boom of the early 1950s restored the fortunes of those involved in commodity production. All three were demanded for military purposes and with the onset of the Korean War, GDP was much higher in 1953 than 1952; thereafter it continued rising due to the effects of the boom (Table 6).

1946 saw a distinct change in the governance of Singapore, which was now run by a governor responsible only to the Colonial Office, as Penang and Malacca were merged into what was first known as the Malayan Union (1946–1948) and then as the Federation of Malaya from 1948 onwards. The British governor of Singapore was given the task of initiating a franchise and expanded elected representation in the legislature. This led to a council of largely elected ministers in 1955 formed from a largely elected legislature. The first chief minister was David Marshall, the leader of a Labour Front alliance.

1959 saw another change in the governance of Singapore, to self-government. Though still a colony, there was now no longer a governor but a nominal head of state

Table 6.   Singapore GDP and its composition, 1950–1959.

	Consumption	Govt.	Investment	Net exports	GDP
$ million at current prices					
1950	912.8	74.4	168.7	−33.4	1122.5
1951	1081.2	91.9	234.3	−24.0	1383.4
1952	1161.2	106.2	194.4	−258.3	1203.6
1953	1368.1	123.8	207.3	−31.9	1667.2
1954	1382.2	143.6	197.7	3.8	1727.4
1955	1393.8	154.5	184.6	−154.5	1578.4
1956	1632.2	164.8	269.6	−114.1	1953.6
1957	1712.3	166.8	252.7	−200.8	1931.1
1958	1779.1	179.6	232.2	−177.3	2013.6
1959	1690.3	186.7	222.5	−65.8	2033.8

Source: Sugimoto (2011, Table 3.1).

with an elected prime minister leading a cabinet answerable to a fully elected legislature. The British government could still suspend such a constitution and was represented by a Commissioner-General for Southeast Asia to whom the governors of Sabah and Sarawak also reported. He was located in Singapore, which still had a sizeable military base comprising land, sea and air force units. Britain was still responsible for defence and foreign affairs, and had the casting vote in matters concerning internal security.

The government elected into power was that of the People's Action Party (PAP), which ran in the 1959 elections on the platform of meeting the domestic needs of the people. In 1957 the majority of Singapore adults were given the vote. The PAP received the mandate of the electorate by winning 43 of the 51 seats in the legislature though with only a 52% share of the votes cast.

A major administrative change effected by the elected government was the development of the island as a whole, abolishing the rural board which administered over three quarters of the island, and the city council which administered the other one quarter in the southeast which housed the business district and port. Electricity, sewage, sanitation and physical infrastructure were then provided to the entire island as an integrated whole. The purpose was to stimulate economic growth which took place except for 1964, when Indonesian Confrontation against the Federation of Malaysia formed in 1963 caused a slight dip.

Previously Singapore was run as part of the Straits Settlements of Penang, Malacca and Singapore, and residents of any one of these three entities could move to any one of the others. There was no need for the British to view Singapore as a separate entity. If urban dwellers in Singapore were not satisfied with their amenities, they could move to Georgetown in Penang or reside in Malacca town. Both Penang and Malacca had rural areas as well, comparable to the rural areas of Singapore.

The new mode of governance of Singapore plus the characteristics of the population, that of many babies being born through marriages which took place with the inflow of single women, enabled this administrative change to take place. With it came the need to mobilize savings for the development of the whole island. This was done through the establishment of the Central Provident Fund (CPF) in 1955 which initially was intended to fund the retirement needs of young workers. However the 1959 government used it to buy newly issued long-term bonds, the proceeds of which were used to acquire land and construct public housing to meet the needs of young families. A development fund was setup to finance long-term projects.

Previously, capital expenditure was on a year-to-year basis as was the practice with most colonial governments. Developing the whole island meant a change to multi-year projects requiring long-term financing. Like the CPF, financial institutions were also compelled to buy long-term bonds, since a percentage of their assets had to be local securities in order to function as financial institutions in Singapore. The percentage was set by the regulator of financial institutions, the Ministry of Finance, for which these bonds represented the liquid portion of the institutions' assets.

With the administrative change of whole-island, physical development came a rise in the share of investment in GDP, from 12% in 1955, when a council of ministers made up the executive of Singapore, to 22% in 1965, the last year that Singapore was in Malaysia. When Singapore joined Malaysia in 1963, it was granted autonomy in labor, education and financial matters, and the government continued its plans laid in 1959 to physically transform the island. A land acquisition act was effected in 1960 enabling the government to acquire the three-quarters of the island then in private ownership for development purposes, at almost confiscatory prices. This land was largely in the rural areas which were then devoted to agriculture and fish farms. The government's Commissioner of Lands valued land at its agricultural value though the potential value due to development would be several times higher. Thus the gain due to development would accrue to the new users of the land who would obtain it for industrial estates and housing for 60 to 99 years.

Investors in factories paid an annual rental equivalent to 6% of the development cost: as the land was acquired at almost confiscatory prices, the effect was a low land cost for new enterprises. Equally dramatic was the effect on wages, due to the public housing constructed on the land thus acquired: workers and their families obtained housing at a price equal to four times their annual salary. Investors found that they need not pay high wages to employ labor, and this made profitable the use of Singapore as a manufacturing production base at a time when industries in the USA, Western Europe and Japan were moving offshore to lower their costs.

The arrival of the jumbo jet meant that components could be shipped to Singapore cheaply and the assembled parts re-exported by air, at a fraction of longer and more expensive shipping. Singapore also took advantage of domestic self-government to connect her telecommunications and transport systems to global networks so that her labor force, previously in danger of being substantially unemployed due to stagnant entrepot trade, now found itself at almost full employment.

The short period that Singapore was in Malaysia meant that Malaysian rule did not adversely affect the internal self-governing capability of the 1959 government. Political disputes between the federal and the Singapore state government led to the expulsion of Singapore from Malaysia in 1965. With that came a new mode of governance, that of full independence as a sovereign nation. Singapore however had been exercising many aspects of sovereignty before that.

5. Singapore as an Independent Republic

Two aspects of sovereignty came to be exercised by the Singapore government with separation from Malaysia in 1965 — defence and foreign affairs. For a short time, the impact of having to provide for defence was not felt though the government was aware of it. After all, the British had a large military base in Singapore with army, navy and air force units. A Ministry of Interior and Defence combined the need to have a Ministry of Defence with the existing Ministry of Home Affairs, so that the Commissioner of Police in effect had to handle some military affairs.

To handle foreign affairs, the government leaned on its former connections as a colony in the then British Empire. Many British Commonwealth countries[6] had close links to Singapore through her being a node in British Empire transport, capital and communication networks. The government had within its own civil service several who had hailed from the Federation of Malaya, and they served in the foreign service: the Singapore cabinet itself comprised of many who were born in the Federation or its predecessor Malay States or British Straits Settlements, but who chose to take up Singapore citizenship and play a role in her development.

A key administrative change was the creation of military conscription as compulsory for all able-bodied males. A small professional defence force would complement it, and assistance in building up the armed forces came from Israel. The task had to be accelerated when the British announced 1970 as the date for withdrawal of their armed forces: however Prime Minister Lee Kuan Yew interceded with the British Prime Minister, Harold Wilson, with whom he was on good terms, and this was postponed to 1971.

---

[6] The British Commonwealth emerged as a network of former countries belonging to the British Empire, with a secretariat in London, as Britain was unlike some other European powers in exercising benign rule in her colonies and protectorates.

Military conscription for two to three years provided the manpower needed for defence at a relatively low cost. The people responded positively due to the granting of the franchise in 1957 to a quarter of the adults who had not been born in the Straits Settlements, least of all Singapore. With the separation of Singapore from the Federation, it was as if Singapore had her back to the wall and new and old citizens alike realized that there would be no Singapore if they did not provide the bodies for military service. In the same way, landowners had given up their land at almost confiscatory values due to land acquisition.

The several years of full internal self-governance from 1959 gave Singaporeans a sense of identity, even though Singapore was not fully independent until 1965. This period had been used by the 1959 elected government to build up a loyalty to Singapore: a state (later national) anthem, state crest and even state (later national) pledge had been initiated in 1959 to build up such a loyalty, including among school-children. Equal treatment to all languages in education and government was effected, with legislative proceedings and many levels of government communication taking place in all four languages of English, Chinese, Malay and Tamil. The free movement of people in and out which characterized the founding of Singapore as an EIC settlement in 1819 was continued, except that now only four "kinds" of people were officially recognized as the people of Singapore, those from India, China and the Federation of Malaya (the use of Malay means that people from the former Dutch East Indies or currently Indonesia were also recognized as being among the people of Singapore). English was an official language although there were few of British ethnicity in Singapore: However the British in their long rule of Singapore as a Straits Settlement had run English-medium schools and even English-medium higher education[7] in order to produce people who could complement the British officials who ran Singapore.

A second administrative change in the newly independent Singapore was the issue of the Singapore dollar in 1967. As mentioned previously, the British issue of the Straits dollar in 1906 stimulated economic connections with the Malay States and the British Borneo territories to the benefit of Singapore's economic growth. Singapore continued to have the Straits dollar (renamed the Malayan dollar after the Malay States joined the currency board agreement) over the time that she was a British colony, then self-governed, and part of Malaysia during 1963–1965.

However the change in governance of Singapore in 1965 brought about this economic change due to disagreement between the two now independent countries, the Federation of Malaysia and the Republic of Singapore, over who was the ultimate holder of currency board assets. Under the currency board agreement, the Federation held a 65% share in the profits of the currency board and Singapore a 29% share,

---

[7] A King Edward VII School of Medicine was started in Singapore in 1905 by the Straits Settlements government to produce doctors, and a Raffles College teaching the humanities was started in 1929 to produce teachers and civil servants.

with the remaining 6% belonging to the British Borneo territories (3.25% to Sarawak, 2% to Sabah and 0.75% to Brunei).[8] These percentages were worked out based on estimates of the currency circulating in each of these territories.

The Singapore government would not have the Federation having final say on currency board assets, as the acrimony from the 1965 separation still remained, and the two finance ministers then, Tan Siew Sin from the Federation and Goh Keng Swee from Singapore, distrusted each other.[9] Hence when the time came for the renewal of the currency board agreement in 1967, both countries chose not to renew and the Malaysian ringgit and the Singapore dollar were born. So also was the Bruneian dollar. All three countries agreed to have an interchangeability agreement so that there was parity between all three new currencies. However that between Singapore and the Federation was not renewed in 1973 while that between Brunei and Singapore continues to be in force today. Brunei, though rich, is small and keeps its reserves in Singapore, so that parity is not a problem. The Federation however has seen its ringgit slide from a 1:1 parity to a 1:3 exchange rate today.

This change of having a Singapore dollar has enabled Singapore to grow its financial sector in the 1970s and up to today, as the world moved from a fixed though adjustable exchange rate system in 1973 to a floating exchange rate system today.[10]

Singapore took advantage of the floating exchange rate system to cultivate financial activity in financial arbitrage, even between time zones, with the introduction of broadband internet in 1999 enabling transactions to be made in seconds. Banks and other financial institutions were attracted to Singapore by various incentives, including the withdrawal of the then 40% income tax on foreign deposits, which enabled the Asian dollar[11] market to be launched in 1968 in Singapore.

One aspect of the change in the Straits dollar of 1906 remains today: the Singapore dollar is still on the currency board system in that its issue is fully backed by foreign assets. This is no longer the single foreign asset of the British pound sterling, but a trade-weighted basket of currencies, not disclosed and periodically adjusted by the Monetary Authority of Singapore (MAS). The reserves of the MAS are used to intervene in the foreign exchange market to keep the exchange rate on a band deemed necessary for Singapore. This rate changes fairly frequently and affects the competitiveness of exports as well as the cost-of-living due to Singapore being a highly open

---

[8] Brunei was not a British colony but a British protectorate i.e., a Malay kingdom "protected" by the British and hence obliged to accept British rule in all matters except religion and customs, as was the case for the nine Malay States.

[9] Tan and Goh were distantly related through families in Malacca where both were born.

[10] The USA abandoned the link of the US dollar to monetary gold at the price of US$35 to an ounce in 1973, and today the US dollar and all other currencies do not have a link to monetary gold. Gold still has a market price, but currencies only have a price to each other but not to gold or any other metal.

[11] This market dealt with US dollars outside the US but located in Asia, hence the term Asian dollar. The Eurodollar market deals with US dollars outside the US but located in Europe.

economy. Singapore thus moved out of the sterling area into monetary independence: Ties with the former British Commonwealth weakened and financial and other ties with other countries strengthened. Singapore became a global city in terms of money as well as in financial matters.

6. Future Changes

How do the governance and economic changes of the past condition Singapore's future policy choices, and what changes are possible or likely? Despite some talk of Singapore eventually rejoining Malaysia, the mode of governance of Singapore is unlikely to change. Singapore will remain an independent republic. However the characteristics of its people will change.

In 1970 with the then forthcoming full withdrawal of British armed forces, the future of Singapore looked bleak and the government initiated an anti-natal population policy. Abortion was liberalized and couples were encouraged to "stop at two". Societal changes were also taking place, with increasing urbanization and enlarged educational opportunities for women. The birth rate fell so drastically that ten years later the government reversed its stance. Abortion though still legal is now discouraged through counseling, and the government embarked on a pro-natal policy, encouraging couples to have three or more children if they can afford it.

The birth rate is now 1.3 which is far below the reproduction rate of 2.2. The economy continued to grow and in 1990 the government liberalized its foreign labor policy. Previously only those from Malaysia could enter for employment purposes, reflecting Singapore's historical ties with the peninsula. Now foreign workers from "non-traditional" sources can enter on work permits for those below a certain salary level and on employment passes for those above that level. The workforce is now more than one-third foreign, so much so there is a backlash among Singaporeans who feel that their salaries are kept low by the inflow of such foreign workers. Thus, the past policy of free movement of people in and out is slowly being replaced by a controlled flow of foreigners. Currently, the government is complementing the 33,000 births a year with the offer of citizenship to 20,000 foreigners every year.

Modifications to other previous changes are possible. For example, a separate Singapore dollar means that maintaining export competitiveness through exchange rate depreciation is now possible.[12] The past policy of free trade might be modified to

---

[12] Competitiveness is much more intense now in a world where giants like India and China are adopting the same policies which helped Singapore succeed in the past, such as attracting multinationals and giving financial incentives to new investors. The present policy keeps the exchange rate strong so that the cost of living is kept down, while manpower costs are kept down through political control of the trade union movement. The alternative can be pursued of keeping the cost of living down through wage control mediated by unions, while keeping exports competitive through a weaker Singapore dollar.

protect some economic activities, such as subsidies to local firms which face difficulties competing in the high-cost environment. The government is already dipping into income from its massive reserves to help the poor among the increasing number of aged: the recent Pioneer Generation package and proposed Silver Support scheme are reversals of the past policy of leaving individuals to take care of themselves. The two years of military conscription can be used to also prepare able-bodied men for their future education and job training.

Certain past administrative changes such as developing the island as a whole are still being pursued, for example through exploring the possibilities of underground caverns. But there are limits to what can be physically done in Singapore itself and Singapore should consider locating more of its economic activities outside the island. There is no need to go too far away as Singapore can invest more in neighboring Malaysia and Indonesia, where there are people and land in abundance. This would require a return to the multilingual policy effected in 1959 when much importance was attached to Malay as the national language, before the switch to a "mother-tongue" policy in the late 1970s when it was felt that Singaporeans were losing touch with Chinese virtues.

Modern Singapore (1819) began by expanding its links with the territories which make up present day Malaysia and Indonesia. A return to its Southeast Asian roots may not accelerate Singapore growth rates, but will help keep economic growth from turning negative. The country's natural locational advantage has been under utilized in much of its more recent history as an independent republic. As the world economy becomes more geographically fragmented, Singapore's future lies more in its Southeast Asian context rather than the global path it pursued in much of the last 50 years.

Administrative changes orienting Singapore back to its roots can start with language instruction and go on to offer Singapore citizenship to those from the neighboring region rather than to those from more distant China, who are now the largest foreign community in Singapore. The Singapore of 1959 which sparked off a few decades of rapid economic growth was dominated by Chinese who limited their ties with the then newly-formed People's Republic of China to make Singapore their home. Now there are many foreigners from nearby countries who may decide to make Singapore their home. The four-language policy of Singapore now may have to change to a multilingual policy in which English and Chinese may still be dominant, but Malay, Tagalog, Bangla and Thai may also be used, alongside French and Japanese. It is not high technology which counts now, but a people-centric policy.

References

Chew, ECT and E Lee (eds.) (1991). *A History of Singapore.* Singapore: Oxford University Press.

Choy, KM and I Sugimoto (2013). Trade, the Staple theory of growth and fluctuations in colonial Singapore, 1900–1939. *Australian Economic History Review*, 53(2), 121–145.

Huff, WC (1994). *Economic Growth of Singapore.* Cambridge: Cambridge University Press.

Saw, SH (1991). Population growth and control. In *A History of Singapore*, Chew and Lee (eds.). Singapore: Oxford University Press.

Sugimoto, I (2011). *Economic Growth of Singapore in the Twentieth Century.* Singapore: World Scientific.

Wong, LK (1991a). The strategic significance of Singapore in modern history. In *A History of Singapore*, Chew and Lee (eds.). Singapore: Oxford University Press.

Wong, LK (1991b). Commercial growth before the Second World War. In *A History of Singapore*, Chew and Lee (eds.). Singapore: Oxford University Press.

CHAPTER 3

Lessons of Singapore's Development for Other Developing Economies

Tilak Abeysinghe

While Singapore is grappling with policy options to sustain its success over the next 50 years, the developing world is wondering what made it such a success so far. By looking at some developing countries that are stuck in a roller-coaster ride of economic development I highlight some policy lessons they can learn from Singapore's success story. In a nutshell, as pointed out by Singapore's economic architect, Dr. Goh Keng Swee, non-economic factors matter more than the economic factors for a successful take-off of a developing economy. The chapter also highlights some complementary development strategies that are instructive to developing economies.

1. Introduction

The developing world is looking at Singapore with a sense of wonder. Wonder it is when juxtaposed against the colonial background.[1] Figure 1 shows real lifetime labor income of Singaporean households at the 20th income percentile.[2] It is very clear that household income, especially at lower levels, stagnated during the colonial era, and rose spectacularly only after the early 1960s. Singapore had a target of reaching the Swiss per capita income level by about 2,000, but surpassed the target earlier than predicted. As of 2011 Singapore's purchasing power parity (PPP)-based real per capita income at 2005 prices was US$51,600, about US$6,800 higher than the Swiss level (Penn World Table Version 8.0, online). All other development indicators tell the same story. For example, the infant mortality rate, the best single indicator of development of a country, that was above 80 per 1,000 live births in 1950 dropped to 1.8 by 2012 and now hovers around 2. In contrast, the infant mortality rate of Switzerland in 1950 was 31 and dropped to 3.6 by 2012 (Switzerland Statistics website). In 1965

---

[1] Singapore's British colonial period spanned over 1819–1959 with self-governance in 1959. Singapore joined the Federation of Malaya in 1963 and unwillingly separated and became independent in 1965.

[2] Lifetime income is computed as the discounted present value at age 20 of labor income over age 20–64. See Abeysinghe and Gu (2011) for computational details.

Figure 1.   Lifetime labor income of a Singapore resident household of the 20th income percentile by birth year of the household head (income at constant 2000 prices).

Source: See footnote 2 for reference to computational details.

only 2% of Singapore's resident labor force had tertiary education (universities and other tertiary institutions). This proportion increased almost at an exponential rate to reach 48% by 2012. In 1965 only 4% of the population owned and lived in public housing. This number increased to more than 80% by 2013 (*Singapore Yearbook of Statistics*).

At the time of independence in 1965, the economic and political challenges Singapore faced were by no means less severe than the challenges that other developing economies faced. Massive unemployment, a low-skilled workforce, a shortage of industrial as opposed to commercial entrepreneurs, lack of domestic savings, wretched housing conditions, militant labor unions, and racial riots were among the challenges. To make matters worse, with the Malaysian hinterland no longer available, Singapore had to face these challenges with hardly any natural resources to depend on except for a relatively miniscule land area of about 580 sq. km., a population size of about 1.9 million people, a deep-water harbor, and perhaps its favorable geographical location.[3] But Singapore made it; the economy took off just within 10 years from 1965 to 1975 and has been moving steadily to higher and higher altitudes since then.

When Mr. Lee Kuan Yew was asked by a foreign journalist "what was the secret of Singapore's success", Mr. Lee replied "There was no secret; we had no choice but to take a chance and sail into rough waters." Singapore worked out its own unique model for development, which cannot be transplanted elsewhere. Its development strategies themselves are evolving. The policies and strategies that served the country

---

[3] By 2014 Singapore's land area increased to 718.3 sq. km. through land reclamations and population size increased to 5.47 million people including long-term foreign residents (SingStat website).

well in the past may fail to sustain the same success in the future. In fact, many recent writings focus on current vulnerabilities of the economy and discuss possible directions for the future.[4] Nevertheless, understanding the key factors that contributed to Singapore's successful transformation from third world to first world status would help developing countries work out their own development strategies.

2. Non-Economic Factors

In a typical production function analysis, the focus is placed on factor inputs, mainly labor, capital and technology as the drivers of growth. In an economy such as that of Singapore, which is driven primarily by international investments, capital and technology are essentially intermediate inputs; what makes Singapore attractive to international capital and technology are the factors that need to be examined. Singapore's economic architect, Dr. Goh Keng Swee, a Ph.D. holder in development economics from the London School of Economics, had the opportunity to test economic theories in real life. He said, "Our experience confirms some of the conventional wisdom of growth theory but refutes much of the rest. The role of government is pivotal. Non-economic factors, which have yet to be reduced to a coherent multi-disciplinary system, are more important than economic variables." (Goh, 2004). The Nobel laureate, Amartya Sen, reiterated these views by arguing that good governance, not less governance, is crucial to addressing the challenges of economic inequality, environmental degradation and terrorism.[5] The importance of political stability and good governance is again re-iterated in the 2008 Growth Report prepared by the Nobel Laureate Michael Spence on behalf of the Commission on Growth and Development (2008).

2.1. *Political Stability and Quality of Governance*

Political stability and good governance played a key role in Singapore's success. Not only the experience of Singapore, but the experience of other East and Southeast Asian economies amply demonstrates the importance of political stability in sustaining growth. Single-party rule over a long period provided the platform for a successful take-off of their economies. The frequent change of power between political parties creates a situation of what the American economist Mancur Olson called a "roving bandit" (Olson, 2000). The role of the roving bandit is to plunder as much as possible during his short stay in power without doing anything in return for the plundered (recall the bandits in the movie "Seven Samurai").

---

[4] See, for example, Low and Vadaketh (2014) and Lim (2014, 2015) and references therein.
[5] Amartya Sen, speech delivered in Singapore.

The problem with a single party rule is that it may become a "stationary bandit". Although both bandits are bad, the stationary bandit is still better than the roving bandit. The stationary bandit has the incentive to make the pie bigger so that he can plunder more while keeping the plundered also better off. This is where the quality of governance comes in.

Political stability is an exogenous variable; leadership matters in providing political stability. However, political stability does not ensure quality of governance. A dictatorship also provides political stability but we do not see their citizenry prospering. Quality of governance is an endogenous variable that emerges through the type of economic system and political process in place. A private sector-driven open economy, open to international trade and investment, is one mechanism that tends to discipline government bureaucracies and enhance the quality of governance. There is a large literature that blames governments for failures in the developing world, and discussions abound on why good governance is essential for development and ethnic peace.[6] However, most of this literature considers quality of governance to be an exogenous variable that needs to be provided by some enlightened leadership.

Although policy-makers are responsible for formulating and implementing good policies, there is no mechanism in closed economies to keep them under check. Even the most promising leaders in closed economies have failed to bring about the changes they desired because of overpowering bureaucracies. The leaders who have succeeded in opening economies have managed to create, perhaps slowly, more responsible bureaucracies. China and India are two recent examples where openness is playing a highly disciplining role on their formidable bureaucracies. In the case of Singapore, although circumstances pushed the adoption of open economy policies and the leadership deserves full credit for its quality of governance, we often forget the role that Singapore's global dependence played in disciplining the country's single-party government. Malaysia and Sri Lanka provide another interesting contrast. Both countries adopted ethnic preference policies but Sri Lanka got embroiled in a crippling separatist war for nearly three decades that ended in 2009. A careful examination of the policies and performance of the two countries suggest that it was the open economy that helped Malaysia move forward despite the constant presence of ethnic tension in the country. It was import substitution (closed economy) policies that paved the way for the ethnic conflict in Sri Lanka, where poverty and relative deprivation became a breeding ground for both communist and ethnic rebellions.

Openness, once set in motion, appears to generate a sustaining feedback loop between government policies and the country's socio-economic environment that will bring about economic growth and ethnic peace. Policy-makers in this setting are more

---

[6] See Collier and Hoeffler (2007) and Nava and Abeysinghe (2008) for some references.

likely to implement socio-economic policies that harness ethnic peace and share the growth dividends. In a study of the factors determining ethnic peace in multi-ethnic societies, we formulated a three-equation regression model to assess the effect of openness on growth, quality of governance and ethnic conflicts. The details are presented in Nava and Abeysinghe (2008) and here I summarize some results. Our panel study covered some conflict-prone countries. We measured quality of governance by a proxy, a corruption index ranging between 0 and 10 with zero indicating the most corrupt (lowest quality) and ten the most clean (highest quality) governments. We used two measures of openness. One is the commonly used trade-GDP ratio. The other is a more comprehensive measure called "composite trade openness index" developed by Gwartney and his co-researchers (Gwartney *et al.*, 2001), which closely captures the legal and institutional framework of openness. This index also ranges between 0 and 10; the larger the value the higher is the openness of a country. The regressions also included an index on democracy, computed based on Marshall and Keith (2002), which ranges between 0 and 20, with 0 indicating autocracy and 20 indicating most democratic.

The regression results show a very robust relationship between the openness indicators and the quality of governance indicator; the higher the openness the higher the quality of governance. The results also show that openness is conducive to higher growth and lowers the probability of ethnic conflicts. We focused only on trade openness. Openness to both international investment and trade is likely to make these results stronger. The results also show that a higher level of democracy tends to improve the quality of governance.

Another finding of our exercise and some others (Collier and Hoeffler, 2007) is that fragile democracies are not very conducive to containing ethnic conflicts. This again points to the importance of political stability. Some developing countries are less likely to settle to a single-party rule for a long enough period for the economy to take off. Given this scenario, an alternative would be for all the political parties to agree upon a long-term economic agenda, a blueprint, that the ruling party cannot deviate from without the consent of the other parties. The objective here is to set the vision beyond a single political term in office and reduce the engagement of the ruling party in crowd-pleasing activities to win the next election. Such an agenda guarantees continuity and keeps room open for branching off to new areas. Obviously the key ingredients of the long-term policy agenda need to be worked out carefully.

2.2. *National Security*

The need for national security should be self-evident. Unfortunately many developing countries have run into trouble and persistent instability when national security was compromised. Countries have more often been derailed by internal threats than by external ones. Singapore's government lays a very high priority on national security and allocates a substantial proportion of the government budget to defence and security (Figure 3). Such high expenditure may appear wasteful, but experience around the globe shows that it is a necessary evil. The Singapore government's stand on this is that economic fortunes may fluctuate but national security cannot be compromised. Peace and stability cannot be taken for granted.

2.3. *Politicians with High Opportunity Cost*

In many developing countries politics has become a profession with zero opportunity cost. In other words, politics is deemed as a profession that does not require specific skills, except perhaps oratorical skills. In contrast, the Singapore cabinet is made up of highly skilled professionals drawn from various professions and paid handsomely to make politics attractive to such professionals. How much a politician should be paid is a contentious issue. The general public likes to see a politician as someone serving the country with a sense of sacrifice. But the reality is far from this ideal. Politicians in many developing countries spend more time enriching themselves through corrupt means than serving the country. In Singapore the top leaders remain non-corrupt and so do the rest.

Having competent politicians makes a difference in terms of foresight and vision. Singapore's government was often criticized in the past by some Western critics for its authoritarian style of governance, harsh actions on some political opponents, diluting the power of labor unions, and a lack of freedom of speech. The government has also been harsh on those who arouse race and religious sensitivities. But all this ensured peace and stability and created an atmosphere conducive for rapid economic development. Singapore is now a developed mature economy and what is heard abroad about Singapore is mostly praise, not criticism. It is Singaporeans now who are demanding more political freedom and asking for more opposition voices in the parliament.

3. Development Strategies

Pragmatism, not ideology, has been the guiding principle of Singapore's development strategy. Many newly independent countries battered by colonial rule resorted to a new path to restart their economies that ended in failure. Singapore, however, adopted the policy of historical continuity and diversification. Under the British, Singapore was an entrepot trading center. This activity has continued to this day and grown in magnitude, though its relative importance declined over time as the economy diversified.

Given Singapore's vulnerability and lack of natural resources, its policy-makers gave priority to policies that promoted economic growth and quickly moved away from the British-style welfare state. In this regard, there are four aspects of Singapore's development strategy that are very instructive to other developing economies: human resources, efficiency infrastructure, international competitiveness and development welfare.[7]

3.1. *Targeted Education and Training*

Singapore has invested heavily in its only resource, human skills. Education and training were targeted for the needs of the economy, so Singapore was able to minimize the mismatch between skills supplied and skills needed by industries. In many developing countries, unemployment among educated youth has been a breeding ground for communist and rebellion activities. Sri Lanka is a classic example in this regard. Almost free education all the way till a university degree is completed expanded rapidly in Sri Lanka in the 1950s and 1960s. Lacking in lab facilities, most of the expansion happened in nontechnical areas like humanities and social sciences. The economy did not grow fast enough to absorb these educated youth and this contributed to the insurgency in 1971 (Obeyesekere, 1974).

In Singapore, as the economy expanded and shifted more towards knowledge-based activities, the proportion of university degree holders in the workforce also increased. Figure 2 shows that this proportion started to increase rapidly only since the early 1990s. In the early 1970s less than 2.4% of the labor force were degree holders, increasing only to 6.3% by 1990. However, over the next two decades, the proportion increased rapidly to 31% by 2013. Table 1 shows the percentage distribution of university enrolment by course and gender. The lion's share of university enrolment has occurred in engineering sciences although there has been a gender difference and a recent downward trend in enrolment in this field. With the expansion of service industries, the university enrolment in business and social science courses has been increasing. By contrast, even as of 2011 the lion's share of university education in Sri Lanka has been in humanities and social sciences (42%).[8]

---

[7] Further discussions of Singapore's development strategies can be found in Ghesquiere (2007), Abeysinghe (2012) and Lim (2014).

[8] Online statistics from University Grants Commission: http://www.statistics.gov.lk/Pocket%20Book/chap13.pdf.

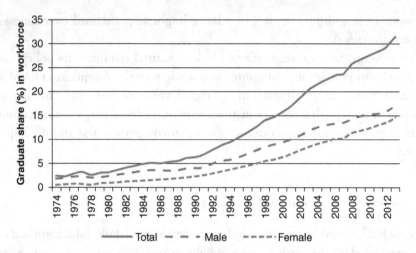

Figure 2. Proportion of economically active university degree holders in Singapore resident labor force.

Source: Department of statistics STS database and *Yearbook of Statistics*.

Table 1. Singapore: Enrolment in university first degree courses (Percentage distribution by gender).

Course	Gender	1995	2000	2005	2010	2013
Engineering sciences	M	50.0	60.7	56.7	43.4	40.7
	F	10.3	23.0	23.9	17.3	17.3
Accountancy, business and administration	M	14.7	9.6	11.8	14.1	15.5
	F	29.5	23.0	21.8	19.6	19.4
Natural, physical and mathematical sciences	M	8.1	6.4	8.5	11.1	10.4
	F	13.1	13.4	15.4	15.6	15.3
Humanities and social sciences	M	9.6	8.2	8.4	11.0	11.8
	F	30.6	24.6	21.7	22.9	23.4
Information technology	M	7.2	6.3	5.5	7.7	8.7
	F	5.0	3.8	3.3	3.6	4.2
Medicine, dentistry, health sciences	M	4.5	3.9	3.6	3.7	4.0
	F	3.1	3.4	4.1	5.3	6.2
Architecture and building	M	3.2	3.0	2.6	2.4	2.5
	F	4.1	4.7	3.9	3.9	3.7
Law	M	2.3	1.3	1.5	2.3	2.5
	F	2.8	1.9	2.3	2.7	2.4
Education, applied arts, mass communication, services	M	0.5	0.8	1.3	4.3	3.8
	F	1.7	2.1	3.6	9.3	8.0

Source: Computed from the Singapore *Yearbook of Statistics*, various years.

3.2. Efficiency Infrastructure

Singapore has become a costly country to do business. What makes it attractive to foreign investors despite the relative cost disadvantage is its "efficiency infrastructure". This refers to not just the quality of the physical infrastructure but also the efficiency of the services that go with it. Efficiency infrastructure is what sets Singapore's port and airport apart from potential competitors who are otherwise geographically more advantaged. Apart from efficient services, Singapore also provides "innovation infrastructure" to carry out innovative and creative work in a legally conducive environment (Koh, 2006; Tan and Phang, 2006).

Constant upgrading of physical infrastructure is a regular phenomenon in Singapore. A negative aspect of these infrastructure developments is that they are built following the demolition of existing structures that are in perfectly good condition. This is a result of the limited land area that constrains Singapore. Nevertheless, from a global perspective, this approach involves a substantial waste of resources and environmental costs.

3.3. International Competitiveness

As a small open economy, international competitiveness plays a very important role in sustaining Singapore's economic growth (Wilson and Abeysinghe, 2002). The 2014–2015 Global Competitiveness Report by World Economic Forum ranked Singapore in second place behind Switzerland in terms of overall competitiveness among 144 countries. The ranking was done based on 11 broad criteria (with many sub categories) that basically capture the level of productivity of a country, which in turn sets the level of prosperity.[9]

While the improvement in productivity is a long term achievement, Singapore utilizes some other policy tools to enhance short term competitiveness. The policy mix can easily be seen through the components of relative unit business cost (RUBC). The log of RUBC for country i against a group of countries j expressed in US dollars can be written as

$$\ln \text{RUBC}_i = \ln\left(\frac{\text{UBC}_i / E_i}{\text{UBC}_j / E_j}\right) = [\ln \text{UBC}_i - \ln \text{UBC}_j] - [\ln E_i - \ln E_j], \quad (1)$$

[9]The 11 criteria with the corresponding ranking of Singapore are: institutions (3), infrastructure (2), macroeconomic environment (15), health and primary education (3), higher education and training (2), goods market efficiency (1), labor market efficiency (2), financial market development (2), technological readiness (7), market size (31), business sophistication (19), and innovation (9). Online: http://www.weforum.org/reports/global-competitiveness-report-2014-2015.

where E is the nominal exchange rate, local currency units per one US dollar. Note that UBC_j and E_j are weighted averages of the corresponding individual components. If UBC is expressed as the weighted geometric average of unit labor cost (ULC) and unit non-labor cost (NLC) and noting that ULC = W/PROD, where W is the nominal wage rate and PROD is labor productivity we can express (1) as

$$\ln RUBC_i = [\alpha \ln W_i - \beta \ln W_j] - [\alpha \ln PROD_i - \beta \ln PROD_j]$$
$$+ [(1-\alpha)\ln NLC_i - (1-\beta)\ln NLC_j][-[\ln E_i - \ln E_i], \tag{2}$$

where α and β are the weights on ULC of country i and country group j respectively.[10] Note that the country loses its international competitiveness if RUBC continues to increase.

If $\alpha \approx \beta$, then (2) can be expressed in terms of relative wage, relative productivity, relative NLC and relative exchange rate. As an economy grows, the wage cost increases and it may increase faster than that of competitors. In the long run, this can be offset only through productivity improvement. In the short run, international competiveness is dominated by the movements of wages (and other costs such as commercial rentals) and the exchange rate.

A unique feature of the Singapore labor market is downward wage flexibility achieved through policy measures. Downward wage rigidity exacerbates an economic downturn and builds up unemployment. Because of extreme dependence on external demand, Singapore is the first country in the region to be hit by a downturn in its major trading partners; it is also the first country to come out of a downturn. This has been made possible partly because of institutionalized wage flexibility. Wages include a variable component that can easily be slashed during a downturn because workers are mentally prepared to forgo it. The government also cuts the employer's central provident fund (CPF) contribution rate to lower the wage cost to the employer. Although these wage policies were aimed at protecting jobs during economic downturns they caused hardships on low income households, especially with regard to mortgage payments that were tied to the CPF. Thus in the wake of the 2008 global financial crisis, the government introduced a novel Jobs Credit Scheme. This entailed paying firms from the government coffers to keep Singaporeans employed during the downturn. Note that these were only short-term policy measures implemented during economic downturns.

As for the exchange rate, the Monetary Authority of Singapore (MAS) has adopted an appreciating exchange rate policy to counter imported inflation, which negatively impacts export competitiveness. However this negative impact is substantially offset by the high import content of exports (Abeysinghe and Choy, 2007).

---

[10] See Abeysinghe and Lee (1998) for some computational details.

During downturns, the MAS lets the exchange rate depreciate or slows down the rate of appreciation. However, the appreciating exchange rate forces exporting firms to be efficient and productive to be competitive.

3.4. *Development Welfare*

Western-style social welfare is something that the Singapore government has long resisted. Instead, it diverts resources to "development welfare" (as opposed to "consumption welfare") to provide education, housing, healthcare and other services at subsidized rates to Singaporeans. Based on the philosophy of equalizing opportunities (not outcomes) through education and training, the government emphasizes self and family responsibility in saving for rainy days and retirement. It has also exercised fiscal prudence and kept both government revenue and expenditure at relatively low levels, below 15% of GDP on average in recent years (down from 25% in the 1980s and 20% in the late 1990s). In contrast, government expenditure of OECD countries exceeds 40% of GDP.

This may appear as excessive frugality on the part of the Singapore government. But the difference arises from consumption welfare, not from development welfare. Figure 3 shows the government social development expenditure (major items like education, health, social and family development and national development) per person of the resident population has trended upward sharply. Figure 3 also shows

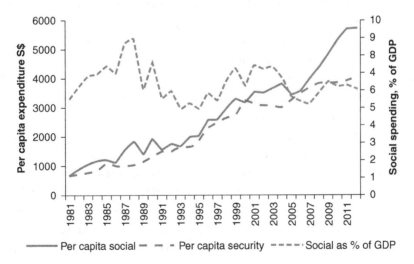

Figure 3. Per capita government expenditure on social development, security and external relations (left scale) and social development spending as % of GDP (right scale).

Note: Per capita figures refer to Singapore resident population, not total population. Expenditure includes both operating and development expenditures.

that social development expenditure as a percent of GDP has not trended downward, instead it has remained steady at around 6.4%. The main reason for fluctuation in this expenditure item is fluctuations of GDP growth. Figure 3 also shows that since 2006 per capita social spending increased much faster than security spending.

Many developing countries run into persistent budget deficits leading to a build-up of a huge public debt burden, both internal and external. From very early on, the Singapore government avoided Keynesian style deficit financing and did not fall into a debt trap. Perhaps driven by Confucian values of thrift and prudence, the government has generated budget surpluses year after year (Abeysinghe and Jayawickrama, 2008). Although public debt in Singapore has increased steadily over the years and stood around 105% of GDP in 2013, public debt in Singapore is a misnomer. The standard government budget constraint $D_t = (1+r)D_{t-1} - S_t$, where D is public debt, r is the interest rate and S is the budget surplus, does not fit the Singapore situation. Growing public debt contradicts a recurrent flow of budget surpluses. But the Singapore government issues government securities simply to develop the domestic bond market. External debt has been zero since 1995, and overall government financial assets far exceed government debt, so there is no net public debt.

Development welfare is growth-enhancing and highly desirable for low income developing countries. With increasing prosperity, however, countries may face the problem of increasing income inequality and therefore relative poverty. Singapore is at such a stage now ((Abeysinghe and Wong, 2014; Low and Vadaketh, 2014), and is addressing the problem of a widening income gap in two fronts. First, the government is moving more toward consumption welfare to help low income groups. This was done on an *ad hoc* basis, but since 2006 special transfers to low income households have become a permanent feature of the budget. The introduction of the Workfare Income Supplement (WIS) scheme is noteworthy. Instead of unemployment benefits, which tend to lengthen unemployment duration, an individual receives a "workfare" allowance from the government only if he or she is employed but earns a low wage. Second, the government is working to equalize educational and training opportunities to increase intergenerational social mobility.

Widening income gaps, especially when non-labor incomes are also taken into account, is a global phenomenon. Income inequality, especially in countries with large populations, can lead to highly undesirable socio-economic consequences (Wilkinson and Pickett, 2009).[11] This has to be factored into the growth strategies of developing economies very early on. A certain amount of consumption welfare,

---

[11] See also their website: http://www.equalitytrust.org.uk/.

whether in the form of "workfare" or direct transfers and subsidies, is essential to prevent relative poverty from becoming socially intolerable and disruptive.

4. Conclusion

There are some features of the Singapore economy that cannot be easily analyzed using standard economic theories. This is because Singapore worked out its own unique model of economic development that cannot be transplanted elsewhere. Moreover, the Singapore model is evolving in the face of new challenges the country is facing. Nevertheless, there are lessons from the Singapore model that are of immense value to developing countries that are struggling to take their economies off the ground. I have highlighted some policy options that other developing countries can learn from Singapore's success story. In essence, the Singapore government played a critical role in combining political stability with market efficiency to produce a win-win solution for the country.

There is much discussion in the literature that a lack of good governance is the cause of the stagnation of developing economies. This literature considers quality of governance as something that has to be provided by some enlightened leadership. What I have argued here is that quality of governance is an endogenous variable that emerges through the type of political and economic system in place.

Finally, I would like to emphasize that the aim of a developing country should not be for faster growth to catch up with others. Rather, the aim should be for sustained growth even at moderate levels. Faster growth comes with a price. Apart from rapid environmental degradation, it also tends to degrade human qualities. The quality of growth matters more than the quantity of growth.

Acknowledgments

I would like to thank Linda Lim for her extensive comments on this essay. Thanks are also due to Chan Kok Hoe for his valuable inputs and my drinking partners (Lee Soo Ann, Choy Keen Meng, Roland Cheo, Yong Soo Keong) for their engaging discussions on the Singapore economy.

References

Abeysinghe, T and KM Choy (2007). *The Singapore Economy: An Econometric Perspective.* London: Routledge (Paperback edition issued in Oct 2008).

Abeysinghe, T (2012). Singapore: Economy. In *The Far East and Australasia*, L Daniel (ed.) Routledge, London: Europa Publications.

Abeysinghe, T and J Gu (2011). Lifetime income and housing affordability in singapore. *Urban Studies*, 48, 1875–1891.

Abeysinghe, T and A Jayawickrama (2008). Singapore's recurrent budget surplus: The role of conservative growth forecasts. *Journal of Asian Economics*, 19, 117–124.

Abeysinghe, T and HC Lee (1998). Singapore's cost competitiveness in the region: A technical note on RULC. *Singapore Economic Review*, 43, 12–23.

Abeysinghe, T and YH Wong (2014). Income inequality in Singapore: Do housing prices play a role? SCAPE Working Chapter 2014/01, Department of Economics, National University of Singapore.

Collier, P and A Hoeffler (2007). Civil war. In *Handbook of Defense Economics*, T Sandler and K Hartley (eds.). Vol. 2. Amsterdam: Elsevier.

Collier, P and D Rohner (2007). Democracy, development and conflict, *The Journal of European Economic Association*, 69(1), 1–27.

Commission on Growth and Development (2008). The Growth Report: Strategies for Sustained Growth and Inclusive Development. Prepared by Michael Spence.

Ghesquiere, H (2007). *Singapore's Success: Engineering Economic Growth*. Singapore: Thomson Learning.

Goh, KS (2004). *The Practice of Economic Growth* (1977, 1st edn., 1995), Singapore: Marshall Cavendish Academic.

Gwartney, J, L Robert, P Walter and S Charles (2001). Economic Freedom of the World, Annual Report, the Fraser Institute, Vancouver.

Koh, WTH (2006). Towards innovation-driven economic growth: R&D capabilities and entrepreneurship in Singapore. In *The Economic Prospects of Singapore*, WTH Koh and R Mariano (eds.). Singapore: Pearson Addison-Wesley.

Lim, L (2014). Singapore's success: After the miracle. In *Handbook of Emerging Economies*, RE Looney (ed.). London: Routledge.

Lim, L (2015). Beyond the "Global City" paradigm. In *Singapore Perspectives 2015: Choices*, S Hoe and C Soon (eds.). Singapore: World Scientific and Institute of Policy Studies (forthcoming).

Low, D and S Vadaketh (eds.) (2014). *Hard Choices: Challenging the Singapore Consensus*. Singapore: National University of Singapore Press.

Marshall, MG and J Keith (2002). Polity IV Project: Political Regime Characteristics and Transitions, 1800–2001, Data set user Manual, University of Maryland, College Park.

Nava, RK and T Abeysinghe (2008). Economic Openness, Disciplined Government and Ethnic Peace, SCAPE Working Chapter 2008/03, Department of Economics, National University of Singapore.

Obeyesekere, G (1974). Some comments on the social background of the April 1971 insurgency in Sri Lanka. *Journal of Asian Studies*, 33(3), 367–384.

Olson, M (2000). *Power and Prosperity: Outgrowing Communist and Capitalist Dictatorships*. New York: Oxford University Press.

Tan, KS and SY Phang (2006). Economic growth and strategic investment in infrastructure: Perspectives from Singapore. In *The Economic Prospects of Singapore*, WTH Koh and R Mariano (eds.), Singapore: Pearson Addison-Wesley.

Wilson, P and T Abeysinghe (2002). International competitiveness. In *Singapore in the 21st Century: Issues and Strategies*, AT Koh, KL Lim, WT Hui, B Rao and MK Chng (eds.). Singapore: McGraw-Hill.

Wilkinson, RG and K Pickett (2009). *The Spirit Level: Why More Equal Societies Almost Always Do Better.* London: Allan Lane.

CHAPTER 4

The Role of the State in Singapore: Pragmatism in Pursuit of Growth

Tan Kim Song and Manu Bhaskaran

This chapter looks at how government intervention shapes the evolution of the Singapore economy and accounts for its successes and failures over the past 50 years. Compared with other dynamic Asian economies, the Singapore government's approach to intervene in the economy is both more extensive and more intrusive, but with a narrow focus on GDP growth and surplus accumulation as the primary objectives. The ruling government's near complete dominance in politics has enabled it to mobilize resources to create the preconditions for strong GDP growth and high savings. But the impact on the broader development of the economy and the long term sustainability of growth is less obvious. High GDP growth and strong savings have been achieved without developing the inherent production and indigenous innovation capacity, securing a larger hinterland and providing a less skewed income distribution and higher quality of life for residents. As the economy enters a new phase where more complex and multi-faceted development is needed, the Singapore government will require more than its vaunted competency in mobilizing resources to deliver the outcome.

1. Introduction: The State in Singapore's Economic Development

Much has been written about the pervasive presence of the state in the Singapore economy and the various forms that government intervention in the economy takes.[1] The government played a pivotal role not only in mapping out the strategic direction for the economy, but also in driving much of its structural transformation over the past 50 years. Hardly any major strategic or structural change in Singapore in the past five decades took place without the involvement of or a strong push from the government. Unlike other economies, the presence of the state (which includes not only the public sector but also the various statutory boards and government linked companies or GLCs) in the Singapore economy has remained pervasive over time, even as the

---

[1] See for example, Lim (2014); World Bank (1993) etc.

economy became more mature and markets and institutions became more developed. To a large extent, the story of Singapore's economic development success can be seen as the story of the government's successful interventions in the economy. Likewise, the weaknesses or failures in the economy also reflect, in many ways, the failures of government intervention.

The state-driven development model has been widely credited for the success of the Singapore economy until the late 1990s. From 1965 till 1998, with the exception of the recession year of 1985, the Singapore economy expanded at near double-digit rates of growth, raising per capita GDP to one of the highest in the world. Strong economic growth and the resources generated allowed the government to invest massively in infrastructure and social amenities that not only improved the living standard of the people but also helped increase the efficiency of the economy and crowd in private investment. The government was not averse to using GLCs to undertake investments that might intrude into the space of the private sector but which it considered strategic for the long term growth of the economy. This robust growth was achieved with persistently high savings and a very strong fiscal position for the government, resulting by the late 1990s in Singapore having one of the highest per capita foreign reserves in the world, providing a strong shield against external shocks.

Together with the other Asian Tigers, Singapore's economic success attracted worldwide attention and was seen as a model for development. Many commentators found Singapore's success particularly fascinating because of the odds that the country had to overcome. As a small city-state with no meaningful resources or hinterland, Singapore had few natural competitive advantages besides its strategic location and the facilities that had been built up during the British colonial times for its role as a regional transport, logistics and trading center.

Compared to the situation in the 1990s, the picture is somewhat different at the half-century mark of nationhood in 2015. Over the past 10 to 15 years, there has been a major strategic shift to transform Singapore into a "global city". While the average GDP growth rate remained high during this period and the per capita income of the country continued to surge, developments in other areas of the economy have been less satisfactory. Today, Singapore has one of the most unequal income distributions (as measured by the Gini coefficient) among developed countries, a large segment of the population suffers from long years of wage stagnation, and productivity growth performance is dismal compared with that of other dynamic Asian economies.[2] Despite the nation's wealth and the high level of savings at the macroeconomic level, there are serious concerns about the adequacy of savings for retirement at the individual level. Meanwhile, the quality of life is seen to have declined significantly over the past 10 to 15 years when the population rose sharply without the necessary

---

[2] See Bhaskaran *et al.* (2012) and Low *et al.* (2013) for a fuller discussion of these issues.

increase in provision of public services, infrastructure and public goods in general.[3] Having progressed "from the Third World to the First World" and moved close to the frontier of production efficiency, there is also less clarity on where future sources of economic growth are likely to come from.

Many of the challenges that confront the Singapore economy today can be seen as a direct result of specific measures taken over the past 10 to 15 years, but some can also be traced to the economic growth strategy pursued in earlier periods. While the economy's growth orientation and the challenges it faced changed over 50 years, the government's basic approach of intervention in the economy has remained consistent. This basic approach is made up of three elements. First is the belief that the government should play an active role in the economy and that such intervention would make a big difference to the performance of the economy and the well-being of citizens. As a small city-state with no hinterland to fall back on, the PAP government lives with an acute sense of vulnerability to the vagaries of the global economy. In its view, taking a laissez faire approach and leaving the fate of the economy to free market forces, as Hong Kong does, would be too risky. The government needs to intervene and forcefully steer the economy in a certain direction. The success of government intervention in the early years of independence reinforced this belief which has since become part of the government's DNA.

Compared with the other dynamic Asian economies, government intervention in the economy in Singapore is both more intrusive and more extensive. Not only does it use the traditional fiscal revenue raising and spending tools to reallocate resources, it also makes extensive use of GLCs to carry out business and economic activities that have significant impact on the private sector. Right from the beginning, the government has not shied away from investing in industries that it deems important to the economy or those that are seen to be "sunrise" industries. In earlier days, state ownership was generally restricted to strategic sectors of the economy such as banking, telecommunications, transportation, defense, infrastructure, airport and port, as well as ownership of land which the government felt had to be treated as a strategic resource in a land scarce country. Through corporations such as DBS Bank, Singtel, Singapore Airlines and ST Engineering, among others, the public sector played a leading role as an investor and catalyst for Singapore's development, and led innovation in nascent but promising fields. In more recent times, GLCs have been used to further Singapore's ambition to grow an "external wing" to its economy by investing directly in the faster growing regions of Asia. State ownership came about as a response to the

---

[3] In a study on the gap between per capita GDP and well-being of the people, Singapore was found to have the greatest gap of all the 134 countries studies. That is, Singapore's per capita GDP figures were the least accurate in measuring the well-being of its people. Singapore had a welfare score of less than half of Hong Kong, despite having a slightly higher per capita GDP. See Jones and Klenow (2010), as cited by Lim (2014).

challenges the government encountered rather than as a result of ideologically driven nationalization.

Second, the government has maintained a near obsessive focus on GDP growth and accumulation of surplus (both of the government and of the nation) as the primary objectives of economic policy. It sees GDP growth as the main measure of economic success and the key to a "better life" for the people. At the same time, it is almost paranoid about the need to save to prepare for rainy days, running large budget surpluses year after year even without including certain revenues (e.g., proceeds from land sales), which underestimates the size of the surpluses.

The primacy of economic growth means that it often takes precedence over other development objectives. Specifically efficiency was prized over equity: discussion of "equity" and "income distribution" was often shunned as it was seen as detrimental to the pursuit of efficiency and economic growth. This has resulted in "producer surplus" being given much greater priority over "consumer surplus". Fiscal policy tends to concentrate on the supply side, to help corporates increase production, rather than be used as countercyclical measures to manage fluctuations in aggregate demand. Policy incentives tend to favor large corporates such as multinational corporations (MNCs) and GLCs as they are seen to be able to generate greater producer surplus through economies of scale. Small and medium enterprises (SMEs) complained for many years that they were neglected by the government. While a Competition Act was adopted in 2004 to help promote market competition and efficiency, a large number of industries were excluded from coverage, effectively giving the firms in these industries a high degree of monopoly power.[4] As the government pointed out, the law aimed to promote market efficiency, not necessarily to enhance consumer surplus. Other than the Consumer Association of Singapore (CASE) which is usually headed by a Member of Parliament from the ruling party, there has been no effort to promote a strong consumer protection and advocacy movement in Singapore.[5]

Third, the government is willing and able to mobilize all resources in the nation to achieve its economic objective. Economic growth takes center stage and social policies are often designed or modified to support the pursuit of economic growth. Social policy objectives would often be subordinated to that of economic growth if the two were in conflict. The near complete dominance that the ruling party enjoys in the political sphere has allowed it to push through growth-centric policies and legislation without much resistance. Strong political control also allows it to take pragmatic and at times unconventional and controversial approaches toward policy making without

---

[4] See the List of Sectoral Exclusion in the Competition Act 2004, Ministry of Trade and Industry, Singapore.

[5] The government tends to discourage the formation of mass grassroots organizations other than those approved by the ruling party. A strong consumer advocacy group could be seen as such a mass organization. See Tan (1995).

having to be concerned about political costs or accusations of inconsistency. The decision to build two casinos in 2005, despite strong opposition from many social groups and the government's own longstanding objection to such a move, was a case in point. The casinos (or what the government prefers to call "Integrated Resorts") were seen as an important component in the effort to transform Singapore into a global city, to provide new sources of growth for the economy.

The decision to peg the remuneration of political office holders and senior civil servants to very top private sector pay, despite disagreement from many quarters, is another example of the government's ability to push through what it considers pragmatic policy measures undeterred by considerations of political costs.[6] Given the important and pervasive role that the government plays in the economy, it argues that the public service sector must be staffed with high caliber people who are equal to the best in the private sector. Matching remuneration to that in the private sector is needed in order to attract and retain such talent without the risk of infesting the system with corruption.[7]

The need to be pragmatic and the ability to experiment with new policies did help foster certain innovativeness in the policy making process. For example, certain key institutions such as the Housing Development Board (HDB), the Central Provident Fund (CPF) and the Economic Development Board (EDB) were encouraged to think out-of-the-box to tackle the unique problems that Singapore faced early on. Their experiences have provided a new benchmark and models for other countries to adopt.

The government's pragmatism is manifest in its willingness to continually calibrate the balance between state intervention and preservation of market discipline. While the government is heavily involved in investment and production activities and competes directly with the private sector in many cases, it is conscious of the need to avoid the inefficiency and wastage associated with many state owned enterprises elsewhere. Efforts are made to ensure sufficient competition (by allowing more than one player in an industry) while providing adequate support for GLCs. The approach was to intervene in the economy forcefully when needed but to leave the rest to the market so long as the balance leads to high economic growth and accumulation of surpluses.

To some extent, this basic approach to government intervention was shaped by the experience in the early days of independence. Singapore's economic prospects looked bleak as it risked losing its traditional hinterland when abruptly forced out of the Federation of Malaysia in 1965 while also subject to near-war or "Confrontation"

---

[6] See the White Paper on Ministerial Salary, 1994 and various revisions subsequently.
[7] The topic continues to be controversial and has been the subject of debate in Parliament a few times over the years.

with Indonesia. There was also capital flight, labor strife, a communist insurgency and ethnic tensions. In the words of a former senior civil servant, Singapore was in 1965 a "stagnant entrepot economy and a crumbling city, with a large slum area and an unemployment rate of over 10%" (Ngiam and Tay, 2006). Thus, as a matter of survival, the PAP government had to urgently create jobs and provide housing, schooling and other basic urban amenities for the people. This required a major role for the state in creating the preconditions for economic growth. In the words of Singapore's first Prime Minister Mr Lee Kuan Yew, the experience not only instilled a "siege mentality" in policymakers, but also forced the government to be pragmatic in managing economic and social problems. It had to adopt whatever policies that worked, even if they ran counter to the conventional wisdom of the day. Hence the decision to adopt an export-oriented policy and embrace MNCs as the driver of economic growth in the 1960s, when the prevailing conventional wisdom was for newly independent countries to follow import substitution policies to develop indigenous productive capacity.

This basic approach to state economic intervention led the Singapore government to run the economy almost like a corporate in relentless pursuit of bottom line figures — in this case, the GDP growth rate and accumulation of surpluses. Political office holders and senior civil servants are even remunerated, in part, according to the GDP growth that they deliver, much like corporates reward their senior management with bonuses linked to profits made. Once the objectives of high economic growth and surplus accumulation are clearly defined, they are implemented efficiently by a task-oriented government bureaucracy. In this single-minded pursuit of short run objectives, certain long term structural issues can get overlooked, and their neglect lies at the root of some of the challenges that the economy faces today.

This chapter looks at how government intervention shapes the evolution of the Singapore economy and accounts for its successes and failures. Section 2 shows how the pragmatic approach helped overcome the constraints that Singapore faced in the early phase of economic development. Section 3 explains how the pragmatic approach was again employed to restructure the economy in the early 2000s so that innovation could take center stage as a driver of growth. Section 4 discusses the problems that the pragmatic growth-centric approach to managing the economy have brought about and what this means for the future of the economy. Section 5 concludes.

2. Providing An Efficient Business Environment for Foreign Investment and Economic Growth

Broadly speaking, the evolution of the Singapore economy can be divided into two phases: Phase One, from 1965 to the late 1990s, could be characterized as a period of "foreign investment driven" growth, and Phase Two, from the early 2000s to date, could be described as one of "foreign talent driven" growth (Tan, 2014; Tan and Phang, 2005). In the first phase, foreign direct investment (FDI) was seen as the key driver of economic growth and job creation. The government sought to attract MNCs by providing an efficient environment for their operations. In the second phase, the government set out to transform the economy from an efficient "MNC hub" to a "global city",[8] one where growth is derived mainly from innovation and creativity. A more creative workforce was seen necessary to support such a growth strategy, so the policy focus shifted from attracting foreign companies to attracting creative foreign talent. Much effort was devoted to making Singapore an attractive living and working environment for such creative workers.

The heavy reliance on inflows of foreign investment and foreign talent reflects the basic constraint that Singapore faces as a small city-state: the lack of economic space, including natural resources and a sizeable domestic market. Even today, despite its strategic location and relatively well-educated workforce, as a city-state economy, Singapore remains "small" relative to other major regional and global cities (see Table 1). How to overcome the constraint of size and expand economic space to achieve sustained GDP growth has been the key question that policymakers in Singapore have had to grapple with from the beginning.

The government's main response to this lack of scale is to try to make a virtue out of necessity by treating the regional and the global economy as its "hinterland", leveraging on their strengths to make up for the lack of economic space in Singapore. It does so by embracing wholeheartedly the policy of "economic openness", openness not only in goods and services trade but also in the movement of capital and labor. Free trade in goods and services helps expand the market for Singapore's products while a liberal policy on factor flows enlarges the supply base of capital and labor that Singapore needs.

Table 1.   Comparison of cities.

City	Nominal GDP (USD bn)	Population (mn)	Physical size (sq.km)	Stock market capitalization (USD bn)*	Number of international airports	Number of universities
Singapore	327	5.5	697	414	1	6
Hong Kong	350	7.2	1108	1108	1	8
London	731	8.6	1572	3019	6	47
New York City	1210	8.4	790	18,668	3	35

Source: Collated by Centennial Asia Advisors using CEIC database and various sources.* 2012 figures.

---

[8] There is no consensus on the definition of a "global city", a term that was first coined by Saskia Sassen. See Phang (2015) for a summary of such views.

While free trade in goods and services is widely considered the optimal policy for small economies, the decisions to open Singapore's door wide to FDI in the 1960s and to allow a liberal inflow of foreign talent in the early 2000s were unconventional and controversial at the time they were made. In the 1960s many developing countries erected protectionist barriers against foreign capitalists who were often vilified as economic imperialists. Singapore, however, went out of its way to woo large foreign companies, enticing them with incentives to locate in Singapore. The Economic Expansion Incentives Act of 1967 granted the EDB, the main government agency charged with bringing MNCs to Singapore, the right to give "pioneer" status to foreign corporations, with five-year tax breaks that were continually extended in the late 1970s.

Likewise, in the early 2000s, when development economists were still debating and disputing Richard Florida's work on The Rise of The Creative Class (Florida, 2002), and there were widespread concerns about the consequences of allowing large-scale cross-border mobility of skilled and unskilled workers, Singapore decided to relax its immigration and foreign worker policy, to allow a massive inflow of creative foreign workers, in a bid to become a "global city".

These decisions to liberalize capital and labor flows despite the controversial nature of the moves were another example of the Singapore government's pragmatic bent, with decisions taken based on the practical needs of the economy as it defined them. They also reflected the political dominance of the ruling party which allowed it to downplay complaints from citizens about the costs that such policies imposed on them. Such negative externalities became especially obvious when not just a large influx of highly skilled "foreign talent" was allowed but, as it turned out, a large number of low skilled foreign workers as well.

The Singapore government's pragmatic approach to intervention in the economy turned out to be enormously successful in attracting FDI in the 1960s. Many MNCs from the U.S., Europe and Japan, because of rising costs at home or the need to find new markets, were looking to relocate to countries that could provide an efficient and low cost operating environment. Building on the country's strategic location and its superior regional and global connectivity, the Singapore government was able to make a series of quick changes to major economic and social policies, as well as a few key strategic investments, to enhance its efficiency edge over other countries in the region, making Singapore the favored regional production and distribution site for MNCs. This approach was refined in subsequent years to help maintain Singapore's attractiveness to MNCs, even as the type of investment targeted changed over time. Specifically, the government was able to provide the following preconditions to make Singapore an efficient operating environment for MNCs.

2.1. *Creating the Political Framework for Sustained Economic Growth and Development*

A critical precondition for sustained economic growth is a certain level of social stability. The PAP government sought to achieve this by establishing, early in the days of independence, a "social contract" between the government and the governed in which some civil rights were traded off against the state powers and political control that it felt were needed to pursue high economic growth. High GDP growth then enabled the PAP to deliver various public services and public goods and legitimize its rule. By maintaining near complete dominance in the political arena, the PAP government was able to continue with such a "social contract" for most of the first 30 years of nationhood, following the single-minded pursuit of GDP growth without being distracted by equity issues and other political concerns.

The state's approach to labor relations is a good example. In the 1960s, labor relations were volatile and industrial strikes were commonplace.[9] In response, the PAP government passed the Industrial Relations Amendment Bill in 1968, limiting the powers of the Industrial Arbitration Court and strengthening the management's rights over the hiring, firing, promotion and transfer of employees.[10] Along with the Employment Act (1968), the Industrial Relations Amendment Bill (1968) cemented government control over the workforce which became more compliant. This helped to reduce labor unrest and thus labor costs for employers, especially MNCs. Labor woes for employers were virtually eliminated. In 1968, over 11,400 man-days were lost in four work stoppages but from 1978 onwards, there was hardly any sign of industrial unrest in Singapore.

At the same time, then Prime Minister Lee Kuan Yew also clamped down on left wing unions, effectively breaking the independent labor movement. The pro-PAP faction of the defunct labor movement formed the National Trade Union Congress (NTUC) which was eventually institutionalized as the only official labor union federation in Singapore. This in turn allowed the government to set up the framework of a "tripartite industrial relations" system (involving employers, employees and the government) including the National Wages Council (NWC) which helped to set wages for the economy. The tripartite system played a large role in minimizing friction among the three parties, helping to preserve the industrial peace important to foreign investors. In the 1985 recession, the government's control over the labor

---

[9] According to a speech by then Minister for Foreign Affairs and Labour S. Rajaratnam in Parliament on 10 July 1968, a total of 1,284,029 man-days were lost as a result of work stoppages between 1960 and 1967, undercutting Singapore's appeal to the MNCs Singapore needed to promote rapid growth.

[10] Retrieved from http://eresources.nlb.gov.sg/infopedia/articles/SIP_ 2014-07-07_133856.html.

unions allowed it to impose wage cuts to help the economy regain competitiveness. Smooth passage of the industrial relations laws and change in the labor movement were possible because of the PAP's near monopoly of parliamentary seats.

The social contract worked well for the PAP which has remained in power since 1959 without interruption. This was because it ensured that the basic needs of the population were met at a pace that far exceeded the citizenry's expectations. The economic strategy produced jobs at such a dynamic pace that full employment was reached by the early 1970s. A massive public housing construction program brought homes of high quality to the vast majority of the population such that by the mid-1990s more than 90% of Singaporeans owned their own homes. A huge effort was made to expand educational opportunities at primary, secondary, vocational and tertiary levels, giving citizens the opportunity for upward social mobility that they had not imagined possible. Such extraordinary success by the PAP government in meeting the citizens' basic needs and aspirations enabled it to retain the support of citizens despite the tough policies pursued. The party's long stint in government also allowed for stability and predictability in national policies and long term planning and continuity in governance, which contributed to the success in attracting FDI and realizing the FDI-driven growth strategy in the first phase of its economic development.

2.2. *Pragmatic Foreign Policy to Maintain Singapore's Strategic Position*

Given its need to expand its economic space by leveraging on the strengths of other economies (both as markets for Singapore's products and as sources of raw materials and other production inputs), Singapore needs to maintain a foreign policy that allows it to be on the best possible terms with as many nations as possible. Dispensing with the anti-colonial rhetoric of other newly independent ex-colonies, the Singapore government developed good relations with advanced economies, helping to ensure an inflow of technology, capital and management skills to Singapore. This inflow of resources came through various technical assistance schemes extended by foreign governments, and through the entry of MNCs which were partly encouraged by the friendly ties that Singapore maintained with their home countries, which helped to reduce perceived political risks.

Singapore was also active in cultivating strong ties with developing countries through various political and economic groupings such as the British Commonwealth and the Non-Aligned Movement. Within Asia, Singapore was one of the key drivers in establishing the Association of Southeast Asian Nations (ASEAN), which plays a critical role in promoting friendly relations among the now 10 member countries, and maintaining regional peace and stability in the region, laying the foundation for sustained regional economic growth and development. Maintaining good ties with as many countries as possible remains a cornerstone of Singapore's foreign policy and it

Table 2.   Singapore's free trade agreements.

FTAs	Year of implementation
Multilateral agreements	
ASEAN Free Trade Area (AFTA)	1993
Singapore-European FTA (ESFTA)	2003
ASEAN-China (ACFTA)	2005
Trans-Pacific SEP (TPFTA)	2006
ASEAN-Korea (ACFTA)	2007
ASEAN-Japan (ACFTA)	2009
ASEAN-India (ACFTA)	2010
ASEAN-Australia-New Zealand FTA (AANZFTA)	2010
Bilateral agreements	
New Zealand (ANZSCEP)	2001
Japan (JSEPA)	2002
United States	2004
India (CECA)	2005
Jordan (SJFTA)	2005
Korea (KSFTA)	2006
Panama (PSFTA)	2006
Peru (PeSFTA)	2009
China (CSFTA)	2009
Australia (SAFTA)	2011
Costa Rica (SCRFTA)	2013
Gulf Cooperation Council (GSFTA)	2013

Sources: http://www.fta.gov.sg/sg_fta.asp.
http://www.mti.gov.sg/MTIInsights/Documents/app.mti.gov.sg/data/article/25542/doc/
FA_2011Q2.pdf.

has been a welcomed member of many bilateral and multilateral free trade agreements in recent years (see Table 2). Even in foreign policy, the streak of pragmatism remains: policymakers have made clear their desire to not rely excessively on a single market for export demand and economic growth, and to constantly look to diversify the country's external markets. While access to the American and Chinese markets has played an important role in Singapore's export-led growth over the decades, it continues to recognize the relevance of enhancing trade ties with ASEAN, Japan and Korea, among others. Such diversified export markets help Singapore to manage fluctuations in global and regional demand: When one regional market slows down, it can be balanced by demand in other regions.

2.3. *Maintaining Macroeconomic Stability Through Prudent Fiscal and Monetary Policies*

Effective management of prudent fiscal and monetary policies helps maintain stable interest rates, exchange rates and inflation, providing the policy predictability that MNCs need for their long-range planning. This helps prevent Singapore from succumbing to a major financial crisis that could set economic development back by many years (Parrado, 2004), as happened to many previously promising countries which then failed to break out of the "middle-income trap". Prudent economic policies increase the resilience of the economy when faced with sudden external shocks. In successive regional and global crises — the 1997–1998 Asian financial meltdown, the 2001 bursting of the dot.com bubble, the 2003 SARS crisis and the more recent 2008 global financial crisis — the government intervened heavily through a plethora of measures, including some unconventional ones (see Table 3).

The government's "siege mentality" leads it to continually scan the horizon to try to pre-empt and nip potential problems in the bud. It carries out large scale scenario planning exercises regularly, in order to stay alert to potential short run and long run risks to the economy.

2.4. *Heavy investment in Strategic Infrastructure to Increase the Efficiency of the Business Environment*

To serve as an efficient production and distribution hub for MNCs, the government invested heavily (in part through GLCs) in a wide array of infrastructure including transportation, logistics, telecommunications systems etc. Such infrastructure was critical to preserving the main natural competitive advantage that Singapore enjoys: its strategic location and its strong regional and global connectivity. For example, the seaport and the airport in Singapore are consistently ranked among the most efficient in the world.

Equally important is public investment in human resources. The government's push to install English as the main official language helped to improve the global competitiveness of the workforce. But more critical were the resources put into vocational and skills training. In the 1960s and 1970s, the EDB's manpower development unit was put in charge of developing vocational training programmes which took place mainly in polytechnics and vocational institutes. These ensured that the workforce was equipped with the right skills for jobs in export-oriented manufacturing industries. Technology transfers from MNCs also played a big role in developing human capital; the government actively leveraged on the training capability of MNCs and their home governments by setting up joint training institutes to provide training

Table 3.   Singapore policy moves in response to crises.

Event	Impact on Singapore	Policy response
The Seventies		
1973: Quadrupling of oil prices and 1979 oil crises.	• Singapore's inflation surged to nearly 30% in 1H74. • Global economic slowdown, Singapore faced stagflation.	*Monetary Policy* • MAS imposed credit ceilings and more stringent credit guidelines on financial institutions. • MAS allowed the Singapore Dollar trade-weighted exchange rate to appreciate by 30% during the 1973–1980 period.
The Eighties		
1985–1987: First recession as global demand weakened just as internal imbalances appeared.	The slump in the construction sector, high domestic savings rate and rigidity in the domestic economy weakened Singapore's competitiveness.	*Fiscal Policy* • Public sector wage restraint. • Business costs reduced by cutting employer CPF contributions plus wage restraint for two years. • Increased depreciation allowance for capital expenditures. • Rebates on personal, corporate and property taxes as well as government fees. *Monetary Policy* • Downward adjustment in the trade-weighted exchange rate.
The Nineties		
1997–1998: Asian Financial Crisis	• Singapore Dollar appreciated significantly against collapsing regional currencies. • Collapse in regional demand and in local business confidence.	*Fiscal Policy* June 1998: S$2bn off-budget package, with three broad objectives: 1. Reduce business costs through property tax, rental and utilities rebates. 2. Accelerate development projects; provide funds to SMEs and skills-upgrading programs to strengthen economic infrastructure. 3. Stabilize property sector by suspending government land sales, deferring stamp duty on uncompleted properties, rental rebates and mortgage rescheduling. • November 1998: additional S$10.5b package to further reduce business costs by 15%. Key measures included: • Cutting wages by 5–8%. • 10% corporate tax rebate for 1999. • Further cuts in government rates and fees. • Further cut of 10% in CPF contribution rate.

(Continued)

Table 3. (*Continued*)

Event	Impact on Singapore	Policy response
		Monetary Policy • July 1997: MAS allowed the SGD to fall against the USD.
The 2000s		
2000–2001: Recession due to global tech slump	• GDP contracted 2.0% in 2001 as manufacturing sector contracted by 12% in 2001 compared to 15% in 2000.	*Fiscal Policy* • New Singapore Shares scheme in August 2001 was a cost-relief measure designed to help less well-off Singaporeans and bolster private consumption. • Off-budget fiscal stimulus measures were announced in October 2001. Measures worth S$7.7bn were disbursed in the economy in 2001–2002. • Measures aimed to stimulate the business sector and pump-prime the economy through public sector infrastructure spending.
2003: SARS	• Tourism, travel-related industries severely hit. Visitor arrivals, hotel occupancy fell. • Weakness in manufacturing and trade-related services, together with ailing global IT market demand compounded the negative effects of SARS, resulting in GDP growth contracting sharply by 7% y/y in 2Q03.	*Fiscal Policy* • S$230m relief package including SARS Relief Tourism Training Assistance grant scheme. • Moral suasion for companies to save jobs by adopting temporary cost-cutting measures; implementation of a shorter work week, temporary layoffs, arrangement for workers to go on leave or undertake skills training and upgrading. Temporary wage cuts were used as a last resort. • The government incurred US$109m (S$192m) in direct operating expenditure related to SARS, and committed another US$60m (S$105m) development expenditure to hospitals for additional isolation rooms and medical facilities to treat SARS and other infectious diseases. • Launched the new Workforce Development Agency (WDA) and gave a second phase of cash injection of S$280m (US$160m) to a Skills Redevelopment Programme to help co-fund the retraining of workers.

(*Continued*)

Table 3.   (*Continued*)

Event	Impact on Singapore	Policy response
2008: Global Financial Crisis	• Debt refinancing was a problem for corporates that had highly illiquid assets and high gearing. • Business and economic activity froze as banks refused to lend while consumers feared a run on banks.	*Fiscal Policy* • S\$20.5b Resilience Package. • Jobs Credit Scheme provided businesses with a cash grant based on the wages of resident employees, set at 12% on up to the first S\$2500 of wages per month. This scheme was only paid out if the workers were still employed by the firm at the end of a 3-month period. • Special Risk-Sharing Initiative: Bridging Loan Programme and a trade finance module. Government took 80% of the loan default risk up to S\$5m, and 75% of the trade financing risk. Together with participating financial institutions, these schemes sought to increase credit availability across the entire supply chain. *Monetary Policy* MAS adopted an accommodative monetary policy that addressed regulatory financial reporting standards, liquidity problems, and property lending limits in order to soften the impact of the GFC. • Entered into a precautionary US \$30b swap with the US Federal Reserve. • Accepted AAA-rated S\$-denominated debt securities as collateral in addition to Singapore government bonds. • MAS entered into cross-border arrangements with other central banks to accept foreign currencies and government debt securities as collateral. • Relaxed leverage ratio requirements and facilitated secondary fund-raising by listed issuers to prevent a disorderly asset fire sale due to a fall in property prices. • Imposed property lending limits. The regulatory 80% loan-to-value limit encouraged home buyers to remain prudent and allowed for sufficient buffer in the loan portfolios of financial institutions. Property sector exposures of commercial banks were capped at 35% in case of a property downturn. • In the absence of sufficient loan loss data, MAS mandated that financial institutions keep 1% of their net loans and receivables as collective impairment provisions.

Source: Collated by Centennial Asia Advisors.

in different skills that were in demand.[11] It responded to the changing needs of MNCs (and the economy) by investing in training for different skills over time. For example, in 1981 the National Computer Board (NCB) was created to drive the learning and application of IT-related skills among companies.

Investment in education and skills training continued even after the economy moved into its second phase, that of foreign talent and innovation driven growth, at the turn of the millennium. The Ministry of Education (MOE) realigned its focus and revised the school curriculum to concentrate on developing students' creativity and critical thinking. A new university, the Singapore Management University, was established to provide a different pedagogical approach to tertiary education.[12] Other new educational institutions were setup to provide for human resource needs in specific industries: for example, a School of the Arts was established to develop the arts and performance industry.

2.5. *Use of State Enterprises to Lead Development of Strategic Sectors*

The government intervened in industries it felt were important but which the private sector either did not have the capability or the resources to develop. GLCs were instrumental in taking the lead in developing nascent and strategic sectors of the domestic economy — banking, telecommunications, industrial estates, port, airport, air and sea transportation, shipbuilding and repair, defense technology, etc. — and continue to have a significant presence in some of these sectors. These investments were important in enhancing the efficiency of the business environment and reducing operating costs for MNCs. State-run enterprises such as Singapore Airlines and Neptune Ocean Lines were started to promote Singapore's international connectivity and trade links while the Development Bank of Singapore (now DBS Bank) was established as a financing institution for development spending. The Post Office Savings Bank (now POSB) served as the main retail bank for the local population; through its deposit-taking activities, it also allowed the government to mobilize high levels of savings for public spending on productive projects. Other GLCs also played and continue to play important roles in increasing the efficiency of the economy. While many GLCs have been privatized, Temasek Holdings — one of Singapore's two sovereign wealth

---

[11] These include for instance, Japan–Singapore Technical Institute, Japan–Singapore Training Centre, Japan–Singapore Institute of Software Technology, French–Singapore Institute, German–Singapore Institute, Philip–Government Training Center, Tata–Government Training Center and Rollei–Government Training Center etc.

[12] Started initially as a collaboration with the Wharton School of the University of Pennsylvania, SMU adopts a US liberal arts type approach to tertiary education, marking a departure from the British educational system followed by the other two main universities (National University of Singapore and Nanyang Technological University).

funds — retains a significant and sometimes controlling minority ownership stake in them, creating the possibility of encouraging or directing investments in projects that could potentially generate substantial positive externalities for the economy.

Statutory boards and GLCs are also mobilized to develop new clusters of economic activity that might not make Singapore more attractive to MNCs, but are seen as important to the realization of the government's vision for the economy. These projects have not always turned out to be resounding successes, pointing to the risks of having the state invest beyond public good provision. Two examples of the state-led development of industrial clusters are described in the Appendix A: while Jurong Island has successfully grown into a globally important cluster of chemical industries, the biotechnology initiative remains a work in progress.

2.6. *Effective State Institutions to Implement Government Policies*

The government has counted on a strong civil service and a system of statutory boards, together with other state institutions, to implement its policies. In general, these institutions, based on meritocratic management and low corruption, have been effective in delivering the desired outcomes. A carrot and stick approach was taken to minimize corruption in the public service. Senior policymakers including Ministers were charged in court for corrupt practices, which together with a few high profile cases in the 1970s served to deter others. At the same time, wages for civil servants were made comparable to private sector wages, to help the government recruit and retain talent, and reduce the incentive to engage in corrupt practices.

Statutory boards provided the government with added flexibility in using the public sector to help achieve its goal of high economic growth. To increase their effectiveness and to reduce bureaucratic inertia, many statutory boards were given significant autonomy to carry out their tasks, with rewards to the officers being aligned with their performance. This flexibility allowed the EDB, the statutory board responsible for attracting MNCs and providing them with a one-stop service to set up operations in Singapore, to be successful, which in turn contributed to the success of the FDI-driven growth strategy (Chan, 2002). When first set up, the EDB was granted extensive powers, initially entrusted with the financing of industries, workforce development and provision of incentives as well as development of industrial estates. This allowed foreign firms to start up in Singapore relatively quickly. To instill confidence, the EDB entered into joint ventures with foreign investors in certain industries. It also took charge of skills training and upgrading of Singaporean workers, investing in the development of human capital to meet the higher skills needs of foreign companies. As the chief marketing agency for Singapore, the EDB set up offices in major cities which it saw as likely sources of target investment; EDB officers were given considerable latitude in their marketing approach, much like marketing in the private sector, and were often able to enlist the help of political office holders in their marketing efforts. The flexibility and resources that the EDB enjoyed provide yet another example of the government's pragmatic but relentless pursuit of its FDI-driven growth strategy.

3. Building an Innovation-Driven Economy

This FDI-driven growth strategy was largely successful in helping to generate growth and create jobs during the first 35 years of Singapore's history as an independent nation. The large and continuous inflows of FDI helped transform Singapore from a trading and logistics hub in the 1960s into a major manufacturing hub by the 1980s. There was also significant skill upgrading in the economy during this process. Over the years, with the inflow of the relevant MNCs, Singapore was able to shift its core manufacturing activities from labor-intensive manufacturing industries such as textiles and electronics to capital-intensive industries like petrochemicals, and then technology-intensive industries such as wafer-fab and telecommunications. At the heart of such success was the government's commitment and ability to maintain Singapore's efficiency edge over other Asian countries.

By the late 1990s, however, the government appeared to have come to the conclusion that the "foreign investment driven" growth model might have run its course, given the changing comparative advantages in the region, the rapid pace at which neighboring countries were catching up with Singapore in providing efficient infrastructure (such as world-class international airports), rising costs in Singapore itself, and the increasingly "footloose" behavior of MNCs. There was general agreement that infrastructure and regulatory efficiency alone would not suffice to sustain Singapore's economic competitiveness in the long run and that the next phase of development had to center on creativity and innovation. Growth should be driven by industries characterized by rapid innovation and productivity increase, with significant agglomeration effects.

In 2003, the Economic Review Committee, a government committee setup to map out the medium term growth strategy for the economy, identified bioscience, global banking and finance, wealth management, lifestyle industries, arts and culture, media and design, education and healthcare, among others, as examples of such industries (ERC, 2003). Manufacturing would continue to be a key pillar of the economy and was envisaged to account for 20% to 25% of GDP, though the emphasis was on encouraging manufacturing with higher innovation content. Greater emphasis was placed on the development of services industries especially exportable services with the capacity to leverage on the size of the global market.

There was also a belief that to attract and build up such innovation-driven industries, efficiency still matters, but even more important is the presence of a critical mass of creative talent. If there was not a sufficient supply of creative talent domestically for the many clusters being simultaneously targeted, then Singapore should be prepared to again leverage on the global economy by sourcing the talent required from abroad. The implicit assumption was that, in an innovation economy, the existence of a critical mass of creative talent would attract companies, rather than the other way round: companies engaged in innovative work would only set up operations with an adequate supply of creative talent.

Indeed, the reports of both the Economic Review Committee (ERC, 2003) and the Economic Strategy Committee (ESC, 2010) emphasized the importance of making Singapore "a leading global city, a hub of talent, enterprise and innovation" and "the most open and cosmopolitan city in Asia, and one of the best places to live and work in".[13] This decision marked a fundamental shift in Singapore's growth strategy: from attracting MNCs to attracting foreign talent. To successfully attract the creative foreign talent it needs, Singapore would have to position itself as a "global city". Instead of investing only in efficiency enhancing infrastructure and policies, the new focus was to increase Singapore's cosmopolitan appeal so that international creative talent would choose to live and work here. The objective of economic policy remained unchanged — high GDP growth and accumulation of surplus — but growth would now be driven by foreign talent instead of foreign investment.

With its pragmatic approach, the Singapore government moved quickly to make a number of major policy changes. First, the immigration and foreign worker policy was substantially liberalized, with the approval criteria and processes for employment passes, permanent residence and citizenship considerably relaxed. The liberalization specifically targeted creative talent, entrepreneurs, professionals, high net worth individuals (HNWIs), and students. A new category of employment pass, the S-Pass, was introduced to speed up the inflow of foreigners who might have the potential to be part of the entrepreneurial and creative class. The number of foreign workers and new residents shot up sharply. Between 2004 and 2014, the size of the nonresident workforce rose 121%, while resident workforce grew by 26% (Ministry of Manpower, Singapore, 2014).

The government also embarked on massive investments in infrastructure to make the business environment more conducive for innovation activities. Intellectual property rights laws were strengthened and government spending on R&D activities substantially increased. The government stepped up its investment in a wide array of industries such as the bioscience industry (e.g., construction of the massive One North project at Buona Vista Road, generous offers of scholarships, job opportunities and permanent residency status for R&D personnel and their spouses, and subsidies, co-investment and other incentives for pharmaceutical companies), wealth

---

[13] See ERC Report (2003), pp. 51–60 and ESC Report (2010), pp. 7–10.

management (e.g., farming out state funds and providing generous fiscal and financial incentives to fund management companies, setting up a wealth management institute to increase the supply of the relevant skills), education (e.g., the EDB's Global School House project to attract well-known foreign academic institutions to set up campuses in Singapore, through generous subsidies and other incentives), among others.

Substantial resources were also poured into the "make-over" of the city, to offer creative talent similar lifestyles that they could enjoy in other global cities like London, Boston and New York. There was extensive renewal of the city landscape and construction of various "iconic" projects e.g., Esplanade, Gardens-by-the-Bay, F1 and Integrated Resorts. There were also efforts to relax the rules for doing business and even attempts to relax political and social rules to allow for more diverse lifestyles. All these policy shifts were aimed at changing Singapore's image as a boring "nanny state", making the city-state a more exciting place to live in.

15 years after the launch of the "foreign talent driven" growth strategy, the results have been mixed at best. The government was able to achieve its GDP growth target: the average annual growth rate from 2000 to 2014 was about 5.4%, higher than in most developed economies. The country's production pattern and industrial landscape did undergo a significant change. Services now account for a larger share of the economy (67% of GDP in 2014 compared with 61% in 2000), and industries such as pharmaceuticals, banking and finance, wealth management (especially private banking), education and creative industries have significantly increased their presence in the economy.

With respect to the objective of surplus accumulation, the government reported smaller fiscal surpluses in this latter period, but this was based on an accounting approach that differed from other countries' which the International Monetary Fund favored. Despite these smaller reported surpluses, the assets owned by the government expanded from $615.9 billion as of March 2009 to $833.7 billion as of March 2014, suggesting that the actual fiscal surpluses were indeed quite large. The country's foreign reserves rose from US$80 billion in 2000 to US$257 billion in 2014. There has also been a significant change in both the physical landscape and the social milieu. Singapore in 2015 is much more cosmopolitan, more of a global city, offering a more diverse culture and lifestyle than in 2000. As in the earlier period, the government's approach to intervention in the economy, with decisive changes in various economic and social policies, helped bring about such a fundamental transformation within a relatively short period of time.

However, the glowing picture at the macroeconomic level masked some worrying trends that emerged during this period, which could also be attributed to the government's approach to managing the economy. First, while the number of high income, creative foreign talent did surge, there was an even bigger increase in the number of low skill, low income foreign workers. The number of employment passes increased from 99,200 in 2007 to 178,900 in 2014, while work permits rose from 757,100 to 991,300, and 887,600 S-passes were issued (Ministry of Manpower). Not surprisingly, the 15-year period saw dismal performance in productivity growth, with labor productivity growth falling from 3.4% a year in the 1990s to 1.1% a year from 2000–2009 (Monetary Authority of Singapore, 2010). From 2009 to 2014, labor productivity grew by only 0.3% a year on average if the exceptional sharp recovery of 2010 is excluded; and in 2014, it declined by 0.8% (Ministry of Trade and Industry, 2014).

Why did the government allow such a sharp inflow of low skill, low productivity foreign workers when the explicit objective of the foreign talent driven growth strategy was to attract only innovative, high-productivity foreign talent? A major reason, as Prime Minister Lee Hsien Loong noted, was that the government did not want to miss out on growth opportunities when they arose.[14] It did not want to turn down demand for work permits for foreign workers in industries such as construction and food and beverages, for fear that doing so would curb production and affect the GDP growth performance. In short, the problem was one of basic "policy inconsistency": the government did what was good for the short term objective of high growth even if this ran counter to its long term objective of structural transformation to an innovation driven economy. This outcome could be attributed to a large extent to its near exclusive focus on yearly GDP growth as the primary objective of economic policy.

A second worrying trend that emerged since 2000 is a sharp rise in income inequality and wage stagnation among lower income groups. This made Singapore (together with Hong Kong and the U.S.) one of the most unequal of developed economies. Singapore's Gini coefficient rose sharply from 0.442 in 2000 to 0.478 in 2012, before falling to 0.464 in 2014. Transfers from government benefits and taxes somewhat moderated this deterioration in inequality: post transfers, the Gini coefficient rose from 0.430 in 2000 to 0.432 in 2012 and fell to 0.412 by 2014. Meanwhile, the ratio of average incomes between the top quintile of employed households and the bottom quintile increased from 10.1 in 2000 to 12.9 in 2010 (Department of Statistics, Singapore, 2011).

Many factors could have contributed to this increase in income inequality. External factors like the forces of globalization and technological change played a large part. But so did domestic factors, most of which could be attributed to the government's approach to intervention in the economy.[15] Its fiscal strategy has generally been to favor the supply side, with a tax regime targeted at increasing the incentives for more work. The shift in policy focus to attract more creative talent added to the

---

[14] At the IPS Year in Perspective Conference, 2013, Dialogue with Guest of Honour Prime Minister Lee Hsien Loong, PM Lee said, in response to a question on managing public infrastructure and population size, that he wanted the country to "make up for lost time" and thus the population, including foreigners, grew faster than expected, placing a strain on infrastructure.

[15] See Bhaskaran *et al.* (2012) for more detailed discussion on this issue.

pressure to reduce income tax rates given competition for talent from other cities such as Hong Kong. Personal income tax rates were aggressively reduced, from a top rate of 28% in 2002 to 20% in 2007. Combined with increases in the Goods and Service Tax (GST), which is regressive in nature, this made the tax system less progressive. Increased government spending on lower income groups has not been sufficient to offset the regressive effects of changes in the tax regime.

Pursuit of the "global city" vision and the foreign talent driven growth strategy probably also contributed to rising inequality. The inflow of high income talent raised average incomes at the top of the income distribution, while the inflow of low-skilled foreign labor depressed wages at the bottom, leading to wider income disparity. This trend might have been accentuated by the government's spending priorities during this period, which focused on making Singapore attractive to the global elites. This could have added to "agglomeration effects" which raise incomes at the higher end of the labor market faster than at the middle and lower end. In addition, there are the negative externalities resulting from the more liberal immigration policy which tend to have a bigger impact on the lower income groups, such as congestion and rising costs of living (Bhaskaran *et al.*, 2012).

A third worrying trend is greater growth volatility in the economy. Between 1998 and 2009, Singapore experienced four recessions. As others have pointed out, the new industries the government bet on to be the leading drivers of growth (e.g., pharmaceuticals, banking and finance) tend to be of the high growth, high volatility type (Choy, 2010; Tan and Phang, 2005). Furthermore, adopting an investment approach almost akin to that of a private equity investor — putting bets on many new industries with the expectation that some would pay off handsomely even if others fail — limited the likelihood of developing sufficient depth and globally competitive scale in any of these industries, since all would be competing for already extremely scarce resources (including skills, thereby pushing up the skill wage premium and contributing to rising inequality).

Fourth, high economic growth since 2000 has been accompanied by a noticeable deterioration in the quality of life as infrastructure provision failed to keep pace with the increase in population, congestion worsened while inflation (especially asset price inflation) rose sharply, arguably reducing the attractiveness and affordability of life in the city-state. Policy and planning failures were to blame here: failure to build up adequate infrastructure before letting in the large number of new immigrants and foreign workers, and poor coordination among various government agencies. More importantly, the near exclusive focus on economic growth rather than on broader measures of citizen well-being, and the ability to shield itself from political pressures due to tight political and media control lie at the root of the problem.

Fifth, if the ultimate aim of economic strategy since 2000 was to build an innovation led economy, the results have yet to be seen. Table 4, which summarizes recent

Table 4.   INSEAD innovation ranking — singapore.

	2014	2013	2012	2011
Overall Ranking	7	8	3	3
Overall Innovation Input	1	1	1	1
Institution	6	7	8	9
Human Capital and Research	2	3	2	1
Infrastructure	2	6	9	9
Market sophistication	4	5	4	2
Business sophistication	1	1	1	1
Overall Innovation Output	25	18	11	17
Knowledge and technology output	13	11	3	15
Creative output	33	40	37	30
Innovation Efficiency	110	121	33	94

Source: https://www.globalinnovationindex.org/content.aspx?page = past-reports.

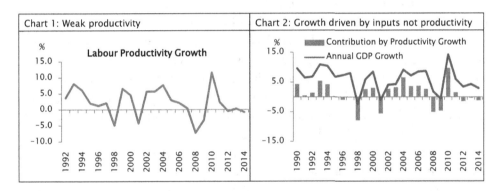

Figure 1.   Labor productivity.

Source: http://www.singstat.gov.sg/statistics/browse-by-theme/labour-employment-wages-and-productivity.

trends in the INSEAD ranking of innovation in countries across the world, shows that Singapore's overall ranking has actually slipped since 2011. More importantly, the ranking still appears high only because Singapore has done well in mobilizing the *inputs* for innovation. The innovation *outcomes* were not as impressive, with the net result that in terms of innovation efficiency, Singapore ranks an abysmal 110th in the world. One possible consequence of this weak innovation capacity is the desultory performance of productivity growth. Ultimately, raising productivity requires an ability of companies to innovate, to re-engineer themselves so as to perform as well with fewer inputs. Charts 1 and 2 in Figure 1 point to Singapore's less-than-satisfactory productivity performance in recent years.

4. Problems with the Singapore Model of State Intervention

The Singapore model of state intervention in the economy has been successful in delivering high growth and transforming a developing economy into a fairly developed economy. However, as time progresses, some of the weaknesses are becoming apparent. In addition to the challenges highlighted in the previous section, in recent years, other problems that result from the growth strategy adopted in the earlier phase of development have come to the surface as well. The dissatisfaction expressed by voters in the 2011 general elections, and continued vocal demands for policy changes across a wide range of areas, point to some fundamental flaws in the government's approach to managing the economy. They also raise serious questions about the sustainability of the same approach in the coming years.

4.1. *Objective of Economic Growth*

The government's narrow economic policy objective of maximizing GDP growth is arguably at the root of many of the problems that the Singapore economy faces, since focusing on too narrow an objective could lead the state into policy errors. Economic growth can come with costs, and the fruits of growth could be poorly distributed. For example, Singapore's share of wages in GDP is much lower than in developed OECD countries, and a significant portion of the higher share of profits in GDP is repatriated to the home countries of MNCs, a result of relying on them as the engine of growth (Bhaskaran *et al.*, 2012). The benefit to the average Singaporeans is much less than GDP growth and per capita GDP would suggest.

The government might have done better if its economic policy objective had been broader, such as maximizing the well-being of Singapore citizens in a manner that can be sustained well into the future. A broader set of indicators which would have better served the interests of the average Singaporean could have been used to measure economic performance, including, for example: (a) median real household income or consumption, with emphasis placed on enhancing the well-being of the most disadvantaged elements of society such as the bottom quartile and with reference to not only a well-researched poverty line defining a minimum basket of goods services but also adequate human capital investment; (b) adequate social security against the volatility of an open global economy, including ensuring adequate funding for retirement and healthcare for all Singaporeans (Stiglitz *et al.*, 2008).[16]

If the objective of economic policy had more truly reflected the overall needs and desires of the citizens of Singapore, then the angst that many Singaporeans feel over a

---

[16] Economists have made various proposals to improve on the measure of economic well-being beyond GDP growth rate. See for example, the report by the Commission on the Measurement of Economic Performance and Social Progress (Stiglitz *et al.*, 2008).

range of issues might have been avoided. In this regard, a quality of living index reflecting key aspects of well-being for the average citizen would have been useful. It is difficult to see how a growth approach that ignores inequality and other issues that matter to the well-being of citizens can be sustainable in the long term, both economically and politically. As has been pointed out, "a more comprehensive measure of the well-being of Singaporeans which incorporates these various economic and social indicators would also help government gauge the impact of its policies on citizens' well-being" (Low *et al.*, 2013). The long-established incentive structure for political office holders and other policymakers (e.g., linking their remuneration to GDP growth rates) would have to be modified to reflect the importance of achieving broader objectives in public policy making.

4.2. *Building "Inherent Production Capacity" and Developing Strong Local Enterprises*

There are also questions about the relevance and effectiveness of the government's current approach in pursuing future economic growth. One outcome of relying excessively on foreign companies and foreign talent to drive the growth of the economy is a serious lack of indigenous production capacity, which could pose challenges for the long-run sustainability of the growth process, given the likelihood of "footloose" behavior on the part of foreign entities and individuals.

Economic development goes beyond just achieving a certain level of per capita income: for example, resource-rich countries may have high per capita incomes but would not qualify as "developed". A core part of economic development includes developing the inherent capacity of citizens and locally-owned companies to create value on a sustainable and durable basis. Inherent capacity could be defined generally as the critical "software" that incorporates the blueprints for successful economic activity held by a country's indigenous workers and companies. This includes accumulated financial capital, workers' skills, locally-owned intellectual property and capacity for innovation, the accumulated intangible experience, management and operating processes, knowledge of markets etc. stored in Singapore-owned companies or other entities such as universities, research centers and industry associations. It would also include the adapted cultural habits and institutions in society that enable economic agents to work together to produce results, including, more broadly, social resilience and cohesiveness.

A growing body of research has discussed the rising importance of elements of "intangible capital" in accounting for the greater part of growth in advanced economies like the United States (Corrado *et al.*, 2006). Such "intangible capital" includes skills, research and development, brand equity etc. which are located within companies. Some argue that it should not matter whether economic value is created by foreign rather than local companies. This is questionable. First, broadening and deepening inherent capacity is important because it makes it more likely that Singapore workers and companies would prosper over the long run, despite unforeseen structural changes in the global economic environment. Second, a diversified economy including local as well as foreign enterprises in a varied range of activities increases structural resilience, enabling a faster recovery to shocks since the economy would not be depending just on MNCs.

Singapore is seen to face two problems in developing its inherent capacity: possible distortions in an ecosystem that might be hindering local enterprises, and lack of economies of scale. Singapore's industrial ecosystem in export manufacturing consists primarily of foreign-owned MNCs with local enterprises forming an essentially supporting industry infrastructure. This contrasts with the export manufacturing structures in Germany, Switzerland, Scandinavia, Japan, Korea or Taiwan, where a core ecosystem of globally competitive SMEs (e.g., Germany's Mittelstand) continually give rise to a few globally competitive national giants. This domestically-owned, medium-sized manufacturing ecosystem has proved its durability and competitiveness over the decades, especially in Germany where it has been the backbone of the world's foremost high value-added export economy since the 1950s. German SMEs account for 40% of German manufactured exports, 85% of industrial output, 75% of industrial patents, and train 80% of German apprentices (Venhor and Meyer, 2007). Similarly, Singapore needs to develop a mixed ecosystem in its globally competitive services sector. Important complementarity exists between manufacturing and services: for example, Hong Kong's domestic manufacturing ecosystem has largely migrated to Shenzhen, but continues to be serviced by Hong Kong-based sales and business services operations, allowing Hong Kong to earn important investment income. This underlines the importance of an industrial hinterland for developing linkages that enable local firms to be globally competitive over time.

The view that Singapore is simply too small to provide economies of scale for local enterprises is not necessarily correct. The Singapore economy is not small, with a GDP almost as large as that of countries with substantially larger populations, such as Pakistan. But Singapore's state dominated economic model has tended to produce an extraordinarily low ratio of private consumption to GDP, thus reducing the potential scale economies for local enterprises that sell to the domestic market. Using analysis from input-output tables, some economists have argued that stimulating private consumption can have larger multipliers and less import leakage than conventionally assumed (Kapur, 2009). Consumption currently constitutes less than 40% of GDP in Singapore, compared with over 60% in Hong Kong, another equally small and open economy. Singapore's large current account surplus, which for decades was above 25% of GDP though it has recently fallen slightly to about 20%, also suggests that local consumption potential is underdeveloped. Another limitation is local enterprises' weak access to neighboring countries' domestic markets: if there were greater ASEAN economic integration, Singapore's local enterprises would have more opportunity to scale up their activities.

The government has setup various committees over the years to promote the growth of SMEs in Singapore, with limited success. One reason for this might be that the actual and effective assistance provided to SMEs paled in comparison to that offered to MNCs and GLCs because of the latter's perceived ability to expand GDP on a larger scale. Following the Economic Strategies Committee (ESC) Report in 2010, a renewed effort has been made to "kick start" the growth of SMEs, with a wider range of assistance being made available to them and a government agency, Spring Singapore, tasked to develop the SME sector. For example, the Productivity and Innovation Credit (PIC) and PIC+ have been rolled out to help SMEs restructure as the supply of foreign workers is reduced. These schemes offer tax deductions and/or cash payouts on qualifying expenditures which boost innovation and productivity. Spring Singapore also partners with third-party investors and co-invests in promising enterprises. It helps SMEs attract talented personnel by sponsoring their studies and guaranteeing them a job after graduation: Participating SMEs are eligible for up to 70% funding support covering the student's tuition fees, monthly allowance and a sign-on bonus for final-year students. Successful students are then bonded to the sponsoring SMEs for two years after graduation (Tan and Gan, 2012).

4.3. *Linkages with the Hinterland*

While Singapore sees the global economy as its hinterland, both as a market for its products and as a source of supply of capital, talent and labor, there is a strong argument for deeper integration with its closer regional neighbors. The right linkages to the right hinterland offer local businesses expanded business opportunities, potential scale economies, and a way to become more cost-competitive.

First, expanded regionalization can provide supply-side economic and social infrastructure for the development of Singapore as a global city, and expand the economic space available for local enterprise. For example, complementary land and labor resources may be available from the neighboring Iskandar region of Malaysia, and land- and labor-intensive parts of port services and manufacturing could be relocated there, releasing valuable land and scarce labor for higher value uses that would produce a net increase in incomes in Singapore. The availability of a cheaper place for retirement or even to live and commute from could directly increase the welfare of Singaporeans as would the availability of cheaper and more diverse recreation facilities, as is increasingly the case in Hong Kong's relationship with the Pearl River Delta area.

Second, regionalization would provide Singapore with a larger, longer-term market for goods and services. The Iskandar region and Riau Islands of Indonesia would give Singapore an effective domestic market of 7 to 8 million, on par with Hong Kong and some highly successful sub-regions in Europe and North America. This would otherwise be impossible to achieve over a similar time frame, even with rapid immigration of unskilled labor and without the attendant social integration problems (Yusof, 2007). A network of more comprehensive free trade arrangements could link Singapore with the larger population centers and future large economies of Indonesia (population 230 m), Indochina (150 m), and even the Greater Mekong Sub-Region (400 m to 500 m, including Southeast China). Development of the Greater Mekong Sub-Region shows the importance of (a) building a wide network of transportation infrastructure so that connectivity is substantially improved; and (b) a comprehensive effort to identify and eliminate bureaucratic and other regulatory impediments to the free flow of goods and services. Appropriate government policies could help Singapore improve its linkages with the regional hinterland. These would include (a) improving relations with Malaysia and Indonesia to the point where all three countries could cooperate on the basis of trust and confidence that mutual benefits would flow,[17] (b) stepping up infrastructure construction and streamlining border controls to improve physical connectivity between Singapore and the Iskandar Region on the one hand and with the Riau Islands on the other.

5. Conclusion

This review of the role of the government in Singapore's economic development highlights a number of issues. First, a state-driven economic development model like Singapore's can succeed in delivering superior economic growth where the government has strong political authority which could be sustained by ensuring that the benefits of such economic development are delivered to the citizenry. Second, the efficacy of such a model of development appears to wane after some time: in the second phase of Singapore's development, economic growth slowed while improvements in living standards appear to have plateaued.

Third, in Singapore's case this decline in economic performance results from a failure to go beyond mobilizing resources and directing them to a narrow objective of economic growth. In a phase of growth where more complex and multi-faceted development is needed, the Singapore state's vaunted core competencies in mobilizing resources has so far not appeared sufficient to the task. These tasks — developing inherent capacity (the skills and capacity of citizens and citizen-owned businesses),

---

[17] In recent years, the government has succeeded in building a stronger relationship of trust with Malaysia, with the result that more efforts are underway to ensure a more seamless integration of Singapore's economy with the Iskandar Region.

tackling a widening income gap, generating an indigenous innovation capacity, and finding bold strategies to secure its neighbors' cooperation in creating a larger hinterland for the Singapore economy — are more complex and may well require skill sets not adequately developed in the government system.

Appendix A

A.1. *Case Study 1: Development of Jurong Island*

One of the most recognized results of the rapid industrialization of Singapore would be the establishment of Singapore's energy and chemicals industry on Jurong Island. In 2012, this key pillar of Singapore's economy contributed an estimated S$100bn or 35% of Singapore's total manufacturing output. More than 100 companies, including ExxonMobil, Shell and Chevron, are located on the man-made island, focused on petrochemicals and specialty chemicals. The industry has attracted cumulative fixed asset investments of more than S$47bn, and reflects Singapore's determination in sharpening its competitive edge with aggressive investments in physical infrastructure to create new synergies.

The success of the Jurong Island development stems from deep collaboration between businesses and government, the ability to execute large, integrated projects, and a keen eye trained on the far horizon to ensure that Singapore is able to ride the waves of global megatrends. Rex W. Tillerson, ExxonMobil's chairman, values the "stable policy course that encouraged international investment, teamwork and advanced technologies". Singapore currently accounts for up to a quarter of ExxonMobil's global chemicals capacity, and will rank as its largest speciality chemicals manufacturing site once two new plants come online.

These qualities are still constantly refined today. Integration of facilities was crucial to Singapore's ability to establish sizeable infrastructure. S$7bn of reclamation work was invested to unite seven small offshore islands into one; physical reclamation work started in 1995 and was completed in 2009, two decades earlier than the initial target completion date of 2030. This tripled the original landmass to 3200 ha, enabling realization of the German concept of *Verbundstandort,* or composite site, where companies could share common facilities, and output from one facility would become the inputs of another. This is crucial for an industry whose margins are affected critically by its feedstock costs. The current flux of energy prices has, however, been challenging. Companies such as Lanxess and Shell have voiced concerns over Singapore's rising costs. The United States is becoming an increasingly attractive location for manufacturing sites due to significantly cheaper feedstock options, while Saudi Arabia has also positioned itself as another destination from which to meet the chemical demand of Asia-Pacific nations.

The government works hard to stay ahead of the curve. The Energy Market Authority is seeking to appoint two more liquefied natural gas (LNG) importers to increase competitiveness, while increasing the capacities of LNG terminals on Jurong Island. The government has also launched initiatives such as the Energy Efficiency Improvement Assistance Scheme and Grant for Energy Efficient Technologies to help bring down relevant costs. This has not been the first display of the government's immense willingness to meet the evolving needs of businesses through the years. When ExxonMobil wanted to build a second plant beside its first, the government spent S$100m over two years diverting 1 km of the Jurong Island Highway, and 17 pipes carrying industrial water, carbon monoxide and natural gas. Besides actively wooing investments in the chemicals industry in Jurong Island, the government goes the extra mile to ensure that these companies have the competitive edge they need to ensure that Singapore remains a premier global chemicals hub.

Moving downstream into specialty chemicals has been a critical development for Singapore's industry positioning. Margins are more stable in this low volume but high margin sector, and the high technical expertise required has translated into well-paying skilled jobs. Government coordination of the construction of mega-complexes helps deepen synergies. The Jurong Town Corporation (JTC) Chemicals Hub at Tuas View will house multiple companies, including local SMEs, involved in further processing of chemicals. Incorporating safety-compliant features and shared facilities will reduce both capital investments and setup time for chemical companies, and increase the accessibility of input materials.

At the same time, the government is implementing productivity improvement schemes. The Process Construction and Maintenance sector (PCM) has teamed up with plant owners and relevant government agencies, forming six working groups to boost productivity further. This will be accomplished through relatively simple initiatives, such as the construction of a dormitory near Jurong Island to reduce travelling time for workers whose increased rest time would in turn lead to higher on-site productivity.

The government's active role in cultivating industry-wide partnerships has been critical in ensuring that the industry remains progressive. A quote from Vince Sinclair, Wood Mackenzie's Asia head of chemicals research, captures the government's mission: "Singapore is different in that the hand of the state is there in enabling things, but not directly involved. It probably makes it more efficient."

A.2. *Case Study 2: The Biomedical Industry in Singapore*

Singapore's reputation as a manufacturer of high quality and complex goods has contributed to the development of the Biomedical Sciences (BMS) industry, with the participation of global pharmaceutical corporations, and partnerships with local enterprises. The government has committed S$3.5b to enhancing current research and development infrastructure, largely by expanding the flagship Biopolis at One North, which houses key research institutes. The BMS industry has seen manufacturing output increase from S$6b in 2000 to S$29.4b in 2012, when it accounted for 25.2% of total manufacturing value-added. Employment also increased from 6000 to 15,700.

Spring has implemented various schemes to involve home-grown medical technology SMEs in the industry. Private Sector Translators, AITbiotech and IPTech work together with the agency to help identify, develop and commercialize intellectual property via a pay-per-use model. This helps to reduce firms' capital expenditure and the incubation period through provision of R&D services such as validation and feasibility studies. The Research, Innovation and Enterprise (RIE) 2015 plan commits S$70m to four accelerators with established records in various medical technologies: they are to identify, and co-invest with Spring Seeds Capital, Spring's investment arm, on a 1:1 basis, in start-ups. A multitude of tax and non-tax incentives have also been lavished on the industry to nurture startups. Angel investors who invest a minimum of S$100,000 in start-up companies for a holding period of two years receive a 50% tax deduction, while start-ups receive tiered tax exemptions in their first three years. Investment allowances, cash grants and reimbursements under various support schemes also reduce research and development expenditures. It is hoped that Singapore's healthcare industry, which requires innovation-led growth to deal with the challenges of an ageing population, will provide a great test-bed for locally-developed technologies.

References

Bhaskaran, M, SC Ho, D Low, KS Tan, S Vadaketh and LK Yeoh (2012). Income inequality in Singapore. In *Singapore Perspectives 2012: Singapore Inclusive, Bridging Divides*, SH Kang and CH Leong (eds.). Singapore: Institute of Policy Studies.

Chan, CB (ed.) (2002). *Heart Work*. Singapore: Economic Development Board.

Choy, KM (2010). Singapore's changing economic model. In *Management of Success: Singapore Revisited*, T Chong (ed.). Singapore: Institute of Southeast Asian Studies.

Corrado, C, C Hulten and D Sichel (2006). *Intangible Capital and Economic Growth*. Washington, DC: Federal Reserve Board.

Department of Statistics, Singapore (2011). Key Household Income Trends 2010.

Economic Review Committee Report (2003). Ministry of Trade and Industry, Singapore.

Economic Strategies Committee Report (2010). Ministry of Trade and Industry, Singapore.

Florida, R (2002). *The Rise of the Creative Class: And How It's Transforming Work Leisure, Community and Everyday Life*. New York: Basic Books.

Jones, C and P Klenow (2010). Beyond GDP? Welfare across Countries and Time. National Bureau of Economic Research, NBER Working Paper 16352. Available at http://www.nber.org/papers/w16352.pdf.

Kapur, B (2009). Making the case for GST rollback. *The Straits Times*, 26 January.

Lim, LYC (2014). Singapore's success: After the miracle. In *Handbook of Emerging Economies*, RE Looney (ed.). London and New York: Routledge.

Low, D, LK Yeoh, KS Tan and M Bhaskaran (2013). Economics Myths in the Great Population Debate, IPSCommons. Institute of Policy Studies, Singapore.

Ministry of Manpower, Singapore (2014). Labour Force in Singapore, 2014.

Ministry of Trade and Industry, Singapore (2014). Drivers of Labour Productivity Growth Trends in Singapore.

Monetary Authority of Singapore (2010). Sources of Singapore's economic growth 1990–2009. *Macroeconomic Review* 9(1) (April), pp. 66–81.

Ngiam, TD and S Tay (2006). *A Mandarin and the Making of Public Policy: Reflections*. Singapore: NUS Press.

Parrado, E (2004). Singapore's Unique Monetary Policy: How Does It Work? International Monetary Fund, IMF Working Paper WP/04/10.

Phang, SY (2015). Global superstar cities, inequality and housing policy. Celia Moh Professorial Chair Public Lecture, Singapore Management University. 23 March.

SingStat (various years). http://www.singstat.gov.sg.

Stiglitz J, A Sen and J Fitoussi (2008). Report by the Commission on Economic Performance and Social Progress. http://www.stiglitz-sen-fitoussi.fr/documents/rapport_anglais.pdf.

Tan, KS (1995). Protecting consumers — how far can CASE go? *The Straits Times*, 26 June.

Tan, KS (2014). Singapore: From MNC Hub to Global City. Paper presented at the Northern Development Summit, ADC Forum. Townsville, Australia, 27 June 2014.

Tan, KS and L Gan (2012). Managing SME development: The Singapore experience. Paper presented at the West Lake International Conference on Small and Medium Business 2012, 12–15 October 2012. Hangzhou, China.

Tan, KS and SY Phang (2005). From Efficiency-Driven to Innovation-Driven Growth: Perspective from Singapore. World Bank, Policy Research Working Paper 3569. Washington, DC.

Venhor, B and K Meyer (2007). The German Miracle Keeps Running: How Germany's Hidden Champions Stay Ahead in the Global Economy. Working Paper No 30, 05/2007, Berlin School of Economics.

World Bank (1993). *The East Asian Miracle: Economic Growth and Public Policy*. U.S: Oxford University Press.

Yusuf, S (2007). The Iskandar Development Region and its impact on Singapore. In *The Eighth Singapore Economic Roundtable*, M Bhaskaran (ed.). Singapore: Straits Times Press.

CHAPTER 5

Monetary Policy and Financial Sector Development

Peter Wilson

This chapter reviews Singapore's monetary policy and financial development since independence, including the immediate challenges in the 1960s, the turbulent years of the 1970s with the collapse of the Bretton Woods fixed exchange rate system and the global oil shocks of 1973 and 1979, the introduction of a unique exchange rate-centered monetary policy in 1981, the Asian financial crisis of 1997–1998 and the global financial crisis of 2007–2009. Despite being a late starter (1971) and given a number of obstacles, not least the high degree of openness of the Singapore economy to trade and capital flows, the Monetary Authority of Singapore has built up a high degree of credibility within a relatively short space of time and delivered low and stable inflation. Although financial development has been "government made" rather than market-driven, proactive and sensible policies have built on Singapore's long history as a regional trading hub to turn Singapore into a premier financial center in terms of foreign exchange trading, offshore money market intermediation and asset management. Nonetheless, some challenges remain: How monetary policy can deal with asset price bubbles and deflationary pressures and steer a careful course to maintain price stability without jeopardizing Singapore's transitory restructuring process to achieve sustainable economic growth.

1. Introduction

When Winston Churchill was asked in 1942 how long it would take to achieve victory in the Far East, his response was: "If we manage it well, it will take only half as long as if we manage it badly." Whilst preparing his memoirs, however, he grudgingly conceded that: "If it had been studied with the intensity with which we examined the European and African operations, these disasters could not have been prevented, but they might at least have been foreseen."[1] Despite external headwinds and some

---

[1] The first quote comes from Jenkins (2001, p. 675) and the second from a timely review of the reasons behind the fall of Singapore to the Japanese in 1942 by Farrell and Hunter (2010, p. 128).

inherent domestic obstacles, monetary policy and financial development in Singapore have been managed well since 1965.[2]

2. The Colonial Legacy: 1965–1969

When Singapore separated from the Malaysian Confederation and gained full independence on 9th August 1965, the landscape in which monetary policy and financial development took place was very different from what it is today. Indeed, Singapore was still trapped in its colonial past (Figure 1) although, as we shall see, this was not necessarily a bad thing.

Founded in 1819 as a trading port by Stamford Raffles, Singapore joined with Penang and Malacca to become the Straits Settlements in 1826. In 1867, it became a British Crown Colony with a legalized silver standard, and in 1897, the Board of Commissioners of Currency for the Straits Settlements was established to issue government notes which were redeemable on demand against silver coins. Following a brief switch to the Gold Standard in 1906, when the First World War broke out in 1914 and gold convertibility was suspended, the Straits Dollar began its long fix to sterling and was renamed the Malayan Dollar in 1939. Following the defeat of Japan in 1945, Singapore returned to the British Currency Board system, which was expanded in 1950 to incorporate Brunei, Sarawak and British North Borneo.

After independence, Singapore chose continuity rather than change and retained the use of the Malaya and British North Borneo dollar as its currency, which was fixed to the pound sterling, and the Malaya, Singapore, Brunei Currency Board had the sole right to issue the currency. Even after the break-up of the 29-year-old common currency board in June 1967, and despite political differences, the member countries continued to fix their new currencies — the Malaysian Ringgit, the Brunei Dollar and the Singapore Dollar (SGD) — to sterling at the prevailing parities and agreed to use each other's currency interchangeably as "customary tender". Although Malaysia exited from the agreement in 1973, Brunei and Singapore have continued this curious currency arrangement to this day. Crucially, Singapore also retained the currency board system, the most "disciplined" monetary arrangement of all, when it setup the Board of Commissioners of Currency Singapore (BCCS) in June 1967. A test of the new currencies came in November 1967 when the pound sterling was devalued by 14.3%, but all three former colonies decided not to devalue, to guard against inflationary pressures and preserve international confidence in the strength and stability of their currencies.

---

[2] For two invaluable surveys of Singapore's monetary history, see Monetary Authority of Singapore (2000, 2012). A review of financial development since the 1960s, including a comparison with Hong Kong, can be found in Tan *et al.* (2004).

1867	The Straits Settlements becomes a British Crown Colony with a legalized silver standard and a currency board is introduced in 1897
1906	Switch to the Gold Standard until 1914 when the Straits Dollar was fixed to sterling and replaced by the Malayan Dollar (1939)
1942–1944	Japanese 'banana money' circulates
1945	Return to the British currency board system which was expanded (1950) to include Sarawak, Brunei and British North Borneo
August 1965	Singapore exits the Malaysian Federation but continues to use the Malaya and British North Borneo dollar
June 1967	Breakup of the Malaysia, Singapore, Brunei currency board system but they continue to fix to sterling and use each other's currency interchangeably as 'customary tender'. Singapore issues the 'Singapore dollar' and sets up its own currency board: the Board of Commissioners of Currency Singapore (BCCS)
November	Sterling is devalued by 14.3%. Singapore, Malaysia and Brunei keep their currencies at their pre-devaluation parities
1968	Asian Dollar Market is established in Singapore
January 1971	MAS is established as a multipurpose central bank but currency issue remains with the BCCS
August	The USA closes the gold window. The Singapore dollar (fixed to sterling) is *de facto* revalued by 8%
June 1972	End of the Sterling Area as the pound floats. The SGD is pegged to the USD
1973	First oil shock. Malaysia exits the Singapore, Brunei, Malaysia currency union Stock Exchange of Singapore (SES) is established
June	Collapse of the Bretton Woods fixed exchange rate system and move to generalized floating, end of the SGD fix to the USD, *de facto* end of Singapore's currency board system
October 1974	MAS raises interest rates to contain inflation following the first oil shock
1975	Singapore monitors a trade-weighted basket of currencies within a band
June 1978	Singapore removes all exchange controls
1979	Second oil shock
1980	Goh Keng Swee appointed Deputy Prime Minister and MAS Chairman
1981	Formal adoption of the present exchange rate-centered monetary policy
May	Government of Singapore Investment Corporation established
1983	MAS Notice 621 codifies the policy of non-internationalization of the SGD
1984	Singapore International Monetary Exchange (SIMEX) setup
1985	First recession since independence. Monetary policy is loosened. On 16 September MAS buys the SGD and raises short-term interest rates to punish speculators
November	Pan-Electric Industries defaults and the SES is suspended
February 1995	Merchant Bank Barings goes into administration due to 'rogue trading' in Singapore by Nick Leeson
May 1997	Asian financial crisis begins with the selling of the Thai Baht
October 1998	MAS adopts a zero appreciation stance and widens the policy band
December 1999	The SES and SIMEX are merged into the SGX
2001	Dot-com bubble bursts and Singapore goes into recession. In April, monetary policy shifts from a gradual and modest appreciation to a zero appreciation stance and the band is widened in October following the September terrorist attacks on the United States
October 2002	Merger of the BCCS with MAS
2003	Severe Acute Respiratory Syndrome epidemic hits Singapore so MAS shifts the policy band down
September 2008	Collapse of Lehman Brothers triggers the global financial crisis and in October monetary policy moves to a neutral stance
April 2009	Singapore in recession. MAS loosens further by re-centering the policy band downwards
February 2010	Economic Strategies Committee recommends restructuring to increase productivity and reduce dependence on unskilled foreign labor
April	Following a strong recovery the policy band is steepened and shifted up
October	The policy band is further steepened and widened
January 2015	MAS surprises the market with an unscheduled announcement to weaken the rate of appreciation of the policy band as inflation forecasts are sharply revised down

Figure 1.   Key events in Singapore's monetary and financial history.

3. Turbulent Years: 1970–1979

1971 was not a good time to be setting up a central bank and sliding down the financial development learning curve, but in Singapore things are different. In August 1971, Richard Nixon closed the gold window, following heavy currency volatility and downward pressure on the US dollar (USD), and at the Smithsonian Institute in December, the USD was *de facto* devalued by 8% against gold. Since the SGD was still fixed to Sterling, it was automatically revalued. With hindsight, this marked the end of the Bretton Woods system of fixed exchange rates, but it was not until the first oil shock in 1973 that it became apparent that fixed rates were untenable in such a volatile global environment. In June 1972, the pound was allowed to float following speculative attacks and capital outflows, marking the end of the sterling area and the SGD was pegged to the USD to reduce inflationary pressures and safeguard the value of Singapore's reserve assets. With the move to generalized floating in June 1973 by the major currencies, the SGD peg to the USD was broken and the currency was floated. This was not welcomed by the authorities at the time, but there seemed little choice.

Notwithstanding the fact that the break with the USD marked the end of the currency board system in Singapore, since the local currency could no longer be exchanged on demand for foreign currency at a fixed rate, when the Monetary Authority of Singapore (MAS) was setup in January 1971, the BCCS was retained as the sole issuer of the currency, and this continued until 2002 when it was finally merged with the MAS. All that then remained of the currency board system was the law that all currency in circulation must be backed 100% or more by reserve assets, which was not, by then, a binding constraint. It appears that MAS was established primarily to preserve the stability and purchasing power of the SGD, supervise and develop the financial system and manage the reserves. Currency issue, however, was deliberately left with the BCCS to signal to the world and to Singaporeans that the fledgling central bank would not be able to print money to finance government deficits, as was common in other newly-independent countries, and that government spending would have to be financed by taxation.[3] The decision to retain the BCCS, despite the fact that the currency board "system" had, for all intents and purposes, disappeared, is thus explicable given Singapore's colonial past. There was no longer a need to fix the exchange rate or supply reserve money at a fixed rate in unlimited quantities, as in Hong Kong after October 1983, but the BCCS was retained to provide confidence that the value of the SGD would be preserved and that the government would not run budget deficits.[4]

---

[3] Even today, although MAS is now a full multi-purpose central bank and enjoys day-to-day independence, technically it is not independent since its Board includes the Finance Minister as non-executive Chairman and other sitting Ministers.

[4] For a comparison between the currency board systems in Singapore and Hong Kong, see Peebles and Wilson (1996, Chap. 5).

When MAS was established in 1970, Singapore's reserve assets were transferred from the Ministry of Finance, with a small amount left at BCCS. By 1970 the reserves per capita had almost tripled since 1965, at S$1,493. This was due to balance of payments surpluses, an inflow of foreign capital, a high domestic savings rate and persistent budget surpluses (Table 1). But this put pressure on the SGD to appreciate, so MAS was obliged to intervene, when necessary, to sell the SGD, usually against the USD, thus accumulating foreign reserves. Once provision had been made for liquidity management, there was a desire to invest the "excess" reserves in a diversified portfolio, including equities, for wealth preservation rather than the "safe" traditional central bank portfolio of cash, bonds and gold, and away from the British pound and USD to currencies, such as the Japanese Yen and West German Mark, for which there was both liquidity and scope for appreciation. Some funds were also farmed out to external fund managers as a forerunner of the asset management policies of the 1980s.

Singapore had long been a regional trading hub providing entrepot and banking services, including the remittance of funds by Chinese merchants back to China, and in the immediate post-independence years financial services were still largely

Table 1. Performance indicators for Singapore: 1960–2014.

	1960–1969	1970–1979	1980–1989	1990–1999	2000–2014
Real GDP Growth (%) 2010 = 100	8.8	9.5	7.8	7.3	5.7
CPI Inflation (%)[1]	1.2[2](n.a)	5.9 (8.6)	2.8 (6.5)	1.9 (2.9)	2.0 (1.9)
Resident Unemployment Rate (%)	n.a.	4.2	3.5	2.7	3.6
Balance of Payments Surplus (% GDP)	5.3[3]	7.4	6.7	7.8	8.7
Growth in Reserves (%)	15.2	17.6	12.0	12.9	6.8

	1965	1970	1980	1990	2000	2013
Real Income Per Capita (S$)	5319	8878	18,159	30,247	45,525	68,472
Reserves Per Capita (S$)	566.3	1493	6028	17,719	42,441	89,662
Insurance and Banking (% GDP)	4.6	5.4	9.2	13.7	10.0	11.8
Reserves (Millions of S$)	1068	3097	13,757	48,478	138,927	344,729

Notes: [1]Advanced countries in brackets; [2]1961–1969; [3]1963–1969.

Sources: www.singstat.gov.sg; International Monetary Fund, International Financial Statistics.

regarded as playing a supporting role in industrialization rather than being developed in their own right.[5]

Nonetheless, a conscious effort was made to make Singapore an offshore trading center for foreign currencies and to develop the domestic banking sector into a regional funding base. This would enable Singapore to go beyond its small domestic market and take advantage of the pool of foreign currency holdings of residents in Asia and the increase in funds coming into the Asian region. It could also capitalize on its favorable time zone enabling round-the-clock over-the-counter trading in the major foreign exchange markets, such as London and New York. A major step in this direction was the establishment of the Asian Dollar Market (ADM) in 1968, which allowed both domestic and foreign-owned banks in Singapore to invest and trade in USD and other foreign currencies without having to convert to SGD. Asian Currency Units (ACUs) were set up to accept deposits from nonresidents and to lend USD and other foreign currencies to finance activities outside Singapore. However, it was understandably felt necessary at this time to protect local banks and financial institutions against foreign competition so the offshore accounts were kept separate from domestic banking units (DBUs) and, initially, Singapore residents were not allowed to transact with ACUs, even in foreign currencies, although this was subsequently relaxed in 1978 when exchange controls were abolished.

At this time, other financial markets remained rather underdeveloped. The Stock Exchange of Singapore (SES) was setup in 1973 with the focus on building up its trading infrastructure to increase its attractiveness as a listing center, while the debt market and asset management were not to become important players until the 2,000s. Nonetheless, MAS had to create an effective supervision system in a short space of time, which posed a steep learning curve to screen and license banks and monitor their activities. Right from the start, it was determined to build up credibility by imposing stringent prudential requirements and rigorous enforcement, supplemented by the effective use of "moral suasion." The chit fund problem in the early 1970s and the Slater Walker Securities episode in 1975 were early challenges to the effectiveness of MAS and were successfully dealt with.[6] MAS also consistently refused to grant banking licenses to the Bank of Credit and Commerce International (BCCI) and National Bank of Brunei, despite political pressure from outside Singapore. BCCI

---

[5] For an excellent history of Singapore from its foundation in 1819 to 1988, see Turnbull (1992).

[6] Chit funds were largely unregulated sources of credit without the collateral requirements of the banks and became popular as the economy grew and the demand for credit increased. In 1972, the Chit Funds Act was passed, but after investigation by MAS, they were banned in 1973. Slater Walker was a prominent British company which specialized in asset-stripping but the government decided to proceed with an investigation into the misuse of company funds by a Slater Walker-controlled company in Singapore, Haw Par International. Jim Slater himself resigned as Chairman in 1975 and was subsequently prosecuted in 1979 for similar offences in the UK.

collapsed spectacularly in 1991 and the National Bank of Brunei was shut down by the Brunei authorities in 1983.

When MAS was set up in 1971, there was no formal monetary framework or experience of managing the exchange rate. Accordingly, MAS developed market instruments and institutions to enable it to carry out traditional monetary policy, including discount houses and treasury bills and certificates of deposit and moved gradually to a reliance on foreign exchange and domestic money market operations rather than the blunter instruments of reserve requirements and credit guidelines.

Throughout the 1970s, conventional monetary policy was used to achieve low inflation in an environment of volatile interest rates and exchange rates, and capital inflows which tended to both appreciate the currency and put upward pressure on asset prices. In the early 1970s, there were no specific targets for money aggregates and interest rates were set by a cartel of banks in consultation with MAS. Only after July 1975, were individual banks free to quote their own deposit and lending rates. Rather, MAS relied on a checklist of indicators, including interest rates, exchange rates, the monetary base and loan growth. In exceptional times, MAS raised interest rates: in October 1974 by 2% points following a sharp rise in inflation in 1973 to 20% in the wake of the first oil shock. In 1975, monetary policy was eased as GDP growth stabilized at 4.6% and inflation at 2.5%, an exchange rate policy band was introduced and movements of the trade-weighted SGD within that band were monitored with a view to reducing SGD volatility. This was the first explorative step toward the more formalized managed floating exchange rate system introduced in 1981.

From 1976 to 1979, monetary policy was mainly used to provide liquidity to support non-inflationary growth and offset the drain in liquidity arising from budget surpluses and capital inflows and to monitor a range of intermediate targets, including interest rates and the exchange rate. After the second oil shock of 1979, global inflation rose sharply (10% in advanced developed countries) and external demand fell as Singapore's major trading partners went into recession. As a result, inflation in Singapore rose to 8.5% in 1980. This was not helped by rising labor costs, partly due to policies to raise wages and boost productivity. Unemployment in 1980 was only 3% but compared to the 1960s and later decades, average inflation in the 1970s in Singapore was relatively high at almost 6% (Table 1). In June 1978 all exchange controls were removed. Individuals and companies could now retain their export proceeds in foreign currency and with overseas institutions indefinitely. This was quite a brave step since it was highly unusual for developing countries to remove these controls and even advanced countries retained some capital controls just in case. It also meant losing some control over currency movements and could have resulted in greater currency volatility. In the event it did not.

4. The Formal Adoption of the Exchange Rate Centered Monetary Policy: 1980–1989

In 1980, Goh Keng Swee was appointed as Deputy Prime Minister and MAS Chairman. This marked the beginning of a remarkable decade for Singapore's monetary policy and financial development with the formal introduction of the exchange rate-centered monetary policy and the creation of the Government of Singapore Investment Corporation (now GIC Private Ltd) to manage Singapore's reserve assets; as well as its first recession since independence.

A tighter approach was introduced to regulation and supervision which was more at arms-length than in the 1970s. The priorities were to allow only reputable financial institutions into Singapore to reduce exposure to global risks and contagion and to have zero tolerance with financial institutions that did not operate in a sound or prudent way. This was to serve Singapore well in the 1990s with the Barings crisis of 1995 and the Asian financial crisis of 1997–1998. The development of Singapore as a funding base and foreign exchange center was also enhanced as trade expanded rapidly and financial deregulation in major industrialized countries proceeded. The Singapore International Monetary Exchange (SIMEX) was set up in 1984 to broaden the equities market by offering currency futures contracts alongside other financial futures and more sophisticated products, such as currency options.

More controversial was the policy of not encouraging the internationalization of the SGD. In 1983, banks in Singapore were required to consult MAS before extending SGD credit above S$5 million to non-residents for purposes other than economic activities related to Singapore, to limit potential speculation against the SGD. Restrictions were also placed on transactions with non-residents in SGD financial derivatives to discourage leveraging or hedging of SGD positions. The rationale was to limit the accumulation of SGD offshore which might compromise the exchange rate-centered monetary policy and lead to excessive currency volatility by providing a pool of funds available for speculation against the SGD. Moreover, in true Singapore style, it was felt that there was a need to send a clear message that speculation would not be tolerated. Whilst this policy undoubtedly helped MAS in its currency management, the side-effects were to prove more troublesome in the 1990s.

In May 1981, the GIC was setup to manage the reserves. MAS would still be responsible for the reserves needed for short-term liquidity and exchange rate management but the rest (including those at the BCCS) would be professionally managed to achieve higher returns in the longer run. The decision was based on the fact that MAS had already accumulated a large stock of reserves and it was a matter of policy that this would continue,[7] but also the sensible view that if there were to be

---

[7] The exact size of the reserves is not public information but according to the published data in Table 1, there has been a persistent accumulation over successive decades. In the early years, the justification was

"excess reserves" they should not be managed in the traditional manner of a central bank in low-risk, low-return assets. At that time, sovereign wealth funds were opaque, largely commodity-based and not designed to invest in a diversified portfolio. GIC would thus focus on investing Singapore's external assets and Temasek Holdings, the government's holding company, would focus more on domestic investment.

Since 1981, Singapore's monetary policy has been centered on the management of the exchange rate with the primary objective of ensuring medium-term price stability as an anchor for macroeconomic stability and a sound basis for sustained economic growth (Wilson, 2008).[8] The rationale is that low and stable price inflation provides a predictable environment for domestic production and consumption, keeps foreign capital operating in Singapore and signals to the rest of the world that Singapore is a stable economy with sound macroeconomic policy and is an economically safe place in which to do business. This also enhances its status as an international financial center. Equally important is the government's long-term commitment to Singaporeans to preserve the purchasing power of the SGD in world markets to protect the value of private savings, compulsory retirement savings with the Central Provident Fund (CPF) and Singapore's reserve assets.

The decision to formally adopt this policy followed a gradual evolution away from the use of direct controls in the early 1970s to one based on a range of intermediate targets, including the exchange rate, between 1975 and 1981. Allowing the SGD to appreciate after the 1979 oil shock also convinced MAS that targeting the exchange rate was more effective in keeping inflation down than the more traditional monetary tightening after the 1973 shock. There was also a growing sense that Singapore's very high trade openness and dependence on imports made traditional monetary policy, based on interest rates or money aggregates, less effective than in other countries. Singapore has always been an exceptionally open economy with a trade to GDP ratio in excess of three and protection has been negligible since the early 1970s. There are other countries in the world that are very open to trade but what singles Singapore out is its very high import content of domestic expenditure and exports. Out of every SGD spent in Singapore, about 64 cents goes to foreigners in payment for imports and a large proportion of the value of a good exported from

---

to build up a "war chest" to be able to cope with political or economic crises, but in more recent decades, the emphasis has switched to the need to fully fund the liabilities of the Central Provident Fund compulsory savings scheme and the expected increase in social spending due to the ageing population (Peebles and Wilson, 2002, Chap. 8). At present, by law the government can draw up to half of the expected long-term real returns from the reserves over its 5-year term and must balance its budget over this period. In an emergency, as in 2009, it can withdraw more only with the permission of the President.

[8] Unlike some central banks, such as the US Federal Reserve, which is under a statutory obligation to achieve maximum employment, stable prices and moderate long-term interest rates, MAS does not have a dual or multiple mandate but targets price stability conducive to sustainable growth of the economy.

Singapore consists of imported intermediate inputs. Out of every SGD of refined petroleum exported from the Republic, approximately 90 cents is accounted for by imported crude oil.

The implication is that Singapore is a classic price-taker in world markets, since it is too small as an exporter or importer to have any discernable impact on international prices, so domestic prices are largely determined by world prices for a given exchange rate. What MAS has done since 1981 has been to turn this import dependence into a virtue by taking advantage of the powerful link between the exchange rate, import prices and domestic prices. If, for instance, consumer price inflation is expected to rise due to a positive domestic output gap and/or a rise in imported inflation, rather than tightening monetary policy by raising interest rates, appreciating the SGD effectively lowers import prices and, subsequently, wholesale and consumer prices, as the effects of the appreciation pass through quickly to the domestic economy.[9] This is the "direct imported inflation channel" but there is a second, "indirect" channel insofar as the currency appreciation reduces the revenues of Singapore-based exporters and lowers their demand for factor inputs, such as manpower and capital goods, and puts downward pressure on local costs and inflation as the output gap is narrowed. Highly export-oriented services and manufacturing will be most affected, compared to domestic-oriented business and financial services, but there will be some consolation for producers in the reduction in costs through the direct channel if they have large import requirements. Insofar as there has been a rise in domestic costs in recent history, exacerbated by the restructuring process (see below), the net effect of the two channels and, therefore, monetary policy may have become weaker.

Another reason for this policy is Singapore's openness to international capital flows. Foreign exchange controls and restrictions on inflows and outflows of capital were removed in 1978 and Singapore has always adopted an open-arms approach to investment by foreign multinationals since 1965. This is not unique to Singapore, but what makes Singapore different is the very high degree of substitutability between the onshore domestic banking system and the offshore ADM, so targeting interest rates would not be very effective. If MAS tried to stimulate the economy by pushing down domestic interest rates through the conventional process of bank intermediation, this would quickly and strongly drive short-term capital offshore and the money supply would fall back to where it was before. Thus, because managing the exchange rate is thought to be more effective than targeting interest rates and Singapore wants to keep

---

[9] Parrado (2004) shows formally that MAS in fact follows a forward-looking reaction function that stabilizes expected inflation and maintains output at potential, which amounts to moving the trade-weighted exchange rate index, the intermediate target of monetary policy, to the left-hand side in a Taylor (1993) type reaction function.

the capital market open to develop the financial sector, monetary autonomy is abandoned and interest rates are essentially determined by global rates.[10] In the jargon of central banks, the exchange rate is a good (controllable) intermediate target for monetary policy and bears a stable and predictable relationship with price stability as the ultimate target of monetary policy over the medium term. Singapore's exchange rate-centered monetary policy may have been born out of necessity and is certainly unorthodox, but it works![11]

Monetary policy in Singapore is thus essentially exchange rate policy and can be summarized in the acronym "BBC" or "basket", "band" and "crawl". The exchange rate is managed against an unpublished trade-weighted basket of currencies (TWS$)[12] of Singapore's major trading partners and competitors, with the weights (not disclosed) updated periodically, as a more stable reference point for monitoring movements in the SGD than a single currency, given that Singapore has a diversified pattern of trade. The TWS$ is permitted to float within a policy band, which allows market forces to absorb short-term market volatility, but without the volatility which might result if the currency were to float freely. However, this is not mechanical and MAS may intervene within the band if, for example, it believes that there is excessive volatility due to manipulation by speculative funds, or to act early to prevent strong momentum building up and pushing the TWS$ outside the band. Finally, the policy stance is reviewed every six months in April and October[13] and embodies John Williamson's famous "crawl" feature which allows policy to be changed if circumstances dictate it, thus preventing the TWS$ from becoming misaligned.

The slope of the policy band can be changed when MAS thinks that the trajectory of economic activity in the medium-term is likely to persist, such as in October

---

[10] This is consistent with the well-known "policy trilemma" (see Obstfeld *et al.*, 2005). Uncovered Interest Parity (UIP) also appears to hold remarkably well for Singapore (Khor *et al.*, 2007) as the SGD Interbank rate (SIBOR) is usually below the USD Interbank rate in Singapore, except when USD rates are artificially pushed down toward zero as a result of FED quantitative easing. For an interesting recent explanation as to why UIP seems to hold for Singapore, see Mihov (2013).

[11] MAS's own research (Khor *et al.*, 2007) and by independent researchers, tends to support the view that targeting the exchange rate is a more effective means of achieving low and stable inflation than targeting interest rates (Abeysinghe and Choy, 2007, Chap. 9). In a recent chapter, Mihov (2013) also argues that in an open economy, such as Singapore, monetary policy based on the exchange rate results in superior welfare outcomes than an interest rate regime.

[12] We will use TWS$ to refer to the MAS' own effective exchange rate index but continue to use S$NEER and S$REER when referring to third-party measures, such as those compiled from IMF data in Figure 2.

[13] There has always been a provision to make an unscheduled policy change within the six month period if circumstances warrant it. This has only happened twice: In October 2001, following the terrorist attacks in the United States and in January 2015, in response to a sharp fall in global commodity prices, including oil.

2008 (downwards) as the global financial crisis unfolded. Shifting the level of the band is a response to a more abrupt shift in the path of economic activity, such as in April 2010 when the band was re-centered upwards in the face of persistent global price pressures and rising domestic costs. Changing the width of the policy band is less common and tends to be a response to market-driven movements that cause an artificial strengthening or weakening of the currency due to short-term currency volatility, such as the widening in October 2001 following the terrorist attacks in the United States.

There are two aspects to the implementation of monetary policy in Singapore: Management of the exchange rate and management of domestic liquidity through money market operations. In anticipation of the Monetary Policy Statement in April and October, the Economic Policy Group at the MAS will calculate several hypothetical exchange rate policy paths, using a mixture of spread-sheet analysis, consultation and more formal macroeconometric modeling, before deciding on the optimum path to be submitted to the Monetary and Investment Policy Meeting, the equivalent of the Monetary Policy Committee of other central banks, for approval.[14] Implementation is then carried out on a 24 h basis in both spot and forward markets.[15]

Although MAS does not attempt to target interest rates or the domestic money supply (which is an endogenous outcome of exchange rate policy), it does carry out daily money market operations to manage liquidity in the domestic banking system. Given Singapore's very high gross savings rate, due primarily to the CPF and large budget surpluses, there tends to be a trend withdrawal of liquidity from the banking system. MAS, therefore, injects liquidity back, where necessary, and might also want to sterilize the effect on the money market of its own foreign exchange intervention, although this is not automatic if there is already sufficient liquidity available.[16] Another motive is to make sure that there is sufficient liquidity to satisfy the banks' demand for cash balances to meet their intra-day settlements amongst themselves and

---

[14] The Committee consists of the Chairman of MAS, the Deputy Chairman, selected Board Members and the Managing Director.

[15] Until 2,000, MAS did not communicate its policy on the exchange rate to the public but since then there has been three main lines of communication. The Monetary Policy Statement is released twice a year in April and October and is accompanied by the publication of the Macroeconomic Review and closed door briefings to the Singapore media and private sector analysts. In recent years, MAS has been more actively engaged with the public through its website, including educational material, and at a workshop in August 2014, it released for the first time substantial details about its suite of econometric models in order to enhance collaboration with academia.

[16] Money market liquidity will change, for example, depending on the net issuance or redemption of government securities. The CPF is also a big player in the market since its net proceeds are placed with MAS for subsequent subscription to special issues of government securities with original maturities of 20 years. These are non-marketable but are used to meet the CPF's investment requirements.

with the central bank, since all banks in Singapore have to maintain cash reserves at the MAS. MAS also offers discount or lending facilities on a daily basis.[17]

The new monetary policy framework was soon to be tested when in 1985 Singapore experienced its first recession since independence. The lagged effects of the second oil shock in 1979 had resulted in slower global growth and higher inflationary pressures in the early 1980s and the spillover effects were felt in Singapore through increased inflation in 1980 (8.6%) and 1981 (8.1%) and slower export growth in 1981 and 1982. This coincided with booming home demand, especially in construction and a sharp rise in unit labor costs from 1980 to 1982. The high wage policy after 1979 to force producers to increase value-added, together with the steady rise in the employer CPF contribution rate to a peak of 25% by 1985 also raised business costs and this was translated into a higher real effective exchange rate (Figure 2). From 1980 to 1984, export growth was still positive but in 1985 and 1986, exports fell and Singapore was particularly affected by a fall in foreign demand for electronic goods, ship repair and oil refining which coincided with a drop in regional tourism and entrepot trade and a sharp contraction in domestic demand, especially construction. The result was negative GDP growth for 1985 of –0.6%.

To cushion the downturn and speed up the recovery, as inflationary pressure eased, the MAS allowed the TWS$ to depreciate (Figure 2), but much of the downward adjustment in the S$REER (real effective exchange rate) came from government-determined cost cuts, including a 15% point cut in the employers' CPF contribution rate, and cuts in wages. On 16th September 1985, there was a sharp attack on the SGD. Between 1980 and 1985, both the S$NEER (nominal effective exchange rate) and S$REER had appreciated quite sharply (Figure 2), partly due to monetary tightening, and there was a perception that the SGD was overvalued and that MAS would intervene to push it down. However, Goh Keng Swee was determined to stick to the strong dollar policy and instructed MAS to buy the SGD with its USD reserves and to raise short-term interest rates to squeeze speculators out of their short positions. Less than 1% of the reserves were spent but the tight liquidity pushed the overnight interbank rate up to 105% on 17 September and 120% the following day and the SGD strengthened by about 5% against the USD in just four days (Monetary Authority of Singapore, 2012, p. 74). The policy of non-internationalization of the SGD may also have helped limit access to the local currency. Since then speculative attacks on the SGD have been rare.[18]

---

[17] Details of these money market operations can be found in the Bi-annual Macroeconomic Review and Monetary Authority of Singapore (2013a).

[18] 1985 was not a good year. In November, Pan-Electric Industries defaulted on a loan installment and went into receivership. All trading on the SES was suspended and MAS arranged a bailout for stock brokers. This was the biggest disaster in the history of Singapore's stock market and the first, and only time, it was closed. According to the Monetary Authority of Singapore (2012, p. 116), the industry may have

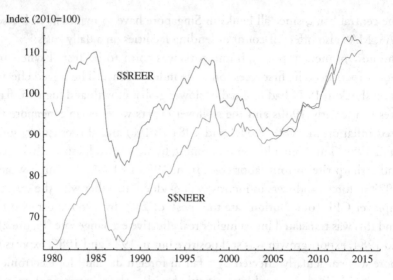

Figure 2.   Singapore's quarterly effective exchange rates: 1980–2014.

Source: International Monetary Fund, International Financial Statistics.

The economy recovered quickly from the recession, with GDP growth in excess of 10% by 1987 and unemployment below 2% by 1990. The following period up to the Asian financial crisis of 1997–1998 was a golden age of strong growth and low unemployment. To offset the build-up of inflationary pressures during this period, the MAS allowed the TWS$ to appreciate (Table 1 and Figure 2).

There was, however, a perception in the late 1980s and into the 1990s that the costs of doing business in Singapore had risen and contributed to a loss of export competitiveness, especially in manufactured goods, such as textiles, electronics and chemicals, to emerging rivals in the region, such as Malaysia, and that this was partly due to the strong SGD policy. The official view was that there was no evidence that aggregate exports had been negatively affected and individual producers should take into account the offsetting fall in the costs of imported intermediate inputs due to the trend appreciation in the S$NEER. In any case, MAS had made it clear that it would not use exchange rate policy to boost export competitiveness because the depreciation would quickly pass through into the consumer price index (CPI) and send wrong signal to exporters and encourage them to neglect supply-side issues, Singapore's exports are more sensitive to global income than price effects via the exchange rate, and a strong depreciation would reduce the value of Singapore's savings.

---

had too much supervisory freedom and there had been overtrading in "forward contracts" after 1981. Subsequent reforms boosted the capital base of stock broking firms and strengthened their prudential requirements. As a result, the fall-out from the Black Monday global stock market crash on 19 October 1987 was small.

It is hard to explain the paradox of substantial periods of strong S$NEER and S$REER appreciation after 1980 yet robust overall export performance, due to the difficulty of unraveling the interplay between aggregate and sectoral export performance and the factors which impinge on international competitiveness, such as nominal exchange rates, relative price levels and relative unit labor costs (ULC).[19] Certainly there was a change in the structure of Singapore's exports between 1988 and 2001 from textiles and lower-end electronic goods toward higher value-added electronics, including integrated circuits, and an evolution away from final goods to intermediate parts and components and pharmaceuticals; whilst at the same time there was rapid aggregate export growth due to strong global and regional demand. With hindsight, this may have been part of a broader and longer process of rapid integration of trade in the Asian region in the 1990s and the development of cross-border production networks in which Singapore's trade is more concentrated, but she is a dominant player, together with China.[20]

5. The Asian Financial Crisis and Major Financial Reform 1990–1999

In the 1990s, there were substantial efforts to speed up the globalization of Singapore's financial sector, to open up the banking sector to more foreign competition, to broaden and deepen the equity and derivatives markets, and to develop the local debt market. The result was a comprehensive set of reforms in the second half of the 1990s to promote Singapore as a full service international financial center, which were relentlessly pursued despite the Barings crisis of 1995 and the worst financial crisis in modern Asian history in 1997–1998.

An important step was the opening up to foreign banks. Given the worldwide trend toward fewer but larger banks, local banks were encouraged to merge and form global alliances and compete on the world stage. By the start of the 21st century, the local banks had been consolidated into three: DBS Group, OCBC Bank and UOB. In October 1999, licenses were given to "qualifying full banks" removing many of the restrictions designed to protect the local banks from competition. These restrictions were further reduced in 2004. Foreign companies were also enticed to setup their treasury and financing operations in Singapore, the telecoms market was liberalized and bank payment systems updated.

---

[19] According to Abeysinghe and Wilson (2002), relative costs in Singapore did fall to offset exchange rate appreciation in the 1980s, but not so much in the 1990s, and was due to the very high import content of Singapore's exports.

[20] For more on this, see Ting *et al.* (2005) and Monetary Authority of Singapore (2013b).

The asset management sector was also targeted. There was a widening of the scope for investment of CPF funds by increasing investment limits on unit trusts and a lifting of fixed commissions in the stock broking sector. The range of retirement products was widened and more government assets were farmed out to selected fund managers located in Singapore.

The SES had evolved into a modern and well-regulated market for raising capital in the region but turnover was not particularly high, derivatives trading was relatively thin and the Straits Times Index tended to be dominated by property market activities. In December 1999, it was merged with SIMEX to form the Singapore Exchange (SGX), in order to offer a broader range of products, including warrants, options and Exchange traded funds.

The debt market was also relatively underdeveloped since budget surpluses meant there was no need for the government to issue debt and companies in Singapore tended to look to the banks or equity market for funding. There was also a shallow secondary market for SGD debt since insurance companies were the biggest buyers and held them to maturity, so the secondary market lacked liquidity. Hence, in 1998, MAS launched the first 10-year government bond to extend the yield curve beyond seven years, regulations for SGD-based interest rate derivatives were liberalized, a repo facility was introduced and the Singapore government securities market was made more accessible to the investing public. Statutory boards and government-linked companies were also encouraged to tap the local bond market for their funding needs.

At the same time, MAS fell in line with global opinion, particularly in the United States, that central banks should focus more on preventing systemic risk, give more autonomy to financial organizations to manage their own risks, and shift the emphasis from regulation and a one-size-fits-all approach to supervision.

The policy of discouraging the internationalization of the SGD may have helped to insulate the domestic financial system and monetary policy from destabilizing speculation by sending a strong signal to speculators, but without good economic fundamentals and credible policy it is unlikely this would have been sufficient on its own to deter speculation given the extreme openness of Singapore to trade and capital flows.[21] Given the actual size of trade and capital flows, including short-term movements, it is unlikely that the policy had any serious impact on Singapore's overall financial development, but as Singapore began to position itself as a premier financial center in the 1990s, it may have impeded the development of the capital markets. There had always been some ambiguity about the policy which may have made local banks reluctant to lend to foreigners, and fund managers, in particular, wanted more freedom to hedge and borrow SGD for reasons other than for direct trade or investment purposes. It also hampered development of the bond market where short sales

---

[21] On this, see Lee (2001).

of securities and access to domestic currency credit are essential to enhance liquidity. There is also the view that by the 1990s, at least, MAS had become overly cautious and that Singapore's strong fundamentals would themselves have provided a sufficient barrier against speculation, and that MAS could have allowed borrowing without restriction in normal times but make it costly for speculators when events required it.[22]

Partly in response to financial market concerns, the SGD bond market was opened up to foreign issuers, the dollar swap market was encouraged, and the policy of non-internationalization was gradually relaxed. By 2004, most of the remaining restrictions were removed and the policy effectively became a restriction on lending SGDs to nonresident financial institutions.[23]

But these reforms did not pass without incident. On 26 February 1995, Britain's oldest merchant bank, Barings, went into administration after it emerged that Nick Leeson, the 28-year-old General Manager and derivatives trader in the bank's Singapore office had lost US$1.3 billion on futures contracts on Japan's Nikkei-225 stock market which he had concealed in a false trading account.[24] But because Barings had been required by MAS to trade futures in Singapore in an entity separate from its merchant banking arm and report directly to London, the bulk of Leeson's trades had been for the accounts of Barings Securities (London) and Barings Securities (Tokyo) so there was no systemic threat to Singapore. SIMEX dealt with the open positions quickly and efficiently and reforms were introduced subsequently to strengthen regulation and the lines of communication between SIMEX and MAS. There was no obvious impact on MAS' integrity or the stability of Singapore's financial sector.[25]

The Asian financial crisis began with a speculative attack on the Thai Baht on 15 May 1997 and quickly spread to other countries in East Asia through currencies, stock markets, and property markets. Even economies such as Singapore and Hong Kong, which were among the strongest in the region and had robust financial systems, were not spared the wave of panic selling and withdrawal of international investment. In 1998, the SGD fell in both nominal and real effective terms over the full year, reversing a long-term appreciation since the second half of the 1980s (Figure 2), GDP growth fell to –2.3% after a positive 8.3% the previous year and inflation was

---

[22] See, for example, Chan and Ngiam (1996) and Chow (2008). The relaxation of the rules is detailed in Ong (2002).

[23] Where a loan is made or SGD equity or bond issue is to be used to fund overseas activity by non-resident financial institutions, the proceeds must be swapped or converted into foreign currency before using outside Singapore.

[24] For details of the crisis, see Mankiw *et al.* (2013, p. 638).

[25] In 1999, Fitch named Singapore's banking system the strongest in Asia, S&P's sovereign rating was AAA throughout the crisis, Moody's AA was subsequently upgraded to AAA a few years later (Monetary Authority of Singapore, 2012).

negative at –0.3%. Accordingly, in October, monetary policy was eased to a zero appreciation stance, supplemented by a widening of the policy band in response to higher financial volatility and an uncertain outlook. As in the past, there was no attempt to depreciate the SGD since this might have triggered a speculative attack and reduced confidence in the exchange rate as the nominal anchor for inflation. Instead, a neutral stance was maintained throughout 1999 and as financial instability receded, the policy band was restored to its narrower pre-crisis level.

With the benefit of hindsight, Singapore emerged from the crisis relatively well compared to other countries in the region in terms of growth, inflation and the balance of payments. The only important negative impact was on the financial sector with falling stock prices, property prices and asset wealth as the currency lost value and incomes fell. Unemployment rose but only to 3.4%. Export growth was negative in 1998 but began to grow again in 1999 and GDP growth rebounded strongly at 6.2% in 1999 and 8.8% in 2000. Apart from the neutral monetary policy and a widening of the policy band to cushion exchange rate volatility, the main thrust of the anti-recessionary policy in 1998 was cost cuts to reduce relative unit labor costs, particularly in manufacturing, and thus the S$REER. In June, a S$10.5 billion off-budget package was introduced, followed in November by a further S$2 billion, including a 10% point reduction in the employer CPF contribution rate, a fall in wages of 5–10% and cuts in government charges for services.

6. Cyclical Volatility and the Global Financial Crisis: 2000–2015

By the beginning of 2,000, it looked as if Singapore had recovered very well from the Asian financial crisis and inflation began to rise. Initially monetary policy reverted to a gradual and modest appreciation of the policy band, but the recovery was short-lived, as Singapore experienced a series of shocks — the dot.com collapse and terrorist attacks in the United States in 2001, the Severe Acute Respiratory Syndrome (SARS) epidemic in 2003 and the much more serious global financial crisis in 2008–2009. On all three occasions, monetary policy was eased as inflationary pressures receded.

In 2001, there was a slowdown in the global electronics market following the bursting of the dot.com bubble. Export-oriented Singapore was badly hit through a fall in global chip sales, a proxy for electronics as a whole, the largest fall in 20 years. Exports fell by 8%, manufacturing output weakened, unemployment rose to 3.7%, and Singapore entered into a full-blown recession with GDP growth of –1.0%. However, as in 1985–1986 and 1997–1998, the recovery was helped by a repeat of policies used to deal with the earlier recessions. In July 2001, a range of cost-cutting and employment enhancement measures were announced and infrastructure investment projects were brought forward. There was a rescheduling of household mortgage repayments and a reduction in the foreign worker levy. Further off-budget policies were introduced in October, including the cancellation of bonuses for civil servants and political appointees, and pay for senior civil servants and government ministers was cut. With inflation expected to remain benign, in April 2001 monetary policy was shifted to a neutral zero percent appreciation stance. Then following the terrorist attacks in the United States in September, MAS widened the band in response to a crash in global financial markets and an increase in global uncertainty. The band was also shifted down to support growth and employment in the wake of the SARS outbreak in 2003 as inflation continued to be subdued but unemployment reached 5.2%.

Between 2004 and 2007, the Singapore economy enjoyed strong growth and job creation and inflation began to rise. Accordingly, monetary policy was tightened gradually using the "crawl" feature and in 2004, MAS reinstated the policy of a gradual and modest appreciation. In 2007, the economy grew by an impressive 9.1% marking the fourth consecutive year of strong growth and the seasonally-adjusted unemployment rate was at a decade low of 1.6% in December. If there was a problem on the horizon, it was from consumer price inflation, which reached an unprecedented 6.5% in 2008, due to rising global food and oil prices, and local wages and rentals. But by September 2008, the situation facing policy-makers in Singapore had changed dramatically. What had hitherto been a US sub-prime mortgage problem had escalated into a full-blown global financial crisis with a concomitant acute contraction of liquidity and credit, necessitating unprecedented emergency counter-cyclical activities by governments in both the developed and developing world.

In the event, Singapore, and Asia in general, appear to have been relatively unscathed as far as the financial fallout is concerned. As the Asian Development Bank (2009) put it: It was more of a "credit hiccup" than a "credit crunch". Share prices did fall in Singapore in 2008 and Singapore's sovereign wealth funds Temasek Holdings and GIC suffered losses on their investments in western banks. Retail investors, including some elderly, were also hit by the failure of Lehman Brothers structured notes and there were suggestions that there had been some mis-selling in Singapore. However, interbank rates in Asia generally did not spike in the latter part of 2008 so the global tightening of credit did not materially disrupt the flow of short-run liquidity. This was partly due to the fact that interbank borrowing is a relatively small source of funding in this region and regional central banks acted quickly to provide the necessary liquidity. Despite the fact that Singapore had introduced substantial financial reforms in the late 1990s, in line with the prevailing view that financial markets were generally efficient, which might have increased the risk of contagion from the crisis, in fact Singapore's banks were not heavily exposed to toxic assets and according to the Asian Development Bank (2009) had sound financial fundamentals.

From the middle of 2008, overall domestic liquidity trended downwards as interest rates in Singapore fell in line with global rates to low levels. At the same time, broad money fell as bank intermediation of reserve money contracted, the banks increased their demand for reserve and settlements balances for precautionary purposes, and the fall in nominal GDP reduced the number of economic transactions taking place in the economy. However, since the money markets continued to operate normally in Singapore, there was no need for the MAS to provide substantial extra liquidity (which would anyway be inconsistent with exchange rate policy), but it did carry out routine money market operations to stabilize interest rates and ensure sufficient liquidity in the banking system. In fact, monetary conditions in Singapore were broadly accommodative from August 2008 as the crisis unfolded (Chow and Wilson, 2011).

MAS also had in place a number of safeguards to help insulate the domestic financial system from the crisis. The priority was to increase liquidity and prevent a mass withdrawal of deposits. Accordingly, all SGD and foreign currency deposits of individual and non-bank customers were fully guaranteed until December 2010 and in October 2008, the MAS arranged a US$30 billion foreign exchange swap with the United States Federal Reserve to provide USD liquidity for financial institutions in Singapore if needed. In the event, this was not needed. Also helpful was the "domestic" nature of the banking system in Singapore, in which local ownership over key financial institutions is predominant, despite the openness of Singapore to trade and capital flows, and the ability of the MAS to provide funds and effect any necessary restructuring through "moral suasion" rather than large bailouts or nationalization.[26]

The financial impact of the crisis on Singapore was also cushioned by the fact that the fall in domestic non-bank loan growth, which occurred alongside the contraction in overall GDP, was less severe than during the Asian financial crisis and 2001 downturn, due to strong demand for credit in the building and construction industry, and the impact on domestic household wealth was cushioned by unusually robust property prices.

The impact of the global crisis on the "real" economy was, however, much more serious as the weighted GDP growth in Singapore's major trading partners fell from 2.9% in 2008 to –0.8% in 2009. Due to the extraordinarily high degree of openness of the Singapore economy, the Republic was severely hit by the fall in its non-oil domestic exports by 11% in 2009. The economy had continued to weaken throughout 2008 with negative fourth quarter growth and sequential contractions

---

[26] AIA, the local subsidiary of the giant insurance company AIG was largely unaffected despite AIG itself being on the verge of collapse in September 2008. To calm panic by AIA policyholders, MAS issued a statement that AIA is required to maintain sufficient funds to meet all its liabilities to policyholders. MAS also made it clear that it would not tolerate rumors about the soundness of particular financial institutions.

for every quarter except the first. Full year growth in 2009 was –0.6% and in September the headline unemployment rate reached 3.4%.

In April 2008, MAS had tightened monetary policy by re-centering the band at the prevailing level (upwards) since at that time, inflation was expected to rise due to persistent global price pressures and rising domestic costs. In October, however, monetary policy reverted to a neutral zero appreciation to accommodate low or negative expected GDP growth and in April 2009 policy was further eased by re-centering the band down. This was justified since inflation was only 0.6% in 2009. In October, this neutral stance was maintained in light of the rebound in economic activity in the second and third quarters. However, the widely expected severe and prolonged contraction did not materialize and by April 2010, Singapore had recovered all the output lost since the peak in the first quarter of 2008, so the recovery this time round was stronger than in the previous two downturns. As in the past, this was driven by trade-related activities, but in sharp contrast to the fall in growth in the G3, in China strong income growth, especially in electronics and electrical products, helped by a substantial fiscal stimulus package, undoubtedly helped the recovery (Monetary Authority of Singapore, 2010a,b). In 2010 GDP growth was 15.2%, well above the average of 5.2% following the previous two recessions.

There were a number of reasons for this. The labor market appears to have been more resilient during this recession, supported by an exodus of foreign workers on short-term contracts and buoyant construction and services, including social infrastructure projects, such as the integrated resorts and MRT Downtown Line. Indeed, by the end of the fourth quarter of 2009 unemployment had fallen to 2.3%, substantially quicker than during the previous two downturns, such that it was almost back to its pre-crisis level and local employment actually expanded in 2009. The impact on the labor market was also cushioned by government initiatives to stem retrenchments, particularly amongst Singaporeans, including a Jobs Credit Scheme in the January 2009 budget and a S$20.5 billion resilience package to stimulate bank lending and support incomes. Meanwhile, wages were also cut aggressively during this downturn, especially in services and in the public sector. Fiscal policy also played a larger countercyclical role during this crisis than in the past and there was an increased use of targeted transfers, including cash, to households and businesses.[27] Simulations by the Monetary Authority of Singapore (2009) suggest that the measures introduced in the budget added approximately 1.5% points to GDP growth in 2009. Monetary policy, by comparison, had a smaller impact, although it may have helped to alleviate some of the burden on exporters' revenue streams at a time when they were being hit by falling sales orders.

---

[27] The fiscal Impulse measure, which takes into account the effects of the cyclical performance of the economy on the budget switched from being contractionary in 2007 to expansionary mode in 2008 and 2009.

Following a much more rapid recovery than expected, in April 2010, MAS once again tightened in anticipation of a build-up of inflationary pressures by steepening the slope of the policy band and moving it up and in October further steepened the policy band and widened it. From April 2012, MAS adopted a policy of a modest and gradual appreciation. However, on 28th January 2015, it surprised the markets when it shifted its inflation forecasts significantly lower, on the back of a sharp drop in global oil prices, coupled with a weaker-than-expected pass-through of business costs to consumer prices, and in a rare unscheduled monetary policy statement, announced that it would reduce the slope of the policy band to allow the TWS$ to appreciate more slowly, while keeping unchanged the width and level at which it is centered.[28]

7. Challenges for Monetary Policy and Financial Development

Given the constraints under which monetary policy has had to operate, including the extreme openness of the economy to trade and capital flows and a fiscal policy which, in normal times, is explicitly targeted at long-term social goals, such as attracting foreign investment, increasing the citizen population and reducing city-center congestion, rather than at medium-term countercyclical goals, monetary policy has been very successful.[29] Most important, it has delivered low and stable consumer price inflation which, on average, has generally been below the benchmark of the advanced developed countries since 1970 (Table 1). If there were a Champions League in central banking, MAS would certainly have qualified! Moreover, the tendency for the S$NEER and S$REER to appreciate over trend (Figure 2) has meant that MAS has clearly fulfilled its mission statement to protect the purchasing power of the SGD and preserve the value of savings over time, ensuring a stable operating environment for consumers and producers, and making Singapore an attractive location for long-term investment and financial transactions.[30]

---

[28] CPI inflation was now projected to come in at −0.5% to 0.5% compared to earlier forecasts of 0.5% to 1.5% and the more stable measure of core inflation, which omits housing and private road transport, was scaled down to 0.5% to 1.5%, compared to 2–3%.

[29] Fiscal policy has always been regarded as relatively ineffective in Singapore as a stabilization tool given the high marginal propensity to import, although in recent decades a higher frequency of downturns has meant that it has been called upon more often. For some estimates of the fiscal multiplier, see Abeysinghe and Choy (2007, Chap. 8).

[30] The standard deviation of quarterly changes in the S$NEER and S$REER between 1980 and 2014 were 1.48 and 1.64, respectively. Against the USD, it was 3.4 compared to an average of 9.4 for the German mark (Euro), Swiss franc, UK pound and Japanese yen against the greenback. Counterfactual experiments, both before and after the Asian financial crisis, also confirm that Singapore's managed floating exchange rate regime has coped well with exchange rate volatility when compared with other countries' exchange rate regimes and a number of hypothetical regimes (Ng and Wilson, 2008).

Although the currency has generally appreciated over the longer run, there have been periods when the exchange rate has needed to adjust to cope with upturns and downturns in the economy, often stemming from external causes. Despite the overriding focus on price stability rather than demand management *per se,* monetary policy has generally been countercyclical and the economy has always recovered quickly from downturns. Moreover, price stability has not been at the expense of economic growth or economic development, given rise to prolonged periods of high unemployment, or in general caused problems for exports and the balance of payments, despite periods of strong S$REER appreciation and the fact that MAS has not intervened to substantially depreciate the currency to enhance export competitiveness, since this would conflict with its long-run mission to protect the purchasing power of the SGD (Table 1).

On the financial front, Singapore has come a long way since 1965. Unlike other more laissez-faire financial centers, such as London, New York and Hong Kong, financial development in Singapore since independence has been government-made. As well as introducing an internationally-competitive tax structure, a sound and stable financial system and tight regulation and corporate governance; there were proactive policies to participate in the ADM in the 1960s and 1970s and to build on Singapore's history as a forex trading center, to develop the fund management industry from the late 1980s, to open up the domestic banking system to global competition in the 1990s and, more recently, to upgrade the debt and equities markets.

In 2010, there were 600 financial institutions in Singapore and the capitalization of the SGX was S$958 billion. Banking and insurance accounted for only 4.6% of GDP in 1965 but by 2013, this was 12% (Table 1) and included high value-added wealth management. Singapore is currently fourth in the world in terms of average daily foreign exchange turnover. There are presently 124 banks operating here and DBS is regularly ranked in the top 100 in the world in terms of assets and both DBS and UOB are ranked highly in Bloomberg's listing of the world's strongest banks. DBU assets were S$973 billion in 2013 and there are 161 Asian currency units with assets which have grown to almost US$1.2 trillion since 1968. Singapore is now a major player in the management of offshore money for investors based overseas. Fund managers had S$1.4 trillion under management in 2010, compared to S$150 billion in 1998. Even the debt market has progressed since the 1990s and has attracted a diverse range of local and foreign issuance. Total debt market capitalization was S$357 billion in 2011, compared to S$135 billion in 2001 with two-thirds in SGD (Monetary Authority of Singapore, 2011).

Despite being a late starter, MAS has built up a high degree of credibility in terms of regulation and supervision within a relatively short time. It has dealt with financial crises effectively and taken a successful long-term view of financial development. The relentless accumulation of the reserves is still a controversial issue[31] but has reinforced Singapore's financial credibility. The published size of the reserves in 2013 is S$345 billion or approximately US$273 billion, with reserves per head of the resident population at S$89,662 in 2013, compared to S$566.3 in 1965 (Table 1). Singapore's sovereign debt rating is triple A for both S&P and Fitch and Aaa for Moody's.

Of course, monetary policy does not work in a vacuum and cannot be given all the credit for Singapore's successful economic performance since 1965. Luckily Singapore has strong supporting macroeconomic institutions which ensure a good degree of consistency in policy and reinforce the credibility of its monetary policy. In particular, because the government generally runs a budget surplus and does not accumulate foreign debt, there is no need for the MAS to finance government debt so it can concentrate on its own longer-run monetary objectives. There is a high degree of coordination between monetary and fiscal policy and the latter has been crucial during severe downturns given the psychological limit to how far monetary policy can be loosened. The ability to push the S$REER down during a downturn is also made easier by the flexibility of the labor market[32] and the use of unorthodox cost-cutting measures, such as cuts in the employer's contribution to the CPF fund and the reduction of utility charges.[33]

Successful though monetary policy and financial development have been, Singapore is currently facing a number of challenges. While the financial fallout from the global financial crisis on Singapore was quite mild, MAS has been active in devising safeguards for investors and strengthening the resilience of banks in line with the Basel III reforms. In February 2010, a cooling-off period was introduced for structured products after an investigation into the sale of structured notes linked to Lehman Brothers. They found some non-compliance and banned some financial institutions from selling them for periods between six months and two years. In June 2014, further measures were announced to enhance the quality and quantity of regulatory capital that banks are required to hold, to strengthen liquidity requirements and to ensure that systemically important banks are subject to higher regulatory standards and conduct regular risk and impact assessments.

---

[31] See, for example, Peebles and Wilson (2002, Chap. 8).

[32] By the end of 2008, about 84% of the private sector was under some form of flexible wage arrangement, including variable monthly components and bonuses, and public sector pay is also linked to the performance of the economy.

[33] Until the global financial crisis, the main focus was on wage and employer CPF cuts and cost cuts for businesses, which meant that the burden of adjustment tended to fall on labor rather than capital, primarily to keep mobile capital in Singapore (Peebles and Wilson, 2005). Only during the global financial crisis was the emphasis changed to keeping Singaporeans employed.

The crisis had also highlighted whether a central bank should tighten monetary policy pre-emptively in order to moderate asset price bubbles in the housing and stock markets before a sudden bust triggers financial instability, such as a large rise in non-performing loans. If the bubbles are big enough, the result could be a very expensive clean-up operation. On the other hand, bubbles are, by definition, extremely difficult to identify *ex ante* and pre-emptive tightening could inflict collateral damage on other parts of the economy. It may also complicate central bank communication to the public. The use of the word "bubble" itself could lead to misinterpretation and cause asset prices to react in unpredictable ways. For example, the tightening of monetary policy by the Bank of China in January 2010 led to a sharp fall in stock prices in Shanghai.

The official view in Singapore is that MAS should keep an eye on financial stability when setting monetary policy and monitor asset prices for secondary effects on consumer prices, but it is better to keep monetary policy focused on price stability and use macro-prudential policies and targeted administrative measures to deal with asset prices or to "target the cracks where specific vulnerabilities are concentrated".[34] Accordingly, in the third quarter of 2009, a 16% surge in property prices in Singapore persuaded the government to release more land for development and disallow borrowers from deferring property payments, to deter speculation. In February 2010, further cooling measures were introduced at a time when the economic outlook was still uncertain and the tightening of monetary policy would have been inappropriate. This marked the beginning of a progressive range of administrative measures to restrain property prices.[35] These seemed to be working by the middle of 2014 as the Urban Redevelopment Authority's private residential price index fell by 0.7% in the third quarter and 1.1% in the fourth, and for the whole year, prices fell by 4% compared to a rise of 1.1% in 2013.

Given the deflationary pressures from the recent fall in commodity prices, especially oil, and the massive quantitative easing by the US Federal Reserve, the European Central Bank and the Bank of Japan, an interesting question arises: Would MAS resort to extensive quantitative easing if a deflationary spiral loomed? Although MAS must, by law, maintain sufficient foreign assets to provide 100% backing for any currency notes it issues, in practice this is not a binding constraint given the extent of its official reserves. Of course, quantitative easing would not be its first choice since this would mean abandoning its exchange-rate centered monetary

---

[34] See, for example, the speech by MAS' Managing Director (Menon, 2014).

[35] Access by foreigners was reduced, as was purchases of second and further properties by foreigners and locals alike. The loan to value ratio was progressively reduced to 60%, the mortgage servicing ratio for public housing was raised, financial institutions were required to consider borrowers' other outgoing debt obligations before granting loans, and quite punitive additional buyers' stamp duties were introduced with different rates for citizens, permanent residents and foreigners.

policy and the subsequent increase in liquidity could depreciate the SGD to an unacceptable level in terms of its purchasing power in international markets. On the other hand, there may be worse things than inflation and the likelihood is that MAS would "do what it takes" if such a scenario were to arise. In the event, demand and incomes are expected to remain strong in 2015, with the GDP growth forecast at 2–4%. The fall in oil prices is also expected to lift real incomes so the issue is unlikely to arise.

The last challenge, however, is not going to disappear any time soon. By 2007, Singapore was facing significant supply-side constraints and a step-up in inflationary pressure which were to signal a fundamental change in its growth strategy and have important implications for monetary policy.[36] In 2009, Singapore began a drive to increase labor productivity growth. A high level Economic Strategies Committee chaired by the Finance Minister published its findings in February 2010.[37] It recognized that Singapore's productivity growth had fallen behind the USA, Japan and Sweden in manufacturing and services, especially retail, and in construction compared to Korea and Hong Kong. Moreover, one of the reasons was the heavy dependence on imported labor, particularly unskilled labor, which accounted for about 35% of the total labor force (excluding domestic workers) at that time. Accordingly a target of 2–3% was set for productivity growth until 2020 in line with a more sustainable GDP growth rate of 3–5%, and a period of restructuring would gradually reduce the inflow of low productivity foreign workers and increase domestic value-added and wages. Existing foreign worker levies and skilled levy differentials would be progressively raised and the Workfare Income Supplement scheme and the National Wages Council would increase incomes and wages for low-paid workers. Since these policies would take some time to bear fruit, there would inevitably be a transitional tightening of the labor market and a rise in domestic costs before productivity improvements filtered through to offset them.

Since domestic costs are becoming more important, inevitably, targeting the exchange rate would be less effective than before. The growth-inflation trade-off would worsen since, not only would growth be slower than in the past, but there would likely be an increase in inflation and a risk of a rise in inflationary expectations. The restructuring process has certainly made monetary policy more difficult because MAS has to steer a careful course to maintain low and stable inflation without jeopardizing the restructuring process and sustainable growth. MAS has also made it clear that it does not intend to fully offset market-driven cost pressures which should be allowed to stimulate the behavioral changes needed for the re-structuring process to take place. Moreover, the restructuring process may take longer than expected.

---

[36] For this and a longer-term perspective on Singapore's growth strategy, see Bhaskaran and Wilson (2011).
[37] The report can be downloaded from www.mti.gov.sg.

A Ministry of Trade and Industry release in February 2015[38] concluded that productivity growth between 2010 and 2014 was 2.6% per annum, on average, but a lackluster 0.3% if the rebound from the global financial crisis in 2010 is excluded. Export-oriented sectors did not do so badly but productivity growth in domestic-oriented activities, especially retail, did. It was acknowledged that "plenty of work needed to be done".

Should MAS re-think its exchange rate-centered monetary policy and switch to a more traditional interest rate-centered policy? It still has the option of widening the policy band to allow more market-determined influence over the exchange rate and in the longer run floating, together with interest rate targeting, would be possible given Singapore's strong economic fundamentals. MAS still believes that targeting the TWS$ is the most effective way to achieve price stability and prevent inflation escalating over the transitory restructuring period. It is true that the impact of the exchange rate on inflation is weaker, insofar as there has been a rise in non-tradable services, but many services, such as financial, information technology and professional, are exportable, and external-oriented manufacturing and services together still account for over half of GDP. Although the contribution of domestic costs to inflation has also increased recently, inflation would have been higher if exchange rate tightening had not been used. Moreover, a substantial hike in interest rates would have been required to achieve the same outcome, which would have attracted even more foreign capital and exacerbated the boom in property prices, as well as appreciating the SGD and increasing interest rate instability.

According to MAS' Managing Director, there does not seem to be any hurry to change Singapore's unique, and very successful, exchange rate-centered monetary policy: "Our exchange rate-centered monetary policy remains fit for purpose and will continue to focus on keeping inflation contained. Our macroprudential policies will complement monetary policy and financial supervisory policies to secure sustainable asset prices and financial stability. Most of all, Singapore's fundamentals remain sound. Fiscal prudence, financial discipline, minimizing debt and living within our means, will provide us policy space and buffers to weather whatever comes ahead. This is an advantage most countries do not have."[39]

Acknowledgments

I would like to thank Edward Robinson and Choy Keen Meng from the Economic Policy Group at the Monetary Authority of Singapore for their very helpful comments. The usual disclaimer applies.

---

[38] As reported in *The Straits Times*, 18 February 2015.

[39] Menon (2013).

References

Abeysinghe, T and P Wilson (2002). International competitiveness. In *The Singapore Economy in the 21st Century: Issues and Strategies*, MK Chng, WT Hui, AT Koh, KL Lim and B Rao (eds.). Singapore: McGraw-Hill.

Abeysinghe, T and KM Choy (2007). *The Singapore Economy: An Econometric Perspective*. London: Routledge.

Asian Development Bank (2009). Asian Development Outlook, Part I. Asian Development Bank, Manila.

Bhaskaran, M and P Wilson (2011). The post-crisis era: Challenges for the Singapore economy. In *The Singapore Economy — Challenges in the Post-Crisis Era*, P Wilson (ed.). Singapore: World Scientific.

Chan, KC and KJ Ngiam (1996). Currency Speculation and the Optimum Control of Bank Lending in the Singapore Dollar: A Case for Partial Liberalization. International Monetary Fund Working Paper 96/95.

Chow, HK (2008). Managing Capital Flows: the Case of Singapore. ADB Institute Discussion Paper No. 86. Asian Development Bank Institute, Tokyo.

Chow, HK and P Wilson (2011). Monetary policy in Singapore and the global financial crisis. In *The Singapore Economy — Challenges in the Post-Crisis Era*, P Wilson (ed.). Singapore: World Scientific.

Farrell, B and S Hunter (2010). *A Great Betrayal? The Fall of Singapore Revisited.* Singapore: Marshall Cavendish.

Jenkins, R (2001). *Churchill.* London: Pan Macmillan.

Khor, HE, J Lee, E Robinson and S Supaat (2007). Managed float exchange rate system: The Singapore experience. *Singapore Economic Review,* 52(1), 7–25.

Lee, J (2001). Evolution of the policy on non-internationalization of the Singapore dollar, In *Singapore: Selected Issues,* International Monetary Fund Country Report (Singapore), pp. 33–43. Washington: International Monetary Fund.

Mankiw, G, E Quah and P Wilson (2013). *Principles of Economics,* 2nd Edition: An Asian Edition. Singapore: Cengage Learning.

Menon, R (2013). Securing price stability as Singapore restructures. Speech at the Asian Bureau of Financial and Economics Research (ABFER) Opening Gala Dinner, http://www.mas.gov.sg/News-and-Publications/Speeches-and-Monetary-Policy-Statements/Speeches/2013/Securing-Price-Stability-as-Singapore-Restructures.aspx.

Menon, R (2014). Getting in all the cracks or targeting the cracks? Securing financial stability in the post-crisis era. Speech at the Asian Monetary Policy Forum (AMPF), http://www.mas.gov.sg/News-and-Publications/Speeches-and-Monetary-Policy-Statements/Speeches/2014/Securing-Financial-Stability-in-the-PostCrisis-era.aspx.

Mihov, I (2013). The exchange rate as an instrument of monetary policy. Monetary Authority of Singapore Macroeconomic Review, Special Feature A, October.

Monetary Authority of Singapore (2000). A Survey of Singapore's Monetary History. Economics Department Occasional Paper (18).

Monetary Authority of Singapore (2009). *Macroeconomic Review,* October.

Monetary Authority of Singapore (2010a). *Macroeconomic Review*, April.

Monetary Authority of Singapore (2010b). *Macroeconomic Review*, October.

Monetary Authority of Singapore (2011). Singapore Bond Market Guide. http://www.sgs.gov.sg/~/media/SGS/MAS_SBondMarketGuide_2012.pdf.

Monetary Authority of Singapore (2012). *Sustaining Stability, Serving Singapore*. Singapore: Straits Times Press.

Monetary Authority of Singapore (2013a). Monetary Policy Operations in Singapore.

Monetary Authority of Singapore (2013b). Shifts in Regional Trade, Box C. *Macroeconomic Review*, October.

Ng SR and P Wilson (2008). The choice of exchange rate regime and the volatility of exchange rates before and after the Asian financial crisis: A counterfactual analysis. Australian Economic Papers, pp. 92–114.

Obstfeld, M, J Shambaugh and A Taylor (2005). The trilemma in history: Tradeoffs among exchange rates, monetary policies and capital mobility. *Review of Economics and Statistics*, 87(3), 423–438.

Ong, CT (2002). Singapore's policy of non-internationalisation of the Singapore dollar and the Asian dollar market. BIS Paper No. 15.

Parrado, E (2004). Singapore's unique monetary policy: How does it work? Monetary Authority of Singapore Staff Paper No. 31.

Peebles, G and P Wilson (1996). *The Singapore Economy*. Cheltenham: Edward Elgar.

Peebles, G and P Wilson (2002). *Economic Growth and Development in Singapore: Past and Future*. Cheltenham: Edward Elgar.

Peebles, G and P Wilson (2005). Don't frighten the horses: The political economy of Singapore's foreign exchange rate regime since 1981. Singapore Centre for Applied and Policy Economics (SCAPE) Working Paper 2005/06.

Tan, CH, J Lim and W Chen (2004). Competing international financial centres: A comparative study between Hong Kong and Singapore. In *Saw Centre for Financial Studies*, Singapore: NUS Business School.

Taylor, J (1993). Discretion versus policy rules in practice. Carnegie-Rochester Conference Series on Public Policy Vol. 39.

Ting, SC, SP Su, E Robinson and P Wilson (2005). Assessing Singapore's export competitiveness through dynamic shift-share analysis. *The ASEAN Economic Bulletin*, 22(2), 160–185.

Turnbull, CM (1992). *A History of Singapore 1819–1988*, Second Edition. Oxford University Press.

Wilson, P (2008). Monetary policy in Singapore: A BBC approach. In *Singapore and Asia in a Globalized World*, WM Chia and Y Sng (eds.). Singapore: World Scientific.

CHAPTER 6

Public Financial Management in Singapore: Key Characteristics and Prospects

Mukul G. Asher, Azad Singh Bali and Chang Yee Kwan

Public financial management (PFM) has played an important role in Singapore's remarkable economic success since its independence. This chapter analyzes select characteristics of Singapore's PFM strategy and prospects for their continuation. An underlying theme has been ensuring that PFM is consistent with and enables Singapore's location-based growth strategy. Other characteristics include conducting economic activities outside the conventional government budget giving rise to a much larger role for the public sector than reflected in the budget; extensive use of non-conventional sources of revenue such as from the lease of land, creating property and usage rights to generate tax like revenue; and limited social risk pooling in financing national spending on healthcare and pensions. As Singapore's business-location-based strategy reaches its limits, and an affluent and ageing population aspires for greater economic and social security, transparency, and effective participation in public policies, current PFM practices will need to undergo significant changes towards a more citizen-centric governance focus. Policymakers' response will not be constrained by lack of fiscal resources, or by institutional and organizational capacities.

1. Introduction

Singapore's public financial management (PFM), that is, its fiscal policy, has played a significant role in its emergence as a high-income country[1] since it became a Republic in 1965. An important implication of this is that Singapore's policymakers have not been, and currently are not, constrained by the availability of fiscal revenues and/or by concerns of debt sustainability for addressing public policy challenges faced by a rapidly ageing, affluent and mature society.

---

[1] In 2013, the World Bank ranked Singapore as fourth globally in per capita GDP, ahead of other small developed economies such as Belgium, Finland, New Zealand, and Switzerland. http://data.worldbank.org/indicator/NY.GDP.PCAP.PP.CD.

The general consensus in the literature is that the main elements of public financial management are: mobilization and generation of financial resources for government expenditure from conventional and non-conventional revenue sources; accounting methods and budgetary systems used in government; allocation of resources on goods and services and on transfers to attain a set of desired outcomes; financial reporting, internal and external auditing, transparency and accountability structures.[2]

Reliable and timely data and supporting information have a significant role in policy formulation, implementation and assessment, and in improving the quality of public policy dialogue (Dilnot, 2012). Several authors (e.g., Asher, 1986, 2003; Lim and Associates, 1988; Blöndal, 2006) have however commented on the relatively limited nature of the relevant information contained in Singapore's budgetary documents, and frequent changes in the manner in which data are presented in official documents. This suggests the need for caution in interpreting Singapore's fiscal data.

This chapter reviews the practice of PFM in Singapore and its objectives that have played a key role in the growth of the country since independence. Lim and Associates (1988) and Asher (2003) have analyzed the trends in Singapore's public finances in its earlier years. This chapter extends the analysis to the decade beginning 2003. However, due to remarkable consistencies in practices, the discussion is applicable across Singapore's history.

The chapter is structured as follows. Section 2 provides a brief overview of the Singapore budget as it forms the context in which data on public finances are organized and analyzed. One of the main features is consistency between management of public finances and the country's location-based growth strategy. This is explored in Section 3. Section 4 discusses the prospects for these to continue, and some recent policy measures, as Singapore becomes accustomed to lower growth prospects, rapid ageing, and altered expectations of the population about the role of government.

2. Organization of the Budget

The annual government budget documents report the revenue estimates and proposed expenditure for each fiscal year beginning in April of the current year to the following March.[3] The structure and format of the annual budget have remained relatively constant over time, with any changes primarily reflecting changes in administrative structure (nomenclature) rather than actual accounting practices. The main features of the organization of Singapore's budget may be summarized as follows.

---

[2] See Cangiano *et al.* (2013) for details.
[3] This fiscal year definition was adopted in 1969. In the years prior, the fiscal year followed the calendar year from January to December.

First, the Accounts of the Government of Singapore are organized around various funds. The major funds are the Consolidated Fund, Development Fund, Sinking Fund, and Skills Development Funds. The Consolidated Fund consists of the Consolidated Loan Account and Consolidated Revenue Account where all proceeds from loans are accounted for in the former. All monies other than loans are in the Consolidated Revenue Account. All government revenues not allocated to any specific purposes by any law are required to be paid into the Consolidated Fund.

Expenditure consists of those charged to the budgetary appropriations for goods and services and for transfer payments, including contributions to the Development and Sinking Funds. Expenditures are classified as statutory and non-statutory, with the former having priority. The main sources of receipts for the Revenue Account of the Consolidated Fund are taxes, receipts from the sale of goods, services, assets, and income from investment, regulatory levies and fines.

Receipts for the Development Fund are loans raised for development, transfers from the Revenue Account of the Consolidated Fund, and income from Development Fund investments. Sinking funds are required to be established under the Developmental Loan Act for the redemption of domestic loans. The receipts of these funds consist of monies appropriated from the Consolidated Fund and income received from Sinking Fund investments. Expenditure from these funds largely consists of interest on public debt and debt redemption.

In such a system of budgetary accounts, evaluation of overall budgetary balance and financial relationships of the government with the rest of the economy should take into account transactions of all funds, thus eliminating double-counting and inter-fund transactions. This is relevant given the importance of inter-fund transactions, especially transfers from the Consolidated Fund to Sinking Funds in Singapore. As will be argued below, both budget documents and budget statements are neither comprehensive nor consistent in the treatment of various items. Therefore, the Budget debate is undertaken without consideration of the overall financial position and macroeconomic impact of the transactions of the general government sector (Asher, 1989).

Second, Singapore's budgeting system has evolved from a line item budget in the first year of independence, to a Program and Performance Based Budgeting System in 1977, and currently relies on a top-down system which emphasizes aggregate limits while granting discretion to ministries on allocations (Blöndal, 2006). Each ministry receives a multi-year spending ceiling (as a share of GDP) for all appropriations (including current and capital expenditures). Funding is fungible across time horizons, and ministries can exercise discretion on the share they wish to appropriate for each fiscal year. The funding ceiling is not made public, and is used as a "tool to assist in budget formulation rather than as a public commitment" (Blöndal, 2006, p. 53). In 2005, the Government introduced a Reinvestment Fund, financed by cuts across the budget. Ministries and agencies are encouraged to "bid" to utilize these funds for special programs.

Third, the budget is also used as an instrument to control manpower and the distribution of civil service personnel across ministries. Each ministry is allocated a share in the number of sanctioned positions in the civil service. Should this share be exceeded, a surcharge of SGD10,000 is payable by the ministry concerned (Blöndal, 2006).

Fourth, the Government of Singapore also operates several funds whose finances are not consolidated or reported as part of the Budget. Revenues, expenditures, and balance sheets of statutory boards are not reported as part of the budget. Some of these statutory boards are of major importance to the economy.[4]

An increasing tendency of Singapore's sovereign wealth funds (largely financed from accumulated budgetary surpluses) to play the roles of a venture capitalist and/or a private equity investor implies an increasing role of the government in (both) Singapore and in the foreign economies it invests in. Thus, the role of the broader public sector in Singapore's economic management is much larger than what is reflected in the government budget and accompanying documents.

Fifth, while there are committees in the Parliament of Singapore that are entrusted to various aspects of PFM, these committees do not play an active role in the parliamentary budgetary process. For instance, while the Estimates Committee discussed "… many of the reforms to the budget formulation process and budget implementation and government management practices… it does not examine the substantive contents of the budget" (Blöndal, 2006, p. 63).

Sixth, the assets and liabilities statement of the government presented in the budget documents are far too aggregated to be useful for analysis or public accountability. Thus, the official data from the latest budget documents indicate that as of 31 March 2014, the assets of the Singapore Government consisted of SGD123.4 billion in cash, Government Stocks SGD215.4 billion, quoted investments SGD307.0 billion and unquoted investments of SGD186.3 billion, for a total of SGD833.7 billion, or more than twice the GDP. Such a large accumulation of budgetary assets substantially increases the fiduciary responsibility of the government, and potentially creates political risk arising from the sizable concentration of funds in the fiscal system.[5]

---

[4] Nearly four-fifths of the population live in public housing and the responsibility for constructing and financing these units is entrusted to the The Housing Development Board (HDB) (Phang, 2001). Budgetary transactions for such a large and important government agency are not reflected in the government budget.

[5] The concentration offunds, and risk, is heightened by the fact that Temasek Holdings alone reports a portfolio value of SGD223 billion, or about 57% of GDP in 2014. The valuation of the other major fund, GIC Private Limited, is not publicly revealed.

Seventh, the accounting basis for reporting the budget to Parliament is on a cash basis for easier understanding of budgetary accounts. However, a modified accrual accounting method, more appropriate for improving budgetary resource allocation decisions, has been used since 1999 within the government.[6]

3. Growth Strategy and Public Financial Management

Singapore's ability to sustain consistency between its growth strategy (the use of specific approaches have been commendably flexible) and its PFM practices is an important achievement, central to its strong performance over the past several decades. Singapore has aggressively focused on a location-based growth strategy emphasizing capital accumulation, attracting foreign firms (MNCs in particular[7]), portfolio investors and foreign workers at all ends of the skills spectrum. This is to ensure that the country remains appealing for businesses while economic activities move up the value chain, and new growth nodes are created to enhance domestic economic resilience and maintain international competitiveness. Historically, the growth strategy has also necessitated tolerance of a high level of income inequality.[8]

To benefit from global trade, technologies, investments, tourism, and manpower flows, Singapore has been flexible in the instruments used in skillfully pursuing its business location strategy. This has required keeping the share of capital substantially higher than the share of labor in national income. The share of labor income averaged 40.4% between 2010 and 2014 with the corresponding capital share at 51.9%.[9] Taxes on capital income have been substantially reduced in the past two decades and there is currently no income tax on interest income, dividends, most capital gains, and foreign-earned income. As capital income usually accrues disproportionately to the top deciles of the population,[10] the tax system is consistent with attracting capital and

---

[6] Cash accounting reports expenditure when the actual expenditure is made and records receipt when the payment is received by the government. The accrual accounting system on the other hand involves recording revenue when payment obligation arises regardless of whether actual cash has been received; and it records expenditure when liability is incurred, regardless if actual payment has been made.

[7] See Ermisch and Huff (1999) for an analysis.

[8] The GINI coefficient fluctuated between a low of 0.460 in 2004 to a high of 0.482 in 2014 before government transfers. After government transfers, this reached a low of 0.409 in 2013 and a high of 0.439 in 2007 (Department of Statistics, 2015a). However, this only includes labor income and, as discussed later, is likely to be understated.

[9] Table A1.11 in Ministry of Trade and Industry (2015).

[10] This suggests that in analyzing the tax burden by income deciles, tax-exempt capital income should be included. As capital income accrues disproportionately to the upper 10% of households by income, its exclusion overstates the tax borne by higher income households. Moreover, it is the economic incidence which requires an explicit model and assumptions about the shifting of the tax burden that matters, and

high-income individuals from abroad, but it contributes systematically to higher inequalities.

Due to falling fertility rates and rising longevity, Singapore's location-based growth strategy also requires a substantial inflow of foreign workers, with domestic wages being suppressed as a result (Hui, 2013), and a relatively inflexible age at which individuals decide to exit the labor force.[11] In 2014, Singapore citizens comprised 61.1% of the total population, with permanent residents comprising 9.6% and foreign workers comprising 29.3% (Department of Statistics, 2015b). The inflow of foreign manpower has been beneficial to Singapore in economic and fiscal terms, but has posed social challenges. These challenges will become more acute, requiring political management as the share of foreigners in the population rises (Yeoh and Lin, 2012).

The Singapore government maintains a significant presence in the economy by direct participation, state-led planning and the use of interventionist policies (Huff, 1995, 1999). This has been facilitated by the fact that in Singapore, there is neither common law nor constitutional right to own land. Government-linked and government-owned companies, and statutory boards, which are outside the budget framework, have been prominent in Singapore's growth strategy and economic management. These are however, run on commercial principles in areas such as healthcare, transportation, utilities, waste management, and finance (Ramirez and Tan, 2004).

An important feature of Singapore's PFM practices is not the predominant role of the public sector in the economy, but that this role has been made consistent with its growth strategy (e.g. by providing complementary public amenities such as power, housing, water, transport, etc. that are needed by businesses), and by generating financial surpluses. These help create confidence in public sector management on the part of foreign enterprises and individuals which are key drivers of the growth strategy pursued. Subsequently, public sector revenue from taxes and other sources increases correspondingly with the growth of the economy. However, in the absence of adjustments to the government's expenditure allocations, budgetary surpluses become self-perpetuating.

3.1. Fiscal Rules

Singapore's growth strategy requires sustained global investor confidence in the government's economic and financial management over a prolonged period. Singapore's

---

not simple arithmetic calculations of the statutory incidence. Note also that the GINI (footnote 8) is thus under-reported and will likely be significantly higher if capital income is included.

[11] The age-specific resident male (female) labor force participation for those aged 55–59 is 87.5 (61.4)% in 2014. Corresponding figures for the age groups of 60–64, 65–69, and those over 70 are even lower at 77.0 (45.5)%, 54.1 (29.5)% and 15.3 (8.8)%, respectively (Ministry of Manpower, 2015).

fiscal rules are therefore designed to demonstrate commitment to address the needs of the investor, and maintaining a resilient economy.

There are four broad fiscal rules which are relevant to Singapore's PFM. First, governments have to work within their period of appointment in managing deficits in the budget, i.e. governments cannot draw on accumulated surpluses in the previous term of government to meet deficits.

Second, under the Net Investment Returns Contribution (NIRC), only half of the expected long-term real rate of return on net assets managed by the GIC Private Limited (formerly the Government of Singapore Investment Corporation) and the Monetary Authority of Singapore (MAS) can be used for financing the budget. Up to half of the Net Investment Income (NII) from remaining assets may also be included in the budget.

Third, should the government wish to draw down accumulated reserves to finance budget deficits, the approval of both the Parliament and the President of the Republic of Singapore are required. However, as Singapore has experienced consistent structural surpluses, approval has rarely been sought,[12] suggesting there has been a relatively disciplined approach in the management of public finances, with an aversion to over-expenditure and incurring of deficits in regular operations of the public sector.[13]

Fourth, only the government can introduce motions to reallocate or change expenditures during the budget process (Blöndal, 2006). While elected members of the Parliament can debate resources devoted and priority areas, the government maintains tight control over the budget.

3.2. Persistent Structural Budget Surpluses

Singapore's growth strategy has resulted in persistent structural budget surpluses, while keeping the level of expenditure and tax revenue relatively low (Figure 1). As mentioned, budget surpluses were necessary to instill investor confidence; it also helps to better manage expectations of macroeconomic stability and to keep the tax burden on capital income low. Low (reported) levels of expenditure and revenue also suggest that the government is committed to a minimalist role in the economy, further strengthening the perception of a business-friendly environment.

---

[12] To date, there appears only to have been one instance where both the President's and Parliament's approvals were sought in 2009 after the collapse of Lehman Brothers in 2008 marked the beginning of a global economic downturn.

[13] Blöndal (2006) in a review of public sector budgeting in Singapore finds a culture of aversion towards any annual deficits in expenditure among civil sector bodies. This is despite a considerably high level of autonomy, with leeway for deficit spending in any year subject to a five year budgetary cap, as to how each department manages its budgets.

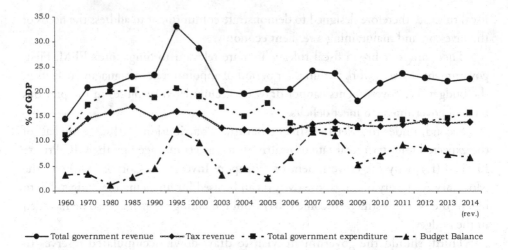

Figure 1. Fiscal indicators, 1960–2014 (selected years).[14]

Sources: Cao and Chew (1996), Asher (2003), and calculations[15] by authors from Ministry of Finance (various years), *The Budget*.

The persistent surpluses imply intergenerational transfers of resources from the immediate past and current generation whose consumption opportunities have been constrained due to the need to generate these surpluses, while consumption opportunities of future generations (with higher incomes) will be larger. This pattern of intergenerational transfers cannot be sustained over a long period particularly in a high-income ageing economy such as Singapore.

The following observations may be made on the basis of the data in Figure 1. First, the budget balance was consistently in surplus between 2003 and 2014,[16] averaging at approximately 7% of GDP a year. Apart for the years 2003–2005, budget surpluses (narrowly defined as revenues less government expenditure) were consistently at 5% of GDP or higher. The tax revenue to GDP ratio has remained relatively

---

[14] Data from pre-2003 is included as a brief guide of the historical trends.

[15] These are calculated using current market prices. Intuitively, constant prices may be more appropriate. However, these are not available for public sector revenue and expenditure. Next, the budgeting is done on a cash basis, and changes in government receipts and expenditures result from various influences such as inflation, tax changes, income rebates, etc, than from changes in real output or economic activity only. Finally, and most importantly, due to the nature of goods and services purchased, the government consumption index will be very different, and publicly unavailable, from either the CPI or the GDP deflator. Thus, using either of the latter to construct a constant price series for government expenditure is unlikely to be informative, or valid, for inference.

[16] Post-1980, the budget balance was negative only in 1986, 1987 and 1998. See Cao and Chew (1996) and Asher (2003).

constant at around 13% since 2003. In contrast, the share of total government revenue to GDP has fluctuated between 20–25% of GDP except during 1995–96 rising above 30% and in 2009 falling to 18%.[17] This suggests there may have been a shift away from relying on taxation as a main revenue instrument; instead, non-tax revenue, including unconventional sources, has become more prominent.

Total government expenditure, which is lower than the outlays, exhibited a similar gradual downward trend over the decade. Total expenditure peaked at 17.7% of GDP in 2005, and fell below 15% between 2006 and 2013. The absence of social security transfers has significantly contributed to the low level of spending in Singapore relative to other developed economies such as the OECD (Asher, 2003). There are other aspects such as not including debt repayment as expenditure, and netting out expenditure incurred in generating capital revenue. This practice is, for reasons which remain unclear, unusual by international reporting conventions. The extensive use of statutory boards and other public organizations have also contributed to Singapore's low reported budgetary expenditure to GDP ratio. These suggest that budgetary revenue and expenditure are inappropriate indicators of the size of Singapore's government.[18]

Various taxes continue to form the core of government finances, but their importance as a revenue instrument appears to be diminishing. With the gradual increase in the share of non-tax revenue, unconventional income sources appear to become an increasingly important avenue for revenue.

3.3. Composition of Government Outlays and Expenditure

Government outlays have largely been oriented towards investments that ensure a high long-term trend rate of economic growth. Thus, the growth strategy has resulted in the composition of government outlays being focused towards development expenditure, as shown in Figure 2.

Outlays differ from expenditure in that expenditure is total outlays minus total consolidated fund outlays, minus total development fund outlays. Each of the latter is itemized to purposes such as land- and investment-related spending, debt servicing, (undefined) loans, etc., and comprises nearly 10% of GDP.[19]

---

[17] In comparison, average tax revenue as share of GDP was 34.9% (ranging from a low of 20.3% to 48.6%) in 2013 for OECD countries.

[18] A more detailed analysis of this issue is out of the scope of this chapter. However, these underline the need to understand the context of a given country, and organizational attributes of its public sector before analyzing cross-country comparative data on public finances.

[19] While total outlays are likely to be a better indicator of government size, classification issues, such as endowment fund transfers inappropriately labeled as expenditure in Singapore's public finances suggests that outlays are, similar to expenditure, unlikely to offer a representative indication about the size of the government (Asher, 1986; Lim and Associates, 1988).

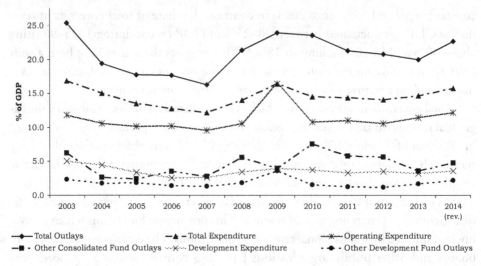

Figure 2.   Total government outlays and composition in Singapore, 2003–2014.

Source: Calculations by authors from Ministry of Finance (various years), *The Budget*.

Figure 3 shows the composition of the government's operating expenditure, with clear indication that the focus is on infrastructure and human capital development, while minimizing general administrative costs and transfer payments for consumption.

Fiscal policy in Singapore has not been primarily used as a countercyclical demand management instrument for macroeconomic stabilization in Singapore's fiscal management. This is because Singapore is a small open economy and a price taker in international markets for goods, services, and capital. Thus, Lim and Associates (1988), Tan (1996) and Lim (2003) have argued that the fiscal multiplier (in this case) will be considerably smaller than what may be derived in less open economies.[20] Instead, supply-side imperatives such as the management of wages and the exchange rate[21] are more suitable for domestic stabilization (Lim, 2003).

3.3.1. *Pensions and healthcare*

Public expenditure on pensions and healthcare in Singapore has been relatively low: In 2014, public expenditure on health was only 1.5% of GDP, less than two-fifths of national health expenditure.[22]

---

[20] See Santoni (1999) for a formal analysis of the fiscal multiplier in a small open economy.

[21] However, note that fiscal policy can still have an indirect effect when used as an instrument for exchange rate management (Nadal-De Simone, 2000). A consideration of this is out of scope here.

[22] National healthcare expenditure as a share of GDP is approximately 4%: https://www.moh.gov.sg/content/moh_web/home/costs_and_financing.html. Retrieved 11 February 2015.

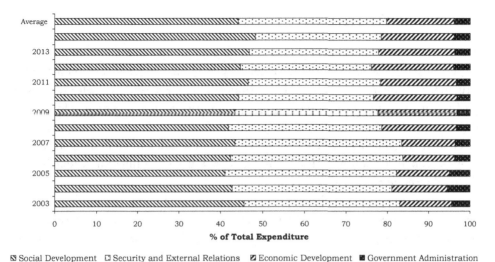

% of Total Expenditure

⊠ Social Development   ⬚ Security and External Relations   ▨ Economic Development   ◼ Government Administration

Figure 3.   Singapore government's operating components and its shares, 2003–2014.

Source: Calculations by authors from the Ministry of Finance (various years), *The Budget*.

Government expenditure on social protection, particularly for retirement and old-age financing, has been similarly low historically. The primary philosophy has been selfdependency from individual contributions to the CPF, supplemented by individual savings. Pension financing in Singapore is based on the assumptions that first, households are able to accumulate sufficient savings, which are micromanaged and intermediated by the state, from income during working years. This leaves households vulnerable to inflation, which lowers the real value of pensions, and women, with lower exposure to the labor market, susceptible to retirement risk. The second is that the role and function of the state is to ensure that households possess sufficient income necessary for only basic necessities and requirements (Williamson *et al.*, 2012; Asher and Bali, 2013).

However, such premises as the basis for retirement financing may no longer be feasible. Globalization, where capital (human, financial, technological) with high locational elasticities moves in search of the highest returns and reduces job security, and rising income inequalities (Hui and Toh, 2014) have greatly reduced the prospects of a fully self-funded retirement for a significant part of the population. There is thus a compelling case for a fundamental rethinking of these premises on both the scope for budgetary-financed social protection in forms such as a social pension on both ethical (Asher, 2003; Asher and Bali, 2014) and theoretical grounds (Molana and Montagna, 2007).[23]

---

[23] Molana and Montagna (2007) do not consider a social pension per se, but the qualitative nature of their results extends easily to consideration of a pension to the elderly and disabled. Recent work by Hoeller *et al.* (2014) provides some empirical validation to their conclusions.

3.4. *Revenue Composition*

The revenue system of Singapore comprises tax revenue and non-tax revenue, including unconventional sources such as regulatory levies and usage fees of public infrastructure and amenities, income from institutions such as sovereign wealth funds and profits from government-linked companies, and duties on activities such as lotteries.[24] Rents from the lease of land use rights are also a major contributor to government revenue in Singapore. The increasing importance of non-tax revenue suggests that its economic incidence on households should be included for a fuller understanding of the total revenue burden of households.

The tax system is based on two major broad-based taxes: the income tax and goods and services tax (GST). The income components of government revenue and their shares are presented in Figure 4. Taxes remain a key source of income, consistently contributing approximately 60% of total revenue. Non-tax or, more generally, unconventionally sourced income, has fluctuated between very sizable shares of 25% and 35% over the period. Thus, policymakers have been successful in reducing the reliance on taxes in favor of unconventional sources of revenue.

In line with other developed economies, Singapore introduced a broad-based tax on consumption, the GST, in 1993. This was officially rationalized as being more equitable with the advent of an aging population, and allowing a corresponding reduction in income taxes to raise economic competitiveness (Cao and Chew, 1996). However, the share of household consumption in income generally exhibits a decline

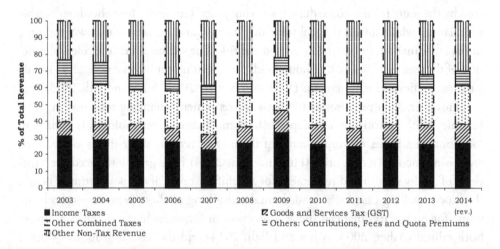

Figure 4.   Composition of total revenue, 2003–2014.

Source: Authors' calculations from the Ministry of Finance (various years), *The Budget*.

---

[24] See Asher (2005) for a fuller discussion.

as income levels increase. To the extent that this is the case in Singapore, the GST burden as a percentage of household income can also be expected to be inversely related.

International experience suggests that the introduction of, or increases in, the rate of value-added tax (VAT) are likely to lead to an increase in the cost-of-living by approximately the same percentage points in well-managed economies, and not lead to inflation, or persistent rises in the price level (Ebrill *et al.*, 2001).

As Singapore did not levy a sales tax when the GST was introduced at a rate of 3% in 1994, even a one-time increase in the cost-of-living[25] would have wealth effects such as a reduction in the real value of accumulated money balances in bank accounts and in CPF accounts of members.[26] The GST also created intergenerational inequalities as the elderly now face an additional GST burden. As a group they are likely to have lower average incomes than the current working population, and are net dis-savers. As a tax on consumption, the GST will thus have a disproportionately large impact on the bundle of goods and services consumed by this group. This suggests a need to not rely too heavily on the GST to meet future expenditure needs. The adverse effects of the GST may have been mitigated partially by GST allowances, but can only be confirmed by quantitative analysis based on disaggregated micro data on individual and household income and consumption patterns, which are not made publicly available in Singapore.

Furthermore, only a relatively small share of the labor force pays individual income tax in Singapore as CPF contributions and interest credited to accounts and withdrawals are all exempt from individual income tax. The ratio of individual income tax payers to labor force, while increasing in recent years is only 37% of the labor force in 2013, that is, nearly three-fifths of the labor force do not benefit from the income tax treatment of the CPF. The extent to which individuals do not benefit from this exemption as their assessed income is within the non-tax threshold, introduces a highly regressive element in the fiscal system. There is merit in considering how this regressive element in the fiscal system can be mitigated by instruments such as an annual tax credit deposited directly into the CPF accounts of those who do not benefit from the tax exemption.

In Singapore's comfortable fiscal position (Figure 1), non-conventional sources of revenue have played an important role. The main contributors to this category are lease of land revenue; investment income generated from past budgetary and

---

[25] The one-time increase in cost-of-living need not be reflected in the reported consumer price index as there are many other factors which simultaneously impact this index.

[26] The GST rebate provided at the time of introduction, and also with each subsequent GST increase, was to ease household expenditure flows, and not for compensating for the negative wealth effect.

balance-of-payment surpluses and by the Monetary Authority of Singapore; and regulatory taxes which allocate property and usage rights.

3.4.1. *Revenue from leasing land use rights*

Singapore has historically utilized revenue from the release of land parcels for development, but actual transfer of land ownership has been small.[27] While the income is considered as sales revenue, land is typically allocated on leases of various durations and acquisitioned in accordance with planning needs as outlined in the Master Plan dictating future land use patterns (Urban Redevelopment Authority, 2014).

The revenue from the lease of land, which is inappropriately labeled in official documents as capital income from "Sales of land" has ranged from a high of 5.5% of GDP in 2011 to a low of 1.1% in 2004. In analytical terms, however, the revenue from the leasing of land is equivalent to a differentiated excise tax, and is better included under tax revenue (Phang, 1995; Asher, 2003). The excise nature of the leasing of land revenue arises due to the following.

The outlay of any business entity on the leasing of land is a part of its cost of production or business activity. This will subsequently be passed on to the buyers of the structures built on the leased land (such as the shopkeepers in a shopping mall). In turn, the latter will attempt to pass on the costs to final consumers, where their ability to do so will depend on factors such as relative elasticities, pricing power, the time period of analysis and other related economic factors.

As businesses pass on some, or all, of the costs from the lease of land, the ratio of the economic burden of these costs to the final retail prices of goods, services and assets is likely to vary. This is the excise tax effect created as a result.[28]

3.4.2. *Investment income*

Investment undertaken by the government largely comes under the purview of Temasek Holdings formed in 1974, and GIC in 1981, as private investment companies mandated to manage surplus government funds (Lim and Associates, 1988) for investment purposes domestically and abroad. Both may thus be viewed as quasi-government bodies since they are recipients of public sector funds and contribute to the annual budget revenue. A statutory limit[29] exists on the proportion of investment incomes that may be apportioned to the budget, but the ambiguity pertaining to their contributions stems from the following: (i) the size and share of the public sector's input; (ii) the true level of returns; and (iii) the proportion of investment income that

---

[27] Recall that there is no Constitutional or Common Law right to own land in Singapore.

[28] To the best of our knowledge, an empirical analysis of the excise effect from the lease of land does not appear to have been undertaken thus far.

[29] See Section 2.

has been apportioned towards the budget. However, as both are incorporated under the Singapore Companies Act (Cap 50) as commercial firms, they are not required to publicly disclose their entire portfolio holdings, financial standing, and governance structure. Yet, their *de facto* quasi-government status suggests the absence of such disclosure presents a shortfall in accountability.

This acquires greater significance as GIC also manages CPF balances[30] which are for financing retirement. This is in contrast to previous speculation that the CPF was a source of funds for domestic projects such as infrastructure and public housing (Lim and Associates, 1988; Cao and Chew, 1996) which carry lower volatility risk than investments in international assets. Furthermore, the institutional design of the CPF has a key role in contributing to the persistent budget surpluses reported. CPF members' balances are invested in non-marketable government securities which form a part of the liabilities of the sovereign wealth funds. However, the (lower) interest credited to members' individual accounts is centrally administered instead of benchmarked against investment returns. As a part of the returns earned by the GIC is included in the government budget as part of the NII component, this revenue in conjunction with the low tax-and-spending mix, further perpetuates the continued budgetary surpluses.

3.4.3. *Regulatory levies and fees*

The government's generation of revenue from unusual property and usage rights has been among the distinguishing characteristics of Singapore's PFM. In particular, the revenue from foreign worker levies are a non-trivial portion of the government's operating revenue taking into account the number of work permits granted.[31] Similarly, generation of revenue from the right to purchase a car for 10 years, called the Certificate of Entitlement (COE), was unusual when introduced in 1990. While these may not be officially classified as tax revenue, their impact nevertheless has tax-like features for households and businesses. Given the revenue importance of revenue from property and usage rights, the overall tax burden in Singapore is much higher than what may be inferred from conventionally defined tax revenue.[32]

---

[30] This was mentioned by Singapore's Deputy Prime Minister and Finance Minister in July 2014. http://news.asiaone.com/news/singapore/cpf-issue-gic-manages-cpf-monies-along-other-govt-funds-dpm-tharman, retrieved 11 February 2015. The budget speech of 2015 proposes inclusion of Temasek Holdings and the Monetary Authority of Singapore's investment returns into the NIR framework.

[31] Total work permits granted in 2014 total 980,800 (Ministry of Manpower, http://www.mom.gov.sg/statistics-publications/others/statistics/Pages/ForeignWorkforceNumbers.aspx, retrieved 11 March 2015). Of this number, foreign domestic workers accounted for 22%, for construction 33%. Thus, over half of foreign work permit holders are in these two sectors.

[32] Note that there may also be a high opportunity cost of public funds (OCPF), but an assessment of this is beyond the scope of this chapter. See Massiani and Picco (2013) for further discussion.

3.5. *Public Debt Management*

Even as Singapore has experienced structural budgetary surpluses over the past decades, it has also accrued high public debt of SGD390 billion (in excess of 107% of GDP) as at the end of 2013. In most countries, public debt is used to finance budget deficits. However, the Government of Singapore's balance sheet as reported in the annual government budget documents has accumulated substantial balances and there appears no economic rationale for the government to issue public debt.[33]

Singapore's entire public debt is held internally (85% through registered stocks and bonds; 9.9% through treasury bills; and the remaining through Advanced Deposits with the Monetary Authority of Singapore).

The Central Provident Fund (CPF) Annual Report for 2013 states that of its total investments of SGD252.9 billion, SGD214 billion (or about 85%) were in hold-to-maturity financial assets: non-marketable government bonds (i.e., Special issues of Singapore Government Securities) and Advanced Deposits with the MAS. Thus, the Central Provident Fund as an institution is the single largest holder of government debt.

The interest on debt held by CPF is administratively benchmarked on return on marketable government bonds. Other holders of Singapore government debt include financial institutions that are required to purchase such debt as part of their prudential norms. Singapore does not face rollover risk as CPF holds government securities till maturity. While Singapore has accumulated large gross public debt, there was SGD401 billion in the Government Securities Fund set aside for repayment of debt. This is higher than the public debt of SGD390 billion. Indeed, if net public debt were measured, Singapore would most likely exhibit a surplus.

Furthermore, under the Protection of Reserves Framework of the Government Securities Act, the Singapore government cannot spend the monies raised from the sale of SGS and SSGS. These funds can however be invested by the government, and the proceeds used to service the debt (Ministry of Finance, various years).

4. Prospects

This chapter thus far has argued that policymakers in Singapore have strived for consistency between their growth strategy and PFM characteristics. The other key characteristics have been: (i) persistent structural budget surpluses to signal to investors the government's determination to manage public expectations about provision of government services, and for generating future revenue to keep the tax burden

---

[33] Issuing of public debt allows an avenue for CPF funds to be transferred to GIC for investment purposes, since these are not marketable, while maintaining management accountability.

on capital income low; (ii) substantial public sector activity outside of the budget; (iii) limited social risk pooling in national spending on pension and healthcare programs; (iv) extensive use of non-conventional sources of revenue; and (v) a stress on accounting and budgeting reforms and e-governance.

The location-based growth strategy historically emphasized by Singapore's policy-makers is dependent on attracting foreign capital and labor, and strong external demand, as determinants for success. However, increasing quality-of-life expectations from the Singapore population, and tougher conditions for labor export set by sending countries in the region, suggest that Singapore can no longer rely on growing the share of foreign labor to sustain growth to the same extent as before.

Moreover, the ratio of global trade growth to world GDP growth was just over 1.5 in 2014 (World Bank, 2015). This is in contrast to a high of 2.4 in 2000, since when there has been a continued downward trend. This suggests that the ability of Singapore to rely on the external sector to generate growth is likely to be considerably lower in the future. Some impact is already observed as Singapore's growth has averaged around 3% in the last few years, in comparison to the 6–8% observed in earlier decades.

Singapore's ageing population also increases the complexity of pursuing innovation and productivity-led growth, and further implies that there will be societal pressures to expand the share of expenditure on public amenities such as healthcare, assistance to hitherto neglected groups such as housewives, singles, the disabled and others.

In general, the balance between the external and domestic sources of growth is likely to shift towards the latter. This will require increasing the share of labor in national income, higher social transfers, including social pensions, more extensive social risk pooling arrangements, particularly for pensions and healthcare programs, from budgetary revenue; and lower tolerance of inequalities. It will also require greater focus on productivity-led rather than resource-intensive growth.[34]

There are some indications of tentative steps being taken in this direction. Since 2012, the year-on-year change in Singapore's budgetary expenditure per capita has been larger (or declined less) than corresponding changes in per capita revenue, thus reversing the general trend of earlier years (Table 1). This trend reversal is expected to continue as there are indications that the government recognizes the need to increase domestic consumption and sources of growth, and strengthen social protection outcomes not just for the low-income, but also for the middle classes. The indications include the following.

First, the government has reversed its earlier policy on CPF contributions by raising the wage ceiling to SGD6,000; increased contribution rates; selectively raised the administered interest rate on CPF balances; and partly addressed longevity risk, the risk that an individual may exhaust retirement savings before death, by appropriately

---

[34] See Pang and Lim (2015) in this volume.

Table 1.   Per capita revenue and expenditure.

	Total revenue per capita		Total expenditure per capita		Tax revenue per capita		Non-tax revenue per capita	
	SGD	Y-o-y change (%)	SGD	Y-o-y change (%)	SGD	Y-o-y change (%)	SGD	Y-o-y change (%)
2003	8250.58	—	6925.93	—	5225.29	—	3025.29	—
2004	9050.95	9.70	6949.68	0.34	5711.76	9.31	3339.19	10.38
2005	10138.62	12.02	8798.97	26.61	6021.59	5.42	4117.03	23.29
2006	10887.27	7.38	7322.60	−16.78	6549.56	8.77	4337.71	5.36
2007	14326.02	31.59	7298.12	−0.33	7982.89	21.88	6343.12	46.23
2008	13288.10	−7.24	7004.77	−4.02	7792.04	−2.39	5496.06	−13.35
2009	10186.68	−23.34	7198.21	2.76	7341.56	−5.78	2845.12	−48.23
2010	13747.74	34.96	9226.91	28.18	8243.10	12.28	5504.64	93.48
2011	15687.75	14.11	9543.91	3.44	8888.67	7.83	6799.08	23.52
2012	15316.48	−2.37	9498.74	−0.47	9434.18	6.14	5882.29	−13.48
2013	15243.11	−0.48	10134.44	6.69	9472.88	0.41	5770.23	−1.91
2014 (rev.)	16064.87	5.39	11248.57	10.99	9936.43	4.89	6128.44	6.21

Source: Authors' calculations from the Government of Singapore Budget documents (various years).

modifying the periodic payment arrangements of CPF members in retirement, and improving income supplement programs for the elderly.

Second, labor costs of low-wage employees are also being subsidized from the budget to a greater extent to increase the purchasing power of low-income households.

Third, the top marginal income tax rate is set to increase from 20% to 22% for high-income individuals from the year of assessment 2017. This has a symbolic significance, as the measure is being taken after many years of declining income tax rates.

Fourth, the 2015–2016 Budget has signaled that more of the investment income will be reflected in the budget, and available for supporting government expenditure. This could reduce reliance on the regressive GST to generate additional revenue.

The mindset of policymakers however appears to be wedded to the requirements of the location-based strategy, explaining the continued reluctance to introduce social insurance principles in pension and healthcare financing arrangements,[35] and to using

---

[35] For example, premiums for MediShield, the state-administered health insurance scheme, remain largely based on commercial principles that vary with age: https://www.moh.gov.sg/content/moh_web/home/costs_and_financing/schemes_subsidies/Medishield/Premiums.html. Retrieved 12 March 2015.

relative income rather than absolute income mitigation in designing public policies. Policymakers are at initial stages of recognizing that transparency, robustness, timeliness and consistency of economic and social data including of broader public sector activities, are needed for greater policy credibility and broader acceptance of policy measures and their rationale by the stakeholders. Disclosure of a tax-expenditure statement with the annual budget documents will be a significant positive step in this direction.

Recent policy measures suggest that the process of overcoming such reluctance has begun, and progress in this direction may be expected over time. A strong indication of the likely success of Singapore's PFM is that this process will not be constrained by a shortage of fiscal resources, or by institutional and organizational capacities of the government.

Acknowledgment

The authors would like to thank Linda Lim for many constructive comments and suggestions that have significantly improved this chapter.

References

Asher, MG (1986). Measurement of the overall budget balance in Singapore. *ASEAN Economic Bulletin*, 3(2), 275–280.

Asher, MG (1989). *Fiscal Systems and Practices in ASEAN: Trends, Impact, and Evaluation.* Singapore: Institute of Southeast Asian Studies.

Asher, MG (2003). Fiscal policy challenges facing a mature Asian economy: The case of Singapore. In *Sustaining Competitiveness in the New Global Economy*, RS Rajan (ed.). UK: Edward Elgar.

Asher, MG (2005). Mobilizing non-conventional budgetary resources in Asia in the 21st century. *Journal of Asian Economics*, 16(6), 947–955.

Asher, MG and AS Bali (2013). Fairness and sustainability of pension arrangements in Singapore: An assessment. *Malaysian Journal of Economic Studies*, 50(2), 175–191.

Asher, MG and AS Bali (2014). Singapore's pension system: Challenges and reform options. In *Designing Equitable and Sustainable Pension Systems in the Post-Crisis World: Challenges and Experience*, S Gupta, F Eich and B Clements (eds.). Washington DC, USA: International Monetary Fund.

Blöndal, JR (2006). Budgeting in Singapore. *OECD Journal on Budgeting*, 6(1), 45–85.

Cangiano, M, TR Curristine and M Lazare (2013). *Public Financial Management and Its Emerging Architecture.* Washington DC, USA: International Monetary Fund.

Cao, Y and SB Chew (1996). GST and tax reform in Singapore. In *Economic Policy Management in Singapore*, CY Lim (ed.). Singapore: Addison-Wesley.

Department of Statistics, Singapore (2015a). Key Household Income Trends, 2014.

Department of Statistics, Singapore (2015b). Monthly Digest of Statistics Singapore, February 2015.

Dilnot, A (2012). Numbers and public policy: The power of official statistics and statistical communication in public policymaking. *Fiscal Studies*, 33(4), 429–448.

Ebrill, L, M Keen, J-P Bodin and V Summers (2001). The Modern VAT. Washington DC, USA: International Monetary Fund.

Ermisch, JF and WG Huff (1999). Hypergrowth in an East Asian NIC: Public policy and capital accumulation in Singapore. *World Development*, 27(1), 21–38.

Hoeller, P, I Joumard and I Koske (2014). Reducing income inequality while boosting economic growth: Can it be done? Evidence from OECD countries. *Singapore Economic Review*, 59(1), 1450001-1–1450001-22.

Huff, WG (1995). What is the Singapore model of economic development? *Cambridge Journal of Economics*, 19(6), 735–759.

Huff, WG (1999). Singapore's economic development: Four lessons and some doubts. *Oxford Development Studies*, 27(1), 33–55.

Hui, WT (2013). Economic growth and inequality in Singapore: The case for a minimum wage. *International Labour Review*, 152(1), 107–123.

Hui, WT and R Toh (2014). Growth with equity in Singapore: Challenges and prospects. Conditions of Work and Employment Series No. 48. International Labor Organization, Geneva, Switzerland.

Lim, CY (2003). Macroeconomic management: Is Keynesianism dead? *Singapore Economic Review*, 48(1), 1–12.

Lim, CY and Associates (1988). *Policy Options for the Singapore Economy*. Singapore: McGraw-Hill.

Massiani, J and G Picco (2013). The opportunity cost of public funds: Concepts and issues. *Public Budgeting & Finance*, 33(3), 96–114.

Ministry of Finance. Singapore (various years). The Budget.

Ministry of Manpower, Singapore (2015). Labour Force Tables 2014.

Ministry of Trade and Industry, Singapore (2015). Economic Survey of Singapore 2014.

Molana, H and C Montagna (2007). Expansionary effects of the welfare state in a small open economy. *North American Journal of Economics and Finance*, 18(3), 231–246.

Nadal-De Simone, FA (2000). Monetary and fiscal policy interaction in a small open economy: The case of Singapore. *Asian Economic Journal*, 4(2), 211–231.

Pang, EF and LYC Lim (2015). Labour, productivity and Singapore's development model. A fifty-year retrospective on Singapore's economy, Special Issue of *Singapore Economic Review*, 60(3), 1550033 (30 pages). DOI: 10.1142/S0217590815500332.

Phang, SY (1995). Economic development and the distribution of land rents in Singapore. *American Journal of Economics and Sociology*, 55(4), 489–501.

Phang, SY (2001). Housing policy, wealth formation and the Singapore economy. *Housing Studies*, 16(14), 443–459.

Ramirez, CD and LH Tan (2004). Singapore Inc. versus the private sector: Are government-linked companies different? *IMF Staff Papers*, 51(3), 510–528.

Santoni, M (1999). Fiscal policy and welfare in a small open economy with imperfect competition. *Bulletin of Economic Research*, 51(4), 287–317.

Tan, KH (1996). A new view of macroeconomic stabilization: The Singapore perspective. In *Economic Policy Management in Singapore*, CY Lim (ed.). Singapore: Addison-Wesley.

Urban Redevelopment Authority (2014), Master Plan 2014, Urban Redevelopment Authority, Singapore. Retrieved 9 February 2015 from http://www.ura.gov.sg/uol/master-plan.aspx?p1=view-master-plan.

Williamson, JB, M Price and C Shen (2012). Pension policy in China, Singapore and South Korea: An assessment of the potential value of the notional defined contribution model. *Journal of Aging Studies*, 26(1), 79–89.

World Bank (2015). *Global Economic Prospects: Having Fiscal Space and Using It*. Washington DC, USA: The World Bank.

Yeoh, B and W Lin (2012). Rapid Growth in Singapore's Immigrant Population Brings Policy Challenges. *Migration Information Source*, 3 April 2012. Retrieved 12 March 2015 from: http://www.migrationpolicy.org/article/rapid-growth-singapores-immigrant-population-bringspolicy-challenges.

CHAPTER 7

Labor, Productivity and Singapore's Development Model

Pang Eng Fong and Linda Y. C. Lim

This chapter discusses how Singapore's labor market policies since independence have been molded by the state-driven, foreign investment-led, export-oriented, manufacturing-focused development model the country has followed over the past fifty years. The literature we review shows that high GDP growth has been achieved through factor accumulation rather than productivity increase, a strategy of extensive growth that has now run into diminishing returns as well as political, social and resource constraints. Prolonged heavy dependence on imports of foreign labor and skills to attract foreign investment has contributed to low, declining and even negative productivity growth, with low real GDP growth in recent years. In response, the government is pursuing renewed economic restructuring, limiting foreign labor inflows, targeting investments more selectively, and promoting productivity and innovation, so far with uncertain results. This chapter suggests that Singapore should let market forces propel the economy toward services, domestic consumption and regional trade, led by domestic private enterprise. But the retreat from established state industrial and social policies will be difficult.

1. Introduction: Singapore's Development Model

Singapore's extraordinary journey from relative poverty to impressive prosperity began with its unplanned independence in August 1965.[1] Along the way from Third World to First, Singapore evolved a distinctive development model based on a large role for multinationals and an extensive involvement of the state in reshaping the economy and society.[2] Local enterprises in Singapore played only a

---

[1] Lee Kuan Yew, Singapore's Prime Minister from 1959 to 1990 said in an interview in *Newsweek* (18 September 1989): "...we did not want an independent Singapore — it went against our logic on how to build a stable long-term future as a multiracial community. We considered Singapore not viable. But we were forced to make it viable".

[2] The central role of the government in the economy is not due to a large public sector or high level of government spending to GDP. The public sector — civil service and statutory boards — employed

supporting role, not the catalytic one that they did in South Korea, Taiwan and Hong Kong.

The dominant role of the state[3] in Singapore's economy and society began after self-government in 1959, when the government led by the People's Action Party (PAP) under Lee Kuan Yew moved swiftly to tackle the serious problems of a stagnating entrepot economy, high unemployment, and urgent housing and educational challenges arising from a rapidly growing population. It embarked on a mass public housing program, introduced family planning, and made plans for industrialization that involved an expanding role for the state. By independence in 1965, the government had become not only a regulator and planner, but also a significant player in the economy, having taken equity stakes in many companies, in large part because the private sector was unable or unwilling to risk its own capital, and it was believed that state enterprises were necessary to create wealth and jobs. Despite these efforts, development achievements in the first half of the 1960s were modest because of political uncertainties and labor unrest. But the period did lay the institutional groundwork for the evolution of a uniquely activist state.

Separation from Malaysia in 1965 meant that the import-substituting industrialization strategy previously envisaged for the larger combined domestic market was no longer feasible, and the newly-born city-state had to turn to export manufacturing instead. But there were few domestic companies that could be nurtured into national industrial champions capable of competing in international markets, given their concentration in the commercial services of a colonial port-city. So, government policy-makers turned to attracting foreign capital, even though much of the developing world then had serious reservations about its long-term positive contribution to industrialization.

Separation did not just cause a change in development strategy. The traumatic event produced in the political leadership a profound sense of psychological insecurity and an acute awareness of Singapore's vulnerable position in Southeast Asia — enduring anxieties that arguably continue to shape the city-state's domestic and foreign policies. On top of the daunting challenge of economic survival, Singapore's political leaders had to build a nation out of an ethnically diverse population descended mostly from immigrants. The struggle for political and economic survival was one and the same thing, leading to policies to promote

---

138,000 persons or 6.2% of the resident workforce of 2.2 million in 2013. In 2012, the government spending to GDP ratio was 17%, one of the lowest among developed economies.

[3]The word "state" encompasses more than "government". It includes all the administrative, legal, bureaucratic and coercive systems that influence relations between a people and those in authority. The state is not a unitary institution and conflicts between parts of the state and different groups of people are inevitable.

social stability and industrial peace which were critical both to attracting foreign capital and to nation building.[4]

In addition to the normal government controls over the macro-economy through monetary, fiscal and exchange rate policies (the colonial-era regimes of free trade and capital flows remaining largely intact), the Singapore state progressively extended its controls over domestic capital (e.g., Central Provident Fund "forced savings", persistent budget surpluses, huge foreign exchange reserves, and world-scale sovereign wealth funds), land and property (e.g., housing over 80% of the population through the Housing Development Board, and developing commercial and residential private properties through state-linked entities), and the labor market (the focus of the rest of this chapter). Government entities including statutory boards and state enterprises (later transformed into government-linked companies (GLCs) through partial divestment or privatization) provide, and profit from providing, infrastructure, finance, and services.[5]

The role of foreign capital or multinationals is itself heavily mediated by state industrial policy, particularly investment promotion led by the Economic Development Board (EDB), which has impacted labor market policy and outcomes, and resource allocation more generally. The basic policy of tax incentives, subsidized infrastructure and labor policies to attract foreign investors has remained unchanged for five decades, with Choy (2012) noting that "Singapore held no attraction then, and now, as a final market; for FDI to keep flowing in, the state has to continually entice investors with tax concessions."[6] At independence, lacking both a domestic market and indigenous industrial expertise, Singapore had "no choice" but to provide state incentives to attract foreign investment for its capital, technology, international market access and the resulting employment creation and income growth. Foreign direct investment (FDI) inflow and the export earnings it generated also covered and then reversed the city-state's longstanding trade deficit. However, there was "no feedback from these beneficial outcomes to investment itself" (Choy, 2012, p. 5), requiring the constant "chasing after" new foreign investments as Singapore's comparative advantage, external demand and international competition changed.

---

[4] Alternate historical explanations are possible for Singapore's unique and persistent dependence on both state and foreign capital. In the colonial and early post-colonial era, most local private enterprise was in the hands of the "Chinese-educated", many of whom supported anti-colonial and then left-wing opposition politics, whereas the more "moderate" PAP was led by "English-educated" professionals. State and foreign enterprises provided an alternative to reliance on potentially contentious domestic private capital, while foreign capital additionally bolstered national security by giving foreign powers a vested interest in Singapore's political survival (Lim, 1987).

[5] See e.g., Lim (1983), Lim et al. (1993) and Huff (1999).

[6] Choy (2012), p. 5.

Specifically, since the late 1970s incentives have been constantly redesigned to encourage industrial restructuring, technological upgrading, higher value-added and "knowledge-intensive" activities which market forces would presumably otherwise not direct to Singapore.

Besides industrial policy, policy in social sectors like housing, healthcare, education and pensions served both to entrench the state and serve the needs of foreign capital (Lim, 1989; Lim and Lee, 2010). Being a city-state (Pang and Lim, 1982b) was an advantage, with concentrated population in a small physical area facilitating both industrial and social policy, from external defense and domestic political control to housing and "social engineering". The government intervened in the social system to promote values and attitudes favorable to nation-building, self-reliance and hard work, over the years imposing a multiplicity of controls and regulations which have profoundly shaped Singapore society.[7] While promoting social order and facilitating economic progress, these social interventions have also arguably bred an aversion to risk-taking, discouraging domestic private entrepreneurship. Citizens came to be increasingly dependent on the government, seeing it as not only the provider of basic needs, but also the generator of wealth and opportunities. Periodically since the 1980s, the state itself has noted the limits of a development model based on two key actors — the state and foreign firms, drawing attention to the need for the local private sector to play a bigger role.

2. Labor Market Policies

At independence, labor was Singapore's only "natural resource", but the labor market had long been characterized by frequent labor unrest which also undermined political stability. Beginning in the early 1960s, the PAP government introduced various legislative and administrative measures to curb rival unionism and promote industrial peace (Vasil, 1989). After independence, to ensure the success of the export-oriented development strategy which hinged on low wages and labor discipline, the government increased its role in the labor market. In 1968, it passed two labor laws to contain labor costs and improve the investment climate. The Employment Act of 1968 standardized terms and conditions of employment and set limits on negotiable fringe benefits. The Industrial Relations (Amendment) Act excluded from collective

---

[7] Singapore's Prime Minister Lee Kuan Yew said in the Straits Times (20 April 1987) that "I am often accused of interfering in the private lives of citizens. Yes, if I did not, had I not done that, we wouldn't be here today. And I say without the slightest remorse, that we wouldn't be here, we would not have made economic progress, if we had not intervened on very personal matters — who your neighbour is, how you live, the noise you make, how you spit, or what language you use. We decide what is right. Never mind what the people think."

bargaining issues such as worker recruitment, retrenchment and dismissal, and dictated new procedures for labor negotiation and conflict resolution.

These laws succeeded in depoliticizing the labor movement, established de facto government control over unions, and gave employers considerable bargaining power over workers. They contributed greatly to the huge expansion of jobs in labor-intensive factories, especially for young women, which initiated major social and demographic changes. In less than a decade, export manufacturing by multinationals had reduced the backlog of unemployment. Since then, with the exception of several short recessions in 1973–1974, 1985–1986, 1997–1998, and 2008–2009, Singapore has enjoyed full employment, as low as 2% of the resident labor force.

In 1972, the government made two major interventions in the labor market. First, it relaxed immigration rules to allow labor-short employers to bring in foreign workers.[8] Second, it formed a tripartite National Wages Council (NWC) as an advisory body with representatives from government, employer groups and labor. The NWC was given three objectives — formulate annual wage guidelines, recommend wage structure adjustments, and advise on incentive systems. In practice, it directed its attention to the first objective. In 1972–1978, the guidelines succeeded in moderating wage pressures, keeping Singapore a competitive location for labor-intensive manufacturing. But they also had unintended effects: across-the-board guidelines meant that actual wage increases did not fully reflect wide sectoral variations in labor demand (Pang and Quek, 1980). The burden of adjustment to changing economic conditions fell on the supply side of the labor market, impairing its efficiency (Pang, 1988). Wage suppression to keep wages in Singapore "internationally competitive" also attracted firms in search of low wages, resulting in more demand for cheap labor (Toh and Low, 1990, p. 264).

The government then became concerned that "orderly" wage increases were leading to a "low-wage equilibrium trap". So, in 1979–1981 it pursued a "wage correction" policy which resulted in high wage increases and slower employment growth, with a greater impact on the mostly local small and medium enterprises (SMEs) than on multinational companies. In the early 1980s, the council dropped its practice of issuing annual wage guidelines and instead became a forum for tripartite discussions on the economy and the labor market.

The policy to import foreign workers has had more profound consequences. In the 1970s, the inflow of unskilled foreign workers represented a small proportion of the labor force — 3.4% in 1970 rising to 7.4% in 1980. They were drawn mostly from Malaysia, the city-state's traditional hinterland, and employed in the manufacturing

---

[8] The transition from a labor-surplus to a labor-importing economy took less than ten years for Singapore. For other rapidly industrializing economies like South Korea and Taiwan, the turning point took longer as they had an agricultural sector (Pang, 1975).

sector. But as labor shortages became widespread, employers were allowed to bring in workers from non-traditional sources and into the non-manufacturing sector. Unskilled foreign workers, less protected by labor laws, provided a useful flexible buffer in economic downturns, and were not subject to the annual leave for military training required of male citizen workers.

Regulations on the importation of skilled and unskilled foreign workers have over the years become increasingly complex, with adjustable levies that vary by industry, dependency ratio ceilings and minimum qualifying salaries for mid-level and high-level pass holders. Until 2004 when employers were allowed to bring in mid-level skilled workers under the S-Pass scheme, there were only two broad categories of foreign workers — highly skilled workers were issued employment passes while unskilled workers were given work permits. The introduction of the S-Pass scheme recognized that manpower shortages had become widespread and were no longer confined to highly-skilled or unskilled groups. It was also a response to representations by labor-short local as well as foreign employers.

The government initially viewed the resort to foreign workers as a temporary solution to manpower shortages. By the late 1970s, it was clear that the growing dependence on unskilled foreign workers could not continue indefinitely without imposing high social and economic costs on Singapore.[9] In 1981, the government announced a policy to phase out unskilled foreign workers by 1991 (Pang and Lim, 1982a). However, the policy allowing the liberal import of skilled people remained unchanged. In fact, the government encouraged (and still encourages) employment pass holders who can be assimilated easily into Singapore to take up permanent residence.

In 1982, the government tightened conditions on the import of unskilled workers from non-traditional sources (that is, other than Malaysia). A year later, in response to employer complaints, it relaxed the deadline for phasing out unskilled workers from non-traditional sources. In 1984, employers were allowed to bring in unskilled workers from four new sources, namely, South Korea, Taiwan, Hong Kong and Macao. The long-term goal of phasing out unskilled foreign workers was set aside in the interest of short-term flexibility even as a variety of incentive measures were introduced to restructure the economy and reduce its need for unskilled labor.

In 1985, Singapore experienced its worst-ever post-independence recession. Its response was to cut costs, particularly employer CPF contributions, and to ease employer access to foreign workers. As the economy recovered in 1986, the upward trend in dependence on foreign workers resumed. The government still recognized the need to reduce reliance on foreign workers in the longer term, but was being

---

[9] As early as 1972, Goh Keng Swee, Singapore's Deputy Prime Minister had spoken of the risk of a rising dependence on foreign workers to sustain economic growth. See Au Yong (2014), Part 1.

"pragmatic" in responding to the short-term labor needs of employers. Thus foreign labor inflows ebbed and flowed with economic conditions, but the net result was a steady rise in the relative and absolute size of the foreign workforce in Singapore.

From the mid-1980s until the introduction of the S-Pass in 2004, the employment pattern of foreign workers differed significantly from that of local workers. Non-citizen, non-resident workers were over-represented at both the top and bottom ends of the skill hierarchy (Pang and Lim, 1982a). With the opening since 2004 of the mid-skilled job market to foreign workers (whose number jumped four-fold from 44,500 in December 2007 to 164,000 in June 2014)[10] the employment pattern of foreign and citizen workers has become more similar. While access to a huge regional pool of unskilled foreign workers has most likely depressed wages of citizen workers at the lower end of the labor market, the opening of the mid-level market to foreigners has enlarged the possibilities for employers to substitute foreigners for citizen workers with similar skills. In theory, employed citizen workers with mid-level skills should not be affected if demand is rising faster than supply. In practice, however, cost-conscious employers seeking greater workforce flexibility find it advantageous to replace older, higher-wage mid-skilled locals with younger replacements from abroad.[11]

The government has long voiced concern about the negative effects of rising dependence on foreign labor. Tony Tan, then Finance Minister, said in his 1985 Budget Speech that "the solution to our labor shortage cannot be an indefinite and ever-growing dependence on foreign workers. The experience of countries, which have indiscriminately allowed large numbers of foreign workers to settle permanently, shows that this gives rise to social and political problems of such a magnitude as to threaten the cohesiveness and stability of their societies." But his speech had little impact on policy. From the mid-1980s to early 2000s, public unease about the rising inflow of foreign workers grew, yet the government did not restrict it, fearing that this would harm the economy. In a 2011 speech at the 50th anniversary of the HDB, Singapore's founding Prime Minister Lee Kuan Yew noted that "we've grown in the last five years by just importing labor. Now, the people feel uncomfortable, there are too many foreigners."[12]

It was only after the PAP suffered its greatest electoral setback in May 2011, when it lost the Aljunied Group Representation Constituency to the Workers' Party, that the government tightened the inflow of foreign workers (excluding domestic workers),

---

[10] As Table 1 shows, in proportionate terms, this jump was much greater than those for work permits (which increased from 757,100 in 2007 to 980,800 in 2014) and employment passes (99,200 to 164,700).

[11] There are also complaints from Singaporeans that foreign employers and hiring managers tend to favor fellow nationals, a practice known among sociologists in U.S. academia as "homosocial reproduction".

[12] For some examples of studies of foreign labor policy in Singapore, see Wong (1997), Huang and Yeoh (2003) and Chia (2011).

Table 1.   Foreign workforce numbers, Singapore, 2007–2014.[1]

Pass type	2007 ('000s)	2008 ('000s)	2009 ('000s)	2010 ('000s)	2011 ('000s)	2012 ('000s)	2013 ('000s)	2014 ('000s)
Employment Pass (EP)	99.2	113.4	114.3	143.3	175.4	173,800	175.1	176.6
S Pass	44.5	74.3	82.8	98.7	113.9	142,400	160.9	164.7
Work Permit (Total)	757.1	870.0	851.2	865.2	901.0	942,800	974.4	980.8
— Work Permit (Foreign Domestic Worker)	183.2	191.4	196.0	201.4	206.3	209,600	214.5	218.3
— Work Permit (Construction)	180.0	229.9	245.7	248.0	264.4	293,300	318.9	321,200
Other Work Passes[2]	—	—	5.2	6.0	7.6	9,300	11.3	14.7
Total Foreign Workforce	900.8	1,057.7	1,053.5	1,113.2	1,197.9	1,268.3	1,321.6	1,336.7
Total Foreign Workforce (excluding Foreign Domestic Workers)	717.6	866.3	857.4	911.8	991.6	1,058.7	1,107.1	1,118.4
Total Foreign Workforce (excluding Foreign Domestic Workers & Construction)	527.1	616.8	588.3	638.9	699.1	731.3	748.1	753.7

Source: http://www.mom.gov.sg/statistics-publications/others/statistics/Pages/ForeignWorkforceNumbers.aspx.

Notes: [1] Data may not add up to the total due to rounding.

[2] "Other Work Passes" includes Letter of Consent (LOC) holders and Training Work Permit (TWP) previously included in published Work Permit (WP) figures. Training Employment Pass (TEP) was included in "Other Work Passes" from Mar 2014 onwards.

slowing the growth rate from 8.8% in 2011 (already down from the 20.7% increase in 2008) to 1% in 2014 (Table 2). Prime Minister Lee Hsien Loong in a speech at the opening of National Productivity Month on 7 October 2014 said "we are controlling foreign worker inflows so that we put pressure on companies to upgrade their workers rather than simply hiring extra bodies. But we still give companies enough access to foreign workers to complement your Singaporean workforce, because if we allow in too few foreign workers, or freeze their numbers, some businesses will not survive, especially SMEs, and many Singaporean jobs will also disappear".[13] Even though the foreign worker inflow has slowed, their absolute number is still rising. Public unhappiness with foreign workers, particularly those competing with Singaporeans for mid-level jobs, has not dissipated, despite new policies like the fair consideration framework (FCF) which came into force in August 2014 to prevent discriminatory hiring practices against Singaporeans (Cabuyao, 2015).

3. Labor Market Outcomes

Singapore's labor market policies contributed to the early attainment of full employment, which has been mostly sustained since. In the early days of independence, domestic labor supply increased largely due to a jump in female labor force participation (FLFP), responding first to new employment opportunities in female-labor-intensive export manufacturing industries, and then to demographic and societal changes, including reduced fertility and increased female education. FLFP rose from 28.2% in 1970 to 43.8% in 1980, then continued a steady climb to 58.6% in 2014, when male LFP was 75.9%, and women accounted for 44.4% of all employed residents. Both participation rates and incomes of women workers remain below those of men, though the gaps have narrowed significantly, and participation continues to decline with marriage, child-bearing and age.[14]

Labor market policies also enabled a long period of high GDP growth based on factor accumulation heavily dependent on imported inputs of both capital and labor. But periodically holding wages below market levels (through the "downward flexibility" afforded by variable CPF contributions), and continually increasing the

---

[13] In a 2012 May Day Rally Speech, PM Lee recognized that employers and workers see the influx of foreigners differently. "The employers… feel that they cannot find enough workers in Singapore, especially workers who will stay on the job. Hence, better to bring in some foreign workers, seize the opportunities, rather than let the business go somewhere else. At least you keep the jobs, the business in Singapore and you keep some jobs in Singapore. The workers often see it differently, that the foreign workers add to competition against them. If there are too many, it may reduce wages and it may even take away some of the jobs which Singaporeans can do. Better we have fewer foreign workers and let our wages rise."

[14] Department of Statistics and Ministry of Manpower. Yap and Gee (2015) note that FLFP in Singapore does not increase after children are older, as it does in most other high-income countries.

Table 2.   Annual percentage change in foreign workforce, Singapore, 2008–2014.[1]

Pass type	2008	2009	2010	2011	2012	2013	2014
Employment Pass (EP)	14.3%	0.8%	25.4%	22.4%	−0.9%	0.8%	0.9%
S Pass	66.9%	11.4%	19.2%	15.4%	25.0%	12.9%	2.4%
Work Permit (Total)	14.9%	−2.2%	1.6%	4.1%	4.6%	3.4%	0.7%
— Work Permit (Foreign Domestic Worker)	4.5%	2.4%	2.8%	2.4%	1.6%	2.3%	1.8%
— Work Permit (Construction)	27.7%	6.9%	0.9%	6.6%	10.9%	8.7%	0.7%
Other Work Passes[2]	—	—	15.4%	26.7%	22.4%	21.5%	30.1%
Total Foreign Workforce	17.4%	−0.4%	5.7%	7.6%	5.9%	4.2%	1.1%
Total Foreign Workforce (excluding Foreign Domestic Workers)	20.7%	−1.0%	6.3%	8.8%	6.8%	4.6%	1.0%
Total Foreign Workforce (excluding Foreign Domestic Workers & Construction)	17.0%	−4.6%	8.6%	9.4%	4.6%	2.3%	0.8%

Source: http://www.mom.gov.sg/statistics-publications/others/statistics/Pages/ForeignWorkforceNumbers.aspx.

Note: [1] Figures have been calculated based upon figures obtained in Decembers of each year.
[2] "Other Work Passes" includes Letter of Consent (LOC) holders and Training Work Permit (TWP) previously included in published Work Permit (WP) figures. Training Employment Pass (TEP) was included in "Other Work Passes" from Mar 2014 onwards.

supply of foreign labor (through liberal immigration policy) discouraged economic restructuring even as a plethora of successive investment incentives and education and skill upgrading measures sought to achieve it. Table 3 shows that real wages of resident workers began stagnating, increasing by 1.5% a year from 2003–2013 (including employer CPF contributions) and by just 1.1% from 2003–2010 and 0.7% from 2010–2013 (excluding employer CPF contributions).[15] Income inequality increased over the same time period: in 2014 Singapore's Gini coefficient before government taxes and transfers was 0.462, one of the highest among developed countries.[16]

---

[15] Real wages are computed for resident workers which include permanent residents who are on average better educated and paid than citizen workers. Data on wage changes for citizens and permanent residents are not publicly available and so it is not possible to analyze the impact of over half a million permanent residents on citizen wages. There are also no publicly available and separate figures on wage changes for unskilled non-resident workers. These data gaps render difficult any attempt to evaluate the effects of the rapid growth of the non-resident population on citizen wages (Basu, 2015).

[16] In 1966, at a much lower level of per capita income, the Gini coefficient was 0.457 (Pang, 1975). It fell by 1973 to 0.415, thanks to rapid employment growth and rising wages for workers at the lower

Still, as the decades passed, education and skill levels, and wages, increased with high growth. In 1980, 83.1% of residents had not completed secondary education, while only 2.7% had a university education; in 2013, 31.2% had less than a full secondary education with 27.3% having a university education (Table 4). These ratios will rise as the existing "stock" of less-educated older workers retires and leaves the labor force. Correspondingly, professional and technical, and administrative and managerial, occupations rose from 13.6% of the labor force in 1980 to 53.1% in 2014 (Table 5). Despite a near-equalization by gender in educational attainment, women are still under-represented in higher-income occupational categories and higher-income levels within occupational categories, while they are over-represented in both mid- and lower-skill occupations.[17]

The sectoral composition of output and employment also changed — first, from regional services to global manufacturing for export from the mid-1960s to the mid-1980s, then back to services, especially high-value global financial and business services, since then. Notably, and contrary to the experience of all other developed economies (except South Korea) and high-income major cities, manufacturing's share of GDP remained high at around one-quarter, though its share of employment predictably declined as state industrial policies targeted specific high-tech and capital-intensive "clusters" such as electronics, chemicals and pharmaceuticals. Unfortunately, these heavily foreign-dependent sectors also contribute to increased volatility and inequality (Choy, 2010), now considered major problems for the economy and society. Industrial restructuring toward male-intensive heavy industry reduced the proportion of women in manufacturing, while the expansion of services increased their representation there.

The proportion of foreign non-resident workers in the Singapore workforce had doubled from 3.2% in 1970 to 7.4% in 1980. Between 1980 and 1990, it doubled again to 16.1% and nearly doubled again to 28.1% in 2000 (Yeoh and Lin, 2012). Between 2004 and 2014, the number of non-resident workers more than doubled from 603,000 to 1.3 million (Table 6), and in 2014, 38.1% or more than a third of the labor force of 3.5 million in Singapore were non-residents.[18]

Very few countries have seen such a surge in foreign workers in recent years or have GDP growth that is driven largely by an influx of foreign labor. In the 1980s when GDP growth averaged 7.8% a year, employment growth was only 2.4% a year.

---

end of the income distribution. Asher *et al.* (2015) argue that the Singapore Gini understates inequality because it is limited to labor income which accounts for only 40% of national income, excluding capital income, which accounts for 52% and accrues disproportionately to the top decile of the population.

[17] See Lim (2015a) for a more detailed analysis of women in the labor force in Singapore, including discussion of how they may be impacted by the foreign labor policy.

[18] Table 3 of Yap and Gee (2015).

Table 3.   Annual percentage change in labour productivity and real wages, Singapore, 2003–2013.

	Labor productivity	Real total wages (incl employer CPF contributions)	Real total wages (excl employer CPF contributions)	Real basic wages
2003	5.7	0.3	1.0	0.7
2004	7.7	−0.1	1.9	1.0
2005	3.0	3.8	3.8	2.6
2006	2.1	3.5	3.5	2.6
2007	0.4	4.5	3.8	2.2
2008	−7.2	−1.7	−2.4	−2.2
2009	−3.3	−1	−1.0	0.7
2010	11.6	2.9	2.7	1.1
2011	2.2	0.9	0.1	−0.8
2012	−1.4	−0.4	−0.8	−0.1
2013	−0.2	2.9	2.9	2.7
2003–2010	2.5	1.5	1.7	1.1
2010–2013	3.1	1.6	1.2	0.7

Source: Survey on annual wage changes, MOM; and data from Department of Statistics (DOS).

Table 4.   Highest qualification attained of residents aged 25 years & over[1] (%).

Education attainment	1980	1990	2000	2010	2013
Below Secondary	83.1	63.3	45.3	34.5	31.2
Secondary	9.5	23.6	24.0	19.0	18.8
Post-Secondary (Non-Tertiary)	4.7[2]	4.7	8.9	9.5	8.7
Diploma & Professional Qualification		3.6	9.8	13.3	14.0
University	2.7	4.7	12.1	23.7	27.3
Total	100.0	100.0	100.0	100.0	100.0

Source: http://www.singstat.gov.sg/statistics/browse-by-theme/population-and-population-structure.

Notes: [1]Data pertain to residents who are not attending educational institutions as full-time students. The data include those who are upgrading their qualifications through part-time courses while working.
[2]Data refer to post-secondary (non-tertiary) and diploma & professional qualification.

In the decade 2000–2010, GDP grew at an average of 5.2% a year while employment expanded by 3.9% a year (Hui and Toh, 2014). Hui and Toh (2014) found that "employment as the driver of growth has increased its share from 31% in the 1970s to 75% in 2000s".

Table 5. Percentage distribution of labor force by occupation (in thousands).

Year occupation	1970		1980		1990		2000		2010		2014	
	No. ('000s)	%	No. ('000s)	%	No. ('000s)	%	No. ('000s)	%	No. ('000s)	%	No. ('000s)	%
Professional & Technical	56.1	8.6	95.1	8.8	240.6	15.6	433.6	29.2	706.9	37.2	1160.341	53.1
Administrative & Managerial	15.5	2.4	52.2	4.8	132.1	8.6	211.8	14.3	250.0	13.2		
Clerical	82.9	12.7	167.5	15.6	201.9	13.1	213.6	14.4	241.8	12.7	541.9296	24.8
Services & Sales	191.3	29.4	244.2	22.7	333.2	21.7	366.0	24.7	252.6	13.3		
Agricultural & Related Workers	26.9	4.1	21.0	1.9	8.9	0.6	1.2	0.1	1.0	0.1	482.9292	22.1
Production & Related Workers	254.9	39.2	435.0	40.4	558.8	36.4	285.5	19.3	254.0	13.4		
Cleaners, Laborers & Related Workers	—	—	—	—	—	—	101.1	6.8	130.3	6.9		
Not Classifiable	23.1	3.6	62.2	5.8	61.4	4.0	52.8	3.6	61.3	3.2		
Total	650.9	100	1,077.1	100	1,537.0	100	1,482.6	100	1,898.0	100	2185.2	100

Source of 1970–2010 data: Saw (2012). In *The Population of Singapore* (3rd ed., p. 291). Singapore: Institute of Southeast Asian Studies.
Source of 2014 data: http://stats.mom.gov.sg/Pages/Labor-Force-Summary-Table.aspx.

Table 6. Resident and non-resident workers in Singapore, 2002–2013.

Mid-year	Total ('000s)	Residents ('000s)	Residents % of total	Resident growth rate %	Foreigners	Foreigners % of total	Foreigner growth rate %
2002	2,223.2	1,573.7	70.8	−0.6	649.5	29.2	−5.2
2003	2,208.1	1,605.4	72.7	2.0	602.7	27.3	−7.2
2004	2,238.1	1,632.1	72.9	1.7	606.0	27.1	0.6
2006	2,505.8	1,796.7	71.7	10.1	709.1	28.3	17.0
2007	2,670.8	1,842.1	69.0	2.5	828.7	31.0	16.9
2007[a]	2,631.9	1,803.2	68.5	−2.1	828.7	31.5	0.0
2008	2,858.1	1,852.0	64.8	2.7	1,006.1	35.2	21.4
2009	2,905.9	1,869.4	64.3	0.9	1,036.5	35.7	3.0
2010	3,047.2	1,962.9*	64.4	5.0	1,084.3	35.6	4.6
2011	3,149.7	1,998.9	63.5	1.8	1,150.8	36.5	6.1
2012	3,274.7	2,040.6	62.3	2.1	1,234.1	37.7	7.2
2013	3,352.9	2,056.1	61.3	0.8	1,296.8	38.7	5.1

Source: Comprehensive labor force survey, Ministry of Manpower, Singapore (2014).

Notes: [1]Data for 1995, 2000 and 2005 are not available as the Comprehensive Labor Force Survey was not conducted in these years due to the conduct of the Census and General Household Survey by Department of Statistics, Ministry of Trade and Industry.

[2]To facilitate comparison with data for 2008 onwards, the 2007 data have been adjusted based on Singapore Department of Statistics' revised population estimates (released in February 2008) which exclude Singapore residents who have been away from Singapore for a continuous period of 12 months or longer. Adjusted data for 2007 are denoted by the symbol *a*.

From 2010 (which was a truly exceptional year of recovery from the global financial crisis with GDP rebounding by more than 14%) to 2014, annual GDP growth averaged about 3%, already at the low end of the 3% to 5% range the Economic Strategies Committee (Ministry of Trade and Industry, 2010) suggested was possible. This was again driven largely by the import of more foreign workers and not by labor productivity growth. The government's own labor productivity growth target set in 2000 of 2% to 3% a year has not been achieved; from 2012–2014, productivity in fact stagnated. The large number of well-funded schemes that the government and its agencies have launched to encourage employers to innovate and substitute capital for labor, and workers to undergo additional training, appear to have had (so far) little effect. Supply-side policies to increase the labor force participation of women and of the elderly have had some success, contributing to a new high resident labor force participation rate of 67% in 2014.[19] But so far there have not been policies to attract back Singaporeans who have emigrated or are working abroad, who are likely to be more highly skilled.[20]

4. Growth with Low Productivity

The story of Singapore's unimpressive productivity record is not a recent phenomenon. As early as the late 1970s, Pang (1977) calculated that Singapore's manufacturing sector had productivity gains (measured as output per worker) of only about 1% a year. Tsao (1982, 1985) found that total factor productivity had stagnated in the 1970s in Singapore manufacturing. She advanced three explanations for this dismal record: the high reliance on foreign capital in manufacturing; the low level of industrial competence; and the use of unskilled foreign labor. A growth accounting study by Young (1992, 1994) suggested that Singapore's economic growth was largely driven by factor accumulation and that the huge influx of capital had not been efficiently used, with Singapore a "victim of its own targeting policies". Krugman (1994) characterized Singapore's rapid economic growth (averaging over 8% between 1966 and 1990) as "an economic twin of the growth of Stalin's Soviet Union growth achieved purely through mobilization of resources", the outcome of perspiration, not inspiration. These conclusions strengthened the government's resolve to intensify the restructuring drive begun in the late 1970s.

The restructuring effort succeeded in attracting sizeable foreign direct investments in knowledge-intensive, high value-added industry clusters including microelectronics, information technology, logistics, aerospace, marine, clean technology, biomedical, chemicals and precision engineering. Also successfully targeted to

---

[19] Tay (2015), citing Ministry of Manpower.
[20] See footnote 45.

broaden the high-value services sector were global finance, wealth management, media, new media, integrated resorts, medical services, logistics, and regional and global multinational headquarters, in addition to the city-state's traditional role as a hub for trade, tourism and transportation. Tax breaks and other incentives were also provided to foreign firms to move more R&D activities to Singapore, in the hope that they would transfer technology to local firms.

These efforts have transformed Singapore's industrial landscape, but they have made little difference to total factor productivity (TFP) growth.[21] According to Vu (2011), annual TFP growth fell from 2% in the 1980s to 1.4% in the 1990s, while from 2000–2008, TFP grew by only 0.5% a year. Using more finely disaggregated data, Nomura and Amano (2012) show that "TFP growth has been poor or even negative" from 1974–2011, while average labor productivity growth of 3.37% per year in the 1980s, 3.33% in the 1990s and 3.54% from 2000–2005 plunged to 0.54% in 2005–2010.[22] A Ministry of Trade and Industry study (2014) says that labor productivity grew by an average of 2.5% a year from 2009–2014 (only 0.3% if the exceptional recovery year of 2010 is excluded); in 2014 it fell by 0.8%.

Singapore's poor productivity performance is not for lack of policy focus or productivity-boosting schemes. Since the 1970s, the government has emphasized higher productivity as the primary engine for raising real wages and so the material standard of living. In developing strategies to increase productivity, it has adopted the approach of giving employers incentives to upgrade their operations through computerization, automation and mechanization and also to invest in manpower development (Au Yong, 2014). One scheme which the government instituted in 2011 and expanded in 2014 is the productivity and innovation credit (PIC), which gives companies tax deductions or cash grants when they invest in machinery and equipment to boost their capabilities. This and other schemes have been criticized for not evaluating their own effectiveness (e.g., how recipient firms have performed), and for subsidizing poor management.[23] The government has also expanded continuing

---

[21] TFP growth measures the efficiency with which an economy uses factor inputs. It reflects technical change — the only long-run source of economic growth.

[22] Nomura and Amano (2012), Table 4, which also shows that TFP growth averaged −0.3% annually from 1974–2010, but 0.53% from 2000–2010. Png (2015) reports that multifactor productivity (MFP) fell by 2.3% in 2012 and 0.7% in 2013, suggesting that "productivity growth seems to have fallen to the point that the level of productivity is dropping."

[23] Png (2015) cites a KPMG survey that found that 30% of survey respondents used the PIC to defray operational expenses rather than to boost productivity. The Singapore Budget 2015 released on 23 February 2015 announced that the PIC Bonus will expire in 2015, but other PIC measures will be extended. Other major productivity-enhancing schemes include the Innovation & Capability Voucher (ICV), the Increase SME Productivity with Infocomm Adoption & Transformation (iSPRINT) and Inclusive Growth Programme (IGP). For a list of productivity-related measures introduced in recent years, see Au Yong (2014), Part 3.

education and training support systems to improve the skills of workers already in the labor market as well as new job entrants from the polytechnics and universities.[24]

One explanation for low productivity growth is that the various government schemes introduced in recent years will take time to bear fruit, even though many similar schemes over the past three decades did not. In the highly labor-intensive restaurant sector, for example, Lim (2015) notes that "Restructuring will be difficult for many, after years of liberal foreign worker policies" due to "entrenched practices".... and "The productivity drive is only just gaining momentum among early adopters."

It can be argued too that the 2% to 3% annual productivity growth target established by the Economic Strategies Committee (Ministry of Trade and Industry, 2010) is too ambitious, given that Singapore is now a developed economy and almost all other economies at a similar per capita income level have a trend TFP rate of 1% to 2%. But as noted above, Singapore experienced low productivity growth even in earlier decades at much lower income levels. Nomura and Amano (2012) estimate that TFP contributed negatively to GDP growth from 1974–1980, and in the 1980s and 1990s; from 1974–2011, capital inputs contributed 63.6% and labor inputs 40.7% to GDP growth; capital deepening explained 83% of the average labor productivity growth from 1970–2010.

These data simply reiterate the long-known "extensive growth" model of development that the Singapore state has followed since independence to maintain a GDP growth rate much higher and for much longer than other economies have managed after maturing into high-income status. Growth in any economy is derived from factor accumulation (adding capital, labor, land to create "extensive growth" or more output from more inputs) and/or increases in total factor productivity (the more efficient use of existing resources, enhanced by technological progress, to create "intensive growth" producing more output per unit of input). Singapore's early post-independence GDP growth was driven by inputs of labor (then primarily domestic and relatively abundant) and capital (readily available, mostly from foreign sources). This continued in the next four decades, with labor quality (human capital and skills) contributing an impressive 1% of the 6.78% annual GDP growth computed by Nomura and Amano (2012), who attribute the slowdown in labor quality improvement after 2005 to the sharp rise in low-skilled foreign workers. A Monetary Authority of Singapore (2010) study which found that labor productivity growth fell from 3.4% per year in the 1990s to 1.1% from 2000–2009 attributed this to "a sharp slowdown in... capital deepening as the economy utilized relatively more labor inputs

---

[24] For example, the SkillsFuture programme will give every Singaporean aged 25 and above an initial S$500 of SkillsFuture Credit which will be topped up at regular intervals and can be used to pay for approved skill-upgrading courses. See Ministry of Finance (2015).

for production" (p. 72), noting that "there is a large increase in physical labor input in recent years, aided by an inflow of foreign workers" (p. 77).

Crucially, despite economic policy-makers' early recognition that a switch toward intensive growth — or increasing productivity — was necessary, the basic model of state-driven multinational-led export manufacturing did not change, but rather was extended through ever more factor accumulation. Industrial upgrading, for example, required more and more capital investment per unit of output, and of labor, with its attendant need for ever-more-generous tax incentives and other state subsidies. When, as economics predicts, rapid growth at full employment caused the prices of complementary inputs (land and labor) to rise, the policy response was to prevent market adjustments from taking place, by continuing to subsidize scarce land (e.g., in state-provided industrial estates) and allowing greater access to foreign labor which depressed the price of competing local labor. In the many instances where the government back-tracked from its own policy intentions to reduce dependence on foreign labor, increase productivity and encourage high wages, the reason given was the repeated short-run need of foreign investors (and local SMEs which were part of their Singapore supply-chain) for "cost competitiveness" in the face of external demand shocks (global recessions), and increasing international supply-side competi-tion (given the tendency of multinationals to relocate production as comparative advantage shifts), to which the traded goods sector (export-oriented manufacturing) is highly vulnerable.

With each successive policy back-tracking and return to the extensive growth model, diminishing returns worsened and opportunity costs rose — again as economics predicts, making it ever more obvious that "meagre factor productivity growth is the Achilles' heel of the Singapore economy" and there is a pressing need to "reduce the Singapore economy's dependence on capital and labor inputs and strive for slower but more sustainable economic growth through productivity gains instead... As the scope for factor accumulation is exhausted, the long-standing model of extensive growth has run into diminishing returns and needs to be replaced by a new paradigm that achieves intensive growth through making better use of existing resources and technological progress."[25]

This result conforms with research by Paul Romer and others suggesting that "the availability of abundant cheap labor not only discourages investment in productivity but also reduces innovation and increases income inequality" (Economist, 2013) The recent large-scale employment of foreign workers in the UK (roughly a third of the increase in employment since 2010) resulted in higher GDP growth than in its European neighbors, but with much lower productivity (20% below French levels) and wages (a third lower), though company profits have soared. "When people are

---

[25] Choy (2012), p. 5. See also Choy (2010).

cheap, firms would rather hire than invest in machines or technology. So productivity is held down" (Economist, 2015).

In Singapore in the end it was political and social constraints, rather than economic inefficiency and unsustainability of the extensive growth model, which led to the most recent and concerted attempt to pursue intensive growth. The sharp increase in the foreign worker population from 2006 was associated with rising housing, healthcare and transportation costs and congestion, and increased "social unease" among Singaporeans at a time when median and lower-end wages were stagnating, and income inequality increasing. This contributed to opposition party electoral and parliamentary gains in the 2011 general election (and subsequent by-elections). Various surveys since then have shown that a very high proportion of Singaporeans ("nearly 9 in 10") believe that the number of foreign workers should be reduced (Wong, 2013), and this proportion has remained high despite the government's policy response to tighten (but not reduce) inflows.[26]

In February 2012, Deputy Prime Minister and Finance Minister Tharman Shanmu-garatnam said, "We have to reduce our dependence on foreign labor, and do much more to build an economy driven by higher skills, innovation and productivity."[27] The absolute number of foreign workers is still being allowed to increase, albeit at a slower rate. This change has imposed hardship on employers, particularly local SMEs which are still struggling to also cope with high commercial rents due to soaring property market values since 2009 (so far only slightly dampened by macro-prudential "cooling measures"). The 8.7% fall in the revenue of the top 1,000 SMEs in 2014 was blamed on difficulties hiring labor and higher wage costs.[28] At the same time, unemployment fell to 1.9% in December 2014, with job vacancies rising to their highest levels in six years, 57.2% of them being in low-skilled jobs such as cleaners, waiters, shop assistants and security guards. Employers themselves cite low pay, unattractive work hours and the physically strenuous nature of work for their difficulty finding locals to fill such jobs, which at a range of S$1,000–S$1,741 per month do not pay enough to cover the high cost of living in Singapore.[29] In 2012, rejecting calls to establish a minimum wage, the government

---

[26] For example, brokerage and investment group CLSA's latest survey of life in Singapore showed that "83% of respondents (believe) there are too many foreigners in Singapore. This view is largely affected by the sight of too much congestion (35%), job losses (20%) and higher costs of living (19%). Only 9% of respondents believe foreigners should be allowed to work in white-collar jobs. Moreover, there is a surprisingly high correlation between positive views of the transport sector and positive opinions of foreigners." The same survey found that 41% of respondents, and 52% of those under the age of 30, said their primary financial concern was the rising costs of living (Singapore Business, 2015).

[27] Quoted in Mahtani and Raghuvanshi (2012).

[28] Lim (2015a) citing the 2014 SME Development Survey by DP Information Group.

[29] Ministry of Manpower (2015a,b); Cabuyao (2015).

instead introduced a progressive wage model to help employers upgrade and raise the wages of lowly-paid workers like security guards and cleaners: this approach has so far had little impact, and it is not clear that productivity in such jobs results from labor skills rather than complementary equipment (capital) and efficient management and operations processes (human capital).[30]

The Ministry of Trade and Industry study (2014) found that domestically-oriented sectors lagged behind export-oriented sectors in productivity gains, and said that the shift of workers to less productive but employment-intensive sectors like food and beverages and construction accounts for the disappointing labor productivity performance of the economy.

But these sectors[31] are not as labor-intensive in other high-income economies as they are in Singapore, suggesting that it is the distortion of relative factors prices which is responsible for their excess demand for low-skilled, low-wage labor. Employers who can "increase output more readily and cheaply by recruiting foreign workers, particularly from lower-income countries, than by investing in capital-labor substitution and upgrading the skills of the domestic labor force" may be expected to do so since "this is an entirely rational decision for profit-maximizing private enterprises" (Lim, 2014a, p. 32). Wage subsidies paid to employers, like the 2012–2015 Wage Credit Scheme (since extended to 2017), may reduce the effectiveness of incentives provided by automation subsidies like the productivity innovation credit to invest in capital-labor substitution and more efficient management and operations processes. Employers may also assume, based on the record of the past four decades, that the government may yield to business pressures to delay, reduce or reverse the tightening of foreign labor inflows: the 2015 Budget already defers increases in foreign worker levies for S-Pass and work permit holders, except for those in manufacturing and construction (the latter the one sector where the net inflow of foreign workers has not slowed).[32]

Besides employers, Singapore consumers, both local and foreign, may have "got used to" what may be called a First World lifestyle facilitated by Third World wages

---

[30] In economic terms, the Progressive Wage Model seeks to lift wages by raising the demand curve for labor, but the wage may still be depressed if the supply curve of labor is not reduced. A minimum wage would simply impose a wage that might be above (employment-reducing) or below (ineffective) the market-clearing wage determined by the demand and supply curves of labor for particular occupations. In the Singapore case, in low-skill occupations the supply curve (heavily influenced by foreign labor imports) is more likely to dominate the demand curve in setting the wage.

[31] Note that given Singapore's extremely open economy, many "domestic" services are in fact provided for foreign customers, including companies, workers and the large quantum of temporary foreign residents and visitors. "Services" in Singapore also include high value-added export-oriented sectors like finance, information and communications technology, healthcare and education.

[32] For details on the 2015 Budget measures, see Ministry of Finance (2015).

and labor conditions in the household, retail and food sectors, developing consumption habits and tastes very different from those prevailing in other high-income societies where businesses and consumers have adjusted to the relative scarcity of low-skilled service workers. For their part, Singapore workers may also shun "low-skilled" jobs not only because wages are too low (the most important, and economically rational, response), but also because of their association with low-wage temporary foreign workers willing and able to tolerate poor working and living conditions that would be unacceptable to locals in other rich countries, and the low social status accorded to such occupations — ironically perhaps partly because of decades of a public policy rhetoric promoting "skills upgrading" to "higher value" jobs associated with higher levels of formal education. Thus, attitudinal changes on the part of consumers and workers may be required in addition to higher wages from employers.[33]

Productivity growth is necessary for real incomes to rise, in any economy. Nomura and Amano (2012) show that Singapore's labor quality growth (in the past, chiefly from rising educational attainment) has declined with the sharp rise in low-skilled foreign workers. Given the ageing population (which limits further improvement in labor quality), they conclude that the prospects for future productivity growth are "bleak", and consequently that Singapore's potential annual GDP growth from 2010–2030 will be around 2%, rising to 3% if TFP growth can be increased.[34] This rate is below the Economic Strategies Committee's (Ministry of Trade and Industry, 2010) projection of 3% to 5% GDP growth, which is very high for a developed economy. In January 2015, Prime Minister Lee Hsien Loong announced that 2% to 3% growth is more likely. With slower growth, greater volatility, stagnant lower-quartile wages and increased income and wealth inequality, the government has recently acceded to social pressures to provide more targeted income support and transfers to the low-income and elderly.[35]

---

[33] For consumers, some such changes include getting used to self-service and clearing up after oneself in eating places, keeping public toilets clean and refraining from littering — habits that in the past were inculcated by vigorous promotional campaigns and fines. For society as a whole it requires letting go of the stigma attached to "manual labor" and "blue-collar" work — which higher wages would help encourage. Singapore has a remarkable 70,000 (mostly foreign) cleaners, whereas Taipei has 5,000, "many of them graduates" (Chang, 2015).

[34] Note that Nomura and Amano's "Business-as-usual" scenario assumes a total fertility rate of 1.24 and annual immigration of 30,000, following a 2011 Institute of Policy Studies scenario. For higher growth in labor quality and average labor productivity, "the low-skilled non-resident workers are required to decrease".

[35] For example, the 2015 Budget contains new targeted measures to help individuals and households, including more financial support for lifelong learning, an income supplement for lower-income Singaporeans and higher CPF contributions for older workers. These follow on earlier wage supplements for low-wage workers, and healthcare subsidies for the elderly. To cover the costs of the 2015 budget

5. Singapore's Development Model Reconsidered

Singapore's economic strategy at independence entrenched its state-driven, foreign-led, export-oriented development model, with a heavy emphasis on manufacturing, well beyond its transition from a developing to a mature high-income economy. High GDP growth has been maintained for over four decades largely through the addition of ever-increasing amounts of capital, labor and skills, much of it foreign, to an initially very small territory and population. This model of extensive growth has been extremely successful in quickly achieving full employment and raising per capita income to one of the world's highest. These results have been achieved with one of the world's highest savings rates and lowest consumption and wage shares of GDP (about 40% each), even compared with other export-led Asian economies (Lim, 2010). Singapore differs in several key respects: much more interventionist state industrial and social policy; much more dependence on foreign capital, labor and talent; and the corresponding relative weakness of domestic private enterprise — which given the small local market and limited resources, has probably been "crowded out" by the large state-linked and multinational sectors in both product and factor markets.

There are several ways in which this development model may have impacted Singapore's labor market and productivity record. Policies to attract and retain internationally mobile foreign manufacturing investments which would otherwise consolidate production in fewer, larger market locations would include liberal visa rules enabling them to bring to Singapore skills and talent from other parts of their global operations. This speeds up set up time, and maximizes MNC employers' human resource allocation flexibility in increasingly dynamic and uncertain global market and technological environments. The more technologically sophisticated their Singapore operations, the less likely MNCs will be to find locals qualified for very specific narrow-skilled niche positions, which also have a long (and thus expensive) training period. Home- and third-country nationals among MNCs' global employee base are unlikely to be interested in staying permanently in Singapore, but will move wherever their personal or corporate career trajectories take them. The dominance of foreigners in the highly-skilled and managerial ranks of MNC subsidiaries may discourage qualified Singaporeans from working for them due to perceptions of a "glass ceiling", leading to even more dependence on "foreign talent". The fact that "big-ticket foreign investments" have been falling "since Singapore tightened its manpower policies and lost its attraction for companies that depend on cheap foreign labor" (Chia, 2015) confirms that many foreign investments were attracted to Singapore because of the ease of employing foreign labor, rather than

deficit (a rare event in Singapore's fiscal history outside of deep recessions) the top rate of income tax is being raised from 20% to 22%, and more resources will be drawn from the (extremely large) foreign reserves.

any intrinsic locational advantages. That the EDB expects "a sharp reduction in the number of skilled jobs created, lower fixed asset investment, and a decline in business expenditure... in line with the Government's restructuring exercise to raise productivity and reduce reliance on foreign workers" (Teng, 2015) also indicates that foreign investors attracted by capital subsidies had been creating skilled jobs mainly for foreigners.

Foreign manufacturers may also be attracted by a local supply chain (including of services) of SMEs which may be more labor-intensive and thus dependent on the import of low- and medium-skill foreign labor, most of whom would not be candidates for permanent residence due to Singapore's own citizenship rules favoring more highly-educated immigrants. SMEs appear to be the most reliant on the low costs of foreign labor for their competitiveness, and its ready availability may discourage them from undertaking the difficult task of restructuring to increase productivity. As Hoon (2013) noted, "The ready access to the supply of foreign workers kept labor costs low while the increase in value-add per worker boosted the profitability of manufacturing firms. This boost to profits very likely benefited both multinational corporations as well as small and medium-sized enterprises." The high (over 50%) capital share of national income, which is very lightly taxed[36] in addition to being heavily subsidized, also suggests that the business sector is highly profitable even though its productivity may be low.

At all skill levels, foreigners from now fast-growing Asian developing countries like China and India may eventually find more preferred employment in their countries of origin, after gaining education and/or relevant work experience in Singapore. Whatever its cause, high labor turnover reduces worker experience and productivity, while increasing employer costs through the need for frequent recruitment and training. The vulnerability to external demand shocks of export-oriented industry in general, and of Singapore's targeted high-tech clusters of electronics, pharmaceuticals and chemicals, in particular, have greatly increased the economy's volatility since the late 1990s (Choy, 2010; Tan, 2015).[37] Volatility itself reduces productivity — from increased labor turnover and the associated loss of skills from worker redundancies or underemployment ("labor hoarding") in downturns, and by discouraging both workers and employers from investing in skills training. The flexibility afforded by the ease of "turning on and off the tap" of foreign worker

---

[36] Asher *et al.* (2015).

[37] Choy notes "While the blame for all this (volatility) cannot be laid on the industrial upgrading measures per se... it is undeniable that the government's pursuit of high growth through restructuring had inadvertently exposed the Singapore economy to new vulnerabilities in the international economy. Ironically too, the SEP (Strategic Economic Plan) had already identified in 1991 the competitive and volatile electronics industry to be a source of vulnerability; as it turned out, the planners' worse fears were confirmed" (Choy, 2010, p. 133).

supply during the labor-intensive era becomes a liability in capital- and skill-intensive sectors when foreign labor mobility in cyclical downturns leads to the shedding of skilled labor which never returns.

In this development model, it is state industrial policy which has pushed capital investment for growth, and targeted particular sectors for ever more generous and capital-and skill-based investment incentives, without which Singapore would not be a competitive location for such investments. At the same time, complementary sectors such as construction (residential, commercial and industrial, some of it under-taken by GLCs), retail, personal services and food-and-beverages were allowed to import low-wage low-skilled foreign labor, thus adding to the subsidies already enjoyed by high-tech industrial (and high-value services) enterprises employing a large number of foreigners with highly specialized skills.

Social policy — and the need for it — have been distorted by this development model. On the one hand, macroeconomic stabilization policies have been con-strained. "The instruments most often deployed in recessions were direct cuts in employers' CPF contributions and reductions in government-controlled fees, charges and rentals. However, econometric research suggests that such measures entail painful adjustments for workers and are inefficacious since export demand is not too responsive to them" (Choy, 2010, p. 134). On the other hand, "low-skilled foreign workers... depress earnings at the lower end of the nominal wage scale because of their low productivity, thus impacting on income distribution adversely. Worse, relying on them indefinitely implies that Singapore's economic progress would still be achieved primarily by increases in labor inputs rather than productiv-ity improvements... a slower pace of economic growth might not be a bad thing if it is achieved through productivity gains and is accompanied by less macroeconomic volatility" (Choy, 2010, p. 135).

Lim (2014) argues that:

> Higher wages would encourage firms to improve productivity and attract more Sin-gaporeans into particular jobs, giving both employers and employees incentive to invest in upgraded skills (since there will be a higher income payoff). Businesses that cannot afford the higher wages would exit, releasing manpower for the businesses that remain. A reduction in demand would alleviate any labor shortage. Fewer for-eign workers would also ease pressures on the housing market and on commercial rents, so businesses may benefit from more moderate rent hikes even as they pay out higher wages. Reduced foreign capital inflows to purchase property, and other invest-ments, would mitigate asset inflation and appreciation of the Singapore dollar, thus helping to maintain cost competitiveness. Higher wages with higher productivity and moderating rents do not necessarily mean higher costs. But if they do, these are costs Singapore's consumers will have to pay. As consumers are also workers, their real incomes may increase with higher salaries, lower rents, and mortgage payments. If

those enjoying higher wages are Singaporeans (rather than foreigners, who typically have higher savings rates and remittance outflows), the multiplier impact of their local spending will be greater. (Lim, 2014, p. 35)

Unwinding Singapore's decades of dependence on foreign labor will affect various groups differently. Some Singaporeans (e.g., business or household employers of low wage labor, property owners — including of HDB flats — and rentiers, shareholders of property companies or REITs, including GLCs) will "lose" even as others (lower-wage workers, first-time home-buyers and renters, more innovative and competitive businesses) gain. The long-established integration of industrial and social policy, while effective in "creating competitiveness" and maintaining the profitability of business (especially for MNCs and GLCs), has created policy inter-connections which are difficult to disentangle one from another. Thus, CPF employer contributions provided for wage flexibility, and CPF savings enabled a very high degree of home-ownership, including of publicly-provided HDB flats. But today nearly half of Singaporeans lack sufficient savings at retirement, the high share of income spent on housing reduces consumption in other sectors and limits the stabilizing effect of domestic demand (Abeysinghe and Choy, 2004; Abeysinghe and Gu, 2011), and the bottom quartile of wage-earners finds it increasingly hard to make ends meet,[38] even as some GLCs make record profits (including from property) and Singapore's world-leading sovereign wealth funds Temasek and the Government of Singapore Investment Corporation (GIC) accumulate valuable assets around the world.

This time the government appears more likely to follow through on slowing (though not stopping) the influx of foreign labor and finally staying the course on productivity growth. It is accepting a more realistic and sustainable lower GDP growth target, and is being more selective in attracting foreign investments (Chia, 2015; Teng, 2015). However Budget 2015 is delaying increases in foreign worker levies, and continuing with state-directed productivity schemes and the practice of state industrial targeting — this time the "new growth clusters" of "advanced manufacturing, applied health sciences, smart and sustainable urban solutions, logistics and aerospace, Asian and global financial services", rather than relying on market forces to reallocate resources.[39] At the same time, the government is increasing its provisions for social security and income support through budget transfers and social subsidies, rather than through higher market wages.

---

[38] Low and Vadaketh (2014) discuss the social policy challenges and alternatives facing Singapore today

[39] Note that increased government expenditure on inputs does not necessarily result in increased output: for example, INSEAD's Global Innovation Index, ranks Singapore No. 1 in Overall Innovation Input each year from 2011 to 2014, but it is only No. 17 in Overall Innovation Output in 2011, declining to No. 25 in 2014, and No. 94 in Innovation Efficiency in 2011, declining to No. 110 in 2014. www.globalinnovationindex.org.

6. Conclusion: Looking Ahead

Singapore's state-driven, foreign-led, export-oriented development model since independence has delivered high GDP growth for over four decades primarily through factor accumulation — chiefly foreign manufacturing investment, high domestic savings, and vast inputs of foreign skilled and unskilled labor. This high-growth achievement, and a very high share for profits in GDP, has occurred at the expense of productivity growth, and more recently, of citizens' social welfare.[40] Singapore economists have long called for a change in this model, recommending a refocus away from subsidized manufacturing for a global market toward market-based services for the Asian and Southeast Asian region, in line with Singapore's unique competitive advantage as a city-state in a fast-growing geography.

We argued in Pang and Lim (1981) that "Singapore has a much stronger international competitive advantage in the export of services — banking, finance, commercial services, transportation and telecommunications — based on its long experience and large human and capital investment in these sectors. Another asset is its location in a rapidly growing regional economy of which it is the service hub. The service sector is intrinsically labor-intensive, and will become more skill-intensive as it upgrades into high-value services... even in export manufacturing industries, Singapore's competitiveness is shifting toward service-oriented activities such as regional warehousing, purchasing, servicing and research and development. Both commercial and industrial services have a demand for skilled professionals that can't be supplied adequately from domestic sources. And, as the Singapore population grows more affluent, it will consume more labor-intensive social and personal services than goods, further increasing the domestic demand for labor. One solution to the long-range problems of labor shortage is to concentrate Singapore's limited domestic resources in the one area in which it has the greatest competitive advantage — the supply of services, including industrial-based services. This would mean the phasing out of production-oriented manufacturing in which Singapore's potential advantage on a global basis is problematic. Unskilled labor would be released for the non-traded services sector, and skilled labor would be available for professional jobs in the highly competitive traded services sector. Reliance on both unskilled and skilled foreign labor would be reduced, and Singapore's historic complementary role to countries in the region would be enhanced." (Pang and

---

[40] The welfare of low-skilled foreign labor in Singapore has also been a matter of international as well as domestic concern, highlighted by spectacular events like the 2012 illegal strike by bus drivers from China, and the 2013 "Little India" riots, as well as longstanding incidents of abuse of foreign domestic workers from the Philippines, Indonesia and elsewhere. It is beyond the scope of this chapter to consider this aspect of the foreign labor situation, on which see, for example, Noorashikin Abdul Rahman (2010) and Low (2015a, b).

Lim, 1981) The Report of the Economic Committee (Ministry of Trade and Industry, 1986) made similar recommendations, saying that Singapore should "move beyond our being a production base, to being an international total business centre... Services account for an increasing share of our GDP, and our service exports have been growing quickly. Scope for growth is still huge."

Choy (2010) points out that services did indeed grow from 60% of output and 67% of employment in 1990 to 63% of output and 77% of employment by 2005, as is typical of all high-income countries. He also notes that the "service economy is less risky... service industries are less dependent on foreign capital and tend to be influenced to a smaller extent by business cycles... a heterogeneous and diversified service sector offers the prospect that monetary policy will be a potent tool for mitigating economic fluctuations, as a result of the greater sensitivity of tradable services to exchange rate movements. Since exportable services have much higher domestic value-added and lower import content compared with manufactured goods... Servicing the needs of the burgeoning middle classes in China and India could easily add a percentage point or two to Singapore's potential growth rate. One should also not neglect to mention the untapped potential of domestically-oriented service industries catering to a richer and ever-growing local population... service industries have the virtue of being relatively more labor-intensive, thus generating more employment and helping to keep both structural and cyclical unemployment at bay" (Choy, 2010, pp. 136–137).

Lim (2015b) argues that the prospects for continued high-tech manufacturing for export in Singapore are poor, given "post-industrial" trends in global market demand and supply, technological change and multinational corporate strategies which "add up to slower growth in output, a lower ratio of goods to services in output, a lower ratio of manufacturing to services value-added in goods, a greater localization of goods and services production, and a much lower employment to output ratio" as well as "spreading global norms like the reduced acceptability of tax-avoidance incentives for multinationals, a major feature of Singapore's attractiveness to foreign investors." But she adds that "The good news is that services for our regional neighborhood are more location-specific and scalable, and less capital- and energy-intensive, than manufacturing for distant markets, less reliant on rare specific technical skills unlikely to be found in adequate scale among our small population, and more open to small entrepreneurs with different levels of formal education, providing a channel for employment creation, upward mobility and reduced inequality (through SME ownership and the capital returns from operating in regional markets)."

Budget 2015 (Ministry of Finance, 2015), like numerous previous budgets and government competitiveness and strategic reports, notes that "Services have also emerged as a major engine of enterprise and jobs", praises the international activities of "our homegrown enterprises" and offers many incentives to develop the capabilities of SMEs and encourage them to go abroad.[41] Singapore has not developed a large cadre of strong local enterprises (outside of the finance, property and GLC sectors) that can venture and compete outside the home country, as South Korea, Hong Kong, Taiwan and even Malaysia and China have. One reason for this could be the lack of incentive in an economy dominated by the state and MNCs for both capital and local talent to undertake the risks of private entrepreneurship. While Singapore's state economic planners have long recognized the limitations of their development model, and from time to time have made determined efforts to transform the economy in other directions, this had mostly been with the addition of new sectors, programs and incentives. To date there has not been any serious attempt to reduce or just stabilize manufacturing or foreign investment, or to re-size the state sector, without which the chronic problem of excess demand for both skilled and unskilled labor, including managers/entrepreneurs and bureaucrats/professionals, cannot be resolved.

Among other Asian countries, even South Korea — which like Singapore has a high ratio of manufacturing to GDP, but with a much larger domestic market, more abundant labor and skills, and strong domestic enterprises which have been successfully globalizing — now "hopes to reduce its heavy dependence on exports for economic growth. Economists see the process as essential for South Korea's long-term prospects... policy-makers in Seoul fret that Korean exports could lose steam in increasingly volatile overseas markets... The government has called for deregulation in six "promising" services industries: health care, tourism, education, finance, logistics and software development" (Jun, 2015).

China, a much larger and lower-income Asian economy that followed a similar state-dominated, high-savings, high-growth, investment-heavy, export-led development model with large foreign participation, has been seeking for some years now to "rebalance" toward "an economy driven by consumers and entrepreneurial vigor and job creation by.innovative small businesses", at a lower growth rate. In unveiling the country's 2015 annual budget, Prime Minister Le Keqiang said:

> The government should be bold in imposing reform on itself so as to leave ample space for the market. The growth in investment in factories, infrastructure and other fixed assets is still running 25% higher than growth in consumption. That means wealth is being transferred from households to the government, rather than the other way around, many economists said, leaving less in consumer pockets. Standing in the

---

[41] Note that following the 1991 Strategic Economic Plan, an official campaign was launched to grow a "second wing" for the economy by encouraging local enterprises to invest in neighboring countries. Several GLCs did do so, with some success, but progress so far has been insufficient to "create a second Singapore outside Singapore" as Teh (2014) points out other developed countries have done through outward investments by their own home-grown multinationals.

way are state enterprises... as well as an extensive bureaucracy that benefits from the government's large sway. Premier Li cited "systemic, institutional and structural problems," calling them "tigers in the road" holding up development."... Key to spurring consumption is directing more money toward pensions, health insurance, unemployment benefits and other social transfers, encouraging citizens to consume more and feel more secure. (Magnier, 2015)

Singapore faces similar challenges. Speculating on why the government has so far clung to its state-dependent, foreign-oriented development model "rather than considering potential alternative market-determined, locally-oriented and private enterprise-led models of post-industrial development," Lim and Lee (2010) suggest that, harking back to the country's reluctant birth, "being important to foreign capital, governments, and "talent" might provide some assurance of security against potential hostile neighbors." Other reasons they suggest include: bureaucratic inertia, self-interest, and incentives tied to delivering top-line GDP growth leading to "growth fetishism" and thus "preference for the easiest route to growth, which is through the addition of inputs of foreign capital, labor and skills. Singapore's continued rapid GDP growth in the post-industrial era has thus been bought at the price of expanding and entrenching the economic as well as political dominance of a one-party state that maintains its power in part by brokering the increased and even privileged participation of foreign capital, talent, and labor in the "local" economy. Foreigners beholden to the state for its beneficence and their own presence are unlikely to challenge its authority, in the way that an independent, globally competitive and non-state-dependent domestic entrepreneurial class — still weak and largely absent in Singapore — might." (Lim and Lee, 2010, pp. 154–155).

But Singapore will continue to rely on foreign labor and especially foreign talent and skills, since it "can certainly do with more managers and professionals in view of its ambition to be a dynamic and cosmopolitan city supplying premium services to the region and the world." (Choy, 2010, p. 135). The number and proportions should be reduced, focusing on skilled immigrants who are likely to settle permanently in the city-state and assimilate into its society, not on short-term low-skilled workers as has been the case so far. At the same time, efforts should continue to maximize the labor force participation of female and elderly workers, including by removing existing gender and age discriminations, and by improved housing, transport, other social amenities, and family-friendly infrastructure and employment practices. Above all, the country should continue to invest in expanding and diversifying the education, skills, opportunities and incomes of all its citizens, not merely to increase productivity and economic growth, but so that all may benefit from living in one of the world's richest nations. It should cease its rigid adherence to persistently large public sector surpluses (which amount to transfers from households to the state) and ideological aversion to properly-structured social insurance,[42] which would lift low domestic consumption, reduce extreme inequality, facilitate macroeconomic stabilization, promote the development of the services sector, and even encourage entrepreneurship by reducing risk aversion.[43]

The city-states of the past were regional in their economic orientation (Pang and Lim, 1982b), and a regional focus in line with that of old city-states and our own economic history,[44] has a chance of enabling Singapore to grow sustainably, if slowly, in the longer run. The very success of the "global city" model in earlier decades is now limited by the lack of land and people, causing rising costs, economic inefficiencies, infrastructure bottlenecks, growing income disparities and social tensions that, if not contained, could compromise the prosperity, stability and identity of the nation-state, and its ability to meet the needs and aspirations of its citizens. There are inherent tensions between being a global city and a nation state. From a labor market perspective, a global city is characterized by two-way labor mobility, especially of the highly-skilled, which would include Singaporeans lacking economic and cultural roots and interests in Southeast Asia being readily pulled or pushed to leave the nation-state for more attractive career opportunities and lifestyles in distant developed locations.[45]

References

Abeysinghe, T and KM Choy (2004). The aggregate consumption puzzle in Singapore. *Journal of Asian Economics*, 15(3), 563–578.

Abeysinghe, T and J Gu (2011). Lifetime income and housing affordability in Singapore. *Urban Studies*, 48(9), 1875–1891.

---

[42] Note that the 17% share of government expenditure in Singapore today is below what it was in the 1990s (over 20%), and much lower than the OECD average of 34%.

[43] In the "start-up nation" of the U.S., for example, taking a second mortgage on one's home is a very common means by which individuals fund entrepreneurial ventures, and housing also consumes a much smaller share of income, savings and wealth than it does in Singapore.

[44] See Lee (2015b).

[45] For example, Hooi (2012) reports on a Mindshare survey showing that 56% of Singaporeans "would like to emigrate", 65% did not believe they would be able to retire comfortably in Singapore, 73% thought that public housing prices are "getting out of hand", 73% agreed that "I should not be spending my entire working life paying off my housing loan", 72% said they "could not afford to get sick due to high medical costs", and 69% said that "there are too many foreign workers taking up job opportunities in our society today." According to the World Bank, there are 300,000 Singaporeans living and working abroad (about 9% of the total native population, although government figures put the number at 200,000 or 6%, a third of whom left in the last 10 years), with Malaysia the top destination, followed by Australia, the UK and USA, all countries with lower per capita incomes than Singapore.

Asher, MG, AS Bali and YK Chang (2015). Public financial management in Singapore: Key characteristics and prospects. A fifty-year retrospective on Singapore's economy. *Singapore Economic Review*, 60(3). DOI: 10.1142/S0217590815500320.

Au Yong, H (2014). Singapore's Productivity Challenge, Part 1-3. Available at http://lkyspp. nus.edu.sg/wp-content/uploads/2014/05/Productivity-challenges-in-Singapore-Part-1. pdf; http:// lkyspp.nus.edu. sg/wp-content/uploads/2014/08/Productivity-challenges-in-Singapore-Part-2.pdf; http://lkyspp.nus.edu.sg/wp-content/uploads/2014/11/Productivity-challenges-in-Singapore-Part-3.pdf.

Basu, R (2015). Make foreigners, PRs count in income data. *The Straits Times*, 26 February.

Cabuyao, P (2015). The Singapore Jobs Market: Data vs Discontent. RSIS Commentary No. 002/ 2015, 3 February. Rajaratnam School of International Studies, Nanyang Technological University, Singapore.

Chang, R (2015). Liak Teng Kit: 5 million people, 70,000 cleaners... that's ridiculous. *The Straits Times*, 16 February.

Chia, SY (2011). Foreign Labour in Singapore: Trends, Policies, Impacts and Challenges. Discussion Paper Series No. 2011-24. Philippine Institute for Development Studies. December.

Chia, YM (2015). Investments down as s'pore chases quality. *The Straits Times*, 3 February.

Choy, KM (2010). Singapore's changing economic model. In *Management of Success: Singapore Revisited*, T Chong (ed.). Singapore: Institute of Southeast Asian Studies.

Choy, KM (ed.) (2012). Introduction. In *Studies on the Singapore Economy*. Singapore: World Scientific.

Economist (2013). Has the Ideas Machine Broken Down? 12 January.

Economist (2015). The Economy and Productivity: Bargain Basement. 14 March.

Hooi, J (2012). Singapore's Emigration Conundrum. Business Times, 6 October.

Hoon, HT (2013). The future of wages in Singapore. *The Straits Times*, 8 February.

Huang, S and BSA Yeoh (2003). The difference gender makes: State policy and contract migrant workers in Singapore. *Asia and Pacific Migration Journal*, 12(1–2), 75–98.

Huff, WG (1999). Singapore's economic development: Four lessons and some doubts. *Oxford Development Studies*, 27(1), 33–55.

Hui WT and R Toh (2014). *Growth with Equity in Singapore: Challenges and Prospects*. Conditions of Work and Employment Series No. 48. Geneva, Switzerland: International Labour Office.

Jun, K (2015). Seoul Swallows Tough Medicine for Economy. Wall Street Journal, 4 March.

Krugman, P (1994). The myth of Asia's miracle. *Foreign Affairs*, 73(6), 62–78.

Lee, M (2015). Top SMEs' revenue "hit by labour woes". *The Straits Times*, 30 January.

Lee, SA (2015). Governance and economic change in Singapore. *Singapore Economic Review*, 60(3). DOI: 10.1142/S0217590815500289.

Lim, J (2015). Fresh ingredients needed to fix eatery troubles. *The Straits Times*, 19 February.

Lim, LYC (1983). Singapore's success: The myth of the free market economy. *Asian Survey*, 23(6), 752–764.

Lim, LYC (1987). The state and private capital in Singapore's economic development. *Political Economy, Studies in the Surplus Approach*, 3(2), 201–222.

Lim, LYC (1989). Social welfare. In *Management of Success: The Moulding of Modern Singapore*, KS Sandhu and P Wheatley (eds.). Singapore: Institute of Southeast Asian Studies.

Lim, LYC (2010). Rebalancing in East Asia. In *Rebalancing the Global Economy: A Primer for Policymaking*, S Claessens, S Evenett and B Hoekman (eds.). London: Centre for Economic Policy-Making.

Lim, L (2014). How land and people fit together in Singapore's economy. In *Hard Choices: Challenging the Singapore Consensus*, D Low and ST Vadaketh (eds.). Singapore: NUS Press.

Lim, LYC (2015a). Beyond gender: The impact of age, ethnicity, nationality and economic growth on women in the Singapore economy. *Singapore Economic Review*, 60(2). DOI: 10.1142/ S0217590815500204.

Lim, LYC (2015b). Beyond the "global city" paradigm. In *Singapore Perspectives 2015: Choices*, S Hoe and C Soon (eds.). Singapore: World Scientific for the Institute of Policy Studies.

Lim, LYC and SA Lee (2010). Globalizing state, disappearing nation: The impact of foreign participation in the Singapore economy. In *Management of Success: Singapore Revisited*, T Chong (ed.). Singapore: Institute of Southeast Asian Studies.

Lim, L, EF Pang and R Findlay (1993). Singapore. In *Five Small Open Economies*, R Findlay and S Wellisz (eds.). New York: Oxford University Press for the World Bank.

Low, D (2015a). Focus on welfare, not wages, of foreign workers. *The Straits Times*, 23 January.

Low, D (2015b). Foreign worker issues: Rethinking assumptions. *The Straits Times*, 10 February.

Low, D and ST Vadaketh (2014). *Hard Choices: Challenging the Singapore Consensus*. Singapore: NUS Press.

Magnier, M (2015). China Chooses a Long, Slow Road to Reform. *Wall Street Journal*, 5 March.

Mahtani, S and G Raghuvanshi (2012). Singapore Restricts Foreigners. *Wall Street Journal*, 10 July. Ministry of Finance, Singapore (2015). Singapore Budget 2015. Available at www. singapor-ebudget.gov.sg.

Ministry of Manpower, Singapore (2014). Comprehensive Labour Force Survey. Available at http://stats.mom.gov.sg/Pages/Labour-Force-Summary-Table.aspx.

Ministry of Manpower, Singapore (2015a). Employment Situation 2014, 30 January.

Ministry of Manpower, Singapore (2015b). Job Vacancies 2014, 27 January.

Ministry of Trade and Industry, Singapore (1986). Report of the Economic Committee. Ministry of Trade and Industry, Singapore (2010). Report of the Economic Strategies Committee. Available at www.mti.gov.sg.

Ministry of Trade and Industry, Singapore (2014). Drivers of Labour Productivity Growth Trends in Singapore. Available at http://www.mti.gov.sg/ResearchRoom/SiteAssets/Pages/ Economic-Survey-of-Singapore-2014/FA_ AES2014.pdf.

Monetary Authority of Singapore (2010). Sources of Singapore's economic growth 1990–2009. *Macroeconomic Review*, 9(1), 66–81.

Nomura, K and T Amano (2012). Labor productivity and quality change in Singapore: Achievements in 1974–2011 and prospects for the next two decades. KIEO Discussion Paper No. 129 (September). Available at http://www.sanken.keio.ac.jp/publication/ KEO-dp/129/KEO-DP129. pdf.

Noorashikin Abdul Rahman (2010). Managing labour flows: Foreign talent, foreign workers and domestic help. In *Management of Success: Singapore Revisited*, T Chong (ed.). Singapore:Institute of Southeast Asian Studies.

Pang, EF (1975). Growth, inequality and race in Singapore. *International Labour Review*, 111(1), 15–28.

Pang, EF (1977). Capitalising on labour. *Singapore Business*, 1(9), 14–16.

Pang, EF (1988). Development strategies and labour market changes in Singapore. In *Labour Market Developments and Structural Change: The Experience of ASEAN and Australia*, EF Pang (ed.), pp. 195–242. Singapore University Press.

Pang, EF (1994). An eclectic approach to turning points in migration. *Asian and Pacific Migration Journal*, 3(1), 81–92.

Pang, EF and L Lim (1981). Singapore's Foreign Workers: Are They Worth the Cost? *Asian Wall Street Journal*, August 4.

Pang, EF and L Lim (1982a). Foreign labor and economic development in Singapore. *International Migration Review*, 16(3), 548–576.

Pang EF and L Lim (1982b). Political Economy of a City-State. Singapore Business Yearbook 1982, pp. 7, 13–33.

Pang, EF and PL Quek (1980). Is the national wages council necessary to Singapore's economic progress? *ASEAN Business Quarterly*, 4(3), 35–37.

Png, I (2015). PIC: move from subsidy to root cause. *The Straits Times*, 7 February.

Tan, KY (2015). Managing Singapore's globalization and its discontents: A long-term perspective. In *Singapore Perspectives 2015: Choices*, S Hoe and C Soon (eds.). Singapore: World Scientific for the Institute of Policy Studies.

Tay, K (2015). More redundancies in 2013 Due to Restructuring. Business Times, 31 January.

Teh, KP (2014). Globalisation and Singapore's Discontent. Talk given at the Asia Pacific Real Estate Association (APREA) Chairman/CEO Series, 5 September.

Teng, A (2015). Fewer Skilled Jobs Expected to be Created This Year. Today, 3 February.

Toh, MH and L Low (1990). *An Economic Framework of Singapore: Principles and Issues.* Singapore: Mc-Graw-Hill.

Tsao, Y (1982). Growth and Productivity in Singapore: A Supply Side Analysis. Ph.D. Dissertation in Economics, Harvard University.

Tsao, Y (1985). Growth without productivity: Singapore manufacturing in the 1970s. *Journal of Development Economics*, 19(1–2), 25–38.

Vasil, R (1989). Trade unions. In Management of Success: The Moulding of Modern Singapore, KS Sandhu and P Wheatley (eds.). Singapore: Institute of Southeast Asian Studies.

Vu, MK (2011). Sources of Singapore's economic growth, 1965–2008: Trends, patterns and policy implications. *ASEAN Economic Bulletin*, 28(3), 315–336, ISSN: 0217–4472.

Wong, D (1997). Transience and settlement: Singapore's foreign labour policy. *Asia and Pacific Migration Journal*, 6(2), 135–167.

Wong, T (2013). Most support curbs on foreigner inflow. *The Straits Times*, 19 March.

Yap, MT and C Gee (2015). Singapore's demographic transition, the labour force and government policies: A fifty-year retrospective on Singapore's economy. *Singapore Economic Review*, 60(3). DOI: 10.1142/S0217590815500356.

Yeoh, B and W Lin (2012). Rapid Growth in Singapore's Immigrant Population Brings Policy Challenges. Migration Information Source (April). Available at http://www.migrationpolicy.org/ article/rapid-growth-singapores-immigrant-population-brings-policy-challenges.

Young, A (1992). A tale of two cities: Factor accumulation and technical change in Hong Kong and Singapore. *National Bureau of Economic Research (NBER), Macroeconomics Annual 1992.* Cambridge, Massachusetts: MIT Press.

Young, A (1994). The Tyranny of Numbers: Confronting the Statistical Realities of the East Asian Growth Experience. NBER Working Paper 4689 (March).

CHAPTER 8

Globalization and Regionalization: Singapore's Trade and FDI

Chia Siow Yue

The Singapore economy has undergone rapid growth and structural transformation from a Third World laggard to a First World sophisticated and dynamic economy. It has overcome constraints of land and natural resources by adopting free trade and investment strategies and building on its global and regional maritime and air links. However, despite its very high per capita income, Singapore's technological, innovative and entrepreneurial capabilities are not on par with the most advanced economies. High dependence on foreign multinational corporations (MNCs) and government-linked-companies (GLCs) has contributed to the underdevelopment of local private enterprise and innovation. High dependence on "foreign talent" has also contributed to the underdevelopment of local talent. For future sustainable development, Singapore has to succeed as an innovative economy, and the state will have an important role as facilitator of local innovation and enterprise.

1. Introduction

For nearly 150 years since 1819, Singapore was a British colonial trading outpost pursuing a free trade strategy. Since political independence in August 1965 the economy has been government-led, export-led and foreign-investment-led. This economic strategy has resulted in economic growth averaging 7.7% annually in the 1965–2013 period, to reach a per capita GDP of US$55,177 by 2013. Total merchandise and service trade is more than triple the size of GNP, reflecting Singapore's role as a major transhipment center and the high import intensity of its production and consumption. The size of the inward foreign direct investment (FDI) stock and high FDI penetration reflect its role as a global export manufacturing base and regional services hub in finance, trade, transportation and logistics, with foreign multinational corporations (MNCs) playing a crucial role in the country's growth success and economic restructuring. But Singapore has lagged in outward FDI, leading the government to spearhead an outward FDI regionalization drive in 1993. Initially led by government-linked-companies (GLCs) focusing on Asia, outward FDI eventually became global.

The economic success of Singapore has been used by neoclassical economists to support the case for market-led development, with minimal price distortions, openness to international trade, investment and technology flows. On the other hand, revisionists argue that Singapore demonstrates the success of government intervention in the economy to create national competitive advantage through selective industrial policy. As this chapter will show, Singapore is neither, as it mixes free trade and investment policies with strong pro-market government intervention and industrial policy.

This chapter evaluates Singapore's trade and foreign direct investment strategies and their effects over the past five decades. Section 2 briefly introduces the different phases of economic restructuring. Section 3 analyzes Singapore's trade strategy, FTAs and trade patterns. Section 4 analyzes Singapore's inward and outward FDI strategies and patterns. Section 5 concludes.

2. Economic Restructuring of Singapore[1]

2.1. *From Entrepot to Manufacturing in the 1960s*

At political independence in 1965, Singapore faced threats to its traditional economic pillars of entrepot trade and servicing the British military base.[2] The very small domestic market, now separated from Malaysia, and policy lessons from failed import substitution experiments elsewhere, led to the choice of an export-led strategy. Lack of manufacturing expertise, and the government's view that transforming trading entrepreneurs into industrial entrepreneurs capable of marketing internationally would be too slow and uncertain, led to reliance on FDI.[3] This would enable Singapore to access foreign investment capital, technology and managerial expertise, and integrate into MNCs' global production networks and supply chains. The government also decided to play a pro-active role in jumpstarting the economy, resulting in the export-led, FDI-led development strategy being government-led as well.

---

[1] See Chia (2011b) for a detailed analysis.

[2] Entrepot trade was threatened by the rise of competing ports in the region and direct trading policies of neighboring countries. Britain announced it would close down its military base in Singapore as part of withdrawing all its troops east of Suez.

[3] South Korea and Taiwan received huge US aid and protected their domestic markets to nurture domestic enterprise and develop technical and scientific manpower capable of absorbing and adapting licensed foreign technologies. Hong Kong was an entrepot experienced in exporting the manufactures of China and benefited from the influx of Chinese industrial entrepreneurs and capital fleeing communism in China after the late 1940s, helping it make a quick and successful transition from entrepot to manufacturing. Singapore was experienced in exporting the raw materials of Southeast Asia.

2.2. *High-tech Manufacturing and Regional Services Hub from the 1980s*

As labor shortage emerged by the late 1970s, Singapore's industrial strategy evolved towards higher-skill and higher-value added manufacturing and services, responding to changing factor endowments and facilitated by government industrial promotion policies. In 1965, the leading industries were domestic market oriented, in printing and publishing, and food and beverage manufacturing. By the 1980s, the leading industries were increasingly export-oriented and were petroleum refining, transport equipment (mainly marine), and electronic products and components. By the 2000s, the leading industries in value added terms were electronic and optical products, pharmaceutical and biological products, transport equipment (mainly marine) and machinery and equipment (Table 1).

Singapore also grew as a regional services hub, linking its Southeast Asian hinterland to the rest of the world through finance, shipping and air transport activities, based on its competitive advantages of a strategic geographical location; well-developed physical and telecommunications infrastructure; expertise in commerce, finance and infrastructure management; well-educated and English-speaking workforce; conducive legal environment; minimal restrictions on right of establishment; favorable tax regime; absence of controls on capital flows and foreign exchange transactions; and political, social and economic stability. It serves as the regional headquarters of many US, European and Japanese MNCs, and the 2003 Economic Review Committee Report identified new hub activities in healthcare, education and creative industries.

3. Trade Strategy, FTAs and Trade Patterns

3.1. *Trade Strategy*

External demand accounts for 60% of Singapore's GDP in value added and 50% in employment terms. Government trade policy aims to: expand the international economic space for Singapore-based companies; secure a predictable and fair trading environment for them; and minimise impediments to the flow of imports and exports. It does this by simultaneously supporting WTO multilateralism and regional and bilateral free trade agreements (FTAs).

3.1.1. *Multilateralism*

The government regards the strong rules-based WTO system as critical for small nation states, as a guardian against protectionism by bigger economies and as a catalyst for economic growth and development. Singapore participates in the Information

Table 1.   Singapore's manufacturing output and value added by industry, 2007 and 2013.

	Output (S$million)		Value added (S$million)		Output (%)		Value added (%)	
	2007	2013	2007	2013	2007	2013	2007	2013
Total manufacturing	244,733	277,854	56,021	57,661	100.0	100.0	100.0	100.0
Food, beverages, tobacco	5,414	8,007	1,270	2,300	2.2	2.9	2.3	4.0
Textiles and wearing apparel	762	500	255	138	0.3	0.2	0.5	0.2
Leather, paper, wood products	1,498	1,530	349	429	0.6	0.6	0.6	0.7
Printing and recorded media	2,953	2,210	1,389	1,168	1.2	0.8	2.5	2.0
Refined petroleum products	47,869	50,901	1,770	72	19.6	18.3	3.2	0.1
Chemical and chemical products	34,033	43,194	5,096	3,744	13.9	15.5	9.1	6.5
Pharma and biological products	20,691	17,979	12,633	9,795	8.5	6.5	22.6	17.0
Rubber and plastic products	2,542	1,801	825	641	1.0	0.6	1.5	1.1
Non-metallic mineral products	1,884	2,381	506	524	0.8	0.9	0.9	0.9
Basic metals and fabricated products	10,223	10,385	2,761	3,149	4.2	3.7	4.9	5.5
Computer, electronic, optical products	77,440	86,807	17,586	19,687	31.6	31.2	31.4	34.1
Electrical equipment	3,000	2,493	703	847	1.2	0.9	1.3	1.5
Machinery and equipment	18,271	25,192	4,597	6,293	7.5	9.1	8.2	10.9
Transport equipment	14,460	17,644	5,427	6,426	5.9	6.4	9.7	11.1
Other manufacturing industries	3,692	6,831	1,273	2,449	1.5	2.5	2.3	4.2

Source: Compiled by author from Singapore Yearbook of Statistics 2014.

Technology Agreement (ITA) and the Government Procurement Agreement (GPA), is a signatory to the General Agreement on Trade in Services (GATS) protocols on telecommunications and financial services, and participates actively in all WTO negotiations.

In goods trade, import duties on most items have been abolished (with liquor, tobacco, petroleum products and motor vehicles remaining dutiable); MFN tariff bindings cover 69.4% of tariff lines, with the simple average bound rate at 7.4%, and the trade-weighted average bound rate on industrial products at 5.1% (WTO, 2012). Import licensing and control provisions are maintained to discharge obligations under international commitments or for public health, environmental, and security considerations. Import of chewing gum for non-therapeutic purposes is prohibited; rice imports are managed through a strategic reserve; and stringent sanitary and phytosanitary (SPS) regulations are maintained. Goods exports are free of export duties, export performance requirements, export credit guarantee and insurance schemes.

Services trade has been liberalized to enhance Singapore's role as a regional services hub, but many restrictions remain: market access for natural persons is unbound, except for the temporary movement of intra-corporate transferees; and commercial presence restrictions apply to foreigners registering their businesses in Singapore. The limited liberalization of services under GATS has enabled Singapore to offer its services markets on a preferential basis to FTA partners in exchange for greater market access for Singapore goods exports.

3.1.2. Regional and bilateral FTAs

Table 2 shows Singapore's network of regional and bilateral FTAs, which are instruments of its foreign economic policy, helping to consolidate relations with selected countries, as well as economically motivated. FTAs open up markets for Singapore's exports, reinforce its role as a regional services hub, attract more inward FDI, and secure preferential treatment and legal protection for Singapore investments abroad. They are legally binding, preventing FTA partners from backtracking on their market access commitments, and produce faster and deeper liberalization than either the WTO or APEC (Asia-Pacific Economic Cooperation forum).

FDI in Singapore is export-oriented, so Singapore negotiators consider the market access interests of Singapore-based foreign MNCs as well as of Singaporean exporters. Rules of origin in Singapore's FTAs recognize the regionally integrated nature of manufacturing, where production is outsourced to low-cost centers, but initial R&D and the final stages of high-end processing and product testing are undertaken in Singapore. Its FTAs incorporate intellectual property (IP) protection and greater cooperation in science and technology to boost R&D.

In addition to the small but high-income Singapore market's own attractions, foreign companies benefit from using Singapore as a gateway to explore opportunities

Table 2.   Singapore's regional and bilateral FTAs as of January 2015.

FTA agreements	Signed or implemented	Under negotiation
ASEAN Free Trade Area	Jan-93	
ASEAN–Australia–NZ FTA	Nov-11	
ASEAN–China FTA	Jul-05 to Feb-10	
ASEAN–India FTA — goods	Aug-11	
ASEAN–Japan CEP — goods	Apr-08	
ASEAN–Korea FTA	Jun-07 to Feb-09	
Singapore–Australia FTA	Jul-03	
Singapore–China FTA	Jan-09	
Singapore–Costa Rica FTA	Apr-10	
Singapore–EFTA FTA	Jan-03	
Singapore–GCC FTA	Sep-13	
Singapore–Jordan FTA	Aug-05	
Singapore–India CECA	Jun-05	
Singapore–Japan EPA	Nov-02	
Singapore–Korea FTA	Mar-06	
Singapore–NZ CEP	Aug-01	
Singapore–Panama FTA	Mar-06	
Singapore–Peru FTA	May-08	
Singapore–US	Jan-04	
TSEP (Brunei, Singapore, NZ, Chile)	May-06	
ASEAN–India services and investment		x
ASEAN–Japan services and investment		x
Singapore–Canada		x
Singapore–Mexico		x
Singapore–Pakistan		x
Singapore–Ukraine		x
RCEP (Singapore + 15 countries)		x
TPP (Singapore + 11 countries)		x

Source: Compiled by author from data on IE Singapore website.

in FTA partner countries, including via partnerships with Singapore companies, enjoying tariff savings, preferential access to certain sectors, and enhanced IP protection.

Singapore's bilateral FTAs are WTO-consistent in that they cover substantially all trade, liberalise within 10 years, and do not raise barriers against non-FTA partners (as under GATT Article XXIV and GATS Article V). They are also WTO-plus as they encompass zero bound tariffs on all goods; liberalize investments beyond trade-related investment measures (TRIMs); enforce IP protection beyond trade-related intellectual property (TRIPs); provide for government procurement beyond GPA limits; and liberalize services beyond GATS commitments. They also include commitments on labor and environmental standards, and development cooperation.

3.1.3. *Customs procedures and rules of origin*

In trade in goods, arbitrary and uncertain customs valuation, and long and tedious customs procedures, are more serious obstacles to trade than import tariffs, now substantially reduced in all FTA countries. This problem has been mitigated by the 2013 ASEAN introduction of "Advance Ruling" from the customs authority of the importing country on the origin of the good. Singapore-based exporters bear the brunt of the burden to comply with rules of origin (ROO) to gain preferential access to the markets of FTA partners, since most products exported from Singapore are manufactured in Singapore from imported materials, parts and components. Singapore's FTAs do not have a common or harmonized ROO system,[4] which complicates matters for exporters.

The web of diverse ROOs in multiple and overlapping FTAs could create a messy "spaghetti bowl" which raises business transaction costs and discourages utilization of FTA provisions.[5] Chia (2011a) surveyed 75 Singapore firms in the electronics, chemicals and pharmaceuticals, and textiles and garments industries and found only 17.3% actual and 28.0% planned utilization of FTA tariff preferences. Reasons for this include: low margin of preference, high administrative cost, and lack of knowledge of FTAs (particularly among SMEs). The "spaghetti bowl" effect is not an apparent problem as exporters generally utilized no more than three FTAs.

3.1.4. *AEC, ASEAN+1 FTAs and RCEP[6]*

Singapore is a member of ASEAN economic integration schemes that began with the ASEAN Free Trade Area (AFTA) in 1992, and will culminate with a single market and production base, with free flow of goods, services and investments,

---

[4] To qualify as "originating" a product must be "wholly obtained" in the originating country or, for manufactured products, have undergone "substantial transformation", with the originating country being the last country where substantial transformation took place. "Substantial transformation" is defined by three main criteria — change in tariff classification (CTC) rule, value added (VA) or local content rule, and process rule.

[5] See for example, Baldwin (2006), JETRO (2007), Bhagwati (2008) and Kawai and Wignaraja (2011).

[6] For an in-depth analysis of this section, see Chia and Plummer (2015).

under the ASEAN Economic Community (AEC) by end-2015. Singapore already has zero tariffs and a "single window" (TradeNet) for all goods, has made extensive services liberalization commitments, and has minimal restrictions on foreign equity ownership and no performance requirements. Despite AEC Mutual Recognition Arrangements (MRAs) to allow the free flow of skilled professionals, employment of such foreigners continues to be restricted in every ASEAN country,[7] including Singapore.

There are five ASEAN+1 FTAs with China, Japan, South Korea, India, Australia and New Zealand. To date there is no ASEAN-US or ASEAN-EU FTA. The templates for these ASEAN-centric agreements are more restrictive than Singapore's bilateral FTAs, since they conform to the needs and sensitivities of 10 ASEAN countries with different levels of development and market- and FDI-openness. Singapore is also negotiating the Regional Comprehensive Economic Partnership (RCEP) together with its ASEAN+1 FTA partners. To have value added beyond the ASEAN+1 FTAs, the RCEP needs to have more comprehensive and deeper integration coverage and resolve some of the "spaghetti bowl" problems.

3.1.5. *Benefits and challenges of FTAs*

Quantitative effects of FTAs are usually determined through computerized general equilibrium (CGE) analysis. But many CGE models on the AEC and ASEAN+1 FTAs[8] are of limited usefulness for Singapore because: they use international sources which provide data on Singapore's total exports (that is, domestic exports plus entrepot exports) though entrepot exports do not qualify as Singapore originating; do not consider the low levels of FTA preferential tariff utilization; and usually have incomplete coverage of the effects of services and investment liberalization. They also usually ignore the effects of multiple and overlapping FTAs. For example, bilateral FTAs unambiguously *increase* Singapore's exports, as tariff reductions lower the prices of Singapore goods to consumers in partner countries, as shown in a 2011 study.[9] But for regional FTAs, there is no significant difference between those that

---

[7] See Chia (2011c) for further analysis. Some ASEAN countries, including the Philippines and Thailand have constitutional and legal restrictions on employment of foreigners, while others have labor market tests and phased-out provisions.

[8] For example, Plummer and Chia (2009) Chapter 2; Kawai and Wignaraja (2007).

[9] Ministry of Trade and Industry (2011). The study used a panel data set comprising country-level annual data for 18 countries from 1987 to 2008. The countries are Australia, China, France, Germany, Hong Kong, India, Indonesia, Japan, Jordan, Malaysia, the Netherlands, New Zealand, Panama, South Korea, Taiwan, Thailand, United Kingdom and United States which together accounted for more than 80% of Singapore's total domestic exports and included countries with which Singapore had (a) bilateral FTAs, (b) regional FTAs, and (c) no FTAs, thereby enabling comparison of export growth rates in these different groupings.

included partners with whom Singapore had a pre-existing bilateral FTA, and those that included partners with whom Singapore had no pre-existing bilateral FTA. With regional FTAs, Singapore exporters enjoy ASEAN cumulation in the determination of rules of origin for FTA preferential tariffs.

The main beneficiaries of Singapore's FTAs are Singapore-based domestic and foreign companies — goods exporters, service providers and investors. Businesses in Singapore are minimally dislocated since they are accustomed to free trade (except for some protected services), but are also unlikely to enjoy efficiency gains from import competition. Singapore consumers benefit little, since imports already enter Singapore duty-free. But services liberalization does lead to inflow of foreign service providers, which improves the efficiency, range and quality of services available to Singapore consumers. There are also indirect benefits as trade and investment expansion leads to higher economic growth, job creation and spin-offs for domestic enterprises. National and preferential treatment and investment protection measures in FTAs will encourage and enable more Singapore-based companies, especially SMEs, to venture abroad, particularly to ASEAN countries.

3.2. *Trade Patterns*

3.2.1. *High import and export dependence*

Singapore's trade in goods and services exceeds three times its GDP, due to its dearth of land and natural resources and small domestic market, and roles as a manufacturing export platform and a regional entrepot, all of which give rise to the high import content of consumption and production. Tables 3 and 4 show Singapore's external trade by commodity and major trading partners for 2007 and 2013. By 2013, domestic exports are dominated by petroleum products (mineral fuels and lubricants), machinery and equipment (mainly electronics and marine transport) and chemical and chemical products. Entrepot exports account for about half of total exports and are dominated by machinery and equipment. The main sources of imports are in Asia, particularly Malaysia and China, as well as the EU and US. The major destinations of exports and domestic exports are also in Asia, particularly China–Hong Kong, Malaysia and Indonesia, as well as EU and US.

Tables 5 and 6 show Singapore's services trade by type and major trading partners. Major service exports are transport, travel and financial services, mainly to Asia, particularly ASEAN, China–Hong Kong, Japan, as well as the EU and US Major service imports are transport, travel and charges for use of IP, mainly from Asia, particularly China–Hong Kong and Japan, as well as the EU, US and Latin America and Caribbean (largely tax havens). Singapore is a net importer of services from EU, Switzerland and the US.

Table 3.   Singapore's external trade by commodity section, 2007 and 2013.

	2007				2013			
	Imports	Exports	Domestic exports	Entrepot exports	Imports	exports	Domestic exports	Entrepot exports
Total (SGD billion)	396.0	450.6	234.9	215.7	466.8	513.4	274.2	239.2
Food	7.8	4.4	2.6	1.8	10.6	7.1	4.9	2.1
Beverages, tobacco	2.7	2.7	0.4	2.3	4.5	4.6	0.6	4.0
Crude materials	2.8	2.9	1.5	1.3	4.2	3.6	1.8	1.8
Mineral fuels, lubricants	83.4	79.7	63.3	16.4	146.3	125.0	106.5	18.5
Animal and vegetable oils	0.7	0.6	0.3	0.3	1.4	0.4	0.2	0.1
Chemicals, chem products	24.0	55.6	45.0	10.6	31.9	63.5	46.4	17.1
Manufactured goods	30.7	21.8	7.2	14.6	29.3	20.2	6.2	13.9
Machinery, equipment	207.6	246.6	94.9	151.7	195.4	237.7	78.9	158.8
Miscell. Manufactures	29.4	29.7	17.1	12.7	36.0	44.7	25.3	19.4
Miscellaneous	7.1	6.6	2.6	4.0	7.2	6.6	3.3	3.3
Total (percent shares)	100.0	100.0	100.0	100.0	100.0	100.0	100.0	100.0
Food	2.0	1.0	1.1	0.8	2.3	1.4	1.8	0.9
Beverages, tobacco	0.7	0.6	0.2	1.1	1.0	0.9	0.2	1.7
Crude materials	0.7	0.6	0.6	0.6	0.9	0.7	0.7	0.8
Mineral fuels, lubricants	21.1	17.7	26.9	7.6	31.3	24.3	38.8	7.7
Animal and vegetable oils	0.2	0.1	0.1	0.1	0.3	0.1	0.1	0.0
Chemicals, chem products	6.1	12.3	19.2	4.9	6.8	12.4	16.9	7.1
Manufactured goods	7.8	4.8	3.1	6.8	6.3	3.9	2.3	5.8
Machinery, equipment	52.4	54.7	40.4	70.3	41.9	46.3	28.8	66.4
Miscell. Manufactures	7.4	6.6	7.3	5.9	7.7	8.7	9.2	8.1
Miscellaneous	1.8	1.5	1.1	1.9	1.5	1.3	1.2	1.4

Source: Compiled by author from data in Singapore Yearbook of Statistics 2014.

Table 4. Singapore's external trade by country, 2007 and 2013.

	2007				2013			
	Total trade	Imports	Exports	Domestic exports	Total trade	Imports	Exports	Domestic exports
Total (SGD billion)	846.6	396.0	450.6	234.9	980.2	466.8	513.4	274.2
Total (percent share)	100.0	100.0	100.0	100.0	100.0	100.0	100.0	100.0
Asia	69.9	70.0	69.8	44.7	70.9	68.5	73.0	65.3
ASEAN9	28.6	25.0	31.7	26.0	26.4	20.9	31.4	28.0
Brunei	0.1	0.1	0.2	0.2	0.3	0.0	0.5	0.7
Cambodia	0.1	0.0	0.1	0.1	0.2	0.0	0.3	0.3
Indonesia	7.8	5.6	9.8	7.3	7.6	5.2	9.9	8.4
Laos	0.0	0.0	0.0	0.0	0.0	0.0	0.0	0.0
Malaysia	13.0	13.1	12.9	9.8	11.6	10.9	12.2	11.5
Myanmar	0.1	0.0	0.3	0.3	0.3	0.0	0.5	0.6
Philippines	2.1	2.2	2.0	2.3	1.5	1.4	1.6	1.4
Thailand	3.7	3.2	4.1	4.0	3.1	2.5	3.7	3.0
Vietnam	1.5	0.8	2.2	2.0	1.8	0.8	2.6	2.2
China	10.8	12.1	9.7	8.5	11.8	11.7	11.8	11.1
Hong Kong	6.3	1.5	10.5	9.1	6.2	0.8	11.2	9.4
Japan	6.4	8.2	4.8	5.3	4.9	5.5	4.3	3.9
South Korea	4.2	4.9	3.5	2.7	5.2	6.4	4.1	3.2
India	2.8	2.2	3.3	2.6	2.6	2.4	2.7	2.3
Bangladesh	0.2	0.0	0.3	0.2	0.3	0.0	0.6	0.6
Pakistan	0.2	0.0	0.3	0.2	0.1	0.0	0.2	0.2

(*Continued*)

Table 4.   (*Continued*)

	2007				2013			
	Total trade	Imports	Exports	Domestic exports	Total trade	Imports	Exports	Domestic exports
Sri Lanka	0.2	0.0	0.3	0.2	0.3	0.0	0.5	0.4
Saudi Arabia	1.7	3.3	0.3	0.3	1.8	3.4	0.3	0.3
UAE	1.4	1.7	1.2	0.8	2.8	4.4	1.4	1.1
Kuwait	0.9	1.9	0.1	0.1	0.5	0.9	0.1	0.0
Bahrain	0.1	0.1	0.0	0.0	0.1	0.1	0.0	0.0
Europe	12.7	14.2	11.3	14.8	11.8	15.4	8.5	10.5
EU	11.5	12.4	10.7	14.1	9.9	12.4	7.6	9.3
Switzerland	0.6	0.9	0.3	0.3	0.7	1.2	0.4	0.4
America	13.0	14.0	12.1	16.9	12.3	14.1	10.5	13.5
US	10.4	12.3	8.8	11.4	7.9	10.3	5.7	6.3
Canada	0.5	0.4	0.7	1.0	0.4	0.3	0.4	0.3
Brazil	0.4	0.3	0.4	0.6	0.6	0.5	0.7	0.3
Oceania	3.4	1.4	5.2	6.6	3.6	1.4	5.6	7.5
Australia	2.6	1.2	3.7	4.6	2.5	1.1	3.8	4.8
New Zealand	0.4	0.2	0.5	0.6	0.3	0.2	0.5	0.6
Africa	1.0	0.5	1.6	1.8	1.4	0.5	7.6	3.1

Source: Compiled by author from data in Singapore Yearbook of Statistics 2014.

Table 5. Singapore's balance of payments trade in services by type.

	2007		2013	
	Imports	Exports	Imports	Exports
Total (SGD billion)	115.3	111.8	161.8	162.8
SA Maintenance and repair services	0.5	6.6	0.8	9.6
Transport	41.2	43.9	46.1	55.2
Travel	20.4	13.6	30.8	23.8
Insurance	3.6	2.5	6.3	5.0
Govt. goods and services	0.3	0.3	0.3	0.4
Construction	0.4	1.1	1.0	2.1
Financial	3.5	15.8	4.8	23.1
Telecomms, computers and information	2.8	2.8	7.1	5.5
Charges for use of intellect. property	14.5	1.1	25.2	2.5
Personal, cultural and recreational	0.4	0.4	0.6	0.5
Other business services	27.7	23.7	38.9	35.0

Source: Compiled by author from data in Singapore Yearbook of Statistics 2014.

Table 6. Singapore's trade in services by major trading partners.

	Imports (S$million)		Exports (S$million)	
	2007	2012	2007	2012
Asia	25,266	35,036	40,853	51,682
ASEAN	5,807	7,794	10,958	15,659
Brunei	104	65	249	552
Cambodia	101	132	89	115
Indonesia	1,630	1,868	3,133	4,203
Malaysia	1,700	2,493	3,499	4,426
Myanmar	70	81	203	228
Philippines	528	876	934	1,243
Thailand	1,165	1,380	1,968	3,310
Vietnam	470	861	748	1,518
China	3,437	6,589	5,127	7,487
Japan	5,778	6,114	7,724	7,734
South Korea	1,653	2,312	2,699	2,697
Hong Kong	3,571	4,008	4,490	5,730
Taiwan	1,603	2,270	2,070	2,070

(Continued)

Table 6.   (*Continued*)

	Imports (S$million)		Exports (S$million)	
	2007	2012	2007	2012
India	1,897	2,922	3,281	4,418
Saudi Arabia	116	162	440	565
UAE	534	1,426	1,660	1,857
Europe	20,598	30,972	21,521	27,644
EU28	16,946	23,711	16,308	21,804
Switzerland	1,861	4,902	2,632	2,651
United States	20,534	24,147	15,083	19,009
Australia	2,438	4,772	4,736	11,484
S&C America, Caribbean	4,167	11,917	3,853	4,446
Africa	773	1,765	1,325	2,692

Source: Compiled by author from data in Singapore Yearbook of Statistics 2014.

3.2.2. *Trade with FTA partners*

Table 7 shows Singapore's domestic exports to FTA partners. Entrepot exports do not qualify for preferential market access, and the high import content of Singapore's domestic exports also mean that some domestic exports fail to qualify under the rules of origin.

Domestic exports to FTA partners account for less than 65% of Singapore's global domestic exports, and domestic exports to some countries are under multiple FTAs. The ASEAN countries are covered under AEC and five ASEAN+1 FTAs, while Brunei is also under Trans-Pacific Strategic Economic Partnership (TSEP). China, Japan, South Korea, India and Australia are covered under ASEAN+1 FTAs as well as bilaterals, while New Zealand is covered under the ASEAN-Australia-NZ FTA, TSEP and a bilateral. ASEAN accounts for a 28% share of Singapore's domestic exports to FTA partners, followed by China (11.2%), US (6.3%) and Australia (4.8%).

4. Inward and Outward FDI Strategies and Patterns

4.1. *Inward FDI and Outward FDI Policy Regimes*

Attracting FDI has been a Singapore policy priority since the mid-1960s, with the government believing that FDI would provide a "package" of finance, technology, management, marketing and integration into global production networks, much

Table 7.   Singapore's domestic exports to FTA partners.

	1996	2001	2005	2007	2013
Total world (SGD million)	103,589	118,444	207,448	234,903	274,192
ASEAN	21,209	24,735	53,672	61,071	76,770
Brunei	388	244	300	356	1,866
Cambodia	264	385	240	286	691
Indonesia	na	na	16,392	17,241	22,964
Laos	4	18	4	3	6
Malaysia	13,299	15,323	20,478	23,130	31,474
Myanmar	na	na	na	599	1,549
Philippines	1,525	2,760	4,027	5,360	3,881
Thailand	4,561	4,087	7,729	9,335	8,193
Vietnam	1,168	1,918	4,502	4,761	6,146
China	2,844	5,288	17,599	19,870	30,568
Japan	9,788	10,504	12,510	12,347	10,614
South Korea	3,019	3,977	5,436	6,385	8,785
India	1,194	1,994	4,726	6,191	6,347
Australia	2,258	3,362	9,721	10,763	13,263
New Zealand	266	437	1,240	1,476	1,555
Jordan	na	na	na	na	na
GCC	686	1,010	2,398	2,967	3,960
Bahrain	17	19	265	44	59
Kuwait	56	67	92	238	113
Saudi Arabia	197	244	367	815	697
UAE	416	680	1,674	1,870	3,091
EFTA	412	451	584	817	1,152
Iceland	na	na	na	na	na
Liechenstein	na	na	na	na	na
Sweden	109	59	132	164	106
Switzerland	303	392	452	653	1,046
United States	25,689	22,031	22,744	26,717	17,330
Chile	na	na	na	na	na
Costa Rica	na	na	na	na	na
Panama	na	na	na	na	na
Peru	na	na	na	na	na
Total FTAs signed	66,679	72,779	128,232	148,604	170,344
As % of domestic exports	64.4	61.4	61.8	63.3	62.1

Source: Singapore Yearbook of Statistics, various years.

quicker than it would take to nurture nascent domestic entrepreneurs. Despite decades of industrialization and growing outward FDI, Singapore remains heavily dependent on inward FDI, having mostly failed to develop a vibrant industrial entrepreneurial class with technological and international marketing capabilities. The country's continued successes in attracting inward FDI are attributed to the following factors as listed in 4.11, 4.12 and 4.13 below.

4.1.1. Conducive business environment

The World Bank's ease of doing business index shows Singapore's core attractions for FDI are the underlying political, social and macroeconomic stability; transparent legal and regulatory framework; strong intellectual property protection; low level of public sector corruption and high level of public sector competence; stable industrial relations; pool of skills and professionals from the country's tertiary education and training institutions supplemented by ready access to foreign professionals and workers; well-developed physical infrastructure of industrial estates, science parks and world-class sea and air transportation and telecommunications; and ready availability of water and energy. From the mid-1980s, emphasis was placed on developing a network of reliable and competent local suppliers for the electronics, chemicals, engineering and precision industries. The small domestic market is augmented by ready access to external markets through an efficient transportation network and logistics and preferential market access secured under numerous FTAs.

4.1.2. Inward FDI policies

Singapore's inward FDI policy regime since the mid-1960s has had the following features: (1) Absence of entry and ownership restrictions and performance requirements; with some exceptions in services, foreign investors are generally accorded right of establishment and national treatment, and are represented on various national advisory and policy making councils and committees. (2) Absence of restrictions on foreign borrowings from the domestic capital market, foreign exchange controls or limits placed on repatriation of capital, dividends, interest and royalties. (3) Ample physical and human infrastructure. (4) Policy consistence and coherence among government agencies and over time, and effective implementation. (5) Initially generous investment incentives to offset disadvantages in manufacturing from high land and labor costs and a small domestic market; tax incentives were later extended to a range of services, innovation and R&D activities to promote Singapore as a services hub and encourage industrial upgrading.

Note that the academic literature is highly critical of the use of tax incentives: They are ineffective in attracting investments, distort resource allocation and lead to loss of tax revenue; cause host economies to compete unnecessarily with each other, raising the extent and cost of subsidies. In Singapore, the large array of tax and financial incentives for manufacturing and services has raised several issues: the need to continually fine-tune incentives as new activities emerge, the growing burden on tax administration; and the questionable ability of the government to pick winners in an increasingly complex technological and business environment. A drop in the corporate income tax rate from 40% in the 1960s to 17% by 2009 also dramatically reduced the margin of preference from tax incentives; both local and foreign investors may prefer a simple and long-term lower uniform rate, rather than selective, conditional and temporary tax incentives. Liberal use of tax incentives could also brand Singapore as a tax haven of government subsidies, which are increasingly subject to international scrutiny and sanctions.

4.1.3. *EDB investment promotion and MNC partnership*

Established in 1961 to spearhead Singapore's industrialization and FDI drive, the Economic Development Board (EDB) maintains a network of overseas promotion offices and an international advisory council which includes global heads of leading MNCs. It functions as a one-stop investment center, offering land and ready factory sites in industrial estates and parks, tax holiday incentives and training subsidies; and post-investment services. Investor satisfaction is evident from the high proportion of Singapore FDI commitments each year including reinvestments and expansions. There is a very high retention rate of foreign MNCs which, even as they relocate more labor-intensive production operations elsewhere, generally maintain in Singapore the technical support, procurement and R&D functions. Thus the nature and role of foreign MNCs in Singapore has changed as the Singapore economy restructures. Those processes and products which are no longer competitive to produce in Singapore are relocated elsewhere, while new investments and reinvestments are in new areas of competitive advantage.

Over the decades, Singapore's public and private sectors have continued to maintain a friendly stance toward foreign investors while the economy and society remain open. Since MNCs are generally engaged in export activities, competition is minimized with local enterprises in the domestic market. But there has been "crowding out" in domestic factor markets (for space, labor, talent), as well as policy neglect towards development of local SMEs and entrepreneurship. In recent years, there have been negative sentiments directed at the large presence of foreign skilled and professional workforce, rather than foreign corporates, following their surge during the 2008–2009 recession when many local professionals and skilled workers were retrenched, and foreigners were seen as taking away jobs from Singaporeans.[10]

---

[10] The growing disaffection was manifested in the parliamentary general elections and presidential elections of 2011 and resulted in significant policy measures to restrict inflows of foreign workers, level the playing field between foreigners and Singaporeans, and provide enhanced benefits for Singaporeans.

4.1.4. *Outward FDI policies*

From the 1960s to the 1990s, Singapore's outward FDI was very limited, reflecting the underdevelopment of domestic private entrepreneurship in an economy dominated by foreign MNCs and GLCs. But in 1993, the government launched an outward investment drive, arguing that Singapore businesses needed to venture abroad for these reasons: (1) A maturing Singapore economy facing severe land and labor shortages and rising costs needed to develop externally to sustain its growth performance: Outward FDI would enable Singapore's growing capital resources to earn higher rates of return, create spill-over benefits from increased trade flows, consolidate Singapore's headquarters functions, and develop and leverage domestic technology, know-how and R&D. (2) With a small domestic market and scarce natural and labor resources, venturing abroad would enable Singapore firms to tap into much larger markets and new sources of labor supply. (3) Trade and investment liberalization under the WTO and regional and bilateral FTAs offer business opportunities around the world, particularly in Asia to which Singapore businesses are more oriented, given the region's growth dynamism, abundant natural resources, low-cost labor and rapidly expanding markets, its geographical proximity and cultural and linguistic familiarity which reduce information, transaction, management, coordination and supervision costs, especially for SMEs. Singaporean investors could enter into partnerships to develop infrastructure in nearby host or third countries, and partner with MNCs to facilitate the allocation of manufacturing value chain segments among countries.

Government measures to promote and facilitate outward FDI include the following: First, promoting change in the mindsets of Singaporean businesses toward overseas ventures through the media and business forums, establishment of bilateral councils to network and exchange business information with overseas counterparts, entering into FTAs and bilateral investment treaties (BITs), and setting up a Committee to Promote Enterprise Overseas in 1993. Second, outreach activities by the EDB, Spring Singapore and International Enterprise (IE) Singapore, providing institutional support, equity and loan financing and administering tax incentive programs.[11] Third, regionalization of GLCs which, because of their acquired specialised expertize and financial muscle, were able to partner with private enterprises and co-lead large infrastructure projects. Fourth, encouraging foreign MNCs in Singapore to enter into joint ventures with Singaporean companies to co-invest in countries such as China, pooling corporate resources and utilizing their various corporate strengths.

---

[11] See Chia (2011b) for detailed listing of measures.

4.1.5. *Inward FDI trends and patterns*[12]

With EDB promotion from the 1960s, inward FDI stock rose rapidly to reach an annual average of US$249.7 billion and 160% of GDP in 2005–2007. Singapore became a mature host economy, with reinvested earnings and expansion investments accounting for a growing share of FDI inflows. Inward FDI stock in manufacturing by 1990 was concentrated in electronic, chemical and petroleum products; by 2000, electronic products became even more dominant with a near 50% share of FDI, followed by chemicals and pharmaceuticals, and petroleum products. As shown in Table 8, in 2012, inward FDI stock was still dominated by these three industry clusters, while manufacturing's share shrank to 17.2% with the corresponding rise of non-manufacturing.

The expanding importance of FDI in services reflects not just Singapore's growing importance as a regional services hub, but also the fact that globally, FDI in services has been expanding much more rapidly than in manufacturing, with the increasing prominence of telecommunications, IT-enabled services, finance and insurance, and air transport. As many services are neither tradable nor storable, they must be produced where consumed, and right of establishment is the dominant means of delivering them to foreign markets. FDI in services in Singapore is concentrated in financial and insurance services, with a near 50% share in 2012, followed by trading activities.

Major sources of inward FDI in 2012 were the advanced economies of the EU (26.7% share in 2012), US (14.3%) and Japan (7.9%), though their share has been declining, while those of China–Hong Kong and Latin America–Caribbean have been rising, the latter reflecting investments from tax havens, whose ultimate ownership is uncertain, concentrated in finance and insurance.

4.1.6. *Outward FDI trends and patterns*

Singapore's outward FDI stock grew from around S$1 billion in 1976 to S$46.2 billion in 1995 and to S$463 billion by 2012, an annual growth rate of 19%. Some outward FDI took place in the 1950s mainly to neighboring Malaya. The increase since the early 1990s is due to several factors: industrial restructuring; the strong Singapore dollar; improvements in investment climate and opportunities in the ASEAN region, China and India; and the government-initiated regionalization program which encouraged Singapore firms to venture abroad. Singapore's outward FDI in finance M&A reflects opportunities in some Asian countries following the 1997–1998 Asian financial crisis, and in manufacturing reflects industrial relocations in the face of domestic land and labor shortages and loss of competitive advantage. As shown in Table 9, outward FDI stock in 2012 was dominated by financial

---

[12] For detailed analysis, see Chia (2011b).

Table 8.   Singapore's stock of inward FDI by sector and source country.

	S$billion		Percent distribution	
	2007	2012	2007	2012
Total Stock	466.6	746.7	100.0	100.0
By Sectors				
Manufacturing	116.5	128.5	25.0	17.2
Computer, electronic, optical	31.6	41.2	6.8	5.5
Pharmaceutical products	47.9	28.5	10.3	3.8
Refined petroleum products	14.1	20.7	3.0	2.8
Construction	1.5	2.6	0.3	0.4
Trade, wholesale & retail	77.1	126.8	16.5	17.0
Accomodation, food services	3.0	4.8	0.6	0.6
Transport & storage	30.5	37.7	6.5	5.1
Information & communications	4.9	7.7	1.0	1.0
Financial & insurance services	195.4	359.6	41.9	48.2
Real estate activities	12.9	27.1	2.8	3.6
Professional, tech, admin support	22.6	39.6	4.8	5.3
Others	2.2	12.2	0.5	1.6
By Source Regions/Countries				
Asia	105.3	182.1	22.6	24.4
ASEAN	16.3	35.1	3.5	4.7
Indonesia	2.0	1.7	0.4	0.2
Malaysia	11.4	27.1	2.4	3.6
Philippines	1.0	2.0	0.2	0.3
Thailand	1.5	3.9	0.3	0.5
China	2.3	14.2	0.5	1.9
Japan	47.5	59.1	10.2	7.9
South Korea	3.0	3.5	0.7	0.5
Hong Kong	6.9	27.7	1.5	3.7
Taiwan	7.7	7.5	1.7	1.0
India	13.0	22.0	2.8	3.0
Europe	198.3	261.3	42.5	35.0
EU28	152.3	199.4	32.6	26.7
Switzerland	27.5	31.1	5.9	4.2
United States	51.6	106.5	11.0	14.3
Australia	4.6	10.3	1.0	1.4
S&C America, Caribbean	91.0	159.3	19.5	21.3

Source: Compiled by author from data in Singapore Yearbook of Statistics 2014.

Table 9.   Singapore's stock of outward FDI by sector and destination country.

	S$billion		Percent distribution	
	2007	2012	2007	2012
Total Stock	317.5	462.7	100.0	100.0
By Sectors				
Manufacturing	69.6	98.9	21.9	21.4
Construction	0.5	1.4	0.2	0.3
Trade, wholesale & retail	14.9	36.8	4.7	8.0
Accomodation, food services	2.6	4.6	0.8	1.0
Transport & storage	9.4	12.5	3.0	2.7
Information & communications	15.2	20.1	4.8	4.4
Financial & insurance services	177.5	207.7	55.9	44.9
Real estate activities	14.6	39.4	4.6	8.5
Professional, tech, admin support	5.5	8.2	1.7	1.8
Others	7.8	33.0	2.5	7.1
By Destination Regions/Countries				
Asia	148.1	262.5	46.6	56.7
ASEAN	68.0	100.7	21.4	21.8
Indonesia	20.1	37.3	6.3	8.1
Malaysia	22.7	32.3	7.1	7.0
Philippines	4.1	5.0	1.3	1.1
Thailand	16.9	18.5	5.3	4.0
BCLMV*	4.2	7.7	1.3	1.7
China	40.3	90.5	12.7	19.6
Japan	3.9	9.0	1.2	1.9
South Korea	3.1	2.9	1.0	0.6
Hong Kong	20.0	39.2	6.3	8.5
Taiwan	5.1	7.0	1.6	1.5
India	4.6	10.0	1.5	2.2
Europe	46.5	68.2	14.6	14.7
EU28	41.2	59.9	13.0	12.9
Switzerland	4.4	3.7	1.4	0.8
United States	13.9	8.8	4.4	1.9
Australia	17.1	38.3	5.4	8.3
S&C America, Caribbean	56.2	60.6	17.7	13.1
Africa	32.5	20.1	10.2	4.3

Source: Compiled by author from Singapore Yearbook of Statistics 2014.
Note: *BCLMV = Brunei, Cambodia, Laos, Myanmar and Vietnam.

and insurance services (44.9% share) followed by manufacturing (21.4%), real estate (8.5% share) and trade (8.0%).

The traditionally strong Asian bias of Singapore's outward FDI declined from a 75.9% share in 1981 to under 50% in the 2000s, rising again to reach a 56.7% share in 2012. The recent rise reflects merges and acquisitions by Singapore financial institutions in Indonesia, Hong Kong, Philippines, Thailand and South Korea, and major telecommunications investments in Indonesia, Thailand and Australia. A large proportion of real estate outward FDI went to Europe through hotel and property investments made by leading Singaporean real estate and hospitality firms. In recent years, Singapore businesses and individuals have also been buying up real estate in neighboring Malaysia following improved bilateral relations.

Singapore is the largest source of regional investment in ASEAN, but the ASEAN share of its outward FDI declined sharply from 64.3% in 1981 to 21.8% in 2012, with the Malaysian share declining from 60% in 1981 to only 7.0% in 2012, reflecting the competing investment attractions of China, and uneasy political relations with Malaysia until recent years. Increased investments in Indonesia reflect development of industrial estates and infrastructure in Batam and Bintan, and acquisitions of shares in Indonesian banks and telecommunications companies. China's share grew rapidly from under 3% in 1985 to 19.6% in 2012. At least half of these investments took place after 1992, following establishment of diplomatic relations in 1990; they include GLC investments in Suzhou Industrial Park, Sino-Singapore Tianjin Eco-City and other infrastructure projects; investments by Temasek Holdings; and property developments and operations of Singapore banks. Outward FDI to non-Asian destinations went mainly to Europe and Australia, reflecting M&A by large Singapore companies desiring access to technology and knowhow. Although the Singapore economy is more US-oriented in trade, Europe is a more prominent destination for its outward FDI.

Singapore's outward FDI is undertaken by Singapore-based foreign MNCs, domestic private enterprises and GLCs. Singapore-based foreign MNCs accounted for 54% share of outward FDI in 1990, falling to 39% in 2002 (Yeung, 2005). Local SMEs are increasingly investing abroad, through greenfield and joint venture activities. Competitive pressure to lower production costs drives them to invest mainly in low-cost destinations such as China, Indonesia, Malaysia, Thailand and Vietnam, where they have some ownership advantages in producing for export markets or supplying large customers locally. While local manufacturing firms tend to invest in China, foreign MNCs tend to relocate to ASEAN, especially Thailand. The top Singapore international companies ranked by overseas revenue shows the dominance of GLCs and service companies in commerce, transport and storage, telecommunications, finance and real estate, and the conspicuous absence of manufacturing companies.

4.1.7. *Effects of inward and outward FDI on the Singapore economy*[13]

Inward FDI in Singapore supplements as well as complements domestic resources. In the 1960s–1970s, investment inflows helped to close the domestic saving-investment gap and finance net imports of goods and services. By the mid-1980s, Singapore had become a net capital exporter and a growing investor abroad. Inward FDI contributed to technological and managerial know-how and integration into regional production networks and global supply chains. Official statistics show that resident foreign companies and resident foreigners contributed to under one-third of GDP in 1990, rising to over 40% by the early years of the 21st century.[14]

Inward FDI contributed importantly to Singapore's value-added and exports of goods and services and their increasing sophistication, particularly in electronics, refined petroleum, chemical and pharmaceutical and financial sectors. Data from the annual manufacturing censuses show that foreign firms (both wholly foreign and joint ventures) have much higher direct export/sales ratios than their domestic counterparts, in part because domestic firms acted as local suppliers to Singapore-based MNCs rather than exporting directly. Wong (2003) divided Singapore's technological development into four phases. (1) From the early 1960s to mid-1970s, there were few innovation links between foreign MNCs and the rest of the Singapore economy. (2) From the mid-1970s to late-1980s, there was rapid growth of local process technological development within MNCs and development of local supporting industries. (3) From the late-1980s to late-1990s, there was rapid expansion of applied R&D by foreign MNCs, local firms and public R&D institutes. (4) Since the late-1990s, there has been emerging emphasis on high-tech startups and basic R&D development, but Singapore's ability to innovate and pioneer new technologies still lags behind the world frontier.

FDI recipient countries are often concerned over the eventual outflows of income exceeding FDI inflows with resultant negative impacts on the balance of payments. In recent decades, there have also been concerns over the volatility of international portfolio flows. Should Singapore be similarly concerned? As noted earlier, Singapore's inward FDI on goods and services are highly export-oriented (albeit with high import content) and will continue to generate a stream of foreign exchange earnings. Further, although Singapore's inward and outward FDI are still very much tilted towards inward flows, Singapore has substantial outward portfolio investments (including by government and quasi-government entities) generating healthy factor income inflows.

---

[13] Drawn largely from Chia (2006).
[14] Data on "indigenous gross national income" has been discontinued in the *Singapore Yearbook of Statistics* in recent years. The 2009 Yearbook stated that "share of resident foreigners and resident foreign companies in GDP" was S$47.8 billion or 35% of GDP in 1998 and S$117.6 billion or 46% of GDP in 2008.

As the Singapore economy matures and outward investments continue to accelerate, economic growth performance would need to be increasingly judged by GNP rather than GDP performance.

5. Conclusion

After 50 years of economic success, the question is whether Singapore can remain internationally competitive and economically dynamic to meet citizens' aspirations for rising incomes, better quality of life and a compassionate and inclusive society. In the next phase of development, Singapore has to transit sustainably to an innovation-driven economy, with innovation-driven policies, innovating and techno-savvy entrepreneurs, and sophisticated domestic consumers.

The focus of this chapter is on Singapore's trade and FDI strategies, trends and patterns. Quo vadis? On the trade front, Singapore has to continue to remain open and balance its global and regional interests. It needs to remain a strong supporter of the rules-based multilateral system of the WTO as well as strong advocate for WTO reforms to revitalise the organization and keep it relevant. Singapore's pursuit of bilateral FTAs has to moderate, as diminishing returns set in with growth in numbers. Instead it should pursue FTA consolidation and harmonization to overcome problems of multiple and overlapping FTAs, and work towards realization of high-quality mega-blocs of Regional Comprehensive Economic Partnership (RCEP), Trans-Pacific Partnership (TPP) and Free Trade Area of Asia and the Pacific (FTAAP).

On FDI, a more even balance between inward and outward FDI will evolve as the Singapore economy matures and has more resources to invest abroad. Should Singapore continue to depend on foreign MNCs to further develop manufacturing? Singapore has a high per capita GDP and cost structures typical of advanced economies, but it still lacks indigenous technological and entrepreneurial capabilities, due in part to past policy and crowding-out effects, as priority was given to attracting inward FDI and foreign talent. Foreign MNCs will continue to bring in much needed technology for new products and processes, and integration into global production networks and supply chains, as well as provide a competitive domestic environment. In recent years many government programs have been initiated and enhanced to support the development of local entrepreneurship and local enterprise. In the Budget announced on 23 February 2015, a range of new government programs and measures are being introduced to develop Singapore's human resources and provide financial, technological, managerial, and internationalization support for SMEs. Changing mindsets and risk calculus require consistent and concerted efforts across time and space, which will be a long uphill battle.

Notwithstanding five decades of industrialization, Singapore's competitive advantage seems to continue to lie in services — its leading corporates are in finance, transportation services, hotels and hospitality services, and business and professional services. These are still very much dependent on the Asian market and vulnerable to regional geopolitics and geoeconomics. To build globally-oriented companies, alliances and M&As are necessary, involving both inward and outward investments. Singaporean private enterprises must integrate and build alliances with foreign MNCs and GLCs to survive and prosper.

In sum, going forward, there is a continuing role for inward and outward FDI in Singapore's development, but the balance will be reversed, with more emphasis on outward and less emphasis on inward FDI. Singapore needs to remain open, not only to international trade flows, but also to international investment flows, to generate a competitive environment for investments and innovations. Industrial policy will remain relevant, but instead of trying to "pick winners", it will facilitate innovations and the market, by removing institutional and regulatory obstacles.

References

Baldwin, R (2006). Managing the Noodle Bowl: The Fragility of East Asian Regionalism, Centre for Economic Policy Research (CEPR), Discussion Paper Series No. 5561.

Bhagwati, JN (2008). *Termites in the Trading System: How Preferential Agreements Undermine Free Trade*. UK: Oxford University Press.

Chia, SY (2006). Inward FDI in Singapore: Policy framework and economic impact. In *Multinationals and Economic Growth in East Asia: Foreign Direct Investment, Corporate Strategies and National Economic Development*, S Urata, SY Chia and F Kimura (eds.). UK: Routledge.

Chia, SY (2011a). Singapore. In *Asia's Free Trade Agreements: How is Business Responding?*, M Kawai and G Wignaraja (eds.). UK: Edward Elgar.

Chia, SY (2011b). Inward and outward FDI and the restructuring of the Singapore economy. In *Foreign Direct Investment in Asia*, C Sussangkarn, YC Park and SJ Kang (eds.). UK: Routledge.

Chia, SY (2011c). Free flow of skilled labour in the AEC. In *Toward a Competitive ASEAN Single Market; Sectoral Analysis*, S Urata and M Okabe (eds.). ERIA Research Project Report 2010–01. ERIA, Jakarta.

Chia, SY and MG Plummer (2015). *ASEAN Economic Cooperation and Integration: Progress, Challenges and Future Direction*. UK: Cambridge University Press.

Department of Statistics, Singapore (2014). *Singapore Yearbook of Statistics 2014*.

Japan External Trade Organisation (JETRO) (2007). FY2006 Survey of Japanese Firms' International Operations. JETRO, Tokyo.

Kawai, M and G Wignaraja (2007). ASEAN+3 or ASEAN+6: Which Way Forward. Asian Development Bank Institute (ADBI) Discussion Paper No. 77.

Kawai, M and G Wignaraja (2011). *Asia's Free Trade Agreements: How is Business Responding?* UK: Edward Elgar.

Ministry of Trade and Industry, Singapore (2003). Economic Review Committee Report.

Ministry of Trade and Industry (2011). Do Free Trade Agreements matter? Evaluating the impact of FTAs on Singapore's domestic exports of goods. Feature Article in *Economic Survey of Singapore, 2011 Second Quarter*.

Plummer, MG and SY Chia (eds.) (2009). *Realizing the ASEAN Economic Community: A Comprehensive Assessment*. Singapore: Institute of Southeast Asian Studies.

Straits Times, Singapore (2015). Reports on Singapore Budget 2015. 24 February.

Wong, PK (2003). From using to creating technology: The evolution of Singapore's national innovation system and the changing role of public policy. In *Competitiveness*, FDI and *Technology Activity in East Asia*, S Lall and S Urata (eds.). UK: Edward Elgar.

World Trade Organisation (2012). *Trade Policy Review of Singapore*. Geneva: World Trade Organisation.

Yeung, HW (2005). Case Study on Outward Foreign Direct Investment by Singaporean Firms: Enterprise, Competitiveness and Development. UNCTAD document TD/B/Com.3/EM.26/2/Add.3

CHAPTER 9

Singapore's Demographic Transition, the Labor Force and Government Policies: The Last Fifty Years

Yap Mui Teng and Christopher Gee

The trajectory of Singapore's population size and composition can be mapped out with its progression through the various phases of demographic transition from high birth and death rates in the post-war years to very low birth and death rates today, all within the context of rapid economic and social development that has taken place in the past 50 years. Population planning has been integral in Singapore's national development strategy, balancing the economy's needs for more and better qualified workers with social considerations such as the dependency burden and the integration of large numbers of foreigners in a global city-state. This chapter considers Singapore's population and manpower planning policies, with an account of the country's passage through the various stages of its demographic transition, and how its working age population composition has evolved. Population and labor force policies are examined with specific consideration of the social, economic and political implications resulting from those policy choices. A final section considers the challenges for the future stemming from these demographic trends.

1. Introduction

Singapore's progression through the various phases of demographic transition (from high birth and death rates to low birth and death rates) occurred against a backdrop of rapid economic and social development, shifting from a very young and fast-growing population with high levels of unemployment to one that is ageing rapidly and which imports labor. This socio-economic transformation is unprecedented, taking place within the lifetime of a single (albeit longer-living) generation. At the time of independence in 1965, unemployment was at 14%, GDP per capita was less than US$2,700 and half the population was illiterate (World Bank, 2009), whilst the total fertility rate was at 4.6 births per woman. By 2014, Singapore was at almost full employment (unemployment rate of 1.9%[1]), GDP per capita had risen more than twenty-fold to US$56,287,[2] 96.7%[3] of the population was literate, and the total fertility rate was 1.25 births per woman (after dropping below the replacement level of 2.1 in 1977).

The government's development planning priorities have consistently incorporated population matters, given the country's constraints of land[4] and lack of natural resources. Whilst resolving high unemployment levels and overcrowded slums were a primary consideration for economic planners in the period immediately after independence 50 years ago, the success of the country's rapid industrialization, sharp declines in birth rates and improvements in education through the 1970s and 1980s rapidly absorbed the surplus labor to the extent that by the mid 1980s, significant reversals in population policy (on family planning and immigration) were steadily introduced. By the time of the publication of the Population White Paper: A Sustainable Population For a Dynamic Singapore (National Population and Talent Division, 2013) however, the rapid pace of population ageing and significant increases in the foreign-born population have shifted the focus of policy-makers towards raising labor force participation rates amongst women and the elderly, productivity improvements and better calibration of the country's intake of foreign labor.

Population planning in Singapore is a complex balancing act between the needs of the economy for more and better-qualified workers and social and political considerations such as the dependency burden, and the ethnic and local/foreign-born composition of the population. Four factors in the balancing equation directly affect population growth: birth rates, death rates, in-migration and out-migration. Over the last 50 years, the government has introduced measures to influence the levels of births and in-migration, and this chapter considers Singapore's population and manpower planning policies in these two areas in the context of its demographic trends over the last half-century. To provide sufficient background for an understanding of the policy choices, we begin with an account of Singapore's passage through the various stages of its demographic transition, and how its working age population composition has evolved. The population and labor force policies are then examined in specific time periods with specific consideration of the social, economic and political implications resulting from those policy choices. The final section considers the challenges for the future resulting from these demographic trends.

---

[1] Ministry of Manpower data, accessible at http://stats.mom.gov.sg/Pages/Unemployment-Summary-Table.aspx.

[2] World Bank data, accessible at http://data.worldbank.org/indicator/NY.GDP.PCAP.CD.

[3] Department of Statistics data, accessible at http://www.singstat.gov.sg/statistics/latest-data#4.

[4] The total land area of Singapore in 1965 was about 585 sq. km., with a population density of 3,000 persons per sq. km.

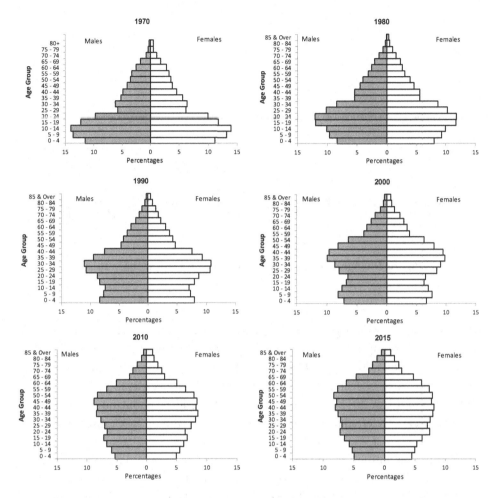

Figure 1.   Age pyramids, 1970–2015.

Source: Department of Statistics, Census 1970, 1980, 1990, 2000 and 2010 for historical data; Institute of Policy Studies 2011, Population Projections 2005–2050, Scenario 2 for 2015. Resident population for all years except 1970, which is for the total population.

2. Singapore's Demographic Transition and its Labor Force

The age composition of a population has a significant effect on the number of people of working-ages and the potential size of the domestic pool of labor. It has also implications for the supply of potential marriage partners and number of births in the future and the dependency ratio. Figure 1 above shows the age composition of the Singapore resident population from 1970 to 2015,[5] with a pyramidal shape in 1970

---

[5] 1970 data from Department of Statistics, Census of Population 1970. 1980–2010 data from Department of Statistics, Population Trends 2014. 2015 age pyramid from Yap and Gee (2014).

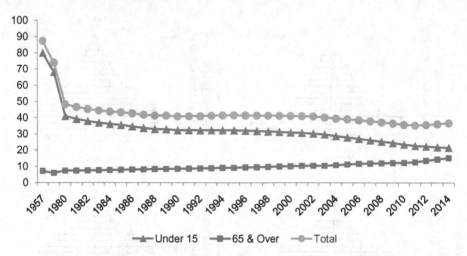

Figure 2.   Age, old-age and young dependency ratios (1957–2014).

(albeit already showing signs of a rapid decline in the number of younger persons) typical of developing countries transforming into a near-pentagonal shape by 2010. From a peak of 804,800 in 1970 (38.8% of the total population), the number of children aged 0–14 years declined sharply over the next two decades to reach 647,400 in 1990 (21.5%) (Saw, 2012). The proportion of the resident population aged between 15 and 64 years,[6] referred to by demographers as the "working ages", rose from 57.8% in 1970 to a high of 73.9% in 2011.

The decline in the proportion of the young and the rise in the proportion of the population in the working ages is a strong indicator of Singapore's demographic dividend. From 1970, the age dependency ratio amongst the resident population declined from 73.9 to a low of 35.3 in 2011 as the decline in the young dependency ratio outweighed increases in the old-age dependency ratio (Figure 2 and Table 1).

The primary cause of the changing age structure of the population has been declining number of births resulting from a sharp fall in the Total Fertility Rate from over six births per woman in 1957 to the replacement level in 1975 (Figure 3). The continuous decline in fertility rates has been the result of a major socio-economic transformation in Singaporean society, and can be attributed to higher levels of

---

[6]The standard age-dependency ratio definition uses the ages between 15 and 64 as the years which best approximate to the working ages, although this has changed over time as average years in schooling and the statutory and practical age of retirement have increased. The young-age dependency ratio is the population aged 14 years and below for 100 persons aged between 15 and 64, whilst the old-age dependency ratio is the population aged 65 years and over for 100 persons aged between 15 and 64. The total dependency ratio is the sum of both the young-age and old-age dependency ratios.

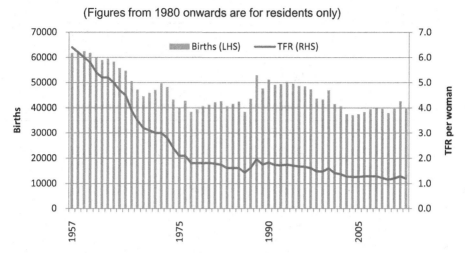

Figure 3.   Live births and total fertility rate 1957–2013.

Source: 1957–1979 data from Saw, S.H. The Population of Singapore, 1980–2013 data from Department of Statistics, Population Trends 2014.

educational attainment particularly amongst women which has elevated their societal status, changing perceptions of the value of children, and aspirations of ever-higher standards of living. These socio-economic changes took place within a population policy context which from its beginning had at its core a strong family planning program which included incentives and disincentives to limit couples to having two children, and the liberalization of sterilization and abortion (discussed in more detail in Section 3).

Proponents of the Second Demographic Transition theory highlight the role of changing societal values and norms in contributing to below replacement fertility levels in developed countries (see inter alia, van de Kaa, 2002). Broader access to education and greater educational attainment, especially amongst women, intensifies human capital formation and changes aspirations, thus contributing to fertility decline in as powerful a way as the population policies may have done (Table 2). However, in the Singapore context, a large majority of Singaporeans cite positive attitudes towards marriage and having children when married: 83% of single respondents to the Marriage and Parenthood Survey 2012 indicated a desire to get married, with 80% indicating a wish to have two or more children, notably with a strong preference for parenthood taking place within the institution of marriage (National Population and Talent Division, 2013).

An alternative perspective views fertility decline in Singapore as resulting from gender inequality in parenting responsibilities, as well as structural impediments and constraints to marriage and family formation (Yap, 2009). Whilst the country's

Table 1.   Total age, young-age and old-age dependency ratios (1970–2014).

Year	Total population ('000)	Resident population ('000)	Age dependency ratio (per hundred residents aged 15–64)		
			Total age dependency ratio	Young-age under 15	Old-age 65 and over
1970	2,074.5	2,013.6	73.9	68.1	5.9
1980	2,413.9	2,282.1	48.2	41.0	7.3
1985	2,736.0	2,482.6	43.3	35.5	7.8
1990	3,047.1	2,735.9	40.8	32.3	8.5
1995	3,524.5	3,013.5	41.6	32.3	9.2
2000	4,027.9	3,273.4	41.1	30.9	10.1
2005	4,265.8	3,467.8	39.1	27.9	11.2
2010	5,076.7	3,771.7	35.7	23.5	12.2
2011	5,183.7	3,789.3	35.3	22.7	12.6
2012	5,312.4	3,818.2	35.7	22.3	13.5
2013	5,399.2	3,844.8	36.1	21.8	14.3
2014	5,469.7	3,870.7	36.7	21.5	15.2

Source: Department of Statistics, Census 1970, Population Trends 2014. Age-dependency ratios for 1970 based on the total population, whilst ratios from 1980 onwards are based on the resident population.

Table 2.   Trends in Singapore's human capital development.

	Mean years of schooling among resident non-students aged 25 and over		Labor-force participation rate (% of resident population aged 15 and over)		Professional, managerial, technical workers (% of employee residents aged 15 and over)		
	Male	Female	Male	Female	Male	Female	M-F
1980	5.6	3.7	81.5	44.3	20.1	13.9	6.2
1990	7.3	5.9	79.0	53.0	27.4	19.5	7.9
2000	9.2	8.1	81.1	55.5	37.8	32.6	5.2
2010	10.6	9.7	76.5	56.5	54.1	49.3	4.8

Sources: Singapore Department of Statistics, 2006, Statistical Highlights (for 1980–2000), Population Trends 2014 and Ministry of Manpower, 2011, Yearbook of Manpower Statistics.

policies encourage married women (especially the better-educated ones) to remain in the work force, given the relatively small size of the work force and labor shortages (from the 1970s onwards), few women return to work once they have left it to raise children. Hence there is the absence of the M-shaped female labor force participation curve evident in other developed countries. Those that return to the workforce soon after child-bearing may find it difficult to balance working life with family commitments (National Population and Talent Division, 2013).

In any case, Wan and Loh (1979, p. 103) noted that "although many of Singapore's social and economic development policies — improving education (particularly of women), health services, and housing; industrialization and urbanization; and increasing employment of women — have probably contributed to fertility decline, these policies were not specifically aimed at fertility reduction."

3. Population and Labor Force Policies

The evolution of Singapore's population and labor force policies since independence may be divided into three broad phases: an initial phase with an anti-natalist population policy and an employment-linked approach to immigration, 1965–1986; a pro-natalist, pro-growth phase from 1987 to 2012; and from 2013 onwards a phase focused on productivity, with a continued pro-natalist emphasis coupled with a more tightly-calibrated foreign labor stance.

3.1. *1965–1986*

The relatively sudden nature of Singapore's independence (Yap, 2001), coupled with high rates of unemployment, prompted the new nation's leadership to lay out a wide-ranging national development programme which, inter alia, included measures on regulating birth rates as well as defining residency and citizenship, and controlling in-migration.

The National Family Planning and Population Programme implemented from 1966 was a comprehensive fertility reduction programme with five basic elements (Wan and Loh, 1979): (1) access to contraception; (2) liberalization of sterilization and abortion; (3) intensive and extensive family planning education efforts; (4) incentives and disincentives and (5) the manipulation of socio-economic determinants of fertility such as improving literacy and education amongst women and encouraging female labor force participation. The central theme of the Programme was "Plan your family", followed by "Plan your family small" (Lim *et al.*, 1998). In the initial stages, the Programme promoted the message of having a "small family" without indicating an optimum size, though a "two-child family norm" was adopted in 1972 with the goal of reducing fertility to the replacement level and thereafter to maintain it at that level indefinitely so as to achieve zero population growth (Yap, 2001). A high-profile public education campaign was also launched with the memorable "Stop at Two" and "Two is Enough" slogans (Wong and Yeoh, 2003).

At about the same time, and catalyzed by the British government's decision in 1967 to withdraw its military presence[7] east of Suez in 1968, industrial development policy took on increased urgency, with the government focusing on speeding up economic growth. This was achieved through the adoption of an external strategy (amidst a recognition that Singapore's small and limited domestic market was insufficient to provide good jobs for the population) by encouraging multinational corporations to set up manufacturing plants in Singapore to serve export markets (Lee, 1979). In-migration was limited with the introduction of a system of national registration for Singapore citizens and a system of work permits for non-citizen workers soon after independence. As explained by Lee (1979, p. 236) the registration process for citizens limited the right of foreigners to move into the country for employment as only registered citizens were permitted to obtain jobs without a permit from the then Ministry of Labor. Second, the work permit system for non-citizen workers linked the growth of the foreign labor force to the state of the economy, as it was the employer that applied for work permits. The foreign labor force declined sharply in the years immediately after the introduction of the system (see Table 3), although the system was relaxed once surplus labor conditions gave way to shortages as Singapore's industrialization drive succeeded in increasing employment.

In particular, the manufacturing sector's expansion from 1967 onwards provided the solution to the country's need for jobs resulting from the high fertility rates experienced in the 1950s (the post-war baby-boom), which according to Lee had become a major policy consideration at that time (Lee, 2007, p. 170). Employment in the manufacturing sector expanded three and a half times between 1967 and 1973, with the largest growth in manufacturing employment coming from the electronics and textile sectors. Employment growth was however propelled by the labor-intensive and low-skilled nature of many of these manufacturing jobs, with the then Finance Minister Dr. Goh Keng Swee noting in the Budget speech[8] of 1970 that "the electronic components we make in Singapore probably require less skill than that required by barbers or cooks, consisting mostly of repetitive manual operations". He went on to emphasize the necessity for the country to upgrade the skills of its workforce "at all levels — from research scientists, engineers, technicians, skilled craftsmen — to standards beyond anything we have achieved now" (Lee, 2007, p. 170).

Maintaining tight control over population growth was thus a major policy objective at that time. The National Family Planning and Population Programme defined specific targets in terms of reductions in births or fertility rates, and the number of "acceptors" (mostly women, and some men, who signed up to the family planning program, which included both contraception and sterilization) to be attained by the

---

[7]The British military expenditure was estimated to have contributed about 15% of Singapore's GNP at that point, and generated employment directly and indirectly to 40,000 Singaporeans (Goh, 1977).

[8]Singapore Parliament Reports, 9 March 1970, Annual Budget Statement Volume 29, Col. 508.

Table 3. Resident and foreign labor force, 1970–2014.

Mid-year	Total	Residents	Foreign	Foreign share of total labor force (%)
1970	723.0	639.9	83.1	11.5
1975	852.0	799.2	52.8	6.2
1980	1,093.0	1013.2	79.8	7.3
1985	1,185.0	1078.4	106.7	9.0
1991	1,673.7	1,372.9	300.8	18.0
1992	1,733.6	1,409.9	323.7	18.7
1993	1,762.7	1,421.7	341.0	19.3
1994	1,842.2	1,456.1	386.1	21.0
1996	2,024.9	1,511.5	513.4	25.4
1997	2,116.0	1,538.3	577.7	27.3
1998	2,187.9	1,546.5	641.4	29.3
1999	2,208.7	1,595.9	612.8	27.7
2001	2,330.5	1,644.3	686.2	29.4
2002	2,320.6	1,667.9	652.7	28.1
2003	2,312.3	1,706.4	605.9	26.2
2004	2,341.9	1,733.4	608.5	26.0
2006	2,594.1	1,880.8	713.3	27.5
2007	2,750.5	1,918.1	832.4	30.3
2008	2,939.9	1,928.3	1,011.6	34.4
2009	3,030.0	1,985.7	1,044.3	34.5
2010	3,135.9	2,047.3	1,088.6	34.7
2011	3,237.1	2,080.1	1,157.0	35.7
2012	3,361.8	2,119.6	1,242.2	37.0
2013	3,443.7	2,138.8	1,304.9	37.9
2014	3,530.8	2,185.2	1,345.6	38.1

Source: Lim *et al*. (1998) Table 6.2, for 1970–1985 data; Department of Statistics, Yearbook of Statistics for 1990 data; Ministry of Manpower Labor Force Time Series for 1991 onwards. Data for 1990, 1995, 2000 and 2005 are unavailable as the Labor Force Survey was not conducted in those years.

end of each five-year plan period (Table 4). An indication of the urgency with which population matters were considered by the government at the time can be found in then Minister for Health Chua Sian Chin's remarks in a speech[9] in 1974 that "(t)he target of the Singapore Family Planning and Population Programme is to achieve a

---

[9] Speech by Mr. Chua Sian Chin, then Minister for Health and Home Affairs, at the Toa Payoh Library, 7 July 1974. Singapore Government Press Statement.

Table 4.   Five-year plan family planning targets and achievements: Singapore Family Planning and Population Board, 1966–1970 to 1976–1980.

Plan and period	Targets	Achievements
1st Five-year plan (1966–1970)	To reduce the Crude Birth Rate from 32 per 1000 in 1964 to around 20 per 1000 in 1970.	Crude Birth Rate reduced to 22.1 per 1000 in 1970.
	To provide family planning services to 60% of all married women aged 15–44 years.	156,556 married women of reproductive ages (62%) accepted family planning with the board's clinics.
2nd Five-year plan (1971–1975)	To reduce the Crude Birth Rate from 22.1 per 1000 in 1970 to 18 per 1000 by 1975.	Crude Birth Rate reached 17.8 per 1000 in 1975.
	To recruit 16,000 new acceptors per year from 1971 to 1975, for a total of 80,000 over the five-year period.	Program recruited 89,501 new acceptors, exceeding the target by 11.9%.
	To retain through sustained service the 156,556 acceptors already registered in the Program.	
	To promote male and female sterilization for those who had completed their family size.	
	To create awareness of family planning's benefits among youths, those of marriageable age, and newlyweds, particularly those in the lower-income and education groups.	
3rd Five-year plan (1976–1980)	To maintain replacement-level fertility so as to achieve zero population growth by 2030.	Total Fertility Rate reached 1.82 children per woman in 1980.

Gross Reproduction Rate of around 1.0 or an average of 2 children per family by 1980. Even if this target is achieved, Singapore will only attain zero population growth and the population stops growing in 50 to 60 years' time after 1980. By then, the population in Singapore will have reached 5 to 7 million" (pp. 3–4). He worried that this would be difficult to achieve as it would require the fertility rate to be reduced by 5% annually "from now onwards" as the fertility rate was already low. However, he argued that "in our overcrowded Singapore, *we have no other choice*" (emphasis added by authors).

From 1966 to 1980, the Singapore Family Planning and Population Board (the statutory agency established under the Ministry of Health which administered the

National Family Planning and Population Programme) provided a range of family planning services through an island-wide network of maternal and child health clinics, which included contraceptive services, home visits and a family planning clinic for men. With the legalization of sterilization in 1970 through the Voluntary Sterilization Act, such services were also offered at government hospitals, and with further liberalization in 1975 to permit on-demand sterilization at affordable cost, this also became available at private hospitals. Between 1970 and 1977, almost 61,000 women and men were sterilized under the program (Saw, 2005) with a peak sterilization rate[10] of 19.0 in 1976. Abortion was also legalized in 1970 (via the Abortion Act 1969) and liberalized in 1975, with some 59,359 legal abortions performed during the period 1970–1977 (Saw, 2005).

Aside from the traditional family planning measures, the most distinctive feature of Singapore's programme was a comprehensive package of social policies made up of disincentives and indirect incentives to encourage the acceptance of small family sizes and to discourage large families. According to Wan and Loh (1979, pp. 102–103), "the basic purpose of many of the social policies ... was to reduce or eliminate heavy government subsidising of certain services ... The rationale is that individuals who use services paid for by other taxpayers should adopt a more responsible reproductive behavior". Amongst the array of disincentives were restrictions on maternity leave, initially for the first three, then for the first two children born; progressively higher accouchement charges for higher-order births; a restriction of income-tax reliefs to the first children born; priority in the allocation of public flats to families with fewer children; and priority in the registration to primary schools to children from families of three or fewer children. Indirect incentives aimed at encouraging voluntary sterilization included paid maternity leave for female civil servants who underwent sterilization after their third or higher order birth, seven days of unrecorded full pay leave for civil servants after sterilization, waiving of delivery charges in government-subsidized wards if they accepted sterilization, and priority in primary school registration for children whose parents were sterilized before age 40 after having no more than two children. Whilst according to Yap (2001) no child was denied a place in school nor a family deprived of public housing due to the family's fertility decisions, the measures aimed at promoting small families were successful in making reductions in third-order births and higher the most important factor in fertility decline in the 1970s (Anderson *et al.*, 1977).

Whilst the government's family planning policies were taking effect in the 1970s, there was strong recognition that the country's high pace of economic growth would nevertheless require the inflow of more highly skilled labor than the domestic workforce

---

[10] Defined as the number of sterilizations per thousand women in the reproductive age groups from 15 to 44 years.

Table 5.   Summary of marriage and parenthood packages 2001, 2004 and 2008.

	2001	2004	2008
Baby bonus			
Cash gift	1st child: n.a. 2nd child: $3,000 3rd child: $6,000 4th child: n.a.	1st child: $3,000 2nd child: $4,000 3rd child: $6,000 4th child: $6,000	1st child: $4,000 2nd child: $4,000 3rd child: $6,000 4th child: $6,000
Co-Savings	1st child: n.a. 2nd child: $6,000 3rd child: $12,000 4th child: n.a. 5th and subsequent child: n.a.	1st child: n.a. 2nd child: $6,000 3rd child: $12,000 4th child: $12,000 5th and subsequent child: n.a.	1st child: $6,000 2nd child: $6,000 3rd child: $12,000 4th child: $12,000 5th and subsequent child: $18,000
Tax measures			
Tax reliefs	Enhanced child relief * Higher relief for children below 12 1st child: 5% of income 2nd child: 10% or 15%* 3rd child: 15% or 20%* 4th child: 15% or 25%* Further Tax Rebate 3rd and 4th child: 15% (capped at $20,000 and $40,000 respectively)	Working mother child relief 1st child: 5% of income 2nd child: 15% 3rd child: 20% 4th child: 25%	Working mother child relief 1st child: 15% of income 2nd child: 20% 3rd child: 25% for each (capped at 100% of mother's earned income)
	Qualifying child relief $2000 per child	Qualifying child relief $2000 per child	Qualifying child relief $4000 per child
	Handicapped child relief	Handicapped child relief	Handicapped child relief
	$3500 per handicapped child	$3500 per handicapped child	$5500 per handicapped child
	Grandparent care-giver relief n.a	Grandparent caregiver relief $3000	Grandparent caregiver relief $3000
Tax rebates	Special tax rebate 1st child: n.a. 2nd child: $5,000–20,000 3rd child: $20,000 4th child: $20,000	Parenthood tax rebate 1st child: n.a. 2nd child: $10,000 3rd child: $20,000 4th child: $20,000	Parenthood tax rebate 1st child: $5000 2nd child: $10,000 3rd child: $20,000 4th child: $20,000

(Continued)

Table 5. (*Continued*)

	2001	2004	2008
Childcare/infant care			
Childcare Subsidy	$150/month	$150/month	$300/month
Infant care subsidy		$400/month	$600/month
Enhance childcare services			• 200 new centers by 2013 • Scholarships and bursaries
Foreign domestic worker levy		$95 concession per month	$95 concession per month
Leave			
Paid maternity leave	8 weeks	12 weeks	16 weeks
Paid childcare leave	n.a.	2 days/year for each parent	6 days/year for each parent
Unpaid infant care leave	n.a.	n.a	6 days/year for each parent
Delivery and fertility			
Medisave maternity package	n.a.	Medisave can be used for delivery and pre-delivery expenses, as well as; Assisted Conception Procedures	
Assisted reproduction technology (ART)	n.a.	n.a.	50% co-funding (up to $3000) for each ART treatment cycle in public hospitals (up to 3 cycles)
Enhanced programmes for singles			
			• Merger of SDU and SDS • Programmes to develop dating industry
Work-life			
	Formation of tripartite committee on work-life strategies	• Organizations can tap into the Work-Life Works! (WOW!) Fund to implement work-life strategies • Five day work week introduced for Civil Service	

Source: National Population and Talent Division.

was then able to supply. Then Finance Minister Dr. Goh Keng Swee pointed out in his 1970 Budget statement that "the demand for engineers, and management and technical personnel will be of a different order of magnitude from what we have been accustomed to. This, then, will be the principal difficulty which we have to overcome ... supply(ing) investors with skilled personnel of all grades, without which modern industry cannot operate. Since it takes four years for an engineering student to graduate and several more years before he acquires sufficient experience to be able to work effectively in an organization, clearly we cannot depend on local supply to meet the demand in these fields ... It is therefore necessary, as a matter of high priority, that we should relax our immigration and work permit restrictions on the inflow of personnel belonging to the categories I have described ... It would be a clear advantage to liberalize the conditions under which such people can come into Singapore, acquire permanent residence and eventual citizenship." Pang (1979) noted that Singapore also gains other advantages beyond sourcing of scarce skilled labor, as it avoids having to pay the "high cost of rearing and educating migrant workers, but it reaps the productive output of the migrants' prime working years". Migrant workers also provide flexibility to the labor market and the economy by being quicker to source in a tight labor market (thus relieving upward pressure on wages) as compared to domestic labor sources that may require many years of forward planning to train and nurture. Furthermore, foreign workers may be more readily repatriated in a downturn.

To enable the intake of higher skilled foreign labor and to promote industrialization, the government introduced various schemes from the late 1960s for foreign entrepreneurs and investors to acquire permanent residence in Singapore, whilst foreign skilled workers and professionals with recognized university degrees who could command a specified minimum basic salary (S$1,500 in 1984) were readily issued with employment passes for temporary work in Singapore for up to three years at a time. Those eligible under these schemes for professionals, entrepreneurs and investors were put on a faster track towards citizenship and were able to apply for Singapore citizenship after at least two years of stay as permanent residents, whilst other permanent residents with acceptable skills and qualifications could apply for citizenship after at least five years of residence. In contrast, the normal requirement for citizenship was ten years of permanent residence. According to Pang and Lim (1982), Chinese from Malaysia, Hong Kong, Taiwan, Indonesia and other Southeast Asian countries were particularly welcomed.

Whilst official government policy favored the intake of skilled foreign labor, there was recognition of the limits to total foreign worker intake which led Dr. Goh in 1972 to posit the question[11] "at what point do we stop importing foreign workers and

---

[11] At an address to the Symposium on "Singapore in the International Economy" at the University of Singapore, 19 March 1972 (as recorded in Goh, K.S. 1995, The Practice of Economic Growth, Singapore: Times Publishing).

cease to encourage foreign entrepreneurs and capital into Singapore?" He quoted Dr. Albert Winsemius (an international economist who consulted for the Singapore government extensively in the 1960s) who suggested the answer to the question be when the number of workers in the manufacturing industries reached 500,000 (in the event, this level was not reached in the 1970s). Pang and Lim (1982) also noted the indirect and social costs of a large foreign worker population, including the costs of providing housing, public transportation, social services and recreational facilities for foreigners. In 1981, a policy to phase out unskilled labor from non-traditional source countries such as Indonesia, Sri Lanka, India and Bangladesh by 1986, and for those from traditional sources (primarily Malaysia) by 1991 was announced (Hui, 2002). This followed the recognition that continued large scale importation of foreign unskilled labor would retard the efforts at restructuring the economy towards higher technology sectors. Administrative measures were introduced to limit the number of industries that could employ foreign workers, with a ratio of foreign to local workers in approved industries. A foreign worker levy was introduced in 1982, with the amount pegged at a level that was slightly above the employers' contribution rate to the Central Provident Fund (the mandatory retirement savings scheme for resident workers, Low *et al.,* 1989). By raising the price of foreign labor to employers, the government hoped that the levy would operate as a price mechanism to regulate the demand for foreign workers and allocate supply accordingly. The Economic Committee set up by the Ministry of Trade and Industry in 1985 however proposed abandoning this policy of phasing out foreign workers because Singapore should "continue to allow a revolving pool of foreign workers on short-term permits [as] ... our industries will require foreign workers to overcome temporary shortages, and to work in jobs where it has proven difficult to employ Singaporeans" (Economic Committee, 1986).

Rapid economic expansion on the back of the success of Singapore's industrialization programme had necessitated a relaxation in foreign worker policies by the late 1960s (Lee, 1979). The importation of foreign labor continued in the 1970s, except for a recession-induced period of retrenchment in 1974/1975, and again in the mid-80s. By 1985, the foreign labor force represented 9% of the total labor force, whilst unemployment was at 4.2%. Whilst overall labor force participation had risen during this initial phase of Singapore's development (from 56.6% in 1970 to 65.6% in 1985), the largest gains came from female labor force participation which increased from 29.5% in 1970 to 47.9% in 1985, with the most substantial gains for females in the prime reproductive age group of 25–44 years.

3.2. *End of the Anti-natalist Period*

Most of the targets of the National Family Planning and Population Programme set in each of the three Five-year Plans were achieved, some well ahead of schedule.

Replacement level fertility was achieved in 1975, five years ahead of the original target date, and the practice of developing five-year plans ended after 1980 (with the conclusion of the 3rd Five-Year Plan) as fertility levels continued to decline below the replacement level. By 1984 the government began to relax its strong anti-natalist stance and introduced selective measures to promote larger family sizes among better-educated women. Better-educated women were having on average fewer than two children, whereas those with no educational qualifications were bearing an average of three. In addition, better-educated women were more likely than others to remain unmarried (Saw, 1990). As a result of this, the then Prime Minister Lee Kuan Yew recommended amending the anti-natalist policies "so that our better-educated women will have more children to be adequately represented in the next generation" (Lee, 1983).

The government amended its policies relating to primary school registration to give priority to children of women who were university graduates and who had at least three children ("the graduate mother scheme"). The level of income-tax relief for mothers with certain academic qualifications was also increased, and at the same time the government established a government agency to promote social interaction among men and women public officers with university degrees, with a view to increasing the marriage rate amongst them. The "graduate mother scheme" was however abandoned in 1985 on account of the controversy it had raised, and the small number of children who were likely to benefit from the measure (Yap, 2001).

The Singapore Family Planning and Population Board was dissolved in June 1986, with the board's staff and functions transferred to the Ministry of Health. With the dissolution of the board (then solely responsible for the National Family Planning and Population Programme), it can be said the anti-natalist phase of Singapore's population policy ended. The total fertility rate in that year was 1.43. Saw (1987) noted that it was "important to recognize that as soon as fertility dropped below (the) replacement level, the strong anti-natalist policies were no longer consistent with the national demographic goal of working toward a stationary population in the 21st century ... If fertility still fails to move back to (the) replacement level, there is little choice but to proceed a step further by introducing pro-natalist policies aimed at influencing couples to produce more children."

Should Singapore's anti-natalist policies be viewed as a mistake? The prevailing view amongst sociologists and demographers in Singapore is that the anti-natalist policies were necessary at the time, with the fertility decline in the early days of Singapore's independence "contributing to, or at least providing breathing space for, development... permitting resources that would otherwise have been spent on merely sustaining a rapidly growing population to be channelled into productive development" (Goh Keng Swee, cited in Yap, 2001). Whilst there were those who called for a change in policy when the replacement level was reached in 1975 (Saw, 1990 amongst others), to be fair to the policymakers then, it was not entirely clear at that time that the fertility decline to replacement level was permanent, or merely a blip.

3.3. *1987–2012*

The transition of Singapore's population policy from anti-natalist to pro-natalist may be marked by the March 1987 announcement by then First Deputy Prime Minister Goh Chok Tong of a new population policy, which encouraged Singaporeans who could afford it to have families of three or more children. The promotion of marriage was integral to the new population policy, which was supported by a package of financial and other incentives for child-rearing. These included tax rebates for the third and fourth child and income tax relief for up to four children; incentives to minimize the conflict between women's work in the formal economy and child-rearing via the establishment of childcare subsidy, a concessionary foreign maid levy for eligible families and paid childcare leave; and the modification of earlier incentives promoting the two-child family such as priority in allocation of housing and primary school registration for families with three rather than two children (Yap, 1995).

The new population policy was put in place after a decade of below replacement level fertility. The seriousness of the demographic challenge that had emerged can be detected in a speech given by then First Deputy Prime Minister Goh Chok Tong in August 1986 (Goh, 1986), noting the country's "changing demographic profile — its size, composition and age distribution" which he portrayed as a "human resource problem". The lack of young workers and productivity growth, the tax burden on smaller cohorts of the young providing for an increasingly older population, and a lack of national servicemen to protect the nation were three main concerns identified in the speech. These concerns reflected what demographers had been highlighting (Yap, 2009). Prolonged below replacement fertility leads to population ageing as fewer babies are born and the proportion of young drops. Over time the population could then decline, once the number of deaths exceeds the number of births. The work force is also subjected to the same processes of ageing and decline as fewer young workers enter the work force to replace those who retire. Population projections showed the size of the population would begin to diminish in the early part of the 21st century in the absence of immigration and a return of fertility to replacement levels, and the ageing and shrinking of the workforce (Manpower 21 Steering Committee, 1999).

Notwithstanding the shift away from an explicitly anti-natalist population policy, the government's approach to fertility in 1990s can be best described as selectively pro-natalist. As Saw (2005, p. 162) noted: "The old anti-natalist measures were not eliminated. They were rendered less severe ... to permit for some additional births. There was still the concern that a complete elimination of the anti-natalist measures might lead to excessive births among certain segments of the population, such as the poor and lesser-educated group."

This period continued to see substantial growth for the Singapore economy, but also substantial volatility, starting amidst the economic restructuring following the mid-1980s recession, and punctuated by the Asian Financial Crisis in 1997/1998, the post-9/11 recession in 2003, and the Global Financial Crisis in 2008/2009. Increasing labor costs from a maturing economy, competition from developed countries with better technology and human capital and from developing countries with lower labor and land costs were chief amongst the challenges the country faced (Thangavelu, 2009). The political leadership believed that Singapore therefore needed to supplement the domestic work force through immigration, which would serve the purpose of both topping up shortfalls in domestic labor supply resulting from the shrinking number of births as well as in skilled labor (Yap, 2009).

In July 1989, a more open immigration policy was announced, lowering the eligibility for permanent residence to the holders of 5 GCE 'O' Levels who earned a monthly income of S$1,500 and had at least five years' work experience. For business investors and entrepreneurs, the value of their proposed investments was also lowered to less than S$1 million. At the time of the announcement,[12] no mention was made of the total number of permanent residents that would be admitted, but 25,000 applicants were specifically allowed from Hong Kong.

Data on immigration flows before 2001 are not publicly available, whilst data for the 2000s is only intermittently provided (see National Population and Talent Division, 2006, 2010 and 2012, March 1). Nevertheless, an estimate of the extent of immigration flows in the period 1987–2013 can be seen in Figure 4, which provides a picture of net migrants obtained via an indirect method of taking the difference between total population growth and the growth due to natural increase. The space between the two lines shows the net in-migration in the years 1987–2013 far exceeded the growth through natural increase (the number of births less the number of deaths in the year), with the exception of the recession year of 2003 (exacerbated by the Severe Acute Respiratory Syndrome, or SARS health scare). The rate of growth in immigrant flows accelerated, particularly in the period 2005–2012 with an average of 48,000 annual increases in the resident population, compared with an average annual natural increase of about 19,000 in those years. Singapore's total population grew at an average annual 140,000 during that period, with a peak increase of 250,797 in 2008, moderating to an annual average rise of about 108,000 in the years 2010–2012.

---

[12]Government of Singapore Press Release, Ministry of Home Affairs, 10 July 1989.

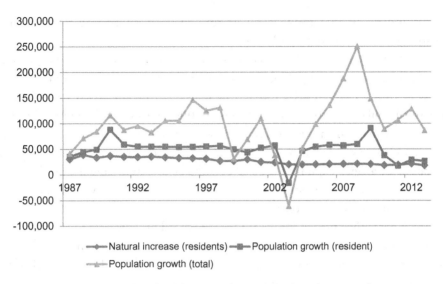

Figure 4.   Singapore total and resident population growth and estimated net migration.

Source: Singapore Department of Statistics, Population Trends 2014.

Continued declines in fertility through the 1990s led to further measures being introduced in a series of Marriage and Parenthood Packages in 2001, 2004 and 2008 (see Table 5). The first of these announced in 2000 introduced the Baby Bonus, comprising a two-tier payment involving an outright cash gift component and a co-saving component matched dollar-for-dollar by the government (subject to a cap) given to second and third children payable over six years to be used for childcare or child development purposes, as well as paid maternity leave for the third child. Other incentives, including paid childcare leave of up to six days in a year for each parent and the co-funding of the use of Assisted Reproductive Technology were introduced in subsequent packages in 2004 and 2008, whilst existing incentives such as the Baby Bonus and maternity leave entitlements were enhanced.

The combination of declining fertility (notwithstanding the enhanced pro-natalist policies) and increased in-migration, especially in the latter half of the 2000s, led to a declining proportion of citizens to the total population. Whilst in 1970, the citizen population accounted for 90.4% of the total population, permanent residents 3.6% and non-permanent resident foreigners 2.9%, by 2010 the citizen population had declined to 63.6%, with permanent residents and non-permanent resident foreigners making up 10.7% and 25.7% respectively (Saw, 2012). With a high pace of naturalization and immigration, 22.7% of the resident population[13] (comprising both

---

[13] From Department of Statistics, Census of Population 2010, Table 11.

citizens and permanent residents) were foreign-born, suggesting that 55.3% of Singapore's total population was local-born.

The sharp increase in the number of foreigner population had by the late 2000s given rise to concern amongst Singaporeans, with the issues arising from the increased inflow of immigrants and its impact on society being discussed in Parliament (National Population and Talent Division, 2010 March 4). An Economic Strategies Committee convened in 2009 recommended in its report in 2010 that Singapore's foreign worker population not exceed about one-third of the total workforce (Economic Strategies Committee, 2010), noting at the same time the need to "raise the quality of the foreign workforce, and give employers incentive to retain experienced and skilled foreign workers".

The General Election in May 2011 was described as a "watershed" election, with cost of living increases in part propelled by population growth in the late 2000s amongst the most important considerations of voters in the 2011 election (Institute of Policy Studies, 2011). The ruling People's Action Party (PAP) won 60.1 % of the votes, its lowest share of the vote since independence, with the PAP behaving like "it had suffered a historic setback" (Janadas Devan, quoted in Institute of Policy Studies, 2011). The government acknowledged the extra-ordinary responses to the crises of 2000s had meant that "the growth in foreign workforce, total population, infrastructure and housing were not aligned", contributing to anxiety amongst the local population, crowdedness and integration problems (National Population and Talent Division, 2013 February 4).

According to the National Population and Talent Division (NPTD), 2012 marked a demographic turning point for Singapore. The first cohort of post-war Baby Boomers born between 1947 and 1965 began to turn 65 years of age in that year, and the NPTD noted that by 2020, the pool of working-age citizens would start to shrink as more citizens exit the working-age band of 20–64 years than would enter it (National Population and Talent Division, 2012). Just a year earlier, Singapore's age dependency ratio reached its lowest point at 35.3 (see Figure 2), marking the end of the country's demographic dividend phase. Prime Minister Lee Hsien Loong noted in his 2012 New Year's Message:[14] "Population is a particularly complex and critical challenge. Like most other developed societies, Singaporeans are having too few babies, and our population is ageing. We must find workable solutions to keep our society vibrant and forward-looking, maintain our economic vitality and strengthen our Singapore core... Singaporeans need to have enough children to replace ourselves, yet getting married and having children are ultimately personal decisions. A vibrant economy needs enough workers and talent, yet we run into physical and social constraints if we admit

---

[14] Prime Minister's Office, 2012 New Year Message 31 Dec 2011. Accessible at http://www.pmo.gov.sg/mediacentre/prime-ministers-2012-new-year-message.

too many foreign workers too quickly. Diversity enriches our society, but only provided new arrivals adopt our values and culture. We need to balance all these conflicting factors, make judicious compromises, and accept the unavoidable tradeoffs." There are in these comments some tacit recognition of the societal limits to a policy of replacement migration, and the need to control the pace and the nature of in-migration.

3.4. *2013 and Beyond*

This phase of Singapore's population policies can best be described as a continuation of pro-natalist policies with a tightly calibrated immigration policy. The Population White Paper: A Sustainable Population for a Dynamic Singapore was published in January 2013 (National Population and Talent Division, 2013), setting out the demographic challenges facing the country: as a result of ultra-low fertility and higher life expectancy, the citizen population and work force would age rapidly and begin declining from 2020 onwards. The simultaneous aging and shrinking trends in the population presaged lower economic growth prospects as well as an impending inability to meet its national security needs (Chong, 2013). The White Paper proposed a significant shift in immigration policy, with a decrease in the rate of workforce and population growth compared to previous decades. Up to 2020, the government proposed an annual rate of workforce growth of between 1% and 2%, compared with a compound annual rate of growth of 3.3% in the three decades from 1980 to 2010. The permanent resident foreign population would be capped at between 500,000 and 600,000 persons, to "ensure a pool of good quality candidates for Singapore citizenship" (National Population and Talent Division, 2013), indicating the continuation of a policy of replacement migration (albeit a more tightly controlled one). The White Paper included a projection of Singapore's total population of between 6.5 and 6.9 million in 2030, which would be used in the government's long-range planning for infrastructure development purposes.

At the same time, the 2013 Marriage and Parenthood Package was announced, further enhancing pro-family initiatives put in place in the earlier Marriage and Parenthood Packages of 2001, 2004 and 2008, but also introducing paid paternity leave of one week which may be taken within 12 months of birth, and significant updates to the incentives for employers to introduce work-life schemes and flexible working arrangements.

Whilst the new population policy as enunciated in the White Paper had been in force for less than 18 months, by mid-2014 workforce growth[15] in Singapore had declined to 2.5%, with a large deceleration in the rate of growth in the foreign workforce to 3.1% (from 5.0% in the year earlier). The Government also reiterated its

---

[15] Ministry of Manpower, Labour Force in Singapore, 2014.

commitment to maintaining the ethnic balance within the citizen population, addressing concerns from minority ethnic groups of the changing composition of the population due to immigration (Singapore Parliament Reports, Hansard). The total fertility rate in 2014 rose to 1.25 births per woman, up from 1.19 the year before, whilst there was a pick-up in the number of marriages involving at least one citizen to 24,037 (the highest since 1997) with the NPTD attributing the increase to an increased availability of flats and the children of Baby Boomers entering marriageable age (Saad, 2015).

Where next for the country's pro-natalist policies? Why have successively enhanced pro-natalist marriage and parenthood initiatives not had the effect of boosting fertility levels further? Indeed in 2013, Singapore's first Prime Minister Lee Kuan Yew expressed exasperation with the idea of monetary incentives to promote fertility, "declaring that he had given up on Singapore's fertility problem" (quoted in Cheam, 2013). It may be that the socio-economic factors underpinning the country's progression through its demographic transition (rising opportunity costs of raising a family, an open economy and labor market exposed to globalization and external competition) have hitherto proved major obstacles to a sustained reversal in the direction of fertility trends since the 1970s. In the absence of evidence proving the counter-factual, it may also be argued that the policies were successful in preventing an even greater decline in fertility levels.

4. Challenges for the Future

Population policy, both those concerning marriage and parenthood as well as those involving the calibration of immigration, will continue to be an integral part of Singapore's national development strategies. The rapid progression of the demographic transition and persistent below replacement fertility level entrenches some of these demographic trends such that within likely reasonable trajectories of fertility, mortality and immigration, Singapore's population size and age structure can be projected. The Population White Paper represents a significant acknowledgement of the need for population policy to be more tightly integrated in the planning process with the country's socio-economic policies, with an increasing focus away from the quantitative aspects of population size and composition towards quality of growth and the productivity of each worker and citizen in the context of an ageing and shrinking population.

Notable is the emphasis on the socio-economic implications of an aging population, with the resident population old-age dependency ratio projected to rise from 15.2 persons to 36.9 by 2050, assuming the Total Fertility Rate remains at 1.24 and annual net in-migration at 30,000 persons (Yap and Gee, 2014). How will an aging workforce be able to sustain productivity levels to ensure a reasonable rate of economic growth? What levels of in-migration, and what kind of foreign labor will be needed?

Policies promoting labor force participation are likely to be central to the next phase, with continuing education opportunities for mid-career and older workers, as well as incentives to encourage mothers to return to the work force after having children. Policies such as extending the retirement age in tandem with improved health and education levels of older workers should also be considered, as should efforts to develop alternative career pathways to offset the effects of delayed entry into the workforce due to an ever increasing number of years spent in education.

References

Anderson, JE, MC Cheng and F Wan (1977). A component analysis of recent fertility decline in Singapore. *Studies in Family Planning*, 8(11), 282–287.

Cheam, J (2013). Baby bonus won't solve our fertility problem. Retrieved from The Straits Times Singapolitics Blog: http://www.singapolitics.sg/views/baby-bonus-wont-solve-our-fertility-problem.

Chong, T (2013). Singapore's population white paper: Impending integration challenges. *ISEAS Perspective*, 1–4.

Economic Committee (1986). *The Singapore Economy: New Directions.* Singapore: Ministry of Trade and Industry.

Economic Strategies Committee (2010). *Report of the Economic Strategies Committee.* Singapore: Ministry of Trade and Industry.

Goh, C (1986). "The second long march." Speech by Mr. Goh Chok Tong, *First Deputy Prime Minister at the Nanyang Technological Institute Forum.* Singapore, Singapore: Singapore Government Press Release No. 20/AUG 05-1/86/08/04.

Hui, W (2002). Foreign manpower policy in Singapore. In *Singapore Economy in the 21st Century — Issues and Strategies*, A Koh, K Lim, W Hui, B Rao and M. Chng (eds.), pp. 29–50. Singapore: McGraw-Hill Education.

Institute of Policy Studies (2011). IPS post-election forum report. Singapore: Institute of Policy Studies. Retrieved from http://lkyspp.nus.edu.sg/ips/wp-content/uploads/sites/2/2013/06/PEF_2011_report.pdf.

Lee, K (1983). *National Day Rally Speech.* Singapore: Government of Singapore.

Lee, S (1979). Population, industrial development, and economic growth. In *Public Policy and Population Change in Singapore*, PS Chen and JT Fawcett (eds.), pp. 229–242. New York: The Population Council.

Lee, S (2007). *Singapore: From Place to Nation.* Singapore: Prentice Hall.

Lim Chong Yah and Associates (1988). *Policy Options for the Singapore Economy.* Singapore: McGraw-Hill.

Low, L, T Soon and M Toh (1989). The foreign worker levy in Singapore's industrial sector: Efficacy and issues. *Southeast Asian Journal of Social Science*, 17(1), 1–20.

Manpower 21 Steering Committee (1999). *Manpower 21 — Vision of a Talent Capital.* Singapore: Ministry of Manpower.

National Population and Talent Division (2006). 16 Aug 2006 — Media interview with DPM Wong Kan Seng on population challenge for Singapore. Retrieved from National

Population and Talent Division — News: http://www.nptd.gov.sg/portals/0/news/Media%20Interview%20with%20DPM%20Wong%20Kan%20Seng%20on%20population%20challenge%20for%20Singapore.pdf.

National Population and Talent Division (2010). Charts. Retrieved from National Population and Talent Division — News: http://www.nptd.gov.sg/portals/0/news/Charts%20for%20DPM's%20speech%20on%20population%20at%20COS%202010%20-%20final.pdf.

National Population and Talent Division (2010). *DPM Wong Kan Seng's Speech on Population at COS.* Singapore: National Population and Talent Division.

National Population and Talent Division (2012). DPM Teo Chee Hean's Speech on Population at the Committee of Supply, 1 March 2012. Retrieved from National Population and Talent Division — News: http://www.nptd.gov.sg/por-tals/0/news/DPM%20Teo%20Chee%20Hean%20-%20speech%20on%20population%20at%20COS%202012.pdf.

National Population and Talent Division (2012). *Occasional Paper on Citizen Population Scenarios.* Singapore: National Population and Talent Division.

National Population and Talent Division (2013). *Marriage and Parenthood Study 2012. Press Release.* Singapore: National Population and Talent Division.

National Population and Talent Division (2013). Speech by Deputy Prime Minister and Minister for Home Affairs Teo Chee Hean. *Parliamentary Debate on Population White Paper.* Singapore, Singapore: National Population and Talent Division.

National Population and Talent Division, Prime Minister's Office (2013). *A Sustainable Population For A Dynamic Singapore — Population White Paper.* Singapore: National Population and Talent Division.

Pang, E (1979). Public policy on population, employment, and immigration. In *Fertility Policies and the National Family Planning and Population Programme*, PS Chen and JT Fawcett (eds.). pp. 205–215. New York: The Population Council.

Pang, E and L Lim (1982). Foreign labor and economic development in Singapore. *International Migration Review*, 16(3), 548–576.

Saad, I (2015). Double happiness: Higher birth, marriage rates in 2014. Retrieved from Channel NewsAsia: http://www.channelnewsasia.com/news/singapore/double-happiness-higher/1661944.html.

Saw, S (1987). *New Population and Labour Force Projections and Policy Implications for Singapore* (Vol. Research Notes and Discussions Paper No. 61). Singapore: Institute of Southeast Asian Studies.

Saw, S (1990). *Changes in the Fertility Policy of Singapore.* Singapore: Times Publishing for the Institute of Policy Studies.

Saw, S (2005). *Population Policies and Programmes in Singapore.* Singapore: Institute of Southeast Asian Studies.

Saw, SH (2012). *The Population of Singapore*, 3rd edn. Singapore: Institute of South East Asian Studies.

Singapore Parliament Reports (Hansard) (2014). *Committee of Supply — Head U — Prime Minister's Office. Budget, 91, 8.* Singapore, Singapore: Parliament of Singapore.

Thangavelu, SM (2009). Spreading the benefits of growth and managing inequality. In *Impressions of the Goh Chok Tong Years in Singapore,* B Welsh, J Chin, A Mahiznan and T Tan (eds.). pp. 230–239. Singapore: NUS Press and the Institute of Policy Studies.

Van de Kaa, DJ (2002). The idea of a second demographic transition in industrialized countries. *Sixth Welfare Policy Seminar of the National Institute of Population and Social Security,* Tokyo, Japan. Tokyo: National Institute of Population and Social Security.

Wan, F and MT Loh (1979). Fertility policies and the national family planning and population programme. In *Public Policy and Population Change in Singapore,* PS Chen and JT Fawcett (eds.). pp. 97–108. New York: The Population Council.

Wong, T and BS Yeoh (2003). *Fertility and the Family: An Overview of Pro-Natalist Population Policies in Singapore.* Singapore: Asia MetaCentre.

Yap, M (1995). Singapore's "Three or More" policy: The first five years. *Asia-Pacific Population Journal,* 10(4), 39–52.

Yap, M (2001). Population policies and programs in Singapore. In *Population Policies and Programs in East Asia,* A Mason (ed.). pp. 89–113. Honolulu: East West Center.

Yap, M (2009). Bolstering population growth: From babies to immigrants. In *Impressions of the Goh Chok Tong Years in Singapore,* B Welsh, J Chin, A Mahiznan and T Tan (eds.). pp. 265–276. Singapore: NUS Press and the Institute of Policy Studies.

Yap, M and C Gee (2014). *Population Outcomes: Singapore 2050.* Singapore: Institute of Policy Studies.

Yeoh, BS and W Lin (2012). Rapid growth in Singapore's Immigrant Population Brings Policy Challenges. Retrieved February 16, 2015, from Migration Information Source: http://www.migrationpolicy.org/article/rapid-growth-singapores-immigrant-population-brings-policy-challenges.

CHAPTER 10

Singapore's Housing Policies: Responding to the Challenges of Economic Transitions

Sock-Yong Phang

Singapore has developed its own unique state-driven housing system, with three-quarters of its housing stock built by the Housing and Development Board and homeownership financed through Central Provident Fund savings. As a result, it has one of the highest homeownership rates amongst market economies. This chapter provides a historical perspective of the main housing problems faced by successive prime ministers and their respective policy responses. Under the leadership of Prime Minister Lee Kuan Yew (1959–1990), the government established an integrated land-housing supply and housing finance framework to channel much needed resources into the housing sector to deal with a chronic housing shortage. Under Prime Minister Goh Chok Tong (1990–2004), asset enhancement schemes to renew aging estates as well as market deregulation measures were implemented. Prime Minister Lee Hsien Loong (2004–present) has been confronted with a different set of challenges — investment demand for housing, rising inequalities and rapidly aging population. These problems have brought about the introduction of carefully crafted macroprudential policies, targeted housing grants to assist low and middle income households, and schemes to help elderly households monetize their housing equity.

1. Introduction

In the five decades since independence, Singapore has developed its own unique housing system, with 75% of the 2014 housing stock built by the Housing and Development Board (HDB), a statutory board established in 1960. In 1968, the Singapore government introduced a significant housing policy innovation when

This chapter draws from Phang (2007, 2013a, 2013b) as well as unpublished papers prepared for the World Bank in 2010, the Asian Development Bank in 2011, and the World Bank Institute and Korea Development Institute in 2013. In particular, I thank Dr. Loic Chiquier of the World Bank for discussions on the problems encountered in countries where governments have adopted or adapted various components of Singapore's housing policies.

Central Provident Fund (CPF) savings were allowed to be used for downpayment and mortgage payments for HDB flats. As a result, 87% of the resident population lived in HDB housing and the homeownership rate had increased to 88% by 1990 — one of the highest rates amongst market economies. The HDB–CPF framework established in the 1960s has transformed the urban form of Singapore and remains largely intact for five decades. The housing challenges confronting each government have however evolved over the years. Singapore's three prime ministers since independence each faced a different set of housing problems during their terms and responded with a different set of housing policies.

This chapter provides a historical perspective of the main housing problems faced by each prime minister and the respective policy responses. Section 2 provides an overview of the integrated land-housing supply and financing framework established by the government of Prime Minister Lee Kuan Yew in the 1960s to channel resources into the housing sector. Section 3 presents the challenges of renewing aging estates and creating a market for HDB flats in the 1990s under the government of Prime Minister Goh Chok Tong. Section 4 describes the housing challenges faced by Prime Minister Lee Hsien Loong — speculative and investment housing demand, rising inequalities and an aging population. These have brought about the introduction of carefully crafted macro-prudential policies, targeted housing grants to assist low and middle income households, and schemes to help elderly households monetize their housing equity. Section 5 concludes with observations on the limited transferability of Singapore's housing model.

2. The Lee Kuan Yew Government, 1959–1990: Laying the Foundations

Mr. Lee Kuan Yew's government is to be credited with laying the foundations for the successful economic development of Singapore in the 1960s. The political turbulence from self-government, merger with Malaysia, and unexpected independence was not conducive to attracting long term investments. On the housing front, the government was faced with a largely immigrant and growing population, a chronic housing shortage as well as insufficient private sector resources and capacity to provide adequate solutions.

The Singapore Improvement Trust (SIT), a statutory board created by the colonial government in 1927, had been established as a town planning authority and also undertook road construction and general improvement of the city. In 1932, the housing shortage led the government to expand the SIT's responsibilities to include the provision of houses and flats for lower income groups. By 1941, SIT had completed construction of only some 2,000 dwellings.[1]

---

[1] See Phang (1992), Chapter 3 for a description of the SIT and other public sector agencies involved in housing development in the 1960s and 1970s.

In the post-war period, the SIT stepped up building activity between 1947 and 1959, building an estimated 21,000 housing units. SIT dwellings housed 8.8% of the population by 1959; a majority of the population resided in overcrowded pre-war shophouses, or slums and tenements without piped water and modern sanitation. Given the appalling overcrowding, the newly elected government took upon itself the task of providing homes on a large scale. In the 1960s, the foundations of Singapore's real estate and housing policies were put in place. Three important components of these were the establishment of the HDB in 1960, the enactment of the Land Acquisition Act (LAA) in 1966 and the expansion of the role of the CPF to become a housing finance institution in 1968.

2.1. *1960: The Housing and Development Board*

The HDB began operations on 1 February 1960. It replaced the SIT and was set up as a statutory board to provide "decent homes equipped with modern amenities for all those who needed them". A target of 110,000 dwelling units to be built was set for 1960–1970. From 1964, the HDB began offering housing units for sale on 99-year leasehold basis, under its "Home Ownership for the People" scheme.[2] HDB priced housing units affordably for households with incomes not exceeding S$800 a month, and offered loans such that owners paid less in monthly mortgage payments than they would have done in rents.

The political and economic motivations for homeownership policies are perhaps best understood in the words of the then Prime Minister, Mr. Lee Kuan Yew:

> My primary preoccupation was to give every citizen a stake in the country and its future. I wanted a home-owning society. I had seen the contrast between the blocks of low-cost rental flats, badly misused and poorly maintained, and those of house-proud owners, and was convinced that if every family owned its home, the country would be more stable ... I had seen how voters in capital cities always tended to vote against the government of the day and was determined that our household-ers should become homeowners, otherwise we would not have political stability. My other important motive was to give all parents whose sons would have to do national service a stake in the Singapore their sons had to defend. If the soldier's family did not own their home, he would soon conclude he would be fighting to protect the properties of the wealthy. I believed this sense of ownership was vital for our new society which had no deep roots in a common historical experience (Lee, 2000, pp. 116–117).

---

[2] Phang (1992) and the HDB website at http://www.hdb.gov.sg.

2.2. *1966: Government Land Acquisition*

The most striking feature of the land system in Singapore is the prevalence of government landholding and the leasehold as a method of land holding.[3] More than 90% of land in Singapore belongs to the state and much of the real estate in Singapore is therefore built on land leased from the state. Land scarcity in Singapore has been used to justify extensive state land ownership and the need for judicious allocation of scarce land by the land use planner among various competing uses. In 1966 the government enacted the LAA which permitted the state and its agencies to acquire land for any public purpose, for any work or an undertaking which is of public benefit or of public utility or in the public interest; or for any residential, commercial or industrial purposes. Thus, the government was and is still empowered to acquire sufficient land from private land owners to develop new public housing flats.

A 1973 amendment set payments independent of market conditions and the landowner's purchase price. Between 1973 and 1987, compensation for acquired land was assessed at the market value as at 30 November 1973 or the date of gazette notification whichever was lower. The existence of rent control further depressed land values for affected properties. Government land acquisition at compensation rates below market values in the 1970s greatly facilitated the industrialization and housing programs. State ownership of land grew from 44% in 1960 to 76% by 1985. This dramatic increase was achieved through a combination of land acquisition, land reclamation[4] and the transfer of British military land.

Subsidiary legislation in the form of State Land Rules 1968 provided that titles for state-owned land should be for terms not exceeding 99 years. Through the LAA, the government cleared low density housing, slums, villages and squatter areas, and assembled land parcels. State land was leased to government agencies for the development of "public" housing which was sold on a 99 year leasehold basis to eligible households, and for the development of industrial estates. Subsequent amendments to the Act from 1987 changed the statutory date used for pegging compensation which is currently at market rates.

Public land leasing generally goes under the term Government Land Sales (GLS). Much urban redevelopment in Singapore has been achieved through the GLS program administered mainly by the Urban Redevelopment Authority (URA) and to a smaller extent — the HDB. Under the program, the government amalgamates land, inserts infrastructure, provides planning and urban design guidelines, and releases the land for sale to private (including foreign) developers. Sites are usually sold on 99-year leases for commercial, hotel and private residential development, whereas leases for

---

[3] Phang (1992), Chapter 2; Phang (1996); Centre for Liveable Cities (2014).

[4] Land reclamation works have increased the land area of Singapore since 1965 by more than one-fifth (see Table 1). The government amended legislation (Foreshores Act) to allow foreshore reclamation works to be undertaken without being subject to claims for loss of shoreline.

industrial sites are usually for 60 years or less. The lease tenure for other types of sites varies depending on the use. The usual sale method is through public tender.

2.3. *1968: Mobilization of Provident Fund Savings for Housing Finance*

While HDB and related construction finance and land policy brought about a trans-formation on the housing supply side, demand for homeownership was "created" by directing savings in the CPF towards housing.[5] The CPF had been in existence before the HDB, having been established as a pension plan in 1955 by the colonial government to provide social security for the working population in Singapore. The scheme required contributions by both employers and employees, respectively, of a certain percentage of the individual employee's monthly salary toward the employee's personal and portable account in the fund. All employers are required to contribute monthly to the fund. The bulk of contributions can only be withdrawn for specific purposes (of which housing dominates), at age 55, or on permanent incapacitation of the contributor concerned.

The CPF became an important institution for financing homeownership from September 1968 when legislation was enacted to allow withdrawals from the fund to finance the purchase of housing sold by the HDB and subsequently sold by other public sector agencies as well. The contribution rates for employees at the inception of the CPF in 1955 were five percent of the monthly salary for employees and five per-cent for employers. From 1968, the rates were adjusted upward and peaked at 25% of wages for both employers and employees from 1984 to 1986 (see Figure 1). Contribution rates are currently 20% of wages for Singapore citizen employees and 17% of wages for employers, up to a salary ceiling of S$6,000. Contribution rates are lower for workers above 50 years of age, and the proportion of contributions allocated for investments, retirement, and healthcare also varies with age. Rates have varied depending on economic conditions and changes to contribution rates have been previously used as a macroeconomic stabilization instrument to limit inflation or to reduce wage cost.

The interest rate on CPF Ordinary Account savings is based on a weighted aver-age of 1-year fixed deposit and month-end savings rates of the local banks, subject to a minimum of 2.5% (the current rate). Savings in the Special, Medisave and Retirement accounts earn additional interest of 1.5 percentage points above the normal CPF inter-est rate (currently 4%). From 1 January 2008, an extra 1% interest per year is paid on the first S$60,000 of a member's combined balances.

Between 1968 and 1981, CPF savings could only be withdrawn for purposes of down payment, stamp duties, mortgage and interest payments incurred for the

---

[5] Detailed information can be found at the CPF website: http://www.cpf.gov.sg.

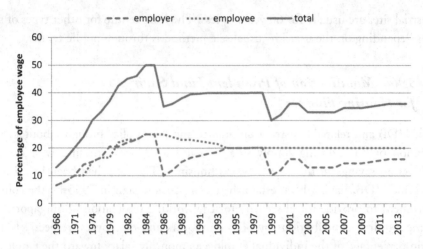

Figure 1.   CPF contribution rates 1968–2014 (percent of employee wage).

Source: Data from Central Provident Fund website at http://www.cpf.gov.sg.

purchase of public-sector-built housing. In 1981, the scheme was extended to allow for withdrawals for mortgage payments for the purchase of private housing. From 1984, rules governing the use of CPF savings have been gradually liberalized to allow for withdrawals for medical and education expenses, insurance, and investments in various financial assets.

The HDB provides mortgage loans and mortgage insurance to purchasers of its leasehold flats (both new and resale). The loan ceiling is 90% of the price of the flat and the maximum repayment period is 25 years.[6] The mortgage interest rate charged by the HDB is pegged at 0.1 percentage points above the CPF ordinary account savings interest rate, which in turn is based on savings rates offered by the commercial banks, subject to a minimum of 2.5%. The HDB is a recipient of government loans to finance its mortgage lending, interest of which is pegged to the prevailing CPF savings rate. The mortgage lending rate charged by the HDB to homeowners is 0.1 percentage point higher than the rate that it borrows from the government, thus ensuring the sustainability of the financing arrangement. A schematic view of how housing is financed in Singapore is shown in Figure 2.

CPF collects member contributions and invests these in special non-tradable government securities that earn the same interest that it pays out to its members:

---

[6] For resale flats, the loan ceiling is 90% of the resale price or 90% of the market value, whichever is lower. The maximum loan repayment period is 65 years minus the buyer's age or 25 years, whichever is shorter. Monthly installments are capped at 30% of the purchaser's gross monthly income. See HDB's website for other terms and conditions at: http://www.hdb.gov.sg/fi10/fi10321p.nsf/w/HLHDBWhat?OpenDocument.

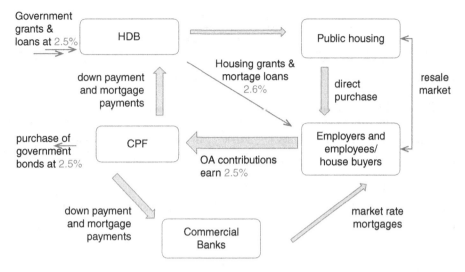

Figure 2. Singapore's CPF mobilization of savings for housing.

Source: Phang (2013a, p. 91).

2.5% and 4%. Each household is eligible to apply twice for new HDB flats (the second application after 10 years of occupying the first, and subject to eligibility conditions) and two loans from the HDB. Housing loans for private housing are provided by commercial banks and finance houses. Housing loans for public housing have also been provided by commercial banks since 2003. With the decline in mortgage interest rates in recent years, commercial banks have been able to offer loans at rates below the HDB loans' 2.6% interest floor and have been increasing their share of mortgage lending.

2.4. *Outcomes of Housing Policy*

Improvements in the urban environment and the standards of housing in Singapore over the next three decades provided very tangible and visible evidence of the success of the economic development and housing strategy adopted by the Singapore government. This overwhelming success has been well documented. Land and properties in the city and rural areas were acquired by the government. Squatter settlements were cleared. Entire neighborhoods and villages were resettled in HDB new towns. HDB's housing stock increased rapidly from 120,138 units in 1970 to 574,443 units in 1990, housing 87% of the resident population (see Table 1). The homeownership rate for the resident population increased from 29% in 1970 to 88% by 1990. Singapore's large public housing sector is therefore in ownership terms, a largely privatized sector. However, ownership tenure of a HDB dwelling differs in many aspects

Table 1.   Key indicators of Singapore's housing sector.

	1970	1980	1990	2000	2010
Total Population (millions)	2.075	2.414	3.047	4.017	5.076
Resident population	2.014	2.282	2.736	3.263	3.772
Non-resident population	0.061	0.132	0.311	0.755	1.304
Resident homeownership rate	29.4%	58.8%	87.5%	92.0%	87.2%
Resident households in HDB dwellings	30.9%	67.8%	85.0%	88.0%	82.4%
Land Area (sq km)	586	618	633	683	712
Macroeconomic Data					
GDP (S$m, 2005 market prices)	$16,556	$39,356	$82,928	$165,358	$286,447
GNP per capita (S$ current)	$2,860	$10,135	$22,868	$40,090	$61,928
Unemployment rate	6%	3.5%	1.4%	3.5%	3.1%
Exchange rate (S$/US$)	S$3.09	S$2.14	S$1.81	S$1.73	$1.36
Gross National Saving/GNP	19.3%	34.2%	43.9%	51.5%	48.4%
Gross Capital Formation/GNP	32.2%	42.2%	31.6%	27.6%	23.6%
Residential construction/GNP	6.2%	5.9%	5.2%	6.2%	6.6%
Housing Loans					
Total housing loans (S$m)	$215	$2,421	$19,151	$102,425	$158,327
Housing loans/GDP	4%	10%	29%	62%	49%
HDB mortgage loans/housing loans	58%	60%	54%	58%	27%
Banks' housing loans*/housing loans	42%	40%	46%	42%	73%
Central Provident Fund					
Balance due members (S$m, current at 31 Dec)	$777	$9,551	$40,646	$90,298	$185,888
Employee contribution rate	8.0%	18.0%	23.0%	20.0%	20.0%
Employer contribution rate	8.0%	20.5%	16.5%	12.0%	15.0%
Prices					
CPI (Nov 97–Oct 98 = 100)	36.5	68.2	85.2	101.1	118.6
Private House Price Index (1998 = 100)	—	27.3	57.7	130.3	194.8
HDB Resale Price Index (1998 = 100)	—	—	34.1	104.9	172
Price of new 4-room HDB flat in new town location (≈ 90 sqm in S$)	$12.500	$24,200	$76,100	$98,000	$260,000

(Continued)

Table 1. (*Continued*)

	1970	1980	1990	2000	2010
Housing Price & Mortgage Affordability					
(4-rm HDB flat price/GNP per capita)	4.42	2.43	3.36	2.32	4.20
15-year housing loan interest rate	n.a	10.83%	7.36%	6.15%	4.41%
HDB mortgage interest rate	6.25%	6.25%	3.98%	2.60%	2.60%
Housing Stock (HS)	305,833	467,142	690,561	1,039,677	1,156,700
Public sector built	120,138	337,198	574,443	846,649	898,532
Private sector built	185,695	129,944	116,118	193,028	258,200
4-room and larger HDB flats/HS (%)	1%	13%	40%	51%	54%
Persons per Dwelling Unit	6.7	5.1	4.4	4.2	4.3

Note: *Includes Finance Houses & Credit POSB.
1984 rate, interest rates refer to average rates compiled from that quoted by 10 leading banks and finance companies; variable rate mortgage loans were available at lower rates.
Sources: Various Singapore government publications and websites.

from ownership of a private dwelling. Ownership rights are limited by numerous regulations concerning eligibility conditions for purchase, resale, subletting and housing loans.

The housing market is highly segmented according to regulations on eligibility of households. Only citizen households are eligible for HDB rental and direct purchase (one unit per household), with current monthly gross household income caps at S$1,500 for rental, S$12,000 for direct purchase of new Build-To-Order (BTO) flats from the HDB and S$14,000 for the Executive Condominium Scheme. The resale HDB sector is open to citizens and permanent residents, with housing grants for purchaser households carefully calibrated according to citizenship, marital status and household income. The private housing sector caters largely to higher income Singapore citizens, permanent residents, expatriates, and foreign investors. Foreign ownership of housing is largely confined to the private flats and condominiums sector.[7]

That a large public housing program could deliver satisfactory housing for the majority in a relatively affluent city testifies to the production efficiency and responsiveness to changes of the Singapore government. This public provision of a private

---

[7] Under the Residential Property Act, foreigners including permanent residents who wish to purchase landed housing have to obtain prior approval from the Minister for Law. If approval is granted, the foreigner or PR is required to use the property for residence only and not for rental or other income-generating purposes. A minimum occupation period of five years and limitation of ownership to only one landed house applies. From 2004, the rule was relaxed for Sentosa Cove landed homes.

good on a large scale was accompanied by numerous regulations on eligibility, resale and financing, which in the earlier decades resulted in some consumption inefficiencies. The public-private hybrid model has however allowed the government to regulate, deregulate and re-regulate the sector with changes in socio-economic as well as market conditions.

Favorable socio-economic effects of Singapore's housing welfare approach include the following[8]:

(i) Increase in savings rate

At the inception of the CPF home ownership scheme in 1968, the Gross National Saving to GNP ratio was less than 20% and insufficient to fund the country's investment needs (32% of GNP). The CPF contributed to a significant leap in the savings rate to 44% of GNP by 1990 (see Table 1) — certainly one of the highest savings rate in the world and more than sufficient to meet the country's investment needs.

(ii) Increase in quantity and quality of housing stock

The housing welfare approach enabled Singapore to mobilize long term resources on the demand side to finance the rapid supply of housing by the public sector with minimal involvement of government expenditure. Although Krugman (1994) has rather critically described Singapore's economic development as "a mobilization of resources that would have done Stalin proud", in the housing sector, it was a mobilization of resources that visibly raised the living standards of the entire population, transformed the built environment of Singapore and resulted in the creation of significant housing and real estate wealth.

(iii) Increase in homeownership rate

The development of well-functioning mortgage markets though desirable in itself is often viewed as a means to achieving a higher homeownership rate. Homeownership is promoted in many countries and various policies and institutional arrangements exist to provide incentives for homeownership by reducing its costs relative to renting (Phang, 2013a). In addition to government provision of affordable subsidized HDB housing and HDB mortgage loans, the policy of allowing high mandatory savings to be used for home purchase and not rental made homeownership the dominant option for almost all Singaporean households. Not surprising, and given sustained income increases and low unemployment rates, the homeownership rate for the resident population increased from 29% in 1970 to 88% by 1990 (see Table 1).

---

[8] See Phang (2007) for details.

(iv) Development of the mortgage sector

Housing policy has contributed in a major way to the development of the mortgage sector in Singapore. In 1970, shortly after the implementation of the CPF Approved Housing Scheme, outstanding housing loans were a mere S$215 million, constituting only 4% of GNP. By 1990, the housing loans to GNP ratio had increased to 29%, with the HDB share at 54% (see Table 1).

(v) Racial integration

The large HDB housing sector has played an extremely important role in the shaping of Singapore society. Singapore is a multi-racial multi-religious country; in 2014, the Chinese majority comprised 74.3% of the resident population, Malays 13.3%, Indians 9.1%, with other races comprising 3.3%. The physical plans of HDB new towns have been designed to integrate the various income and racial groups within the public housing program, and this has prevented the development of low-income or ethnic ghettos. The colonial administration had in its early days of town planning, followed a policy of racial segregation. Beginning in the 1970s, the HDB allocated new flats in a manner that would give a "good distribution of races" to different new towns. However, by 1988, a trend of ethnic regrouping through the resale market, was highlighted as a housing problem which would lead to the re-emergence of ethnic enclaves. In 1989, the HDB implemented an Ethnic Integration Policy under which racial limits were set for HDB neighborhoods and blocks. When the set racial limits for a neighborhood/block is reached, those wishing to sell their HDB flats in the particular neighborhood/block had to sell it to another household of the same ethnic group. The government had emphasized that "our multiracial policies must continue if we are to develop a more cohesive, better integrated society. Singapore's racial harmony, long term stability, and even viability as a nation depend on it" (Ooi *et al.*, 1993, p. 14).

(vi) Impact on economic distribution

The vast majority of households including low income households in Singapore have benefited from access to ownership of affordable public housing. The active resale market allows for mobility within and out of the market and for the benefits of price discounts to be capitalized after a minimum occupancy period. Each household is allowed to apply twice for a "housing subsidy" that has been described as "a ticket to an easier life for the HDB heartlander" (The Straits Times, 19 April 1997).

Given the massive program, trade-offs were inevitable. The housing approach adopted in Singapore undoubtedly increased savings and homeownership rates, mobilized resources for the housing sector and contributed to an increase in housing loans and development of the primary mortgage market. However, the approach is not without its detractors. Singapore's housing strategy is inherently policy driven and centrally controlled, with major decisions on savings rate, savings allocation, land use, housing production, and housing prices being largely determined by the government. Pugh (1985), in the context of providing a set of operating guidelines for a good housing system, and advocating Singapore's strategy as a good model, writes:

> ... do not be too perturbed if some orthodox (neo-classical) economists argue that housing is over-allocated by subsidy. Show them that 'subsidy' is a concept which cannot be fitted easily to housing, and produce counter arguments, which are respectable in economics, and which are readily available.

3. The Goh Government, 1990–2004: Market Deregulation and Asset Enhancement

When Mr. Goh Chok Tong succeeded Mr. Lee Kuan Yew as Prime Minister in 1990, the housing shortage problem had been solved. With 88% of households owning their own homes, 87% in HDB flats, the property-owning democracy had become a reality. In the 1990s, the HDB shifted its focus to providing larger and better quality flats for existing HDB and upper-middle income households, redevelopment of older estates, and retrofitting existing flats. Upgrading by households to larger flats within the HDB sector has been facilitated by the development of an active secondary market and a system that allowed an eligible household to apply for a second (usually larger) subsidized flat after a minimum occupation period.

The land planning focus in the early 1990s correspondingly shifted to one that was more visionary and which provided a larger market space for private sector developers to meet the aspirations of a growing segment of the population for more exclusive housing. This was the period when government land sales to private developers resulted in a marked increase in the supply of private housing. Revenue from sale of state land leases constituted a significant proportion of government revenue, particularly during the "boom" years of the 1990s.

Housing policy under Goh Chok Tong's term as Prime Minister was marked by market deregulation, "asset enhancement" and "upgrading" policies. The Goh government came to view Singaporean homes as an asset and potential source of security for their old age (Centre for Liveable Cities and HDB, 2013, p. 15). Policies implemented included deregulation of the HDB resale market including increased housing loans for HDB resale flats which facilitated mobility, physical upgrading of HDB flats and neighborhoods, and the introduction of demand side subsidies in the form of CPF housing grants. These policies partly contributed to the rapid escalation of housing prices in the early half of the 1990s.

3.1. *Resale Market Deregulation*

The desirability of any asset is determined to a large extent by its liquidity, while ease of trade determines the efficiency of a market. The promotion of ownership of subsidized new HDB dwellings was therefore accompanied by policies concerning the secondary market for that housing. From the perspective of public policy, there was early concern that given the then general housing shortage, HDB dwellings should not become a vehicle for speculation by allowing the price subsidies to be capitalized on a secondary market. Resale regulations were therefore extremely onerous in the early days of the housing program. With the easing of the housing shortage, the HDB housing sector was ready for deregulation.

Prior to 1971, there was no resale market for owner-occupied HDB dwellings. HDB required owners who wished to sell their flats to return them to the HDB at the original purchase price plus the depreciated cost of improvements. In 1971, a resale market was created when the HDB allowed owners who had resided in their flats for a minimum of three years to sell their flats at market prices to buyers of their choice who satisfied the HDB eligibility requirements for homeownership. However, these households were debarred from applying for public housing for a year. The debarment period was increased to two and a half years in 1975. The minimum occupancy period before resale was increased to five years in 1973 and has remained in place since.

The debarment period, a great deterrent for any household considering sale of its dwelling, was abolished in 1979 thereby greatly facilitating exchanges within the public housing sector. This was replaced by a five percent levy on the transacted price of the dwelling to "reduce windfall profits". A graded resale levy based on flat type was introduced in 1982, and rules regarding circumstances under which levies could be waived were fine-tuned in the 1980s. The resale levy system ensures that the subsidy on the second new flat purchased by the household from the HDB is smaller than that for the first time HDB flat buyer.

Only citizens, non-owners of any other residential property, households with a minimum size of two persons with household incomes below the income ceiling set by the HDB were eligible to purchase new or resale HDB flats prior to 1989. In 1989, residential mobility was enhanced when the income ceiling restriction was removed for HDB resale flats; the resale market was opened to permanent residents as well as private property owners who had to owner-occupy their HDB flat. HDB flat-owners who could not own any other residential property before, could also invest in private sector built dwellings. From 1991, single citizens above the age of 35 have been allowed to purchase HDB resale flats for owner-occupancy.

The HDB also provides loans to buyers of resale HDB flats. Loan financing prior to 1993 was based on 80% of 1984 HDB new flat (posted) prices. As both new and

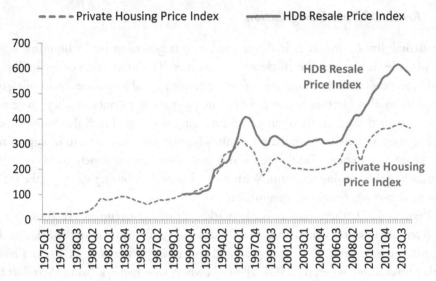

Figure 3.   Nominal house price indices.

Notes: Private house price index, 1975–2014 (1990 Q1=100); HDB resale price index, 1990–2014 (1990 Q1=100).

Sources: Singapore government agencies: Urban Redevelopment Authority, Real Estate Information System REALIS; Housing and Development Board website.

resale prices rose (see Figure 3), households purchasing resale flats had to pay an increasingly larger proportion of the price in cash. In 1993, HDB moved its mortgage financing terms closer to market practice by granting loan financing of up to 80% of current valuation or the declared resale price of the flat, whichever is lower. In 1993, the CPF Board also began to allow withdrawals of CPF savings to be used to meet interest payments on mortgage loans for resale HDB and private housing purchases. Before this, CPF members were allowed to withdraw only up to 100% of the value of these properties at the time of purchase.

Deregulation of the HDB resale market was accompanied by an increase in the number of resale HDB transactions. The transaction volume of resale HDB flats increased from fewer than 800 units in 1979, to 13,000 units in 1987, 60,000 units in 1999, and 31,000 in 2004 (HDB Annual Reports). Resale transactions as a proportion of total (new and resale) owner-occupied public housing transactions, were three %, 37%, 64% and 68% in 1979, 1987, 1999 and 2004 respectively. The increase in the demand for resale flats in the later half of the 1990s was in part due to the introduction of demand side housing grants.

3.2. *CPF Housing Grants*

In 1994, demand-side subsidies in the form of CPF housing grants for the purchase of resale HDB flats were introduced. This represented a shift from total reliance on subsidies tied to new flats to a hybrid system of partial reliance on subsidies tied to resale flats. The subsidy is deposited into the CPF account of the eligible household when it applies to purchase a resale HDB flat. Under the scheme, the government provided the first time applicant household with a grant of S$30,000 to purchase a HDB resale flat close to either parents' or married child's residence. In 1995, the grant was increased to S$50,000. The government also introduced a more general grant of S$40,000 for eligible households that purchase a resale flat which does not need to satisfy the criterion of being close to parents' or married child's residence.

The shift towards constrained housing grants for the purchase of housing on the secondary market was necessary for the following reasons. In the first three decades of the HDB's existence, annual supply of new public housing added substantially to the housing stock particularly in the early 1980s. It was a rapid rate that was consistent with high income and population growth in a situation of grave housing shortage. The supply policies of the HDB that were suitable under the above circumstances had to be reviewed as population growth stabilized and basic housing needs were generally met.

3.3. *HDB Upgrading and Selective En Bloc Redevelopment Schemes*

By the late 1980s, a spatial age gradient for HDB estates had become evident. Older estates had been built closer to the central business district (CBD) and new towns were built at distances further away from the CBD. Also evident was the trend of younger families moving out of older HDB towns as they were allocated new flats in outlying new towns. In 1989, the government announced an ambitious long term HDB Upgrading Programme to upgrade existing HDB estates. The upgrading programs varied in nature and scale (see Table 2) and were subsidized by the government by between 53% and 93% depending on flat type (Centre for Liveable Cities and HDB, 2013, p. 20). The Goh government also launched the Selective En bloc Redevelopment Scheme (SERS) in 1995 under which older low density blocks of HDB flats were demolished and occupants moved to brand new and high density developments within the same estate.

3.4. *Housing Bubble, the EC Scheme and the Asian Financial Crisis*

Financial liberalization as well as positive macroeconomic factors resulted in rapidly rising housing prices in the early 1990s (see Figure 3). In response to growing concern over the affordability of private housing, the government in 1995 introduced the Executive Condominium (EC) scheme, a hybrid public-private house type. The EC scheme also facilitated the HDB's withdrawal from the upper-middle-income housing market, allowing it to discontinue its building of Executive Flats. The EC's similarity with 99-year leasehold private condominiums provided the government with another

Table 2.   HDB upgrading programmes.

Selective En bloc Redevelopment Scheme
- Launched in August 1995
- Old estates with high redevelopment potential identified
- Government acquires flats by compensating flat owners the prevailing market price plus removal expense
- Flat owners guaranteed new replacement flat priced below market value
- Old blocks demolished and new higher density developments built

Main Upgrading Programme (MUP)
- Launched in 1989 to enhance overall living environment of estate
- Residents offered 'standard package' comprising improvements to precinct, block and within flat
- Option of space adding item i.e. extra bathroom, balcony or kitchen extension
- Proceed only if 75% of Singapore Citizen eligible households vote in favor of upgrading works

Lift Upgrading Programme (LUP)
- Launched in 2001 to provide direct lift access, where feasible, to existing HDB blocks without 100 percent direct lift access
- Proceed only if 75% of Singapore Citizen eligible households in a block vote in favor of it

Home Improvement Programme
- Replaced the MUP since August 2007
- *Essential improvements* include replacement of waste pipes, repair of structural cracks, spalling concrete and ceiling leaks, as well as upgrading of electrical supply which are fully funded by the government
- Residents may opt for *improvements works* such as replacement of entrance door, grille gate and refuse hopper, as well as upgrading of toilets/bathrooms, at highly subsidized costs (Singapore citizen residents in 3-room flats pay 5% of the cost, while those in 5-room flat contribute 10% of the costs)

Interim Upgrading Programme (IUP) and IUP Plus
- Launched in 1993
- Provides pedestrian covered linkways, repainting of blocks and new letter boxes
- Fully funded by the government
- Combined with LUP as 'IUP Plus' in May 2002

Neighborhood Renewal Programme
- Replaced the IUP Plus in August 2007
- Focus on block and neighborhood improvements and can be implemented on a larger area basis of two or more contiguous precincts
- All costs borne by government and implemented by town councils
- Examples of improvements include residents' corners and lift lobby tiling, drop-off porch, linkways, soccer pitch, fitness corners and jogging track at neighborhood level
- Proceed if at least 75% of eligible flat owners in the neighborhood indicate their support

---

Source: Summarized from Centre for Liveable Cities and HDB (2013), Appendix B.

instrument on the supply side to impact private housing prices. The government auctions land for the development of EC units to housing developers (private as well as government-linked companies) who are responsible for design, construction, pricing, arrangements for financing and estate management. Applicant households have to satisfy eligibility conditions and abide by resale and other regulations governing these units.

Despite an increase in the supply of new HDB housing, the introduction of the EC scheme, and increased government land sales for private housing development, housing prices continued to soar (with the private housing price index more than tripling between 1990 and 1996). On 15 May 1996, the government introduced a package of measures to curb real estate speculation. These included capital gains taxes on the sale of any property within three years of purchase, stamp duty on every sale and sub-sale of property, limitation of housing loans to 80% of property value, as well as limiting foreigners to non S$ denominated housing loans. The HDB also tightened various regulations. In April 1997, HDB flat buyers were limited to two loans from the HDB where there had been no limit before. In May 1997, the HDB implemented various measures to curb housing demand of upgraders (households applying for a second new subsidized flat from the HDB), including lengthening the time period before flat lessees are eligible to purchase a second new flat from the HDB from five to ten years, and revising the graded resale levy system.

The immediate effect of these measures was to cool the property market which then entered a slump with the onset of the Asian economic crisis in 1997 (see Figure 3). In response to the fall in demand that was particularly pronounced in 1998, the government halted land sales and also ended its long standing policy of not providing housing subsidies for singles by introducing a S$15,000 CPF housing grant for eligible single persons to purchase resale 3-room or smaller flats. As housing prices declined further, the CPF housing grant was reduced in stages over ten months from January to October 1999 — S$500 reduction per month for the Single Citizen housing grant, and S$1,000 reduction per month for other housing grants.

Both the private and public housing sectors were faced with a situation of declining prices and unsold units. The Monetary Authority of Singapore (2001) estimated unsold housing stock of about 19,800 units for the private sector. With more than 17,500 unsold new flats in early 2002, the HDB suspended its Registration for Flat or queuing system, diverting remaining and new applicants to its built-to-order program under which flats are built only when there is sufficient demand for them. In July 2003, in a major restructuring exercise, the HDB's 3,000 strong Building and Development Division[9] was re-organized and the HDB Corporation Private Limited (HDB Corp.) set up as a fully-owned subsidiary of HDB. In November 2004, HDB divested its 100% shareholding in HDB Corp. to the government's investment holding company, Temasek Holdings. HDB Corp. was rebranded as Surbana Corporation

---

[9] At the time of restructuring HDB's staff strength was 8,000, including 3,000 in the Building and Development Division. The new HDB Corp took in about 800 to 1,000 staff. Ministry of National Development, Housing and Development Board Press Release, 26 February 2003.

Private Limited and is now partly owned by CapitaLand, a public listed company which is also partly owned by Temasek Holdings.

In his memoirs, Mr. Lee Kuan Yew (who remained in the Cabinet as Minister Mentor to Goh's government) recalled this episode as one in which the government yielded to popular pressure:

> I should have known that it does not pay to yield to popular pressure beyond our capacity to deliver. Yet I was party to a similar mistake in the early 1990s. As property prices rose, everybody wanted to make a profit on the sale of their old flat and then upgrade to a new one, the biggest they could afford. Instead of choking off demand by charging a levy to reduce their windfall profits, I agreed that we accommodate the voters by increasing the number of flats built. That aggravated the real estate bubble and made it more painful when the currency crisis struck in 1997. Had we choked off the demand earlier, in 1995, we would have been immensely better off (Lee, 2000, p. 121).

4. The Lee Hsien Loong Government, from 2004: Managing Housing Demand and Equity Withdrawal to Finance Retirement

Mr. Lee Hsien Loong became Singapore's third Prime Minister in August 2004, having served as a Member of Parliament since 1984 and a member of the cabinet since 1987. The housing market at the start of his term appeared to be stabilizing at the trough of the property cycle (see Figure 3). The HDB had been restructured and downsized. The economy was still recovering from the shock of the SARS crisis of 2003. The Asian economic crisis of 1997 and the subsequent fall in property prices had demonstrated the risks of housing bubbles, unemployment, and reliance on housing as an asset to finance retirement. A rapidly aging population and declines in total fertility rate over the years posed a major demographic challenge. Policy attention shifted to ways in which elderly households could monetize their housing asset, better targeting of housing grants to benefit lower income households, and regulation of the housing market and housing loans.

In 2005, the government decided to proceed with the development of two casino-based integrated resorts. This decision could be said to mark another phase in the economic development of Singapore as a global city. On the population front, immigration and foreign worker policies resulted in a rapid growth in the number of foreigners in Singapore. But the global financial crisis of 2008–2009 and the uncertainties it engendered led the government to hold off increasing housing supply. This subsequently resulted in a housing shortage that was acutely felt in 2010 — the year when the two integrated resorts opened and the economy rebounded sharply (with real GDP growth of 14.8%).

Housing price increases in excess of median income growth, a younger generation facing housing affordability problems and ineligible or repeatedly unsuccessful in ballots to purchase HDB flats, rising income inequality, over-crowding problems on public transport and other facilities, contributed to a decline in electoral support for the ruling People's Action Party (PAP). The PAP's vote share declined from 66.6% at the 2006 election to 60.1% at the 2011 election, with the opposition Workers' Party winning 6 of the 87 seats for elected Members of Parliament. Since 2011, Prime Minister Lee Hsien Loong has implemented several measures to address the housing problems of elderly and lower income households, increase housing supply, as well as curb speculative and investment demand for housing.

4.1. *Elderly Households: Monetizing Housing Assets*

The typical household in Singapore has the bulk of its wealth invested in housing. McCarthy *et al.* (2002) show through simulations that the average worker in Singapore is likely to be "asset-rich and cash-poor" upon retirement, with 75% of his retirement wealth in housing, provided housing values continue to rise in real terms. In contrast, an American elderly household would have only 20% of its retirement wealth in housing. This raises the problematic issue of over-concentration of household assets in housing resulting in a risky under-diversified portfolio at retirement.

The government-appointed Economic Review Committee in 2002 arrived at a similar conclusion that CPF members were "asset rich and cash-poor" and made recommendations to limit CPF withdrawals for housing, and for the government to explore ways for homeowners to monetize their property.[10] Agreeing with the committee's recommendations, the government moved to cap CPF withdrawals for housing at 150% of the value of the property, with the cap moving down gradually to 120% over five years for new private housing loans.

To address the problem of "Asset Rich and Cash Poor" faced by a segment of the population in their old age, the HDB introduced the Lease Buyback Scheme (LBS) in 2009 to allow the low income elderly (age 63 or older) living in 3-room or smaller flats to unlock the equity in their homes. The proceeds of the part sale will be used to top up their CPF Retirement Accounts and to purchase an annuity plan to provide a monthly income for life. The amount of monthly income would be determined by the market value of the flat, the length of the remaining lease, amount of outstanding loan on the flat, and the age and gender of the elderly owner(s). Under this scheme, HDB buys back the tail lease of the flat, with the elderly flat owner retaining a 30-year lease, and provides a bonus (up to S$20,000) in addition to the unlocked housing equity. The LBS thus allow the elderly to continue to stay in their

---

[10] Economic Review Committee: Sub-committee on policies related to taxation, the CPF system, wages and land (2002).

flat allowing them to age in place. In 2015, the LBS was extended to 4-room flats (Lee, 2014).

Other monetization options for eligible elderly households include:

- a Silver Housing Bonus incentive (of up to S$20,000) to sell their current flat and buy a smaller flat (right-sizing);
- the 2-room Flexi Scheme which allows households over the age of 55 to buy 2-room HDB flats on shorter leases ranging from 15 to 45 years (this replaces the 2-room and earlier Studio Apartment schemes);
- sublet a room or put their flat up for rental for a steady flow of income.

4.2. *Lower Income Households: Additional and Special Housing Grants*

With eligibility for HDB new subsidized flats and CPF Housing Grants (of S$40,000) extending to over 80% of Singapore citizen households, subsidies needed to be better calibrated to household incomes. Housing grants which allowed the HDB to better price discriminate based on household incomes became a feature of HDB pricing policy.

Additional Housing Grants were introduced in 2006 (and enhanced in 2007 and 2009) to allow families with lower incomes to receive a higher grant amount which could be used for either a new flat or a resale flat. The amount of the Additional Housing Grant depends on the average gross monthly household income (see Table 3).

The Special Housing Grant (SHG) was introduced in 2011 to help households buy 4-room or smaller new flats in non-mature estates directly from the HDB. The

Table 3.   Additional CPF housing grants (from February 2009).

Average monthly household income S$	Additional CPF housing grant S$
$1,500 or less	$40,000
$1,501–$2,000	$35,000
$2,001–$2,500	$30,000
$2,501–$3,000	$25,000
$3,001–$3,500	$20,000
$3,501–$4,000	$15,000
$4,001–$4,500	$10,000
$4,501–$5,000	$5,000

Source: HDB website.

Table 4.   Special housing grant* (from November 2015).

Average monthly household income S$	Special housing grant amount S$
Up to $5,000	$40,000
$5,001–$5,500	$35,000
$5,501–$6,000	$30,000
$6,001–$6,500	$25,000
$6,501–$7,000	$20,000
$7,001–$7,500	$15,000
$7,501–$8,000	$10,000
$8,001–$8,501	$5,000

*Available for 2-room, 3-room and 4-room flat applications in non-mature estates.
Source: HDB website.

SHG was enhanced in 2012, significantly expanded in 2013, and expanded again in 2015 when the maximum grant amount was increased from S$20,000 to S$40,000. The income ceiling for household to qualify to receive the SHG was also raised from S$6,500 to S$8,500. The amount of SHG depends on the average gross monthly household income (see Table 4). A Step-Up Housing Grant (of S$15,000) was introduced in 2013 to help families in subsidized 2-room HDB flats in non-mature estates upgrade to purchase 3-room HDB flats in non-mature estates.

4.3. *Property Investors: Curbing Housing Investment Demand*

In the post Global Financial Crisis period, rapid population increase, the low interest rate environment and high global liquidity resulting from the very accommodative monetary policies of Central Banks in developed economies, led to accelerated price increases of Singapore property (see Figure 3). The upward trend in Singapore real estate prices had caused housing to be viewed as an attractive investment as compared to other asset classes. In the past two decades, based on price indices, the returns on both private housing and HDB resale flat sectors have out-performed the stock exchange's Straits Times Index on a risk-adjusted basis (see Tables 5 and 6). Leverage in real estate and Singapore Dollar appreciation further magnify the returns. The superior performance of the HDB sector is based on the resale price index alone, and does not include the added benefits of generous subsidies, attractive rental yields (6–8%) or imputed income from owner-occupancy.

The relatively attractive returns on housing assets drew the attention of both local and foreign investors. The continuous upward trend in prices has posed difficulties and exerted tremendous pressure on policy makers to react with counter-cyclical and

Table 5.   Risk-adjusted return ratio (nominal).

		Average nominal return*	Standard deviation	Risk-adjusted return ratio
1990–1999	Private housing	12.1	23.2	0.52
	HDB resale	15.2	25.9	0.59
	STI	12.2	35.3	0.35
2000–2012	Private housing	4.1	10.8	0.38
	HDB resale	5.1	8.1	0.63
	STI	6.0	29.5	0.20

*Based on price index only.
Note: Gross rental income yields for HDB in the range of 6% to 8%.

Table 6.   Risk-adjusted return ratio (real).

		Average real return*	Standard deviation	Risk-adjusted return ratio
1990–1999	Private housing	10.1	22.7	0.45
	HDB resale	13.3	25.7	0.52
	STI	10.3	35.7	0.29
2000–2012	Private housing	1.9	10.9	0.18
	HDB resale	3.0	7.1	0.42
	STI	3.9	30.5	0.13

*Based on price index only.
Source: Phang (2013b).

cooling measures. Since 2006, the Singapore government has announced several consecutive rounds of "cooling" measures to curb demand for housing (see Table 7). These measures can be viewed as macro-prudential policies to stabilize housing prices, reduce the returns for housing investors, and pre-empt a housing bubble from developing. Numerous additional transaction taxes for both buyers and sellers have been introduced. These, together with HDB rules and CPF housing grants, have resulted in a housing tax-and-subsidy framework which exceeds the income tax code in complexity. Table 8 provides a simplified picture of the progressivity of the housing tax-and-subsidy framework.

In addition to the numerous demand-curbing measures, the government has been ramping up the supply of HDB flats since 2011. While HDB dwelling units under management increased by a mere 23,000 units from 2006 to 2011,[11] about

---

[11] HDB, Annual Report 2005–2006. http://www.hdb.gov.sg/fi10/fi10221p.nsf/Attachment/AR0506/$file/index.html; HDB, "Annual Report 2010/11", http://www10.hdb.gov.sg/ebook/ar2011/main.html.

Table 7. List of government measures affecting the property sector (2006–2013).

December 2006	In December 2006, the government withdrew the Buyer Stamp Duty Concession (which allowed payment to be deferred until Temporary Occupation Permit date or completion for purchasers of uncompleted properties), and all property buyers had to pay their stamp duties within 14 days of the date of excising their purchase options.
October 2007	In October 2007, a Deferred Payment Scheme introduced by developers, which allowed buyers to defer making payments for properties under construction to the date of issue of Temporary Occupation Permit, was disallowed by the government.
September 2009	In September 2009, an Interest Absorption Scheme introduced by developers, which allowed buyers to transfer their interest-servicing burden on a housing loan to the developers for properties under construction until the completion date, and Interest-Only housing loan scheme, which allowed buyers to make only interest payments on their housing loans, were disallowed by the government.
February 2010	In February 2010, seller stamp duty was re-introduced for sale of properties within one year of purchase and LTV ratio was lowered from 90% to 80%.
August 2010	In August 2010, the holding period for imposition of seller stamp duty was increased to three years. For borrowers with existing housing loan(s), their LTV ratio was lowered from 80% to 70% and minimum cash-component down-payment was raised to 10% from 5%.
January 2011	In January 2011, the holding period for imposition of seller stamp duty was increased to four years. The seller stamp duty rate was increased to 16%, 12%, 8% and 4% for properties sold within the first, second, third and fourth year of purchase, respectively. For borrowers with existing housing loan(s), their LTV ratio was lowered from 70% to 60%.
December 2011	In December 2011, additional buyer stamp duty was imposed; Singapore citizens buying their third and subsequent residential property pay 3%, Singapore permanent residents buying their second and subsequent residential property pay 3%, and foreigners buying their first and subsequent residential property pay 10%.
October 2012	In October 2012, the Monetary Authority of Singapore (MAS) imposed a 35-year tenor restriction for housing loans on new residential properties. For borrowers without any existing housing loan(s) and where loan tenors exceed 30-year or extend beyond borrowers' retirement age of 65 years old, the LTV ratio was lowered to 60%. LTV ratio was lowered to 40% for borrowers with existing housing loan(s) where the loan tenors exceed 30-year or extend beyond borrowers' retirement age of 65 years old.
January 2013	In January 2013, additional buyer stamp duty was raised; Singapore citizens buying their second residential property pay 7% and those buying their third and subsequent residential property pay 10%, Singapore permanent residents buying their first residential property pay 5% and those buying their second and subsequent residential property pay 10%, and foreigners buying their first and subsequent residential property pay 15%.

(Continued)

Table 7. (*Continued*)

	LTV ratio was lowered to 50% and 40% for borrowers applying for their second and third or subsequent housing loan, respectively, where loan tenors do not exceed 30-year or do not extend beyond borrowers' retirement age of 65 years old. In cases where loan tenors exceed 30-year or extend beyond borrowers' retirement age of 65 years old, LTV ratios of 30% and 20% apply for borrowers applying for their second and third or subsequent housing loan respectively. The minimum cash-component down-payment was also raised to 25% from 10% for buyers taking their second or subsequent housing loan.
June 2013	The MAS introduced the Total Debt Servicing Ratio (TDSR) for homebuyers with the intention that the measure "…will help strengthen credit underwriting practices by [financial institutions, FIs] and encourage financial prudence among borrowers". The TDSR is the total monthly debt service as a percentage of the borrower's income and is capped at 60%. In computation of TDSR, FIs will need to take into account the monthly repayment for the property loan that the borrower is applying for plus the monthly repayments on all other outstanding property and non-property debt obligations of the borrower; apply a specified medium-term interest rate or the prevailing market interest rate, whichever is higher, to the property loan that the borrower is applying for when calculating the TDSR; apply a haircut of at least 30% to all variable income (e.g. bonuses) and rental income; and apply haircuts to and amortize the value of any eligible financial assets taken into consideration in assessing the borrower's debt servicing ability, in order to convert them into "income streams".
	MAS also required borrowers named on a property loan to be the mortgagors of the residential property for which the loan is taken; "guarantors" who are standing guarantee for borrowers otherwise assessed by the FI at the point of application for the housing loan not to meet the TDSR threshold for a property loan to be brought in as co-borrowers; and in the case of joint borrowers, that FIs use the income-weighted average age of borrowers when applying the rules on loan tenure.
August 2013	Effective August 27, 2013, new Singapore Permanent Residents have to wait for 3 years before they are eligible to purchase resale HDB flats. The maximum tenure for HDB housing loans was reduced from 30 years to 25 years. The mortgage servicing ratio limit was reduced from 35% to 30% of the borrower's gross monthly income. The maximum tenure of new housing loans and re-financing facilities granted by financial institutions for the purchase of HDB flats was reduced from 35 to 30 years.
December 2013	From December 2013, the government required second-timer applicants who buy Executive Condominium units directly from property developers to pay a resale levy, similar to second-timer applicants who buy HDB BTO flats. The Mortgage Servicing Ratio for housing loans granted by financial institutions for EC units bought directly from property developers was capped at 30% of a borrower's gross monthly income.

Sources: Lee *et al.* (2013); Monetary Authority of Singapore website at http://www.mas.gov.sg/newsand- publications/press-releases/2013/mas-introduces-debt-servicing-framework-for-property-loans.aspx; and Ministry of National Development press release 9 December 2013 at http://app.mnd.gov.sg/Newsroom/NewsPage.aspx?ID=5023&category=Press%20Release&year=2013&RA1=&RA2=&RA3.

Table 8. Grants and taxes for housing purchase (from November 2015).

Average gross monthly household income	Grant amounts for eligible citizen households (CPF + Additional + Special housing grants)*	
Eligible first time buyers who purchase HDB flats	Direct from HDB	In HDB resale market^
$1,500 or less	$80,000	$70,000
$1,501–$2,000	$75,000	$65,000
$2,001–$2,500	$70,000	$60,000
$2,501–$3,000	$65,000	$55,000
$3,001–$3,500	$60,000	$50,000
$3,501–$4,000	$55,000	$45,000
$4,001–$4,500	$50,000	$40,000
$4,501–$5,000	$45,000	$35,000
$5,001–$5,500	$35,000	$30,000
$5,501–$6,000	$30,000	$30,000
$6,001–$6,500	$25,000	$30,000
$6,500–$7,000	$20,000	$30,000
$7,001–$7,500	$15,000	$0
$$7,501–$8,000	$10,000	$0
$8,001–$8,500	$5,000	$0
$8,500–$12,000	$0	$0
Above $12,000	Not eligible	$0
Eligible first time buyers of new executive condominium flats		
up to $10,000	$30,000	$0
$10,001 to $11,000	$20,000	$0
$11,001 to $12,000	$10,000	$0
$12,001–$14,000	$0	$0
Above $14,000	Not eligible	$0
Private housing — additional buyer stamp duties (ABSD) payable#		
Singaporean		
First property	No ABSD	
Concurrent 2nd property	7%	
Concurrent 3rd and subsequent	10%	
Permanent Residents (for private and HDB resale)		
First property	5%	
2nd and subsequent	10%	
Foreigner (any property)	15%	

Notes: * These grant amounts are for households where both husband and wife are citizens. Amounts will be less for singles and for citizen and PR/foreigner couples.
^ does not include proximity housing grant of $20,000 for households that live close to family.
# % of actual price paid or market value of property, whichever is the higher.
Sources: Compiled from HDB and Inland Revenue Authority of Singapore (IRAS) websites.

25,000 HDB flats were launched for sale in 2011, followed by 27,000 units in 2012, 25,000 in 2013, 22,000 in 2014 and 15,000 in 2015. With the increase in supply of both HDB and private housing, the shortage has eased and prices have started to decline.[12] Housing, though, remains an attractive investment, given the underlying housing framework in place, careful regulation of the sector and the long term plans and prospects for Singapore.

5. Concluding Observations

The success of Singapore's housing welfare model demonstrates what can be achieved with strategic planning to mobilize resources and guide key investments. Complemented by close attention to the supply part of the equation as well as policies which created markets over time and accommodated private initiatives to fill the gaps, the process has helped Singapore to avoid the worst outcomes of the extremes of central planning and unplanned growth. Numerous city governments in former socialist countries and in Asia are also major landowners, yet the absence of markets often makes these cities inefficient. Those cities can learn much from Singapore's planning processes, policies to remove real estate gridlocks, and the state's active role in creating markets. It can also be seen that the Singapore government has deployed multiple mitigations in parallel to reduce the risk of housing becoming a source of financial sector instability.

- Housing markets are carefully segmented and carefully regulated.
- The main source of capital for housing finance comes from domestic savings.
- Price subsidies and housing grants are given to eligible households at the point of purchase and not deferred.
- The HDB relies on government loans to fund mortgage loans.
- HDB mortgage financing is not subsidized and over time, market share has been shifting to commercial banks.
- The use of compulsory savings lowers default risks.
- Government housing institutions do not have conflicting missions.
- The government has control over land and housing supply.

However, deregulation of housing finance and HDB markets in the 1990s, and supply lagging behind population increases recently did contribute to recent episodes of rapid housing price increases. Since then, the government has carefully restrained housing credit growth by caps on Loan to Value Ratio, Debt Service Ratio, and use of

---

[12] *The Straits Times*, 21 February 2015.

CPF savings for mortgages. It has actively intervened in the housing market to curb foreign demand and speculative demand by using HDB regulations, and fiscal and macro-prudential tools when price increases threatened to develop into a bubble.

The transferability of Singapore's experience needs to be juxtaposed with the local, political and social context. A housing provident fund is relatively simple to set up if designed as a savings and payments institution. The more complex institution to replicate is the HDB, in particular its ability to comprehensively and effectively intervene to affect many aspects of housing demand, supply and prices. Moreover, the tactics on which Singapore relies — compulsory savings, state land ownership, and state provision of housing, complemented with an extensive public sector — could easily have spawned widespread inefficiency and corruption.

Singapore's effective implementation of such planning and regulation is attributable to a network of competent and reliable organizations that together provide rich public sector capacity. The quality of public administration in Singapore is a result of recruitment based on merit, competitive pay benchmarked against private-sector salaries, extensive computerization, and a civil service culture of zero tolerance for corruption. Where governments and public sector leadership are weak and/or corrupt, such extensive intervention and government control over resource allocation can be potentially abused and may carry a higher cost than inaction.

Despite its rather unique context, there are elements of Singapore's housing system that can provide helpful pointers for housing policy makers generally.

First, despite the very visible hand of government, markets are very important and creating and/or enabling markets to work more efficiently is a very important aspect of housing policy.

Second, government involvement can be very helpful for providing timely real estate market information, establishing sustainable housing supply regimes and mortgage institutions, and in improving the liquidity of housing assets. The short and long term implications of housing subsidies, explicit or implicit, supply or demand-side, within the entire system, need to be fully understood.

Third, retirement savings may be mobilized for housing mortgage payments. However, the CPF itself does not make loans to its own members. It is not a good practice for a Housing Provident Fund to become a direct lender for housing due to potentially conflicting objectives.

Fourth, the government regulates the housing markets extensively and has in place an array of instruments to curb speculative demand and mitigate the development of asset bubbles.

Finally, the need for strong legislation and a proper fund governance structure to ensure that the interests of provident fund members are adequately protected cannot be overemphasized.

References

Centre for Liveable Cities (2014). *Land Acquisition and Resettlement: Securing Resources for Development*. Singapore: Centre for Liveable Cities.

Centre for Liveable Cities and Housing Development Board (2013). *Housing: Turning Squatters into Stakeholders*. Singapore: Cengage Learning.

Economic Review Committee: Sub-Committee on Policies Related to Taxation, the CPF System, Wages and Land (2002). Refocusing the CPF System for Enhanced Security in Retirement and Economic Flexibility.

Krugman, P (1994). The myth of Asia's miracle. *Foreign Affairs*, 73, 62–78.

Lee, D, SY Phang, KF Phoon and K Wee (2013). Evaluating the Effectiveness of Cooling Measures on Property Prices: An Exploration of Alternative Econometric Techniques. Paper presented at the 2013 Asian Meeting of the Econometric Society, Singapore, 2–4 August 2013.

Lee, HL (2014). National Day Rally Speech.

Lee, KY (2000). *From Third World to First: The Singapore Story 1965–2000*. Singapore: Singapore Press Holdings.

McCarthy, D, OS Mitchell and J Piggott (2002). Asset rich and cash poor: Retirement provision and housing policy in Singapore. *Journal of Pension Economics and Finance*, 1, 197–222.

Monetary Authority of Singapore (2001). Quarterly Bulletin, III (1), March.

Ooi, GL, S Siddique and KC Soh (1993). *The Management of Ethnic Relations in Public Housing Estates*. Singapore: Times Academic Press.

Phang, SY (1992). *Housing Markets and Urban Transportation: Economic Theory, Econometrics and Policy Analysis for Singapore*. Singapore: McGraw Hill.

Phang, SY (1996). Economic development and the distribution of land rents in Singapore: A Georgist implementation. *American Journal of Economics and Sociology*, 55, 489–501.

Phang, SY (2007). The Singapore model of housing and the welfare state. In *Housing and the New Welfare State*. Groves, R, A Murie and C Watson (eds.), pp. 15–44. UK: Ashgate.

Phang, SY (2013a). *Housing Finance Systems: Market Failures and Government Failures*. UK: Palgrave Macmillan.

Phang, SY (2013b). Do Singaporeans Spend Too Much on Housing? Presentation at IPS Closed Door Discussion, 10 May 2013.

Pugh, C (1985). Housing and development in Singapore. *Contemporary Southeast Asia*, 6, 275–307.

The Straits Times. Singapore. Various dates.

Urban Redevelopment Authority, Singapore. Real Estate Information System, REALIS. https://spring.ura.gov.sg/lad/ore/login/index.cfm.

CHAPTER 11

Adding a Basic Pillar to the Central Provident Fund System: An Actuarial Analysis

Ngee-Choon Chia

The Central Provident Fund (CPF) system has worked well for majority of Singaporeans who are able to work consistently over their life cycle and have made prudent housing choices. However, the inherent structure of CPF, which is based purely on contributions, is unable to address retirement adequacy for its vulnerable members. Adding a means-tested non-contributory basic pillar to the system will make the system more inclusive. This paper studies the pension cost of a targeted old-age income support system for needy elderly to help meet their basic living expenses. A Lee–Carter stochastic model is used to forecast the elderly population. Pension costs depend on coverage and benefit levels and the cost of living adjustments. The viability of a basic retirement support scheme would also depend on the speed of aging and the rate of economic growth.

1. History of CPF and Social Protection

The Central Provident Fund (CPF) was established under the CPF Ordinance in 1953 and came into operation on 1st July 1955. Shortly after its inception, a contentious issue emerged.[1] There were concerns that the provident fund system which covered only employed workers would not provide social protection for all, particularly the vulnerable segments of society — the elderly, disabled and unemployed. A committee headed by Sir Sydney Caine was appointed to study the desirability and feasibility of measures to establish a "minimum standard of livelihood for the people of Singapore" (Caine, 1957, para. 1). The Caine Committee unanimously agreed that there should be an integrated social security system that would include a contributory Social Insurance (pension) Scheme to cover all workers, including the self-employed, and a Public Assistance Scheme to provide social protection to the unemployed, needy and vulnerable. Benefits payable should be the same in all

---

[1] The narrative on the history of CPF draws heavily from Chia (2015).

categories, whether receipt be based on old age, survivorship, sickness, maternity or unemployment (Caine, 1957, p. 42).

The Colonial Government sought alternative views and solicited technical assistance from G. J. Brocklehurst, an International Labor Organization expert on social security measures. Brocklehurst proposed terminating the provident fund system, which had operated briefly, and to start a compulsory contributory insurance scheme with a redistributive defined benefits structure (Brocklehurst, 1957, p. 79). A Select Committee of Government Officials, chaired by Gillespie, was set up on 14 January 1958 to examine and correlate the reports submitted by the Caine Committee and Brocklehurst. The Select Committee unanimously endorsed the recommendations by Caine and Brocklehurst, and was keen to start a new social security system integrating the social insurance and public assistance schemes. The main stumbling block, however, was how to dispose of the money already paid to the CPF as it "would be impracticable to wind up the Fund and return to members their balances" (Gillespie, 1959, p. 34). The Select Committee was also mindful that the new scheme would be administratively challenging, particularly with the new redistributive contribution and benefit structures.

By early 1959, a legislation for the new social insurance scheme was drafted and ready for approval. The provident fund system would be replaced by the new scheme. The scope of the proposed integrated social insurance scheme was expanded to cover loss of income due to illness and unemployment, maternity benefits and a public assistance program. The draft bill outlined the set-up of a new social security department, and also gave administrative details on the transference of CPF contributions and assets to the new scheme. There were detailed directives on how CPF Board personnel at that time would fit into the new social security department. Contributions to CPF would cease and contributions to the Social Insurance Fund would start (ILO, 1959, pp. 19, 84). Pension benefits were to be paid out from the Social Insurance Fund. Existing contributions to the CPF (with minor exceptions) would be transferred to the Social Insurance (Reserve) Fund. The transferred balances of existing contributors to the CPF were treated as contributions to the Social Insurance Fund.

However, when Singapore achieved self-government in June 1959, the new government chose to allocate the then scarce capital resources to more urgent economic investments, and to postpone spending on less urgent social investments (MOF, 1961, p. 6). The immediate task was to increase employment to address the double-digit unemployment at that time. Under the new directives, economic development made up about 58% of total capital requirements and social development 40% (MOF, 1961, p. 34).

Mr. Lee Kuan Yew in his memoirs said that he and his fellow leaders aimed at creating a "fair society not a welfare society." Drawing from the experience of advanced

Western countries that adopted welfare states which developed many problems, the government explicitly pursued a different philosophy and path to avoid debilitating the system.[2] In terms of social development, priority was given to housing, education and health, with housing given the biggest share under the 1961–1964 Singapore Development Plan. The strategy was to provide low-cost housing under the Singapore Improvement Trust/Housing and Development Board (MOF, 1961, p. 29).

The provident fund was preferred over an integrated social insurance scheme as the population at that time was relatively young, with many migrant workers. This choice was also consistent with McFadzean's observation that "the problem of retirement benefits was only a part, and possibly not the most important part of the overall social problem confronting the Government of Singapore. The expansion of the education and medical services and an improvement in the squalid housing conditions in which so many people are forced to live are social problems which rank at least as high in priority as the provision of retirement benefits." (McFadzean, 1952, p. 3).

Economic development thus took precedence over the establishment of a welfare state. Social protection was mainly targeted at providing housing, education and medical services for Singaporeans. The provident fund system was not replaced and became the bedrock of social security arrangements in Singapore.

Currently, CPF operates as a fully funded mandatory system, with working Singaporeans and their employers making monthly contributions to individualized CPF savings accounts. Contributions are channeled into three different accounts for different purposes. Savings in the Special Account (SA) and Medisave Account (MA) are earmarked for retirement and healthcare expenses, respectively. Savings in the Ordinary Account (OA) can be withdrawn for pre-retirement uses, notably to finance housing. This becomes a unique feature of CPF. Whether CPF can successfully provide an adequate retirement income and protect against longevity risk depends on the designs of both the accumulation and the payout phases. Retirement wealth depends on the net accumulation of pre-retirement CPF savings. This in turn depends on the worker's wage level and the amount withdrawn to finance housing mortgages. Hence, the accumulation is sensitive to the labor market and macroeconomic environments that affect salary, salary growth and employability. How much is accumulated depends on CPF policy variables such as contribution rates, contribution period, allocations to the various accounts, and returns to CPF savings.

---

[2] "We have used to advantage what Britain left behind: the English language, the legal system, parliamentary government, and impartial administration. However, we have studiously avoided the practices of welfare state. We saw how a great people reduced themselves to mediocrity be leveling down. The less enterprising and less hardworking cannot be made equal simply by cutting down the achievements of enterprising and the striving. And we have seen how difficult it is to dismantle a system of subsidized living once people get accustomed to a government providing for them." Utterance by Mr. Lee K. Y. in 1985, see Lee (2013, p. 138).

Chia (2015) narrates how the net accumulation of CPF savings is also sensitive to CPF policies, such as pre-retirement withdrawal rules and allocation of contribution among different accounts. These policy changes were made at different times of Singapore's economic history to address the social and economic needs. For example, when Singapore became a new nation, the top national priority was to help Singaporeans acquire housing assets under the Home Ownership Scheme. The CPF Act was amended in 1968 to allow the worker's entire CPF savings to be withdrawn to buy government flats. CPF contributions were used to build up housing asset as retirement nest egg.[3] It was only in 1977 that the CPF Board implemented a new account named the Special Account, into which part of the worker's monthly contribution is required to be deposited. Savings in the Special Account are earmarked for retirement only and cannot be withdrawn before retirement. This change marks the beginning of re-aligning CPF policy toward retirement.

Before 1987, upon reaching the age of 55, members were able to withdraw the full amount of their CPF savings. The Howe Report (MOH, 1984) precipitated the rethinking of the decumulation of CPF savings which led to the tweaking of the withdrawal rule. In addressing the problem of the aged, Howe proposed that the age at which a person can withdraw his CPF savings should be raised from 55 to 60 and then to 65, in line with a higher retirement age. As people work longer, the drawdown age has to be postponed. The Howe Committee wrote: "withdrawal before retirement would encourage unnecessary consumption, and in some cases, misuse of savings, resulting in little or no balance for retirement" (MOH, 1984, p. 26). But this proposal was met with great resistance.

Besides the accumulation phase, the design of the CPF payout phase increasingly becomes more important. How and when to drawdown the accumulated savings are important to ensure retirement adequacy and to minimize longevity and inflation risks. To raise retirement adequacy, in 1987 an innovative scheme — the minimum sum (MS) scheme was introduced. The MS is the amount that must be set aside at age 55 to safeguard CPF members' retirement nest egg. The decreed sum has increased progressively to yield higher payouts. The amount that can be cashed out by using property pledge is now up to 50% of the MS. To address longevity risk, in 2009 a life annuity CPF LIFE scheme was introduced to ensure that the nest egg can last a member's whole lifespan. Although CPF LIFE helps to address longevity risk, inflation risk remains because CPF LIFE payouts are fixed, with no cost of living adjustment.

---

[3] This view prevailed even into 2010s as seen in the articulation by Prime Minister Mr. Lee Hsien Loong that "home, an appreciating asset in Singapore, is a nest egg … It's for you to live in, it's for your investment, it's for you for your old age." (*The Straits Times*, 21 February 2010).

Adopting a provident fund system has helped Singapore to focus on economic development. Singapore has successfully transited from a third world developing country to a first world developed country within one generation. The working population at the time of Singapore's independence are now retirees in first-world Singapore. Singaporeans have become wealthier and most are asset-rich. Home ownership increased from 29.4% in 1970 to 90.5% in 2013,[4] a rate unparalleled in anywhere else.

The CPF system has worked well for the broad majority of Singaporeans who have had consistent employment and good salary earnings, and have made a prudent housing choice.[5] It has helped many Singaporeans to own a house, save for healthcare and prepare for retirement. But improvement is required to meet the needs of those who do not have enough CPF savings and to address inflation risks.[6] Among other issues, the CPF Advisory Panel, which was set up in 2014, has been tasked with studying how to help CPF payouts keep pace with the cost of living.

However, the current inherent structure of the CPF based purely on contributions is unable to address retirement adequacy for its vulnerable members. These include workers in low-wage and casual jobs, stay-at-home mothers and older CPF members, for whom there is no social safety net. Adding a non-contributory basic pillar to the system will make the system more inclusive. Currently, low-wage workers receive support from the Workfare scheme. The poorest of the elderly poor receive public assistance administered by the Ministry of Social and Family Development (MSF). Government transfers have increased significantly since 2007.[7] Some are regular transfers, others are ad hoc and irregular. For example, transfers such as rebates on utilities, GST (goods and services tax) Vouchers and Workfare Income Supplement disbursements are regular; while transfers such as senior citizen bonuses, CPF top-ups and progress/economic growth packages are disbursed on an ad hoc, irregular basis over a specific period. Adding a more structured first pillar, such as a means-tested basic pension, will allay uncertainties and anxieties and give peace of mind to the vulnerable.

Currently CPF is the bedrock of social security in Singapore, with four pillars of support for housing, healthcare, retirement and income enhancement for older

---

[4] National Population and Talent Division (NPTD) Singapore (2014). 2014 Population in Brief (Singapore).

[5] Chia and Tsui (2014), through simulations, demonstrate that by making prudent choice on housing, CPF savings will yield adequate retirement for young entrant workers.

[6] In the recent national survey of senior citizens, 72.6% of the male elderly have CPF savings. Less than half of the female elderly (47.3%) have any CPF savings. Furthermore, older Singaporeans tend not to have CPF savings. Only 37.3% of those aged 75 and above have CPF savings, compared to 50.6% of those aged 65 to 74 (Kang et al., 2013, p. 57).

[7] See Chia (2014) for the shifting trend in government social expenditures and the unique way of funding these expenditures through funds.

low-wage workers. This chapter explores the viability of adding another pillar — a basic pension scheme to provide income support for vulnerable elderly to help them meet their basic needs. The main concern inevitably will be the fiscal sustainability of such a scheme. The experiences of aging developed countries show that a universal pension system can become a fiscal burden and may not be compatible with incentive to work. With an aging population, the base of the recipients will grow and the system becomes costly. The basic pension proposed in this chapter is not a universal system but a more targeted system with means-testing. The basic pension cost is estimated using an actuarial approach. The Lee–Carter stochastic forecasting model is used to project the demographic landscape taking into consideration mortality and fertility rates and immigration assumptions. The chapter is organized as follows. Section 2 narrates the patterns of retirement financing and expenditure of current retiree households based on data published in the recent household expenditure survey of DOS (2014a). Retiree households living in 1- and 2-room government public housing are the least prepared for retirement. Section 3 explains the choice of parameter assumptions used in the proposed income support scheme, and presents the demographic landscape derived from the Lee–Carter population projection model. Singapore's population is aging fast and the proportion of population aged 65 and above is increasing. Section 4 presents the computations of pension cost and analyzes the viability of pension costs. Sensitivities of the cost computations to the parameter assumptions are also reported. These include sensitivity to the rate of growth in real per capita GDP, cost of living adjustments and the design of the basic pension scheme. Section 4 gives some concluding remarks.

2. State of Current Elderly and Pattern of Retirement Financing

When CPF was instituted, many of the current elderly, especially the males, were at their prime working age. Many were migrant workers who stayed on in Singapore. Additionally, the first wave of baby boomers (born between 1947 and 1964) are now age 65 and above. Some of these are CPF members who have experienced the benefits and pitfalls of CPF policy changes. Many would have used their retirement savings to finance housing and are now home-owners. They are asset-rich but could be cash-poor as many were low-wage earners with small CPF accumulation. Some who were informal and irregular workers would have little or no CPF savings. Many elderly women have low or no CPF balances as they had limited or no participation in the labor force as many are stay-at-home mothers.

The government has provided various options for the "asset-rich and cash-poor" elderly to unlock housing equity to supplement their retirement incomes: lease buy-back scheme (LBS), reverse mortgage (RM), subletting and downsizing. Under LBS, homeowners sell the tail-end of the flat lease to HDB. They can age in place in their own flats and have their remaining lease monetized. But they are unable to leave a bequest. Under RM, homeowners receive a steady stream of cash flows by borrowing against the value of their homes, repay the loans upon death and possibly are able to leave a bequest. With downsizing, the elderly homeowner sells the flat to buy either a smaller HDB flat from the resale market or a studio apartment from HDB. The amount unlocked is then annuitized. However, the elderly may have to move and may not be able to leave a bequest if they buy a studio apartment. With subletting, only the rental service of the flat is unleashed; the housing asset remains, making it possible to continue to age in place and leave a bequest, but there will be exposure to the volatility of the rental market. The elderly have to choose the option that best matches their preferences, such as ability to age in place and leave a bequest. But each option would entail a trade-off.[8]

Responses to these monetization options have been lukewarm. For example, since its inception in 2009, only 471 household took part in the lease buyback scheme, representing only 0.6% of total retiree households in 2012. After the government relaxes the rules and opens the scheme to include homeowners who have enjoyed more than one housing subsidy and/or who have been private property owners, another 312 households signed up, bringing the proportion of retiree households that has signed up to about 1%. As of August 2015, the LBS will be extended to 4-room flats.

The low take-up rate could be because these instruments were too complicated to understand for the current elderly. A large proportion of the current elderly has low or no education qualifications and lacks basic financial knowledge. Retirement planning products must be framed in such a way so that it is easily understood. Subletting is the most easily understood and is the most utilized option. Information on rents is readily available as HDB publishes the median rent by town and flat types on its website. Elderly homeowners could use this information as a guide before entering into a rental agreement. Subletting allows the elderly to monetize part of their flat into cash and they can age in place while retaining the option to leave the flat as a bequest. Elderly homeowners with other housing alternatives, such as moving in with their married children, can unlock more housing equity by subletting the whole flat. However, incomes generated from subletting will depend on the economic condition of the rental market.

Elderly retirees are averse to the lease buyback and reverse mortgage schemes as they exhibit what behavioral economists call the "endowment effect". In behavioral economics, endowment effect is the hypothesis that people ascribe more value to things they own, and "it's hard for people to give up what they owned." It is difficult to give up a large lump sum of housing equity in exchange for small monthly payouts. Monetization schemes entail annuitization, with lump sum housing wealth being

---

[8] For economic analysis of the monetization options, see Chia and Tsui (2009).

converted into monthly payouts. This helps transform the risk and uncertainty of potentially outliving one's resources to receiving a guaranteed monthly income for life. Yet people decline buying such a product. Economists call this "annuity puzzle". Eminent behavioral economist Thaler offered several explanations for the unpopularity of annuities. For the elderly, "buying annuity is scary and complicated. Shopping for an annuity with hundreds of thousands of dollars at stake can be daunting, even for an economist" (Thaler, 2011). Another reason is that people are loss averse, or simply "*kia su*" (afraid to suffer loss). Instead of seeing annuities as part of the overall optimization of their retirement portfolio, individuals doubt they will live long enough to make back their initial investment. Annuities appear unattractive because the pain of "losses" from the annuity (if the annuitant dies early) would be relatively larger compared to the gratification of potential "gains" from living a long time, even past life expectancy. Furthermore, not being able to leave a bequest does not jibe well with people's preferences.

Housing wealth is a large proportion of the elderly's retirement wealth. In a sample household survey conducted by HDB in 2008, 83% of the elderly (aged 65 and over at the time of the survey) considered the HDB flat they lived in as their main personal asset, followed by savings or fixed deposits. CPF savings was their third main source of retirement wealth (HDB, 2010, p. 180). A higher proportion, about 93% of the future elderly (aged 55 to 64 at the time of the survey) regarded the HDB flat they lived in as their major asset, followed by CPF savings. Based on the National Survey of senior citizens in 2011, which covered 5,000 senior citizens, slightly more than a quarter of the respondents encountered some degree of financial inadequacy while about one third perceived that they have inadequate financial resources. "Low or no income" and "high cost of living" are the two most cited reasons for their financial inadequacy (Kang *et al.*, 2013, p. 8).

The Department of Statistics conducts the household expenditure survey. In 2012/13, 11,000 households were polled, and for the first time the survey reports in great detail the income and expenditure patterns of retiree households, those comprising solely non-working persons aged 60 and above. About 70% of the retiree households live in HDB flats, about a third in 3-room flats, a fifth in 4-room, and 16.5% in 1- and 2-room flats, including HDB studio apartments. Table 1 shows the sources of retiree household incomes by housing type. Retiree households' incomes are from non-work sources. These include rental and investment income, transfers and contributions from relatives and friends, annuities and CPF monthly payouts, and social assistance and government transfers.

Government transfers and rebates/subsidies comprise regular transfers, with rebates/subsidies reflected as reduced prices of services offered, and as ad-hoc transfers. The average monthly income for retiree households living in HDB flats, excluding imputed rent of owner-occupied housing, was S$1,735. This puts them on par

Table 1. Source of retiree household incomes by type of dwelling.[1]

Source of household income	Total[3]	HDB dwellings						Condominiums and other apartments	Landed properties
		Total[4]	1- & 2-room flats[5]	3-room flats	4-room flats	5-room and executive flats			
Average monthly household income excluding imputed rental of owner-occupied accommodation	1,735	1,147	647	1,069	1,233	1,806		3,851	5,306
Rental income, excluding imputed rental of owner-occupied accommodation	322	93	0	102	125	146		1,179	1,681
Investment income	457	207	17	233	200	318		988	2,351
Contributions from relatives and friends not staying in the same household	458	433	255	389	514	662		490	670
Annuities and monthly payouts from CPF minimum sum scheme, CPF LIFE	208	160	93	145	173	250		513	368
Others[2]	290	254	282	199	220	431		682	237

Source: DOS (2014a, Table 50).

Notes:

[1] Retiree households are those comprising solely non-working persons aged 60 years and over.

[2] Others include income from pension, social welfare grant, regular payment from insurance protection policies and regular government transfers.

[3] Total includes other types of dwellings not shown, e.g., non-HDB shop, houses, etc.

[4] Total HDB includes non-privatized Housing and Urban Development Corporation (HUDC) flats.

[5] 1- and 2-room flats include HDB studio apartments.

with the first (lowest) income decile of employed households, which had an average monthly income of S$1,644 in 2012 and S$1,711 in 2013 (Singstat, 2015,
Table 12A). The average monthly non-work income for retiree households living
in private apartments and landed property was S$3,800 and S$5,300, respectively.
This would put them, respectively, on par with those in the 30th and 50th percen-
tiles of resident employed households, whose median household income from work
was S$7,570 in 2012 and S$7,870 in 2013 (DOS, 2014a, p. 4).

Figure 1 plots the composition of income for retiree households according to
housing type. Payout from CPF savings is not an important source of income for the
wealthier retiree households in landed property, contributing only about 7% to their
total non-work income, with investment and rental income contributing 44% and
32%, respectively. For retiree households in condominiums and private apartments,
rental income contributes 30% and investment income 26% of non-work income.

The composition of income sources for retiree households in 3-room, 4-room
and 5-room HDB flats is quite similar. On average, rental income contributes about
9%, and CPF payouts approximately 14%, of total non-work income. Monthly CPF
payouts are S$145, S$173 and S$250 for retiree households in 3-, 4- and 5-room
flats, respectively. The average payout from the CPF minimum sum scheme for these
retirees is S$164. The low payouts could be due to low net savings because of large

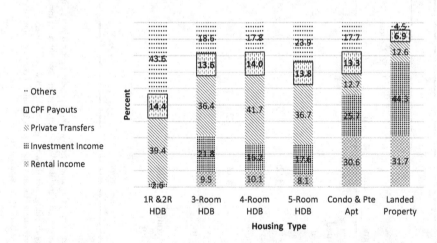

Figure 1.   Composition of income for retiree households according to dwelling types.

Source: Author's Calculation using DOS (2014a), Chart 1.9 and Table 50.

Notes:

1. Retiree households are those comprising solely non-working persons aged 60 years and over.
2. Others include income from pension, social welfare grant, regular payment from insurance protection
   policies and regular government transfers.
3. 1- & 2-room flats include HDB studio apartments.

pre-retirement withdrawals from CPF savings. Given the CPF policies that prevailed accumulation phase, these elderly were able to withdraw almost all their CPF savings for housing, and were also allowed to make lump sum withdrawals at the age of 55. When the Minimum Sum (MS) was incepted in 1987, it was estimated that a MS of S$30,000 in cash would yield a monthly payout of S$230. In 2003, although the MS was higher at S$80,000, half of the decreed MS would yield S$252 a month to last 18 years.

From the reported amount of CPF payouts received, we infer that most elderly were unable to meet even half of the decreed cohort-specific MS in cash. Furthermore, retirees who were age 60 and above in 2012 would have belonged to the cohorts who turned 55 in 2007 or earlier. In 2007, only 36% could meet the MS (including using property pledge). Figure 2 plots the proportion of CPF members who were able to meet the cohort-specific MS at age of 55. Figure 2 also shows the prevailing cohort-specific MS for the year. Between 1996 and 2004, with the revision of MS upward, the proportion of CPF members able to meet the MS fell. Even for those who were able to meet the MS, they could have done so using property pledge and would have cashed out most of their CPF monies.

Traditionally, familial financial support, particularly from children, is the most important source of income for the elderly. In Table 1, private income transfers refer to contributions received from relatives and friends not staying in the same household. For retiree households living in HDB, income transfer is a major source of

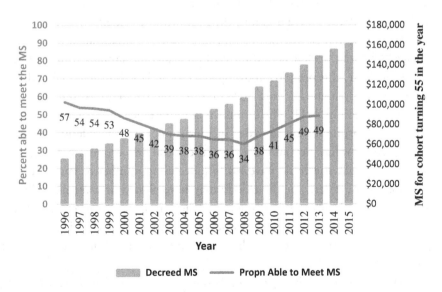

Figure 2.   Proportion of CPF members able to meet the cohort-specific minimum sum.

Source: CPF Annual Reports, various years.

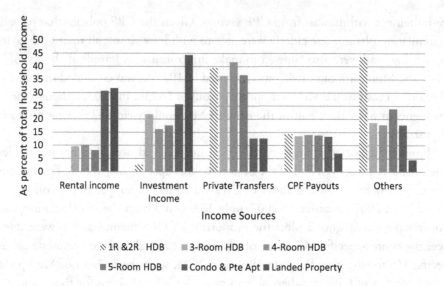

Figure 3.   Income source of retiree household by housing type.

Source: Author's calculation using DOS (2014, Table 50).

non-work income, surpassing incomes from rent, investment and CPF payouts. Figure 3 shows that private transfer is the most important income source for HDB retiree households, contributing a third of their non-work income.

While familial transfers are still important, these are trending down. This is evidenced from the three rounds of national survey of senior citizens conducted in 1995, 2005 and 2011. Figure 4 graphs the proportion of elderly who cited income transfers from children as the most important source of financial support. Among elderly aged 65 to 74, 79% received most of their income support from children in 1995. But by 2011, this proportion dropped to 45%. For those aged 75 and above, the drop was less dramatic — from 86% in 1995 to 64% in 2000, and remained at the same proportion in 2011. The diminishing importance of income transfer from children as the most important source of income support for the elderly could be due to shifting family values or/and changes in the social and economic environment. Shrinking household size could have led to a declining number of family members able to care for the elderly, or the elderly may have gained or want more financial independence. Work income also becomes a more important source of income as people work longer, particularly for those aged from 55 to 64. This group works longer because of postponement of the retirement age and implementation of the Re-employment Act.

But retiree households living in 1- or 2-room HDB flats are the least prepared for retirement. They rely heavily on private transfers and social assistance for financial support. As seen in Figure 1, almost 84% of their non-work incomes were private

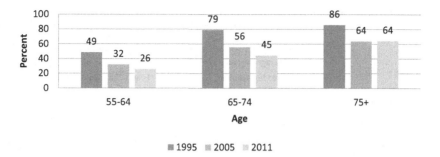

Figure 4.   Proportion of elderly who cited income transfers from children as the most important source of financial support.

Source: Compiled from MCYS (2005, p. 28) and Kang *et al.* (2013, p. 54).

transfers from relatives and friends (40%) and others (44%). The category of 'Others' includes income from pensions, social welfare grants, regular payment from insurance protection policies and regular government transfers. Without these transfers and social assistance, these households would experience significant economic hardship.

The ComCare Endowment Fund has been the key source of funding for needy Singaporeans. The ComCare Fund started in 2005 with a capital injection of S$250 million from the government, and with top-ups from budget surpluses. The fund stood at S$1.7 billion in 2014 (MSF, 2014, p. 4). The ComCare Long Term Assistance program targets the "most needy who are unable to work due to old age, illness or disability have limited or no means of income and have little or no family support" (MSF, 2014, p. 7). In FY2013, S$17.33 million was disbursed to 3,187 households, with each household receiving S$5,437 per year or S$453 per month for daily living expenses. The level of income support for public assistance is S$450 per month. Some elderly are recipients under the public assistance scheme administered by MSF. The need for public assistance by elderly has gone up. In 2005, only 0.6% of the respondents in the National Survey of Senior Citizens cited public assistance as their main source of income. But the proportion doubled to 1.1% in 2011 (Kang *et al.*, 2013, p. 54).

3. Means-Tested Basic Retirement Support

This chapter proposes formalizing a system of income support for the elderly poor.[9] The proposed basic pension is means-tested and adjusted for cost of living. The income

---

[9] This research was completed independently before the announcement of the Silver Support Scheme announced in Budget 2015. The Silver Support Scheme is a means tested cash support for the elderly poor. The means-tested basic pension scheme share many similar features with the Silver Support Scheme.

Table 2.   Average monthly expenditure per household member among retiree households.

	Average over all retiree households	HDB dwellings			
		Average	1- and 2-Room	3-Room	4-Room
Average monthly expenditure[1]					
Excluding imputed rental	$1,012	$819	$624	$726	$879
Including imputed rental	$1,610	$1,256	$722	$1,212	$1,421
Average monthly basic expenditure[2]					
Excluding imputed rental		$590	$532	$587	$650
Including imputed rental		$965	$630	$1,073	$1,191
Basic expenditure component[3]					
Food and non-alcoholic beverages	$167	$137	$94	$132	$187
Clothing and footwear	$18	$12	$5	$11	$21
Housing and utilities					
Imputed rentals[3]	$598	$375	$98	$486	$541
Utilities	$169	$115	$103	$119	$123
Furnishings, equipment and house Maintenance	$71	$44	$29	$42	$60
Health	$141	$120	$159	$114	$86
Transport	$71	$30	$17	$29	$43
Communication	$35	$25	$18	$26	$29
Food serving services[4]	$120	$108	$108	$114	$102
Number of retiree households in HDB	77,481	54,058	12,819	26,051	15,188
HDB retiree households as proportion of total retiree households		69.8%	16.5%	33.6%	19.6%

Source: Data from DOS (2014, p. 267).
Notes:
[1] Average monthly expenditure per household member as reported in DOS (2014, p. 267).
[2] Average monthly basic expenditure after excluding "non-basic" expenditures. The latter includes personal care services, recreation and culture, educational services, accommodation services, alcoholic beverages and tobacco and other non-assignable expenditure.
[3] Imputed rentals for owner-occupied accommodations facilitate the comparison between homeowners and renters.
[4] Food servicing services include meals bought from restaurants, hawker centers, food courts, etc.

and expenditure patterns for retiree household in 1- to 4-room HDB reported in the Household Expenditure Survey 2012/2013 (DOS, 2014a) will be used to estimate the benefit level and coverage of such a scheme. Table 2 presents the average monthly expenditure per household member among retiree households living in 1- to 4-room HDB. Excluding imputed rentals of owner-occupied accommodations, the average monthly expenditure per household member is S$1,012 for all retiree households (both HDB and non-HDB dwellers), and S$819 for HDB dwellers.

The proposed income support is to help needy elderly meet their basic needs.[10] We therefore exclude expenses on "non-basic" goods and services from the expenditure components in the household expenditure survey. The following categories of expenditures are excluded: personal care services, recreation and culture, educational services, accommodation services, alcoholic beverages and tobacco, other non-assignable expenditure. However, expenses on "food servicing services" are kept as basic expenditure. "Food servicing services" includes meals bought from restaurants, hawker centers, food courts, etc. Cooked food, particularly meals bought from hawker centers and food courts, are convenient, and sometimes necessary substitutes for prepared food for many elderly in Singapore. As there is no detailed breakdown, we are unable to exclude meals from restaurants. We assume that "expenses from restaurants" are small for the less well-to-do elderly.

The average monthly basic expenditure excluding imputed rentals for each household member living in 1- and 2-room, 3-room and 4-room HDB are respectively S$532, S$587 and S$650. The average expenditure is about S$590. We therefore consider S$600 per month to be a good estimate of the average basic living expenses for home-owning retirees. Retirees living in 1- and 2-room HDB flats may be renters. If rental cost is included, the average monthly basic expenditure outlay for the elderly in 1- and 2-room HDB will be higher, at S$630.[11] As discussed earlier, almost 84% of their non-work incomes come from private and government transfers. Assuming familial support to continue and the current government in-kind transfer programs to remain, a monthly payout of S$500 per person will be a good estimate for income support to meet basic living expenses. For sensitivity analysis, we also compute pension cost at varying benefit levels to reflect more generous and more conservative support. The benefit level is also adjusted for the cost of living. As there is no published CPI for elderly only, we use the core inflation index which averaged 1.7% from 2002 to 2013. For the sensitivity analysis, we will use different cost-of-living adjustments (COLA) assumptions.

The proposed income support is not universal but covers needy elderly. The eligibility age of recipient is set at age 65 which is the definition used for elderly. Based on DOS (2014a, p. 247), the least prepared retiree households live in 1- or 2-room

---

[10] There is a need to calibrate "basic expenditure" as Singapore does not use a defined poverty line to reach out to the needy. Instead a "multiple lines of assistance" is used to identify people in need of support. See the website of the Ministry of Social and Family Development at: http://app.msf.gov.sg/Press-Room/Poverty-Line-in-Singapore; accessed on 23 January 2015.

[11] HDB provides limited rental flats to the poor and needy citizen families without any housing options. The monthly rentals are heavily subsidized and means-tested: S$26 to S$33 for 1-room and S$44 to S$75 for 2-room.

HDB. Assuming a two person household, we set the coverage to be the poorest 30% of the total elderly population.

4. Support Cost — Actuarial Calculation

We estimate the pension cost for the year 2015 and project it to 2050. At time t, the pension cost at time $t(C_t)$ is represented by the following equation:

$$C_t = b\beta \sum_{x=\alpha}^{100} (N_{x,t}^m + N_{x,t}^f)t = 15,\dots,50.$$

We set C_{15} as the pension cost in year 2015 and C_{50} as the projected cost in year 2050. Pension recipients will start receiving payout b at age α. Recipients of the basic pension must be at least age α. The basic pension targets the poorest β percentage of the eligible population. The total cost in year t will depend on the proportion covered (β) and the number of elderly who are age α and older in year t.

Given the phenomenon of feminization of aging, we compute pension costs for different genders. Let $N_{x,t}^m$ and $N_{x,t}^f$ respectively represent the number of male and female population who are age x in time t. This together with the proportion of poor (β) covered will give the forecasted cost of the basic pension. To forecast the number of pension recipients, we use the well-established Lee–Carter stochastic demographic model to forecast mortality to obtain the number of elderly residents in each age group as the population ages. This is presented in Appendix A. The population projection is based on the historical mortality rates obtained from Singapore's Complete Life tables from 2003 to 2013 from DOS (2014b). The demography package in R written by Hyndman is used to forecast future mortality rates. The demographic forecast results are in line with expectations of improving mortality over time as shown in the forecasted survival functions.

In the population projection, instead of total fertility rate, a parametric model is used to fit the age-specific fertility rates for 2013. Immigration assumptions are also incorporated. Currently 20,000 new citizens from the pool of permanent residents are added to the population each year. We assume the current immigration policy to continue in order to keep the citizen population from shrinking (NPTD, 2014, p. 13). Since the majority of the permanent residents are in the prime working ages of 25 to 49 years, these residents are distributed uniformly to the existing population, equally between genders and across 25 to 49 years old. In 2013, non-residents account for 28.8% of total population and are capped at 20% of the total population. This is in line with the manpower policy of reducing reliance on foreign manpower and improving labor productivity, with the non-resident population required to meet manpower needs in the healthcare sector, and for construction workers and foreign domestic

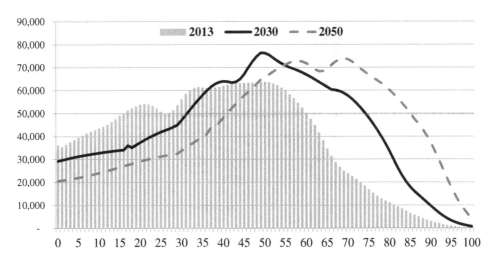

Figure 5.   Demographic landscape of Singapore in 2013, 2030 and 2050.

Source: Author's computation.

workers[12] (NPTD, 2012). In the simulation, we assume the non-resident population to moderate at a rate of 3% per annum. The forecasted resident population would reach about 4.4 million in 2030, which corroborates with the government's projections in the Population White Paper (NPTD, 2013).

Figure 5 shows the changing demographic landscape for Singapore from 2013 to 2050. Over time, the population distribution shifts to the right, indicating an aging population. The right tail also becomes fatter through time, indicating a larger proportion of elderly population. Figure 6 shows that by 2050, the population pyramid would be fully inverted. Indeed, elderly population as a proportion of resident population will increase at an unprecedented rate, reaching 14% by 2019 and 20% by 2026. It will have taken Singapore 19 years to transit from an "aging" to an "aged" population.[13] But the transition to a "super aged" population will be much quicker, in less than 10 years. In contrast, Japan took nearly 25 years to transit from an "aging" to an "aged" population structure while the US took nearly 66 years.

Figure 7 plots the age pyramids of the elderly population (age 65 and above) for 2013, 2030 and 2050. Compared to the elderly population pyramid in 2013, the

---

[12] The Economic Strategies Committee had recommended maintaining foreign workforce at about one-third of the workforce (MTI, 2010, p. 7). Given the recent shift in manpower policy, in our simulation, we set foreign workforce at a fifth of the population.

[13] An aging, aged, and super-aged society is defined by the United Nations to be when the proportion of a population aged 65 and above exceeds the 7%, 14% and 20% levels respectively. If elderly population is computed as a proportion of total population, that is, including non-residents and foreigners, then becoming "aged" and "super-aged" will occur later.

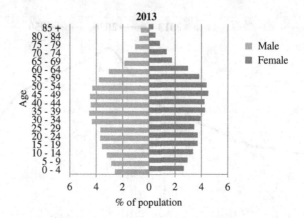

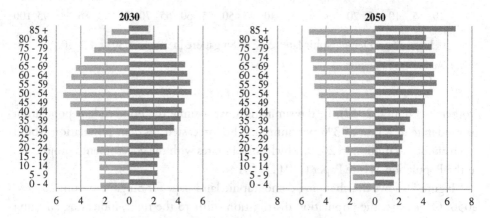

Figure 6.   Resident population pyramid.

Source: Author's projections.

pyramids in 2030 and 2030 show that the "oldest old" (age 85 and above) is the fastest growing age group. By 2030, the youngest cohort of the baby boomers will be the "young old" at age 65 and in 2050, they will become the "oldest old". By 2030, the youngest of the pioneer generation will be 80 years old and by 2050 they would have exited the population.[14] We will report pension costs for these years: 2015, 2030 and 2050. The age pyramids of the elderly population show evidence of feminization of aging, with more female elderly than male elderly, especially at older ages.

With mortality improvement and aging population, the number of basic income support recipients will go up and so will pension cost. The viability of providing a

---

[14] The pioneer generation refers to the 450,000 Singaporeans who are aged 65 and above in 2014, and who belong to the birth cohorts of 1949 or earlier.

2013   **2030**   **2050**

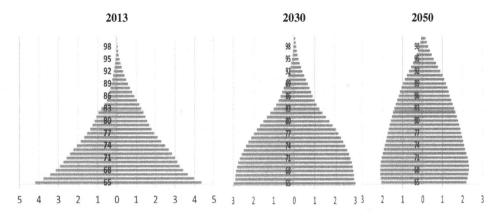

Figure 7. Population pyramid of elderly aged 65 and above percent of resident population. *Source*: Author's projection.

basic pension is evaluated in terms of its cost relative to GDP. This is because fiscal strength is premised on economic growth. As expected of a mature economy, economic growth rates will be lower. In this chapter, we project GDP taking the actuarial approach. We first apply growth rates to the base GDP per capita in 2013 to project GDP per capita. The projected GDP per capita for year t is then multiplied by the forecasted population in year t to yield projected GDP at year t. The projected population is generated from the Lee–Carter mortality forecasting model. Using the GDP per capita in 2013 at S$69,050 as the starting value, we project GDP to the year 2050.

Table 3 presents a sample of aging and more mature economies that have experienced falling real GDP per capita growth rates. In the past decade, Singapore's annual real GDP per capita growth has slowed to about 3% to 3.5%. In the base case, we assume a rather optimistic real GDP per capita growth rate to be 2.5%. For sensitivity, we assume a more optimistic real growth rate of 3% and slower real growth rate of 0.5% to 2%.

4.1. *Pension Cost Under Base Case and Sensitivity Analyses*

Table 4 gives the parameters used in the pension cost calculations. In the benchmark, the monthly pension benefit is $500 per month which is adjusted annually by the cost of living at 1.7% per annum. In the benchmark computation, the basic pension covers 30% of the elderly population. Table 5 presents the projected pension cost for 2020, 2030 and 2050 under the base case assumptions. With an aging population, the projected elderly aged 65+ as a proportion of resident population increases from 15.4% in 2020 to 23.6% in 2030 and then to 38.5% in 2050. The projected life

Table 3.   Historical real per capita GDP growth rate for some advanced aging society.

	1961–1965	1966–1970	1971–1975	1976–1980	1981–1985	1986–1990	1991–1995	1996–2000	2001–2005	2006–2010
Singapore	4.52	10.71	7.58	7.2	4.26	6.35	5.46	3.12	3.67	2.93
Japan	7.93	9.1	3.15	3.51	3.59	4.53	1.1	0.75	1.16	0.46
Switzerland	3.19	2.82	0.44	1.98	1.05	2.16	−0.85	1.64	0.62	0.93
United States	0	0	1.77	2.66	2.33	2.24	1.22	3.14	1.46	0.07
United Kingdom	2.38	2.09	1.93	1.75	2.05	3.08	1.39	3.13	2.04	−0.29
France	0.43	4.7	3.24	2.93	1	2.66	0.8	2.27	0.87	0.09
Germany	0	0	2.19	3.47	1.53	2.85	1.66	1.87	0.53	1.37
Netherlands	4.11	4.08	2.43	2.15	0.66	2.71	1.62	3.43	0.83	1.05

Source: World Bank (2014) downloaded from http://data.worldbank.org/indicator/NY.GDP.PCAP.KD.ZG/.

Table 4. Model parameters and assumptions.

Basic pension structure and eligibility	Benchmark	Conservative	Generous
Monthly pension benefit	$500	$450	$600
Minimum eligible age	65	65	65
Target (proportion of elderly)	30%	20%	50%
Cost of living adjustment	1.7%	1.0%	1.7%
Macroeconomics GDP per capita growth rate	2.5%	2.5%	2.5%

Source: Author's computation.

Table 5. Projected pension cost under base case assumptions.

	2015	2020	2030	2050
Percent of resident population aged 65+	11.7%	15.4%	23.6%	38.5%
Projected recipients	137,688	189,381	310,046	525,611
Female life expectancy	85.6	87.0	89.2	92.6
Male life expectancy	81.6	83.2	86.1	90.5
Pension cost using base case assumptions				
Pension Cost, Female ($ millions)	$453	$664	$1,259	$3,024
Pension Cost, Male ($ millions)	$374	$572	$1,136	$2,666
Total Pension Cost ($ millions)	$826	$1,236	$2,395	$5,689
Pension cost as percent of GDP				
2.5% real GDP per capita growth	0.209%	0.274%	0.414%	0.580%

Source: Author's computation.

expectancy rates for males are 83.2 years in 2020, 86.1 in 2030 and 90.5 in 2050; and for females 87 years in 2020, 89.2 in 2030 and 92.6 in 2050. With an aging population, the cost of providing basic pension rises. Pension cost increases from S$0.83 billion to S$1.24 bn in 2020 and then to S$2.40 bn in 2030 and S$5.69 bn in 2050. Pension costs, however, are well below 1% of GDP as long as GDP per capita growth rate is well above 1% per annum.

Figure 8 compares the projected costs of basic income support for elderly men and women. Given the feminization of aging, the pension costs for women are higher than for men. On average, the cost of providing income support for female elderly is about 10% to 15% higher than for male elderly.

The viability of the pension scheme, which is evaluated as percent of GDP, depends on economic growth. We perform sensitivity analyses of the pension cost as percent of GDP (C/Y) to the real growth rates of GDP per capita (g). Pension cost as

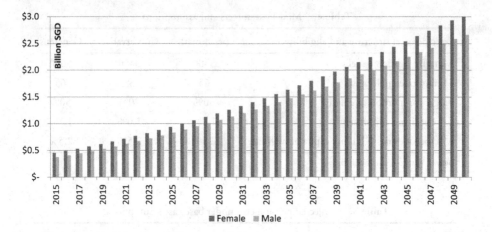

Figure 8.   Projected cost of basic pension provision to elderly males and females using base case assumptions.

Source: Author's computation.

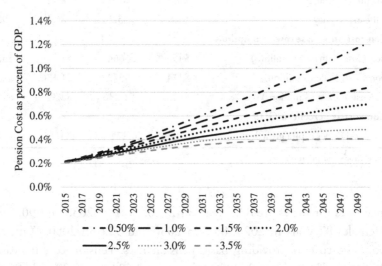

Figure 9.   Projected pension cost as percent of GDP (C/Y) using different scenarios of real per capita GDP growth rates (g).

Source: Author's computation.

percent of GDP increases gradually when the economic growth rate exceeds the pace of aging. As can be gleaned from Figure 9, when the economic growth rate is low, the cost of providing pensions is higher. When g is 2% or higher, pension cost as a percent of GDP increases gradually over time. At slower growth rates, for example when g is below 1.5%, C/Y increases steadily.

Table 6. Sensitivity of pension cost as percent of GDP to the real growth rate of GDP per capita, using base case assumptions.

Real GDP per capita growth rate (g) (%)	Pension costs as percent of GDP (C/Y)			
	2015 (%)	2020 (%)	2030 (%)	2050 (%)
0.5	0.218	0.315	0.578	1.203
1.0	0.215	0.304	0.531	1.001
1.5	0.213	0.294	0.489	0.834
2.0	0.211	0.284	0.450	0.695
2.5	0.209	0.274	0.414	0.580
3.0	0.207	0.265	0.381	0.485
3.5	0.205	0.256	0.351	0.405
Difference in C/Y when $g = 0.5$ and $g = 2.5$	0.010	0.048	0.181	0.596

Source: Author's computation.

Table 6 shows that when at g = 1%, pension cost is 0.3% of GDP in 2020, increasing to 0.5% of GDP in 2030 and reaching about 1% of GDP in 2050. But when g is below 1%, for example at g = 0.5%, by 2050, the cost will exceed 1% of GDP, at 1.2%. The increase of C/Y over time is more gradual when g is higher. When g = 3.5%, C/Y is 0.26% in 2020, increasing gradually to 0.35% in 2030 and 0.41% in 2050. It is observed that as time advances, the sensitivity of C/Y to g magnifies. The last row computes the difference in C/Y under the most pessimistic growth rate (g = 0.5%) and the benchmark growth rate (g = 2.5%). Note that the difference in C/Y from different g becomes magnified over time.

In 2020, the difference was 0.048%, which widens to 0.181% in 2030. Therefore, the viability of providing pensions when the population is aging depends on the long term economic performance.

Next we perform sensitivity of pension costs to the cost of living adjustments (COLA) using the parameterization in the base case. In the benchmark, we set COLA to the average core inflation, which was 1.7% from 2002 to 2013. Figures 10 and 11 show that adjusting the benefit payout by using a smaller COLA factor will significantly dampen the size of the pension cost and the pension cost as percent of GDP.

4.2. Sensitivity Analyses

We also compute pension costs assuming more conservative and more generous income supports. For more conservative income support, the benefit level is set at

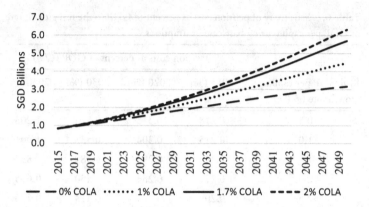

Figure 10.   Sensitivity of pension cost to cost of living adjustments (COLA).

Source: Author's computation.

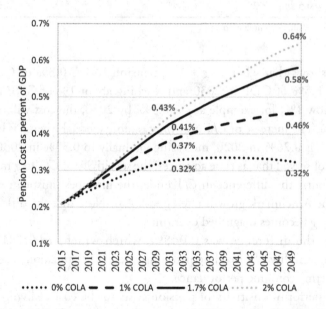

Figure 11.   Sensitivity of pension cost as percent of GDP to cost of living adjustments.

Source: Author's computation.

the current level of subsistence monthly income support under public assistance, at S$450. The cost of living adjustment is set at 1 percent, lower than the average core inflation. Basic pension income support covers only the poorest 20% of the elderly population aged 65 and above. For a more generous income support scheme, the monthly pension benefit is set at S$600 per month, with an annual cost of living adjustment of 1.7% per annum covering half of the elderly population.

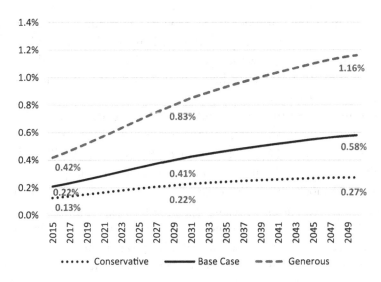

Figure 12. Projected pension cost as percent of GDP using varying coverage and benefit level.

Source: Author's computation.
Note: See Table 4 for the parameter assumptions for the different cases.

Using the same macroeconomic variables, a more generous scheme will increase the pension cost considerably, as shown in Figure 12. Under the benchmark scenario, a benefit level of S$500 per month, covering the poorest 30% of the elderly population, yields a projected pension cost of 0.41% of GDP in 2030 and 0.58% of GDP in 2050. When the benefit level is increased to S$600 per month and covers the bottom half of the elderly population, the pension cost as percent of GDP will be higher — at 0.83% in 2030 and 1.16% in 2050. The pension cost will exceed one percent of GDP using the benchmark real growth of GDP per capita at 2.5%. Under the more conservative scenario, a lower monthly benefit level of S$450 covering the poorest 20% of the elderly population will keep the pension cost to around 0.3% of GDP.

5. Conclusion

As a fully funded and defined contribution system, the CPF system is financially sustainable. The CPF system has worked well for Singaporeans who were fully employed, enjoyed good income and exercised prudent housing consumption. The CPF system has helped these Singaporeans to own a home, save for health care and prepare for retirement. However, there is room for improvement, to meet the needs of those who do not have enough CPF savings, and to address inflation risks. The CPF system maintains a one-to-one correspondence between contributions and withdrawals. Being a work-based system, it cannot ensure retirement adequacy for its vulnerable members. These are low-wage workers with low CPF accumulation, those unable to work because of disabilities, stay-at- home mothers without CPF savings, and elderly without any familial support.

Interestingly, after fifty years of independence, we are revisiting issues raised before Singapore became independent. These issues were discussed in various reports, for example, McFadzean (1952), Brocklehurst (1957), Caine (1957), and others. In the last fifty years, the social and economic landscapes of Singapore have changed. Changes in the demographic landscape are particularly significant and Singapore will soon achieve the status of "an aged society". Establishing a dignified and minimum standard of living for the vulnerable increasingly require active policy interventions.

The expansion of government redistributive programmes through the various government transfer schemes is a step in the right direction to address social inclusivity and income inequality. Although the Gini coefficient has improved with recent transfer programmes, retirement inadequacy still looms. Of CPF members who turn 55 in 2013, only about half can meet the cohort-specific minimum sum. Of these, 15% are able to do so only by using the property pledge. Adding a basic pillar to the CPF structure will help the elderly poor meet their basic expenditure to enable them to live independently with self-respect and dignity. The proposed support scheme is not a universal scheme but will be means-tested to keep it viable. As long as the real growth rate stays higher than 1% per annum, and using the base case assumptions for immigration and foreign worker population, the cost of the means-tested pension will be kept within 1% of GDP. The cost will be higher if more restrictive immigration and foreign population assumptions are made. Furthermore, measures must be put in place so that the scheme will be incentive compatible and minimize disincentives to work, save and annuitize.[15]

Financing an aging population is indeed challenging. Generally, welfare provisions in Singapore are targeted schemes which are funded using endowment or trust funds with capital injections from accumulated budget surpluses. For endowment funds, only interest and investment earnings on the funds are allowed to be used to provide welfare benefits; the fund capital is untouched. For trust funds, the capital amount can be spent down. In 2014, the government set aside $8 billion as the Pioneer Generation Trust Fund to meet the long term medical needs of the pioneer generation. A similar trust/endowment fund can be set up from capital injections

---

[15] The fiscal sustainability of such a system is sensitive to economic growth. As alerted by the late Mr. Lee Kuan Yew in 1996 regarding the view that the government is not doing enough to help the poor, that doing so is "the easiest way to destroy self-reliance which has been a driving force for high performance. Many Singaporeans feel that the government can afford it. This is precisely the trap which the advanced countries fell into when the economic growth was robust and compassion was believed to be always affordable" (Lee, 2013).

from the accumulated budget surpluses or reserves, if necessary. The experience of implementing the Medishield Life means-tested scheme will provide the government with the necessary machinery to implement a means-tested basic pension scheme.

In conclusion, the CPF machinery has evolved to adapt to the changing demographic landscape and the shifting ideology on building a more inclusive society. By including more risk-pooling in the CPF LIFE scheme and by adding basic retirement cash supplements through the budgetary system, the form and functions of CPF have changed. Nonetheless, even with these changes and shifts, the CPF Board still adheres to its original mission of maintaining and ensuring a sustainable system. There is no move toward a collective social insurance scheme, such as the pay-as-you-go system, which is unsustainable, distorts retirement decisions, and generates both inter- and intra-generational inequities. CPF is a pure defined contribution scheme, and CPF members need not make their own investment choices but enjoy a capital protected guaranteed return. With the implementation of the CPF LIFE scheme, the CPF system allows for risk pooling and addresses longevity risk.

The introduction of a means-tested Silver Support Scheme is a step forward. In his roundup speech for budget 2015, Deputy Prime Minister Tharman Shanmugaratnam said, "a strong element of collective responsibility built into the CPF scheme. The Government provides support through the Budget to lower income members and provides assurance to all."[16] Current social protection in Singapore, in terms of retirement adequacy, has incorporated some measures to establish a "minimum standard of livelihood for the people of Singapore" (Caine, 1957), though in different forms. The CPF system has evolved to become both individual and collective to ensure sustainability with greater inclusivity. It is "individual" as it is based on individual savings and responsibility. And it is "collective" as a means-tested basic retirement support is built into the CPF system.[17]

Appendix A. Lee–Carter Stochastic Mortality Forecasting

To project mortality rates, we use the widely established Lee–Carter model (Lee and Carter, 1992). The Lee–Carter model has been successfully applied to the G7 countries to forecast life expectancy at birth. The model assumes that the log of the central mortality rate follows a stochastic random walk with drift which is expressed as:

$$\ln m_{xt} = a_x + b_x k_t + \varepsilon_{xt},$$
$$k_t = \mu + \varphi k_{t-1} + \eta_t,$$

---

[16] Budget 2015 Roundup Speech by Deputy Prime Minister and Minster for Finance (Shanmugaratnam, 2015).

[17] *Ibid.*

where m_{xt} is the central death rate in age class x in year t; a_x is the additive age-specific constant, reflecting the general shape of the age schedule; b_x is the responsiveness of mortality at age class x to variations in the general level; k_t is a time-specific index of the general level of mortality; μ and φ are parameters; ε_{xt} is the error to the actual age schedule, assuming to follow a normal distribution with zero mean and a constant variance; and η_t is the white noise.

Assuming a uniform distribution of death, the central mortality rate is related to the mortality rate defined as $q_{x,t}$ by:

$$m_{x,t} = \frac{q_{x,t}}{1 - 0.5 q_{x,t}}.$$

We input historical mortality rates from Singapore's Complete Life tables from 2003–2013 provided by the Department of Statistics (2014b). We calculate the number of residents aged x at year t with the equation:

$$N_{x,t} = N_{x-1,\ t-1}\ (1 - q_{x,t}).$$

References

Brocklehurst, GJ (1957). *Report to the Government of Singapore on Social Security Measures.* International Labor Office ILO/TAP/Singapore/R.3.Government Printing Office, Singapore.

Caine, S (1957). *Report of the Committee on Minimum Standards of Livelihood, (Chairman S. Caine).* Government Printing Office, Singapore.

Chia, NC (2014). Uniquely Singapore budgetary system and social protection financing schemes. *Singapore Economic Review*, 59(3), 1–22.

Chia, NC (2015). The CPF Story: Reflecting the Social and Economic History of Singapore. Manuscript.

Chia, NC and A Tsui (2009). Monetizing Housing Equity to Generate Retirement Incomes. SCAPE Working Paper No. 2009/01.NUS Economics: Singapore Center for Applied Policy and Economics.

Department of Statistics (DOS), Singapore (2014a). *Report on the Household Expenditure Survey, 2012/2013.*

Department of Statistics (DOS), Singapore (2014b). Complete Life Tables 2008–2013 for Singapore Resident Population.

Gillespie, RD (1959). *Committee of Officials Established to Examine the Recommendations of the Brocklehurst and Caine Committee Reports.* Singapore. Interim Report by R. D. Gillespie. Government Printing Office, Office.

Housing Development Board (HDB), Singapore (2010). Public housing in Singapore: Well-being of communities, families and the elderly. HDB Sample household survey 2008. HDB Research and Planning Department, March.

International Labor Office (1959). *Report to the Government of Singapore on a Proposed Social Security Scheme*, ILO/TAP/Singapore/R.5. International Labor Office, Geneva.

Kang, SH, ES Tan and MT Yap (2013). National survey of senior citizens 2011. Retrieved 16 January 2015 from http://app.msf.gov.sg/Publications/National-Survey-of-Senior-Citizens-2011.

Lee, KY (2013). *The Wit and Wisdom of Lee Kuan Yew*. Didier Millet Pte. Editions (ebook).

Lee, RD and LR Carter (1992). Modeling and forecasting US mortality. *Journal of the American Statistical Association*, 87(419), 659–671.

McFadzean, FS (1952). *Report of the Retirement Benefits Commission*. Singapore, Government Printer, Singapore.

Ministry of Community Development, Youth and Sports (MCYS), Singapore (2005). The national survey of senior citizens in Singapore, 1995 and 2005. Retrieved 15 January 2015 from http://app.msf.gov.sg/Research-Room/Research-Statistics/National-Survey-of-Senior-Citizens.

Ministry of Finance (MOF), Singapore (1961). State of Singapore Development Plan, 1961–1964. Government Publication Bureau.

Ministry of Health (MOH), Singapore (1984). [Howe Report] Report of the Committee on the Problems of the Aged.

Ministry of Social and Family Development (MSF), Singapore (2014). ComCare Annual Report for Financial Year 2013.

Ministry of Trade and Industry (MTI), Singapore (2010). Report of the Economic Strategies Committee, February.

National Population and Talent Division (NPTD), Singapore (2012). Projection of foreign manpower demand for healthcare sector, construction workers and foreign domestic workers.

National Population and Talent Division (NPTD), Singapore (2013). *A Sustainable Population for a Dynamic Singapore: Population White Paper*, Singapore, January. Available at http://population.sg/whitepaper/resource-files/population-white-paper.pdf.

National Population and Talent Division (NPTD), Singapore (2014). 2014 Population in Brief. September.

Shanmugaratnam, T (2015). Deputy Prime Minister and Minister for Finance. Budget 2015 Debate Round-up Speech, 5 March 2015, Singapore.

Thaler, RH (2011). The annuity puzzle. *The New York Times*, 4 June.

CHAPTER 12

Being Poor in a Rich "Nanny State": Developments in Singapore Social Welfare

Irene Y. H. Ng

This chapter reviews the trends in poverty and inequality in Singapore since independence, as well as policy recommendations adopted through the years, and their results. Poverty is discussed not only in terms of wage earnings, but also in relation to employment conditions, social challenges that pile up together with income poverty, and intergenerational mobility. The chapter finds that notwithstanding improvements in early decades, after fifty years, the problems of a social divide and poverty have come full circle. Social policy in Singapore retains its fundamentally productivist philosophical orientation, but the recent deterioration in poverty, inequality and mobility trends is leading to adoption of more welfare-oriented and universalist policy solutions. Social inclusion is now a national priority, and policy redirection for the future needs to take place in wide-ranging policy domains, including the labor market and economic growth.

1. Introduction

Singapore has become a stratified society. Years of unevenly distributed growth in a neoliberal growth regime has led to emergence of a class of working and non-working poor who face insurmountable challenges in uplifting themselves from a cycle of poverty. This chapter attempts to trace Singapore's developments in social welfare policy and services, in response to trends in poverty and inequality. The word "attempts" is important as there is scant information on poverty and inequality in Singapore. Poverty estimates were made from the early post-independence years to the 1980s. Thereafter, there was a period of "silence" until recent resurgence in efforts to make inferences on the magnitude of poverty.

As social welfare policy veteran Richard Titmuss argued for the United Kingdom, the lack of data on poverty in Singapore reflects a lack of priority given to poverty alleviation. Titmuss says in "the Irresponsible Society" (1960): "No effort has been made by government to discover the real incidence of poverty and levels of living among the old and other dependent groups. This to me is one of the more striking signs of irresponsibility of the 1950s. In so far as a society fails to identify, by fact and not by inference, its contemporary and changing social problems it must expect its social conscience and its democratic values to languish." (p. 69) His criticism of the British welfare system was strong, based on his value orientation discussed at the end of this chapter. What he pointed out about the British system in the 1950s has also been true in Singapore from the 1950s till today. While there are other reasons for not focusing on deriving good measures of poverty, such as the belief that poverty has been solved by strong economic growth in the 1990s, the lack of official poverty data also reflects the Singaporean value orientation in our choice of welfare system.

From the early colonial choice of a provident fund over a social insurance scheme, the prime priority of social welfare policy appeared to be minimizing the financial burden on the state (Low and Aw, 2004). Recommendations made then for more wide-ranging supports, such as benefits for old age, survivorship, sickness, maternity or unemployment, were set aside. When the People's Action Party (PAP) took over the government, the Central Provident Fund (CPF), originally created to improve retirement security, took on larger political economy objectives. Priority was given to social development goals, namely housing, education, and healthcare (Low and Aw, 2004; Chia, 2015). Holliday (2000) referred to such a welfare system, observed in East Asian economies including Singapore, as "productivist". The productivist model prioritizes "human capital investments" to yield human resource inputs for economic development.

The choice of the productivist model for social welfare relies on belief in the effectiveness of "trickle down economics". It also reflects the greater urgency given to solving problems such as poor housing conditions and an uneducated population, than to income security especially for old age. Thus, besides choosing a defined contribution compulsory savings scheme over social insurance, the role of the CPF was also incrementally expanded to be used for financing home ownership, personal healthcare insurance, and (higher) education.

The public assistance scheme retained from the British era was only for those without any means of earnings and sources of social support — selected groups such as destitute elderly and people with disabilities. Except for this one program, a productivist welfare model was seen as a more viable source of social protection than a more universalist approach to cash relief. It relies on the notion that individuals should take advantage of the opportunities provided by high subsidies for their social development (in health, education and so on) to be self-reliant. Not only is income inequality not prioritized in a productivist model, the ideology underpinning such a system depends on inequality to sustain the individual's incentive to strive in order to support oneself.

This emphasis on self-reliance has pervaded policy thinking in Singapore till today. It is a laissez-faire philosophy rooted in the belief that even if bottom earners get a lower share of economic gains, their lot would be worse without the strong growth premised on an open and competitive economy. But with social inclusion now considered a national priority, welfare policies have greatly expanded in recent years. The criteria for public assistance, for example, have been relaxed to also include the elderly poor with low-income children. Other programs to address poverty, such as Workfare and CPF Life, have also been introduced. Still, Singapore's policy response has lagged the responsiveness to "inclusive" growth in the international community (Asian Development Bank, 2004; United Nations, 2010).

This chapter proceeds as follows. The next two sections discuss inequality and poverty in turn, making inferences on the magnitude of each problem and discussing policy responses. Poverty is framed not only in terms of wage earnings, but also employment conditions. The chapter then extends the understanding of poverty to include social challenges that pile up together with income poverty, and to the intergenerational transmission of poverty. It concludes with a discussion of past and present policy frameworks and recommendations that have implications for future policy redirection.

2. Inequality

Figure 1 provides a time trend of income inequality, as measured by the Gini Index. A full time series is not possible due to different data sources and measurement changes through the years. However, from the different sources, a general trend line can be approximated, showing that income inequality decreased from post-independence in the 1960s and 1970s, bottomed out in the late 1970s, before increasing from the 1980s until 2007. The trend seems to be plateauing after 2007 and reversing in 2013 before turning up ever so slightly again in 2014.

The Gini trend line reveals four facts. First, it shows that reducing inequality was easy in the early years, and challenging thereafter. The transformation from Third World to First World in the 1960s and 1970s, with massive social and physical infrastructural investments and labor-intensive employment creation, was able to uplift incomes for the mass of the population. But as the economy moved increasingly up the value chain toward targeted capital- and skill-intensive sectors, there were winners and losers, the losers being the low-skilled in the bottom income pool. Second, the Gini trend line shows the correlation between economic growth and inequality, with inequality narrowing in the recessionary years of 1985, 1998 and 2008/2009. Third, the trend times well with the introduction of Workfare in 2006/2007 and the Progressive Wage Model in 2012. Fourth, the short-lived effects of these policies

Figure 1.   Singapore's Gini index, 1966–2014.

Notes: 1966–2000: From World Institute of Development Economics Research (WIDER), based on household survey in 1966 and labor force survey the rest of the years. Years 1995 and 2000 are omitted from this chart because they are from different sources, resulting in points that did not align with the time trend (1995: 44.3 from General Household Survey; 2000: 48.1 from Census of Population). 2001–2014: From Department of Statistics Household Income Survey, various years.

suggest that more aggressive policies are required to reverse the trend of increasing inequality.

Indeed, policy to address income inequality has been increasingly aggressive and direct. For example, ComCare temporary financial assistance for working adults was introduced in 2005 and incrementally expanded. Other measures such as progressive tax rebates and subsidies for utilities were also introduced. Figure 2 shows that redistributive policies appear to be increasingly narrowing inequality. The left vertical axis measures the Gini Index. The blue line with the triangle markers gives the Gini Index before taxes-and-transfers, and the red line with the square markers gives that for after taxes-and-transfers. The right vertical axis and green lines show the trend in the difference between the Gini indices before and after taxes-and-transfers. The dotted line with the round markers gives the ratio of the Gini Index after taxes-and-transfers (2) to that before taxes-and-transfers (1). The continuous straight line gives the linear trend of the green ratio line. This line is downward sloping, indicating that (2)/(1) is lower through the years and therefore the after-taxes-and-transfers Gini is further and further below the before-taxes- and-transfers Gini. But this downward trend becomes apparent only when the latest two years 2013 and 2014 are included. The line was almost flat up to 2009 (Ng, 2011).

In sum, redistributive policies are narrowing the income divide. However, even as these policies are incrementally expanded, the general trend of an increase in inequality seems to defy remedial policies. Further, income inequality in Singapore has never been low in comparative context (Ramesh, 2003). The published Gini Indices, based on labor force and household surveys, also only give inequality in terms of earnings

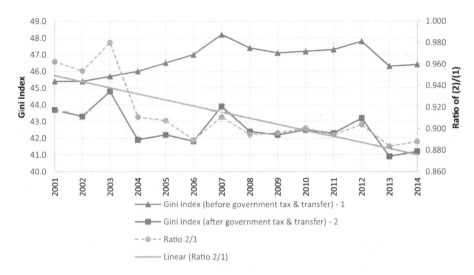

Figure 2.   Gini index before and after government taxes and transfers, 2001–2014.

from work, which account for less than half of total national income. Property income, which accounts for most of the remainder, can be expected to be much more unequally distributed, as wealth is typically more unequally distributed than income from work.

The government has recognized the need for more redistribution through the tax system by not only transfers such as the Workfare Income Supplement (WIS), but also by increasing taxes of top earners (Ministry of Finance, 2015a). Different forms of wealth taxes might also be introduced in future. Besides remedial redistribution, direct intervention to correct wages and labour market imbalances are also vital at this point, and thus the necessity for persisting with productivity overhaul and wage correction.

3. Poverty, Wage Stagnation and Precarious Job Conditions

While income inequality is reported through the years, there has been no report of poverty rates in Singapore, except for sporadic estimates by researchers. According to Lim Chong Yah's (1988) estimates based on the poverty line from the Amalgated Union of Public Employees (AUPE) of $240 per month per household of four persons, absolute poverty plunged from 30.8% in 1972/1973 to 7.4% in 1982/1983. Lim attributed the poverty reduction to "family size reduction, employment expansion and real income increases supported by rapid economic growth" (p. 395), factors that present-day Singapore can no longer count on to alleviate poverty. After Lim (1988), there were no reports of poverty rates for two decades. This period of "silence" was accompanied by a perception that with the success of economic development, poverty had been eradicated.

Recently, poverty has returned to the radar screen of policy-makers and the public. Donaldson *et al.* (2013) estimate that the absolute poverty rate in 2012 was between 10% to 14%. This was based on thresholds for minimum monthly expenditure of $1,250 or qualification for government assistance at $1,500 for households with four members. These poverty lines are high compared to the $240 estimated by Lim (1988). However, costs of living have also risen rather dramatically in Singapore especially in the last decade.

The problem with using absolute measures of poverty is that any poverty line is arguably arbitrary, based on the assessors' criteria of what should be basic expenses needed for survival. Even so, the ball park figures above, with generous margins of error, suggest that poverty in absolute terms did fall drastically from post-independence to the 1980s. Compared to then, absolute poverty has risen again, although not back to the extremely high levels in the 1960s and 1970s.

For comparability across nations, countries have used relative measures of poverty, with the view that a society should be looking out for the most vulnerable amongst us. Donaldson *et al.* (2013) and Hui (2013a) estimated that the relative poverty rate, defined as 50% of median income, is 20–22% in Singapore (Yeoh, 2012; Hui, 2013a). Comparison with East Asian and OECD countries suggests that Singapore's relative poverty rate is high (Ng, 2015).

Singapore's labor market structure and lean welfare system are factors contributing to the high poverty rates. First, labor market trends in wages and employment indicate that low-skilled wages have stagnated until recent wage correction measures. Figure 3 shows the stagnation of gross wages of selected occupations in the period 2000–2010, and Figure 4 shows the decline in real wages during this period. The occupation categories and types are selected based on the common occupations reported by beneficiaries of the Work Support Programme (WSP) disbursed by the Ministry of Social and Family Development (MSF); these include driver, cleaner, security guard, factory worker and waiter/waitress (Ng *et al.*, 2015).

Wage stagnation is not the only economic vulnerability faced by low-wage workers. As noted in a United Nations report, "the free-market orientation of development policy in the last decades is associated with expanding labor market inequalities, persistent informalization and the emergence of precarious forms of employment in many countries" (United Nations, 2010, p. 29). One indicator of informalization is part-time and contract work, which Figure 5 shows increased greatly from 1996–2001, particularly in the services sector where the proportion of part-time work among cleaners, laborers and related workers surged from 8% in 1996 to 32% in 2011. The rise in part-time work is not entirely employer determined; it is also related to increased female labor force participation, since greater flexibility in working hours enables

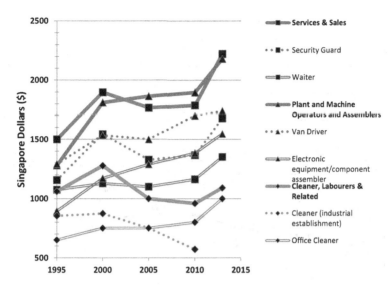

Figure 3.   Gross median monthly wages of selected occupations, 1995–2015.
Source: Ministry of Manpower, various years. Singapore Yearbook of Manpower Statistics.

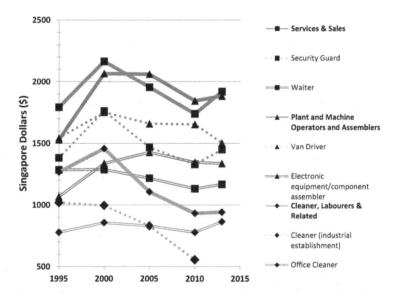

Figure 4.   Real median monthly wages of selected occupations, 1995–2015 (2009 = 100).
Source: Ministry of Manpower various years. Singapore Yearbook of Manpower Statistics.

women to meet their caregiving duties and other family obligations. However, the higher proportion of low-income and female workers employed in part-time positions suggests their greater economic vulnerability, because part-time work offers fewer benefits — such as CPF contribution, bonuses, and annual and medical leave — than

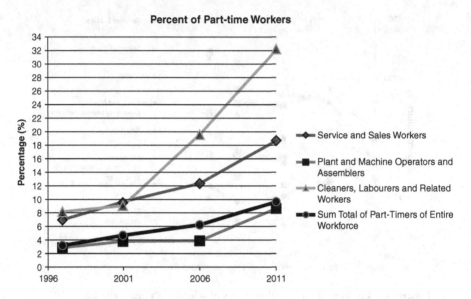

Figure 5.   Percent of part-time work in selected occupations.

Source: Ministry of Manpower, various years. Report on Labor Force in Singapore.

full-time work. These vulnerabilities of part-time work is compounded by the long and shift hours of service jobs, and the fact that many low-income households experience multiple family challenges that act as barriers to employment.

Singapore's lean welfare system also puts low-income individuals at risk, especially the elderly poor. While there is no data on poverty by life stage in Singapore, inferences can be made from data in similar economies. A comparative analysis of trends and welfare systems in East Asian economies (Hong Kong, South Korea and Taiwan) suggests that they have high elderly poverty relative to other industrialized economies, but lower child poverty. Four reasons given for this are: (i) labor markets where the jobs of low-educated elderly are facing wage depression whereas younger families with children experience this less; (ii) relatively underdeveloped pension systems; (iii) "familial" welfare systems (Teo, 2013) that emphasize family rather than state support; and (iv) productivist welfare systems that focus more on child-oriented development such as education (Ng, 2015). Singapore shares these four characteristics, which would explain its relatively high elderly and low child poverty rates.

Singapore's policy-makers are recognizing the need to strengthen the safety net for elderly Singaporeans. New initiatives such as Medishield Life (a form of universal healthcare) and Silver Support (a form of universal pension) are being rolled out. These are important, even if they lag other East Asian economies. At the same time, labor market reforms and wage correction measures are also crucial to address poverty in relation to wage stagnation and work informalization.

4. Social Challenges and Psychological Well-Being

Besides economic vulnerabilities, research has established that poverty risks occur in interaction with social challenges. Poor families are more likely than higher income families to face multiple challenges that act as barriers to employment, thus putting them in a downward poverty spiral (Danziger *et al.*, 2000; Ng, 2013a).

Ng (2013a) proposes a model of the pile-up and interaction of different types of stressors faced by low-income families in Singapore. The starting point is low education, which in today's high-tech and globalized economy depresses the wages of lowly educated individuals. Other factors lead to as well as result from low income: health problems; mental health issues; spousal relations issues including divorce; child issues such as child health, child behavior, and caregiving; and criminal history. Ng (2013a) found that the 466 WSP beneficiaries studied were facing at least two of the six types of stressors, with prevalence rates for each type of stressor being higher than national averages (Table 1).

The pile-up of multiple challenges experienced by poor households while living on the economic margins takes a toll on individuals' psychological outlook and cognitive functioning. This makes breaking the cycle of poverty more challenging than simply providing temporary financial relief. Successful policy intervention to break the cycle requires holistic multi-pronged approaches that recognize that each family unit experiences the various economic-social-psychosocial challenges together as one unit, and not as separate individual entities. Worded differently by Ng *et al.* (2014), "a plethora of separate and independent programmes does not gel with the reality that the family is one entity experiencing different types of needs simultaneously and in interaction. Therefore, the different challenges faced by a family unit

Table 1.   Prevalence rates of social stressors faced by 466 WSP beneficiaries.

Type of stressor	Percent
% with primary education and below	40.85
% divorced, separated, single or widowed	20.60
% with chronic health condition	40.22
% who are generally depressed	24.89
% with generalized anxiety	38.63
% with criminal record	18.89
% who has a child with a health condition that limits regular activities	20.82
% who has a child with difficult behavior	29.40

Source: Ng (2013a).

need to be dealt with holistically through increased integration and merger of services." (p. 157)

An example of more coordinated help is the greater connection between financial, psycho-social and employment assistance. ComCare financial assistance that used to be disbursed by the Community Development Councils (CDCs) under the People's Association was moved to the Ministry of Social and Family Development (MSF). From five CDCs, the provision of financial assistance was distributed out to 24 social service offices (SSOs) located in neighborhoods with higher concentrations of low-income households. At the same time, the oversight of family service centers (FSCs), which are the main providers of family and psychosocial assistance, was transferred from the National Council of Social Services (NCSS) to MSF, in an attempt to better coordinate the linkages between SSOs and FSCs. MSF also collaborates closely with the Workforce Development Agency (WDA) in providing employment assistance through joint case management in some cases, and colocation in others.

5. Intergenerational Mobility

Perhaps of greater concern than the magnitude of poverty at a point in time is the transmission of poverty through generations. In his round-up speech of the Budget 2015 debate, Deputy Prime Minister Tharman Shanmugaratnam articulated his concern for social mobility as the "defining challenge in every advanced country today" (Ministry of Finance, 2015b). While the Minister provided statistics indicating greater upward mobility for young adults in the bottom 20% in Singapore than even the welfare state of Denmark, he warned that "it will get more difficult as society gets more settled". Furthermore, the statistics he cited were generated for a young cohort at the particular income distribution threshold of 20%. Studies of the overall mobility of an earlier cohort of Singaporeans who were in their 20s and 30s in the 2000s (Ng, 2013b; Yip, 2012) suggest that intergenerational mobility for this cohort was moderate to moderately low. A more complete and accurate picture will require information on intergenerational mobility across the income distribution and of older individuals when incomes are more stable.

With data on intergenerational mobility lacking, lessons might be learned by comparing Singapore's institutions with factors that international research has shown lowers mobility in other countries. First, income inequality lowers intergenerational mobility because of the greater distance that one has to overcome in order to move between income classes. Second, strong welfare states improve intergenerational mobility, because they provide stronger protection for recovering beyond basic living needs. Third, differentiated and more privately-run education systems, where spending is less progressive, lower intergenerational mobility (Ng, 2013b, 2014).

On this last factor, there is extensive research evidence on the cumulative effects of parental advantage or disadvantage at significant life stages from pre-school, to middle school, tertiary education, and finally at the stage of transition to work (Pekkarinen *et al.*, 2009; Park, 2013; Ermisch *et al.*, 2012; Blanden and Machin, 2004; Yeoh, 2012; Hong Kong Institute of Education, 2013). Strikingly, these studies show the unequalizing effects of sorting or streaming; thus local analyses such as Ng *et al.* (2014) and Ng (2015) point to the need to review educational streaming due to its possible immobility-generating effects. Ng (2015) finds that in the Program for International Assessment (PISA), there was a larger than average gap in the performance of Singapore students as well as a greater than average dependence of their performance on parental socio-economic status.

Social science theories provide possible reasons for how differentiated education decreases mobility. Ng (2015) summarizes as follows: "The increasing differentiation of education through the introduction of streaming (Express, Normal Academic and Normal Technical) programmes (e.g., Integrated Programme, gifted education) and school types (e.g., independent, autonomous, specialized), with different schools offering different streams and programmes and charging different fees, results in three processes that lower intergenerational mobility. First, differential labels of different schools and programmes create perceptions of prestige and stigma, leading to the self-fulfilling prophecy of students behaving and performing according to the expected labels on them. Second, differential resources to the different schools and programmes leads to virtuous cycles of more resources for the preferred tracks and vicious cycles of fewer resources for the stigmatized tracks. Third, as the prestigious tracks attract students from more well-endowed families and the stigmatized tracks are shunned, differential networks lead to differential access to current and future connections and resources (see Ng (2014) for a fuller treatment of the three theoretical processes)."

It is further possible that, through these social science theoretical processes, early segregation of students solidifies in-group versus out-group experiences, views, and networks. Such segregation reduces the understanding and empathy that students have of others who are not within their narrow social spheres. This leads in turn to a socially divided society that makes collective responsibility hard to achieve.

The natural implication of this body of research on education and mobility would be to dismantle sorting and reduce educational stratification. This, however, is orthogonal to the policy directive in the Budget 2015 round-up speech by Mr. Shanmugaratnam, where diverse pathways are seen as the solution to social mobility, because they "cater to every talent and inclination, and even different learning styles….". The two opposite policy prescriptions are obviously based on very different theoretical starting points. It is possible that the empirical evidence on the negative effects of differentiated education on intergenerational mobility is not applicable to Singapore because differentiation here occurs with high state support for each pathway. Still, the international evidence should not be ignored. If education is to be a main tool to improve mobility, then different educational policies should be researched and evaluated to help us understand their effects on mobility in Singapore.

6. Policy Redirection

As discussed above, the issues around poverty, inequality and mobility are complex, inter-related and challenging. Not only is the wide income inequality in Singapore a matter of social concern by itself, but it is accompanied by the resurgence of poverty, wage stagnation and general economic vulnerability among a significant proportion of the population. Economic poverty is further compounded with social disadvantages which isolate families in poverty.

One challenge of poverty alleviation in contemporary Singapore is that our society has become stratified. Ironically, when poverty was rampant, it meant many people were in the same boat. Now, however, those who are poor risk social isolation in a segregated society where gaps are wide, so that powerful elites have less and less understanding of those at the bottom.

Another challenge is that poverty today is more structural in nature. The gains in social development achieved in the early post-independence years are no longer as easily attainable. Poverty today also results from the inter-related forces of globalization and technological change that caused policy-makers to embrace high growth, open immigration and economic restructuring towards targeted high-tech industries on one end, and services on the other end (Tan, 2015; Lim and Lee, 2010; Hoon, 2013). The choice of the social welfare model anchored on self-responsibility through the CPF as the main source of income security and on the social development goals of education, healthcare, and housing, have turned out to offer weak protection against enhanced economic risks. Lim (1989) suggested that the multiplicity of goals in the welfare services imply a lack of priority toward welfare, and that the partial privatization of health and education has resulted in regressivity in these basic welfare services.

The regressivity of public health and educational services was also asserted by Richard Titmuss (1965), hailed as "one of the world's leading public analysts and philosophers" (Glennester, 2014, p. 1). Titmuss' framework for welfare continues to be incisively relevant today: it was partly political and partly economic, but "unabashedly moral" (Glennester, 2014, p. 5). While he criticized the inefficiency of stringent "negative" means-testing (to prevent "undeserving" applicants from receiving social services), Titmuss' main argument for a strong universalist system of welfare was moral. He lauded the basic principle of universal healthcare in Britain as "making services available and accessible to the whole population in such ways as would not involve users in any humiliating loss of status, dignity or self-respect. There should be no sense of inferiority, pauperism, shame or stigma in the use of publicly provided service". He opposed the "past" system which invoked "a sense of personal fault, or personal failure" to deter welfare dependence.

Titmuss' promotion of universalism was premised on "the fundamental fact that for many consumers the services used.... represent partial compensations for dis-services, for social costs and social insecurities which are the product of a rapidly changing industrial urban society. They are part of the price we pay to some people for bearing part of the costs of other people's progress; the obsolescence of skills, redundancies, premature retirements, accidents, many categories of disease and handicap.... They are socially caused diswelfares, the losses involved in aggregate welfare gains".

These ideas are relevant to Singapore (as they still are in Britain) today. As our economy has become rich and our society has matured, it may be time to consider if social welfare should now be based on moral rather than just pragmatic principles. The moral imperative of universalist services is actually not devoid of pragmatism. Ng *et al.* (2014) point out that an over-reliance on self-reliance based on multiple bureaucratic layers and points of meanstesting is inefficient. A system based on unfettered economic growth which stigmatizes welfare recipients may also unleash its ugly side when a group of citizens are socially excluded. This point parallels that made by Tan (2015) when he compared the economic and political divisions between London and Scotland in Britain to those between Shenton Way and Hougang in Singapore. He proposed that to pre-empt the lower-middle class from declaring "independence", social welfare should focus on the "relative losers" of globalization and economic growth. He suggested the development of an "early warning system" to monitor median income relative to the costs of living of necessities such as housing, transport, food and healthcare. However, Tan stops short of recommending a measure of poverty, which would be a more direct indicator of economic hardship.

Perhaps the quote from Titmuss (1960) at the beginning of this chapter is too harsh in claiming that a society which identifies poverty by inference and not by real data leaves its "social conscience and its democratic values to languish". Perhaps the pragmatic approach to policy in Singapore leads us to address poverty and inequality in layered and flexible ways that avoid the cliff effects of a poverty measure. After all, there are today extensive poverty measures in Britain, yet poverty continues to be a persistent problem. However, it is probably not far off the mark to conclude that the lack of poverty measures reflects the low priority given to poverty alleviation, and that absence of poverty measures prevents more decisive and effective interventions, in particular toward different types of poor individuals such as the elderly, the young, or other vulnerable groups.

It is noteworthy that there have been repeated calls in Singapore for more comprehensive and responsive income support policies. The recommendation at independence for a social insurance model instead of the CPF, is a case in point. Examples of other recommendations made through the years include: Lim's (1988) recommendation that (i) immigration policy take into account wage and equity impacts, while at the same time avoiding "manpower import" by enhancing "factor substitution and mechanization so as to improve labor productivity", and that (ii) wage guidelines by the National Wages Council (NWS) contain fixed quantums besides percentage changes; and Asher and Nandy's (2008) recommendation that social protection in Singapore move from a single-tiered system based on the CPF to a multi-tiered system that relies more on social risk-pooling.

Recent policies appear to be responding to these recommendations. As the problems of elderly poverty, wage depression and inequality deepen, welfare policies have been expanded. The Workfare Income Supplement was introduced, followed by Medishield Life, a form of basic universal health insurance, and the Silver Support Scheme, a form of basic pension. With these more universalist schemes, policies are becoming more similar to Titmuss' framework of having a strong universalist foundation, followed by selective services. Yet, the message of self-reliance continues to be emphasized (Ministry of Finance, 2015a). Perhaps the test of the new systems is Titmuss' yardstick of whether beneficiaries are stigmatized in the process of accessing services.

These policy initiatives, alongside increased taxes on top income earners to help pay for them, have made our overall system less regressive and more redistributive. Directly addressing inequality will require redistribution through further tax revisions, for example by taxing other sources of wealth besides earnings. Policy-makers have signalled that such tax revisions will take place in future.

Remedial policies alone are insufficient. Addressing wage depression head on requires interventions in the labor market and the economy. Thus, the productivity and innovation drive that stalled in the 1990s is now being renewed despite low productivity gains so far. However, wages have been so depressed that wage correction is also needed. So far, it has taken shape as part of a Progressive Wage Model (PWM) spearheaded by the National Trades Union Congress (NTUC), which recommends a minimum monthly wage of S$1,000 beginning in the cleaning and security sectors, gradually moving to cover other sectors with low-paying jobs (Employment and Employability Institute, 2014).

This model of wage correction through the tripartite system of unions, employers and policy-makers is uniquely Singaporean. It is considered to be more flexible and responsive than legislating a blanket minimum wage, which proponents such as economist Hui Weng Tat and former Ambassador Tommy Koh have recommended (Hui, 2012; Koh, 2012). Opponents to a minimum wage — including economist Lim Chin, employers, and NTUC itself — cite the risk of unemployment, increased costs and thus loss of competitiveness as some reasons that a minimum wage would be detrimental (Lim, 2010; Kor, 2010; Cai, 2010). They suggest that WIS does a better job of uplifting wages and maintaining firm competitiveness. Hui (2013b), however, argued that unemployment risk is minimal in labor-scarce Singapore where foreign workers provide a buffer. Acknowledging the unique value of the tripartite wage-setting model through the National Wages Council (NWC), Lim (2012) recommended a three-prong strategy: (i) quantitative wage increase guidelines for low-wage workers; (ii) a temporary three-year wage freeze for top executives; and (iii) a minimum wage "should the wages of the lowest paid resident workers remain stubbornly very low".

The current model of a proposed baseline wage of $1,000 tied to the PWM is an amalgamation of the above recommendations. It seems to have made progress in the cleaning sector (National Trades Union Congress, n.d.); it remains to be seen if this moral suasion approach will work in other sectors. Going forward, further wage correction, not necessarily commensurate with productivity increases, will be required, as is also happening in other developed countries like the U.S. and Japan (Ton, 2014). The transition period when wages jump will be difficult, and may result in some firms folding.

Beyond wages, sustaining employment to reduce poverty and inequality also means good jobs with career prospects, not just part-time informal jobs with no benefits. In an increasingly flexible labor market, it might be time to provide benefits for casual positions. Initiatives such as the Progressive Wage Model, Skills Future, and good sourcing will need to be calibrated to ensure that the target beneficiaries will indeed benefit. For example, anecdotal examples of training that does not lead to higher paying jobs, and progressive wages that conflict with outsourcing processes, should be investigated to improve on implementations details. With respect to the economy as a whole, Lim (2015) questions the continued viability of the "global city" model that has defined Singapore's development; she proposes a shift to becoming a "primary regional city" leveraging on natural market-based rather than policy-directed advantages that could yield more opportunities for higher-wage employment and entrepreneurial income in the services sector.

More fundamentally, Singapore's main pillars of social development, namely education, healthcare, housing and CPF, have matured and become more structured; they should be reviewed for the ways they might be reinforcing inequity rather than promoting growth as in the past. Interestingly, Lim (1988), Lim (1989) and Titmuss (1965) have all been critical of streaming and the increasing differentiation of basic education, raising concerns of elitism. There should also be concern that stratification in education, healthcare and housing has stigmatizing effects that perpetuate intergenerational immobility. Bhaskaran *et al.* (2012) also highlight the market (and government) failures in these key sectors of social development. They suggest a rethinking of the design and the ideologies behind the tools of social welfare and social development, arguing for a "new social compact" premised on maximizing the well-being of Singaporeans. "This means a Singapore which treasures its citizens, where its citizens live in a secure society in which the worth of every one of its diverse citizenry is valued, and where every citizen has as much opportunity to rise as is practically possible" (p. 17).

Fifty years, and the problems of poverty and a social divide in Singapore have come full circle. Applying the wisdom of experience and hindsight to changed economic and social circumstances, more attention can and should now be paid to the alleviation of poverty and the narrowing of economic inequalities which could otherwise undermine the social cohesion and national unity previously so successfully developed through post-independence social policy. The discussion here suggests that policy redirection should cover all policy domains. The wide range of solutions to poverty, inequality and social mobility recommended by the various authors cited in this chapter have sound economic bases. However, the "good society" envisioned by Bhaskaran *et al.* (2012) and the non-stigmatizing services proposed by Titmuss, are ultimately moral imperatives. It is perhaps apt to end with yet another quote from Titmuss (1960): "More of us, as individuals, can now afford to be moral in our attitudes to the great problems of world inequality and racial intolerance. But for this to happen it surely means that those who hold positions of power and influence in our society should set examples for the younger generation in moral leadership and higher standards of social responsibility."

Acknowledgments

I thank Chong Yen Kiat and Lee Poh Choo for research assistance.

References

Asian Development Bank (2004). Enhancing the fight against poverty in Asia and the Pacific: The poverty reduction strategy of the Asian Development Bank. Available at http://www.adb.org/ Documents/Policies/Poverty_Reduction/2004/prs-2004.pdf.

Bhaskaran, M, KS Ho, D Low, KS Tan, S Vadaketh and LK Yeoh (2012). Paper: Inequality and the need for a new social compact. Background paper, Singapore Perspectives 2012: Singapore Inclusive: Bridging Divides. Institute of Policy Studies, Lee Kuan Yew School of Public Policy, National University of Singapore.

Blanden, J and S Machin (2004). Educational inequality and the expansion of UK higher education. *Scottish Journal of Political Economy*, 51(2), 230–249.

Cai, H (2010). SNEF on why minimum wage won't work. *The Straits Times*, 13 October.

Chia, NC (2015). The CPF Story: Reflecting the Social and Economic History of Singapore. Book Manuscript.

Danziger, SK, A Kalil and NJ Anderson (2000). Human capital, health, and mental health needs of welfare recipients: Co-occurrence and correlates. *Journal of Social Issues*, 56(4), 635–654.

Donaldson, JA, J Loh, S Mudaliar, M Kadir, B Wu and LK Yeoh (2013). Measuring poverty in Singapore: Frameworks for consideration. Social Space Issue 6. Singapore Management University. Available at https://centres.smu.edu.sg/lien/files/2013/11/SocialSpace2013-2014_ SanushkaMudaliar.pdf.

Employment and Employability Institute (2014). NTUC pushes for adoption of progressive wage model in the cleaning, landscape and security sectors. Available at http://e2i.com.sg/ntuc-pushes-for-adoption-of-progressive-wage-model-in-the-cleaning-landscape-and-security-sectors/.

Ermisch, J, M Jantti and T Smeeding (2012). *From Parents to Children: The Intergenerational Transmission of Advantage*. New York: Russell Sage Foundation.

Glennester, H (2014). Richard Titmuss: Forty Years On. Centre for Analysis of Social Exclusion, London School of Economics.

Hanushek, EA and L Woessmann (2005). Does Educational Tracking Affect Performance and Inequality? Differences-in-Differences Evidence Across Countries. CESifo Working Papers, No. 1415. Available at http://hdl.handle.net/10419/18779.

Hong Kong Institute of Education (2013). HKIED study: Disparity in higher education attainment is widening between rich and poor. Available at https://www.ied.edu.hk/media/news.php?id=20130131.

Hoon, HT (2013). Relook link between low wages and foreign workers. *The Straits Times*, 27 November.

Hui, WT (2013a). Working Poor in Singapore [Powerpoint slides], FASS Forum on Building an Inclusive Society: Understanding and Empowering the Poor in Singapore, 23 September.

Hui, WT (2013b). Economic growth and inequality in Singapore: The case for a minimum wage. *International Labour Review*, 152(1), 107–123.

Hui, WT (2010). Minimum wage law works. *The Straits Times*, 2 September.

Koh, T (2010). By invitation: What Singapore can learn from Europe. *The Straits Times*, 2 September.

Kor, KB (2010). Minimum wage policy won't work: Employers, labour chief. *The Straits Times*, 13 October.

Lim, C (2010). Workfare does a better job. *The Straits Times*, 2 September.

Lim, CY (1988). *Policy Options for the Singapore Economy*. Singapore: McGraw Hill.

Lim, CY (2012). Shock Therapy II Revisited (No. 1204). Nanyang Technological University, School of Humanities and Social Sciences, Economic Growth Centre.

Lim, LYC (1989). Social welfare. In *The Management of Success: The Moulding of Modern Singapore*, KS Sandu and P Wheatley (eds.). Singapore: Institute of Southeast Asian Studies.

Lim, LYC (2015). Beyond the "Global City" paradigm. To appear in *Singapore Perspectives 2015: Choices*, S Hoe and C Soon (eds.). Singapore: World Scientific and Institute of Policy Studies.

Lim, LYC and SA Lee (2010). Globalizing state, disappearing nation: The impact of foreign participation in the Singapore economy. In *Management of Success: Singapore Revisited*, T Chong (ed.). Singapore: Institute of Southeast Asian Studies.

Low, L and TC Aw (2004). *Social Insecurity in the New Millennium: The Central Provident Fund in Singapore*. Singapore: Marshall Cavendish.

Ministry of Finance (2015a). Budget 2015: Building Our Future, Strengthening Social Security. http://singaporebudget.gov.sg/data/budget_2015/download/FY2015_Budget_Statement.pdf.

Ministry of Finance (2015b). Transcript of Budget 2015 Debate Round-Up Speech by Deputy Prime Minister and Minister for Finance, Mr. Tharman Shanmugaratnam on 5 March 2015. Available at http://www.singaporebudget.gov.sg/data/budget_2015/download/FY2015_Budget_Debate_Round_Up_Speech.pdf.

National Trades Union Congress (n.d.). Recommendations of the tripartite cluster for cleaners on progressive wages. Available at http://ntuc.org.sg/wps/wcm/connect/01fb4b004d2266b39a32da36e20ded97/TripartiteClusterforCleaners_Report.pdf?MOD=AJPERES&CACHEID=01fb4b004d2266b39a32da36e20ded97.

Ng, IYH (2011). Workfare in Singapore. In *Welfare Reform in East Asia: Towards Workfare?* KC Chak and K Ngok (eds.). U.K.: Routledge.

Ng, IYH (2013a). Multi-stressed low-earning families in contemporary policy context: Lessons from work support recipients in Singapore. *Journal of Poverty*, 17(1), 86–109.

Ng, IYH (2013b). The political economy of intergenerational mobility in Singapore. *International Journal of Social Welfare*, 22(2), 207–218.

Ng, IYH (2014). The political economy of intergenerational mobility: Implications for Singapore's skills strategy. In *Skills Strategies for an Inclusive Society: The Roles of the State, the Enterprise and the Worker*, J Sung (ed.). Singapore: Institute for Adult Learning.

Ng, IYH (2015). Intergenerational Mobility: Reflections for Singapore from International Research. *Critical Studies in Singapore Education: Unfolding History, Culture and Politics*, A Koh and J Tan (eds.). Singapore: Routledge.

Ng, IYH *et al.* (2014). Social infrastructure development. In Population Outcomes: Singapore 2050. IPS Exchange Series Number 1. Available at http://lkyspp.nus.edu.sg/ips/news/the-population-outcomes-singapore-2050-project.

Ng, IYH, KW Ho, M Mathews and IS Sarjune (2015). Longitudinal study of families placed on longer term assistance under the work support programme. Fifth Annual Report (January to December 2014). Unpublished Report Submitted to the Ministry of Ministry of Social and Family Development. National University of Singapore.

Park, H (2013). *Re-Evaluating Education in Korea and Japan: Demystifying Stereotypes*. USA/Canada: Routledge.

Pekkarinen, T, R Uusitalo and S Kerr (2009). School tracking and intergenerational mobility: Evidence from the Finnish comprehensive school reform. *Journal of Public Economics*, 93(7–8), 965–973.

Prime Minister's Office Singapore (2011). Speech by Prime Minister Lee Hsien Loong at the Debate on the President's Address, 20 October 2011, at Parliament. Available at http://www.pmo.gov.sg/content/pmosite/mediacentre/speechesninterviews/primeminister/2011/October/Speech_by_Prime_Minister_Lee_Hsien_Loong_at_the_Debate_on_The_President_Address.html#.U-yyHfOwpLM.

Ramesh, M (2003). *Social Policy in East and Southeast Asia: Education, Health, Housing and Income Maintenance*. New York: RoutledgeCurzon.

Tan, KY (2015). Managing Singapore's globalization and its discontents: A long term perspective. *Singapore Perspectives 2015*: Choices, S Hoe and C Soon (eds.). Singapore: World Scientific and Institute of Policy Studies.

Teo, YY (2013). Support for deserving families: Inventing the anti-welfare familialist state in Singapore. *Social Politics: International Studies in Gender, State & Society*, 20(3), 387–406.

Titmuss, RM (1960). *The Irresponsible Society*, Vol. 323. London: Fabian Society.

Titmuss, RM (1965). The role of redistribution in social policy. *Social Security Bulletin*, 28, 14.

Titmuss, RM (1968). *Commitment to Welfare*. London: Allen and Unwin.

Ton, Z (2014). *The Good Jobs Strategy: How the Smartest Companies Invest in Employees to Lower Costs and Boost Profits*. USA: New Harvest Books.

United Nations Research Institute for Social Development (2010). Combating poverty and inequality: Structural change, social policy and politics.

Yeoh, LK (2012). Presentation at cycle and psyche of poverty workshop: A caritas dialogue [PowerPoint slides].

Yeung, J (2012). Implications of the college expansion policy for China's social stratification. SMU Social Sciences and Humanities Seminar Series. Singapore Management University, November 2.

Yip, CS (2012). Intergenerational income mobility in Singapore: Available at http://app/mof.gov.sg/data/cmsresource/Feature%20Articles/Intergenerational%20Income%20Mobility%20In%20Singssapore_13%20Jan%202012.pdf.

CHAPTER 13

Energy and Environmental Policy

Youngho Chang

Energy and environmental policies in Singapore have had two goals — to help the Singapore economy grow, and to keep Singapore clean and green. Energy policies such as development of an energy industry and an energy trading hub have contributed to economic growth and high per capita income, while enhancing energy security. There has been clear success toward achieving water self-sufficiency while providing water for all, and Singapore has become a global leader in the development and commercialization of water reclamation technologies. On the environmental front, indicators such as the share of green space, the ratio of wastes recycled, and decrease in some air pollutants show progress toward being clean and green. Per capita energy consumption has jumped to a high level by international standards, due to industrial structure, but energy efficiency and carbon emissions (per capita and per $ of GDP), have improved.

1. Introduction

Energy and environmental policies have been integrated into Singapore's economic policies since independence in 1965. As an established entrepot trading center and port at a strategic maritime location, Singapore then already had well-developed oil storage and blending facilities. Early energy policy built on this by offering "tax free operation in refineries" to attract foreign investments which built five refineries in 12 years (Horsnell, 1997). Separation from Malaysia made water policy a national security as well as public utility issue, since Singapore relied on piped water from Johor for most of its water needs. Broader environmental concerns, for example, over littering and pollution, started with the campaign to "Keep Singapore Clean" in 1968, followed by "Keep Singapore Green" in later years (Science Council of Singapore, 1980).

Energy was initially viewed as a commodity that could be acquired so long as economic growth could purchase the quantities required, hence the focus was on growth. Commodity prices fluctuated, with the crude oil price spiking during the two oil shocks in 1973 and 1979, and again during the 1991 Gulf War, collapsing in 1986 and after the 1997 Asian financial crisis, bottoming out around 1999. The economics of energy security started to be discussed globally (Toman, 1993; Bohi and Toman, 1996), and by the late 1990s, the premise of policy in Singapore seemed to shift to the belief that economic ability-to-pay alone was insufficient to ensure security of supply, leading to diversification of fuel sources and suppliers. The 1992 Earth Summit had alerted the world to the looming danger of global warming, and Singapore started to use natural gas which had emerged as a new source of fuel, cleaner than coal or oil. Oil's overwhelming 96% share of Singapore's fuel mix in 1992 declined to 87% in 2013 while the share of natural gas increased from 4% in 1992 to 13% in 2013 (BP, 2014).[1] A terminal for receiving liquefied natural gas (LNG) was constructed in 2005. In 2010, a pre-feasibility study was conducted to explore more energy options; it concluded in 2012 that while current nuclear energy technologies were not yet suitable, Singapore should continue to participate in global and regional discussions on nuclear safety, and a Nuclear Policy Research Programme was established (NUS News, 2014).

Securing water supply to meet the demand for water in Singapore was and remains the pre-eminent goal of water policy. The Public Utility Board (PUB), once responsible for both electricity and water, became solely responsible for supplying water after responsibility for overseeing the electricity sector was transferred to Singapore Power in 1995, and then to the Energy Marketing Authority in 2001. Water policies have three main goals: to increase the capacity of water supply, to make water available for all, and to promote development of water technologies. On the supply side, major efforts are made to develop water technologies including recycling and reclaiming water, and desalinating sea water, while on the demand side, water conservation fees control excess consumption and block water tariffs ensure water availability for low income households. In 2013, Singapore imported up to 250 million gallons of water per day from Malaysia, about 63% of total demand; it currently consumes about 400 million gallons per day (mgd), 45% of this going to homes. Water continues to be imported from Johor under the 1962 Water Agreement that allows Singapore to draw up to 250 mgd from the Johor River until 2061. NEWater, reclaimed water introduced in 2003, meets 30% of demand,

---

[1] Oil consumption includes inland demand plus international aviation, marine bunkers and refinery fuel and loss. Coal was consumed but the amount was less than 0.05 million tons oil equivalent in the 1960s and the early 1970s and nil for the rest of periods. Tuas Power (Tembusu Multi-Utilities Complex) started to use coal for getting heat in 2009 (Tuas Power, 2015).

desalinated water introduced in 2005 meets 10% of demand and the rest is met by water from local catchment (PUB, 2013).

The goal of environmental policy in Singapore during the 1960s and 1970s was "to keep Singapore clean and green". As the economy grew, controlling pollution became the most important policy goal (Science Council of Singapore, 1980). Four plans — the Singapore Green Plan (SGP) 1992, SGP 2012, the Sustainable Singapore Blueprint (SSB) 2009 and SSB 2015 — were developed to keep Singapore green. Later, environmental policies were embedded in climate change policies such as the National Climate Change Strategy 2012 (NCCS, 2012).

This chapter identifies five broadly defined goals for energy policies, three for water policies, and two for environmental policies. Table 1 summarizes the key policy goals and indicators on which energy, water and environmental policies will be evaluated. Section 2 examines how energy policies have been implemented, and

Table 1.   Policy areas, goals and indicators.

Policy areas	Policy goals	Indicators
Energy	Improve energy efficiency	Energy intensity
	Promote energy conservation	Per capita and total primary energy consumption
	Ensure energy security/ Diversification	Fuel mix
	Sustain competitive edge	Linkage between global and domestic oil price
	Energy for growth	Share of oil sector in manufacturing; value-added; employment
Water	Ensure sustainable water supply or self-sufficiency	Share of water sources: local catchment, imported, reclamation, desalination
	Water for all	Per capita water consumption; water tariffs
	Promote innovation in water technologies	Reclamation, desalination, local catchment
Environment	Keep Singapore Clean	Emissions of various pollutants: CO_2, SO_2, NO_x, PM_{10}, $PM_{2.5}$
		Municipal solid waste generated: total and per capita
		Waste recycling rate
	Keep Singapore Green	Share of green space and per capita green space

whether their intended goals were met. Section 3 does the same for water policies, and Section 4 for environmental policies. Section 5 concludes.

2. Energy Policy

2.1. *Energy Policy and Economic Growth*

As noted above, Singapore at independence lacked an industrial base, so energy policy was harnessed to economic policy by attracting foreign investment in the refinery industry through tax exemption. Later, following the successful establishment of a refinery centre in the region, oil and other commodity trader programmes were introduced: the Approved Oil Trader (AOT) scheme for oil trading in 1989, and the Approved International Trader (AIT) scheme for other commodities such as grains and metals, in 1990 (Horsnell, 1997). Both AOT and AIT offered a concessionary tax rate and were replaced in 2002 by the Global Trade Programme (GTP) which still provides a concessionary tax rate on qualifying trade incomes (Chang, 2014). These trader programmes helped the oil sector contribute to domestic exports, as shown in Table 2.

It accounted for 50% of domestic exports in 1976 and close to 50% in 1984 (MTI, 2002b), shrinking to about 25% in 1991 and then to below 20%, before increasing to over 30% at a still sizable S$106,476 million in 2013 (Table 3). The oil sector was one of the key demand engines that contributed to economic growth in the first two decades after independence, adding 1.1% points to GDP annually from 1965 to 1974, and 0.4% points from 1975 to 1984, eventually petering out after 1985 (Table 4).

Table 2.   Domestic exports by commodity (unit: %).

Period	Oil	Elec	M&T	MG	Chem	F&BT	Misc.
1976	50.0	16.3	10.2	6.7	2.9	2.5	11.2
1984	47.6	22.2	10.9	3.6	4.0	1.8	9.9
1991	26.1	42.4	9.9	3.4	6.4	2.3	9.7
2001	18.3	48.0	10.0	2.4	10.2	1.4	9.7

Source: MTI (2002b).

Notes: Oil indicates the oil sector, Elec electronics, M&T machinery and transport, MG manufactured goods, Chem chemicals, F&BT food, beverage and tobacco and Misc miscellaneous.

Table 3.   Contribution of oil to domestic exports (unit: million dollars).

	Domestic exports	Oil	Non-oil	Oil share (%)
1996	103,589	16,551	87,038	15.98
2001	118,444	21,716	96,728	18.33
2002	119,438	20,859	98,579	17.46
2003	150,558	27,459	123,099	18.24
2004	180,200	37,310	142,891	20.70
2005	207,448	52,798	154,650	25.45
2006	227,378	59,605	167,773	26.21
2007	234,903	63,271	171,632	26.93
2008	247,618	89,526	158,092	36.15
2009	200,003	58,655	141,348	29.33
2010	248,610	75,011	173,599	30.17
2011	281,350	103,954	177,396	36.95
2012	285,147	106,814	178,333	37.46
2013	274,192	106,476	167,716	38.83

Source: Yearbook of Statistics Singapore 2007, 2014.

Table 4.   Demand engines and growth contributions (unit: percentage point).

Period	ASEAN-2	US	Japan	CW	Oil	WS	Average GDP (%)
1965–1974	2.8	0.8	5.3	1.2	1.1	0.0	10.9
1975–1984	2.9	0.6	2.7	1.7	0.4	0.0	7.6
1985–1991	2.8	0.5	3.1	0.5	0.0	1.2	6.5
1992–2001	1.1	3.8	0.0	0.9	0.0	1.1	6.7

Source: MTI (2002b).

Notes: ASEAN-2 means Indonesia and Malaysia combined economy, the US economy, the Japan economy, CW the domestic construction and works, the oil sector and world semiconductor sales.

2.2. *Energy Efficiency and Conservation*

Promoting energy efficiency and energy conservation then became, and still remains, the key thrust of energy policies (IACEE, 1999). The Inter-Agency Committee on Energy Efficiency (IACEE) was formed in 1998, renamed the National Energy Efficiency Committee (NEEC) in 2001, and expanded in 2006 to deal with issues relating to climate change, when it was renamed the National Climate Change Committee (N3C). The N3C was dissolved upon formation of the National Climate Change Secretariat (NCCS) in 2010.

The IACEE's May 2000 Report on Energy Efficiency in Singapore identified four objectives of energy policy: pricing, energy conservation, efficiency in energy production, and diversification in fuel supplies. For pricing, two detailed policy measures were established: (i) market forces of supply and demand were to determine energy price to ensure that energy is used more efficiently; (ii) electricity and gas tariffs would be reviewed regularly to ensure that they reflect costs. For energy conservation: (i) conservation would be promoted through financial incentives and disincentives, and through education; (ii) energy conservation standards for building design would be incorporated into the Building Regulations; (iii) fiscal policies would be designed to encourage the public to use smaller, more energy efficient vehicles; (iv) use of public transport would be encouraged. Greater efficiency in energy production would be achieved through market competition in the generation and sale of electricity. Diversification of energy supplies would be achieved by adding use of natural gas.

Promoting energy efficiency and energy conservation boil down to decreasing energy intensity, defined as the amount of energy in tons of oil equivalent per million S$ of Gross Domestic Product (GDP). This is a good proxy for measuring the energy efficiency of an economy, since it indicates how much energy is required to produce one unit of GDP: higher energy intensity implies lower energy efficiency. Figure 1 shows that energy intensity in Singapore has been decreasing, implying improving energy efficiency. As shown in Table 5, comparing per capita energy consumption with those of other developed economies at the same income level shows that by 1990, Singapore under-performs (consumes more energy per capita than) all the countries listed except the U.S., a situation that persists in 2011. Moreover,

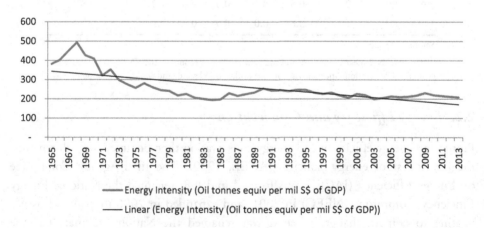

Figure 1.   Energy intensity (unit: tons of oil equivalent per million S$ of GDP).

Source: BP Statistical Review of World Energy and DOS, Yearbook of Statistics of Singapore, various issues.

Table 5   Per capita energy consumption (unit: kg of oil equivalent) year.

Year	Singapore	US	Japan	Korea	Hong Kong	Denmark	Switzerland
1971	1,292.24	7,644.53	2,531.09	516.11	741.96	3,728.54	2,637.67
1975	1,640.49	7,656.26	2,725.16	693.27	813.40	3,453.21	2,710.77
1980	2,126.01	7,942.25	2,950.14	1,080.98	914.01	3,735.14	3,170.58
1985	2,472.93	7,456.59	3,005.31	1,311.78	1,204.84	3,774.11	3,412.39
1990	3,778.94	7,671.55	3,556.22	2,171.42	1,517.71	3,377.02	3,627.66
1995	5,337.16	7,763.37	3,956.20	3,210.16	1,729.98	3,705.40	3,422.56
2000	4,640.75	8,056.82	4,090.52	4,002.74	2,009.29	3,489.70	3,480.46
2005	5,144.85	7,846.81	4,073.95	4,366.12	1,858.73	3,485.15	3,488.02
2011	6,452.33	7,032.47	3,610.37	5,231.87	2,106.12	3,230.79	3,206.96

Source: World Bank.

between 1995 and 2011, the U.S., Japan, Denmark and Switzerland all reduced per capita energy consumption, whereas Singapore, Korea and Hong Kong increased theirs, Singapore to the highest level next to the U.S. (Table 5). For both Korea and Singapore, this probably reflects industrial restructuring and technological upgrading into more capital- and hence energy-intensive industries, in Singapore's case particularly the growth of the chemical industry since the 1990s. Of note, Singapore's per capita energy consumption is three times higher than that of similarly dense urban Hong Kong, reflecting the high share of manufacturing in Singapore's GDP as compared with the services-oriented Hong Kong economy.

Singapore does better in terms of energy intensity (the amount of energy required to produce a particular amount of GDP in purchasing power parity). As shown in Table 6 and Figures 1 and 2, Singapore's energy intensity as measured in oil equivalents has been declining, due to reduced dependence on oil as expenditure on oil consumption as a percentage of GDP decreased (Chang and Wong, 2003). Declining energy intensity is also observed in other developed economies, presumably reflecting energy-saving technological change, conservation practices, and a relative decline in manufacturing's share of GDP relative to that of less energy-intensive services as incomes rise. Singapore's absolute level of energy intensity is lower than in the U.S., Japan and Korea, but higher than in the small high-income economies of Hong Kong, Denmark and Switzerland.

The Energy Conservation Act of 2013 seeks to make energy conservation practices the norm for large energy users in Singapore. The Act's objectives are: (i) achieving the target of a 35% improvement in energy intensity by 2030 from 2005 levels; (ii) improving the energy performance of companies to make them more competitive in the global economy; (iii) complementing existing schemes and

Table 6.   Energy intensity in kg of oil equivalent per $1,000 of GDP in constant 2011 PPP.

Year	Energy use (kg of oil equivalent) per $1,000 GDP (constant 2011 PPP)						
	Singapore	US	Japan	Korea	Hong Kong	Denmark	Switzerland
1990	110.49	220.35	120.35	179.65	56.25	102.76	78.33
1995	119.31	196.83	126.70	191.10	53.45	102.25	76.98
2000	90.13	175.20	127.09	192.84	59.05	84.70	71.35
2005	83.36	157.68	120.12	170.94	45.41	80.30	68.72
2010	94.02	145.06	113.27	166.19	40.94	81.91	62.18
2011	86.50	141.20	105.21	167.01	42.05	75.48	59.15
2012	—	134.31	101.16	164.87	—	71.94	58.79

Source: World Bank.

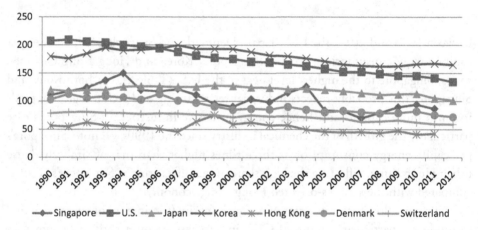

Figure 2.   Energy intensity in kg of oil equivalent per $1,000 of GDP in constant 2011 PPP.
Source: World Bank.

capability-building programmes which provide support for companies investing in energy efficiency; (iv) ensuring a coordinated approach to standards setting for energy efficiency across all sectors. The Act requires mandatory energy management practices for companies that consume more than 15 giga watt hour (GWh) or 1.29 kilo ton oil equivalent (ktoe) of energy annually. Declining energy intensity suggests that Singapore is already making progress in this area.

2.3. *Energy Diversification and Market Deregulation*

Besides improving energy efficiency and encouraging conservation, Singapore has tried to diversify its fuel mix and to use energy policy to sustain economic

competiveness. Singapore used only oil until 1992, when it started importing natural gas from Indonesia and Malaysia. Its oil-based electricity generation
capacity was replaced with one based on natural gas. The sources of fuel suppliers were also diversified by constructing a liquefied natural gas (LNG) terminal,
enabling the import of natural gas from countries other than its two neighbors,
particularly the Middle East. Table 7 shows the fuel mix in Singapore in selected
years. Diversification improves energy security while the LNG terminal enables
Singapore to become a LNG trading hub in the region.

Table 7.   Fuel mix in Singapore.

Year	Oil	Natural Gas	Renewables
1991	23.7 (99.6)	0(0)	0.1 (0.4)
1992	24.6 (95.7)	1.0 (3.9)	0.1 (0.4)
2002	38.0 (91.6)	3.2 (7.7)	0.2 (0.7)
2012	65.4 (88.2)	8.5 (11.4)	0.3 (0.4)
2013	65.9 (87.1)	9.5 (12.5)	0.3 (0.4)

Source: BP Statistical Review of World Energy, various issues.
Notes: Renewables include geothermal, biomass and others.

To sustain cost competitiveness, competition was introduced into the energy
market (Chang and Tay, 2006). This involved relocating electricity and gas functions
from the PUB to Singapore Power in 1995, and then to a newly created statutory
board, the Energy Market Authority (EMA) in 2001. The Singapore Electricity Pool
(SEP) was created in 1998 to facilitate electricity trading, and operated until super-
seded in 2003 by the New Electricity Market of Singapore (NEMS). The movements of electricity and fuel prices suggest that competition did increase. Figure 3
shows that the annual average Uniform Singapore Energy Price (USEP) and fuel
price appear to move in tandem, suggesting that the global fuel price is fully reflected
in the USEP.

The EMA has implemented vesting contracts in the new electricity market since
2004: these are contractual agreements between generation companies and the regulator to supply a certain portion of electricity capacity to the market. The quantity of
vesting contracts ranged from 55% to 65% of the total electricity load, reduced to
30% of the total electricity load for the first half of 2015, 25% for the second half of
2015 and 20% for 2016 in the deregulated market (EMA, 2014a). The price of the
vesting contracts is determined by a formula set by the regulator. Between 2005 and
2012 there was a less than 10% difference between USEP and the competitive
marginal cost of electricity generation at every hour (Dang and Chang, 2013). This
modest price-cost mark-up (shown in Table 8) indicates that competition appears to

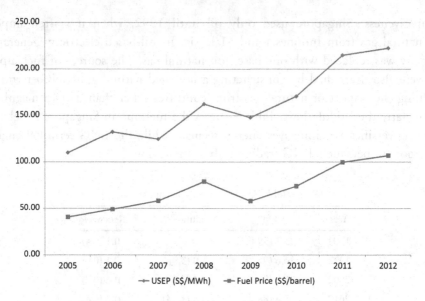

Figure 3.   USEP (S$/MWh) and fuel price (s$/barrel).

Source: Dang and Chang (2013).

Table 8.   PCMI, USEP and fuel price in Singapore electricity market.

Year	PCMI (%)	USEP (S$/MWh)	Fuel price (S$/barrel)
2005	5.87	109.90	40.63
2006	0.35	132.42	49.09
2007	2.50	124.58	58.31
2008	2.56	162.25	78.91
2009	6.17	147.75	57.91
2010	0.20	170.50	73.90
2011	8.66	214.84	99.59
2012	2.04	222.49	106.76

Source: Dang and Chang (2013).

Notes: PCMI refers to price-cost mark-up index and USEP refers to uniform Singapore energy price.

be working in the electricity sector, contributing to Singapore's global competitiveness by stabilizing the electricity price.

2.4. *Energy for Growth Revisited*

Oil was an engine of economic growth in Singapore from independence until the mid-1980s (MTI, 2002a,b). After more than two decades, the government revived energy as a growth engine. The National Energy Policy Report (NEPR) published in 2007 articulated an overall policy framework to secure "Energy for Growth". As previously noted in Table 2, oil's contribution to manufacturing output dropped from 40% in the 1960s and 1970s to less than 20% in the late 1980s and 1990s, and has ranged from 15% to 20% since 2000. Contribution to manufacturing value-added was around 5% until the mid-2000s, dropping to around 1% to 2% in the late 2000s and early 2010s. Contribution to manufacturing employment is about 1% (Figure 4).

The NEPR presented three policy objectives — economic competitiveness, energy security and environmental sustainability — and specified six strategies in its energy policy framework: to promote competitive markets, diversify energy supplies, improve energy efficiency, build an energy industry and invest in energy R&D, step up international cooperation, and develop a whole-of-government approach. It created several government agencies and an energy research institute, put more effort into research and development, promoted regional cooperation and integration through the Association of Southeast Asian Nations (ASEAN), the Asia-Pacific Economic Forum (APEC) and the East Asia Summit (EAS), and committed to international activities through the UN Framework Convention on Climate Change (UNFCCC) (Chang and Putra, 2012).

The Economic Strategies Committee's (ESC) 2010 report suggested six strategies in the energy arena: diversifying energy supplies, enhancing infrastructure and systems, increasing energy efficiency, strengthening the green economy, and

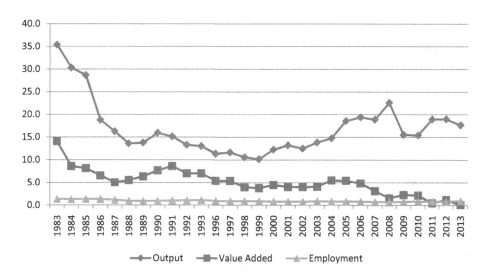

Figure 4. Share of the oil sector to output, value-added and employment.

Source: DOS, Yearbook of Statistics Singapore, various volumes.

continuation of pricing energy right. It made three recommendations for further energy diversification: allow the market-based entry of new energy options, develop renewable energy sources, study the feasibility of nuclear energy and develop expertise in nuclear energy technologies. The two recommendations for enhancing infrastructure and systems were: invest in critical energy infrastructure ahead of demand, and develop Jurong Island as an energy-optimized industrial cluster. The two recommendations for increasing energy efficiency were: promote energy efficiency for buildings, homes and industries, and support clean and efficient technologies in transportation. The two recommendations for strengthening the green economy were: establish energy as a key national R&D priority and build capabilities for the green economy, and apply a green lens to government procurement. The recommendation for pricing energy right was to price energy to reflect its total cost (Chang and Putra, 2012). It remains to be seen if these NEPR and ESC recommendations will strengthen the Singapore energy sector and bring positive and sizable benefits to the Singapore economy such as lower costs of doing business and a larger share of GDP from the energy sector.

3. Water Policy

3.1. *A Sustainable Supply of Water*

A secure water supply is a key national security priority for Singapore. Utmost effort has been made to secure all available amounts of water from natural sources by building local catchment, to reduce water usage, and to develop new water technologies. Table 9 shows the number of reservoirs, and the amounts of potable, reclaimed and industrial water sold. The amount of reclaimed water sold has increased five-fold in 2013 from its first introduction in 2004, which has increased the capacity of sustainable water supply.

Table 9.   Water supply.

	2004	2005	2006	2007	2008	2009	2010	2011	2012	2013
No. of reservoirs	14	14	14	14	15	15	17	17	17	17
Sale of potable water	440.3	440.2	449.0	155.5	462.6	467.9	476.1	478.5	490.9	498.6
Sale of NEWater	19.0	26.6	29.6	49.2	66.0	72.0	96.4	102.4	111.4	114.1
Sale of Industrial water	38.1	39.1	40.1	29.3	23.7	21.9	24.5	23.1	25.3	27.6

Source: MEWR, Key Environmental Statistics, various volumes.

3.2. *Water for All*

To ensure that all Singaporeans get a sufficient amount of clean water, the government adopted an increasing block tariff system for domestic customers whereby three water tariffs were applied according to the amount of water consumed. Until June 2000, the tariff for the first 20 m³ was $0.56 and $0.80 for the next 20 m³ and $1.17 for the amount above 40 m³. In July 2000, the number of blocks was reduced to two, and the amount of the lowest block increased to 40 m³ guaranteeing the essential amount of water for living at the lowest tariff possible.

Water consumption in Singapore shows a decreasing trend over time. Table 10 shows domestic water consumption per person per day since 2003. The government has set 147 liters per person per day as a target for 2020 and 140 liters per person per day for 2030. The 2013 level of water consumption per capita per day is already quite close to the 2020, which is thus well within reach.

Table 10.   The level of water consumption.

Year	Water consumption (liter per capita per day)
2003	165
2004	162
2005	160
2006	158
2007	157
2008	156
2009	155
2010	154
2011	153
2012	152
2013	151

Source: MEWR, Key Environmental Statistics, various volumes.

3.3. *Development of Water Technologies*

Table 11 shows the start and capacity increase of water reclamation and desalination capacity. Development of new technologies resulted in water reclamation, with NEWater plants meeting 30% of water demand and desalination plants meeting 25%

Table 11.   Starting year and capacity of NEWater and desalination plant.

Name of plant	Year started	Capacity (m³/day)
Hyflux Bedok NEWater Plant	2003	32,000
Hyflux Seletar NEWater Plant	2004	24,000
Veolia Kranji NEWater Plant	2003	41,400
Keppel Seghers Ulu Pandan NEWater Plant	2007	148,000
SembCorp Changi NEWater Plant	2010	228,000
	Total	473,400
Hyflux SingSpring Desalination Plant	2005	136,380
Hyflux Tuas Desalination Plant	2013	318,500
	Total	454,800

Source: Compiled from PUB and company websites.

in 2013. By 2030, the government aims to supply 50% of demand by NEWater and 20% by desalination, with these ratios rising to 55% and 25% respectively, by 2060 (Public Utilities Board, 2013). Currently water from local catchment, reclamation and desalination is not enough to meet demand so Singapore still depends on water supply from Malaysia, with that agreement valid until 2062.

Besides increasing and diversifying the sources of water supply, policies are also hinged on reducing water consumption. Over the years, the Public Utilities Board (PUB) has built up a comprehensive water conservation programme to reach out to the 3P (People, Private and Public) sectors. The price of water in Singapore is set to reflect its scarcity value — the cost of producing clean water from the next available source after all the rainwater collected has been used. To encourage conservation, there is a water conservation tax ranging from 30% to 45% of the tariff, to encourage conservation. PUB remains the sole provider of water, but Singapore is also known for the successful commercialization of water technologies. The best known example, Hyflux, is a global environmental solutions company listed on the Singapore Stock Exchange (SGX), with operations in China, India, the Middle East and North Africa, as well as Singapore and Southeast Asia. In 2006, the company was given the global "Water Company of the Year" award by Global Water Intelligence, U.K. (Hyflux, 2015).

4. Environmental Policy

4.1. *Keep Singapore Clean: Awareness Campaigns*

Environmental policies in Singapore started with increasing environmental awareness, and awareness campaigns started even before independence, focused on cleaning the city or beach and anti-cholera measures. The first grand-scale campaign came with the theme of "Keep Singapore Clean" in 1968, and was followed by "Keep Singapore Green" (Science Council of Singapore, 1980). Table 12 shows the list of various campaigns since 1958. The early campaigns (accompanied by fines) were successful for a while, but did not succeed in changing the habits and attitudes of the population.[2] The "Keep Singapore Clean" Movement — led by the Public

Table 12.   "Keep Singapore clean" campaign slogans.

Year	Campaign slogan
1958	Keep Your City Clean
1959	Gerakkan Pembersehan Bandar Raya Singapura
1960	Operation Clean-up
1961	Anti-cholera campaign
1963	Keep Our State Clean
1964	Help Keep Our City Clean
1966	Keep Your Beach Clean
1967	Big Sweep
1968	Keep Singapore Clean
1969	Keep Singapore Clean and Mosquito Free
1970	Keep Singapore Clean and Pollution Free
1971	Tree Planting campaign
1973	Keep Our Water Clean
1978	Use Your Hands
1979	Keep Your Factory Clean
1983	Keep the Toilet Clean
1984	Please Keep My Park Clean
1988	Singapore is Our Home — Let's Keep It Clean and Beautiful
1988	Keep Our Buses and Interchange Clean
1990	Clean & Green Singapore (CGS)
2005	Youth Environment Envoy
2010	Do the Right Thing. Let's Bin It!
2010	Litter-Free Ambassador (LFA) programme
2011	Keep Singapore Beautiful Movement
2014	Keep Singapore Clean Movement

Sources: Singapore Infopedia.

---

[2] The NEA issued about 19,000 tickets for littering in 2014, almost double the number in 2013 even though the maximum fine for littering was doubled for a first conviction (*The Straits Times,* 20 February 2015).

Hygiene Council (PHC), Singapore Kindness Movement (SKM), and Keep Singapore Beautiful Movement (KSBM) and supported by the National Environment Agency (NEA) — was a national rallying call for Singapore to move from being a "cleaned city to a truly clean city", but has yet to show results.[3]

In 2001, the "3R: Reduce, Recycle and Reuse" campaign and the National Recycling Programme (NRP) were launched. A "Schools Recycling Corner Programme" launched in 2002 and a "Recycling Programme for JTC Industrial Estates" was implemented in 2003. The Ministry of the Environment and Water Resources (MEWR), National Environmental Agency (NEA) and SembWaste Pte Ltd jointly initiated a pilot programme of "Save-As-You-Reduce" from April 2013 to February 2014.

For the "3R: Reduce, Recycle and Reuse" campaign, Public Waste Collectors (private companies licensed by the NEA) were mandated to provide recycling bins and recycling collection service to all households in Housing Development Board (HDB) flats and private landed property estates. From November 2008, management councils of condominiums and private apartments also had to provide recycling bins and send the recyclables collected for recycling. The Schools Recycling Corner Programme aimed to educate and inculcate the recycling habit among school children by setting up a Recycling Corner where students could recycle chapter cans and plastic bottles and can get educational materials. A Preschool 3R Awareness Kit was also provided to increase preschoolers' awareness. The Recycling Programme for JTC Industrial Estates set up collection points for wood waste for reuse and recycling bins to collect chapter, aluminum cans, plastics, metals and glass at strategic locations in each industrial estate. The "Save-As-You-Reduce" pilot programme which ran from April 2013 to February 2014, covered HDB flats, condominiums and landed property households, and rebated the amount of waste reduced to the participants through reduced households' refuse removal charges.[4] Table 13 shows that the total amount of waste generated increased, but the ratio recycled also increased, approaching the recycling goal of 65% by 2020.

The first Singapore Green Plan (SGP) released in 1992 aimed to ensure economic development along with sound environmental management which would meet the

---

[3] For example, Singapore employs 70,000 (mostly foreign) cleaners compared with only 5,000 for the city of Taipei, Taiwan (*The Straits Times*, 16 February 2015).

[4] Four months after the start of the "Save-As-You-Reduce" pilot scheme in Punggol, some HDB blocks there did not reduce waste significantly, with some generating even more waste than in the previous year.

Table 13.   Solid waste generated and recycled.

Wastes	Unit	2004	2005	2006	2007	2008	2009	2010	2011	2012	2013
Generated	Million tons/year	4.79	5.01	5.22	5.60	5.97	6.11	6.52	6.90	7.27	7.85
Recycled	Million tons/year	2.31	2.47	2.66	3.03	3.34	3.49	3.76	4.04	4.34	4.83
	%	48	49	51	54	56	57	58	59	60	61

Sources: DOS, Yearbook of Statistics Singapore, various issues.

needs of the current generation without compromising the needs of future genera-tions. The second SGP released in 2002 as SGP2002, and revised in March 2006, aimed to move beyond being "clean and green" to attain environmental sustainability. The Sustainable Singapore Blueprint released in 2009 set out a national framework and strategies for sustainable development for the next two decades until 2030. In 2013 Singapore had 9,707 ha of green space, about 14% of total land area, or 18.0 m^2 per person (NParks, 2014). Of this, 3,380 ha are nature reserves, 2,362 ha are parks, playgrounds, open spaces, fitness corners and park connectors, and 2,550 ha are roadside greenery.

Pollution control was and is part of "Keep Singapore Clean". Recognizing the negative environmental consequences of rapid industrialization, Singapore attempted to curb pollution, beginning with the Anti-Pollution Unit established under the Prime Minister's Office in 1970 to curb air pollution. In 1972, the Ministry of the Environment was formed and started to control water quality and industrial effluents. The Clean Air Act of 1971 was amended over time to make for more effective enforcement and better control of air pollution; it was repealed and replaced with the Environmental Pollution Control Act in 1999.

Table 14 shows the emission levels of various pollutants such as CO_2, SO_2, NO_2, $PM_{2.5}$ and PM_{10}. Carbon emission levels fluctuated with economic activity — they were high during good economic years and low during economic downturns (except for 2009). SO_2 emissions increased slightly in recent years while those of NO_2 stabilized from 2007 to 2009 but have increased since 2010. Both $PM_{2.5}$ and PM_{10} fluctuated or increased slightly (except for 2006), affected by domestic activities and transboundary pollutants such as haze. Motor vehicles are other key sources of such pollutants.

Table 14.   Level of various pollutants in Singapore.

Year	CO_2	SO_2	NO_2	$PM_{2.5}$	PM_{10}
2006	30,799	11	24	23	33
2007	17,866	12	22	19	27
2008	19,637	11	22	16	25
2009	24,767	9	22	19	29
2010	13,520	11	23	17	26
2011	N/A	10	25	17	27
2012	N/A	13	25	19	29
2013	N/A	14	25	20	31

Source: World Bank, MEWR, Key Environmental Statistics, various issues.

Notes: Unit for CO_2 is kilo ton, ug/m³ for SO_2, NO_2, $PM_{2.5}$ and PM_{10}.

4.2. *Keep Singapore Green and a National Strategy for Climate Change*

Climate change issues were handled together with energy related issues. Following the IACEE (mentioned in Section 2.2), the government set up the National Energy Efficiency Committee (NEEC) in 2001. This was a public-private partnership (3P) which aimed to promote energy conservation through improving energy efficiency, using clean energy and developing Singapore as a location for test bedding of new energy technologies and a hub for development and commercialization of clean energy technologies. In 2006 the NEEC was renamed the National Climate Change Committee (N3C) and continued to promote energy conservation while developing the National Climate Change Strategy (NCCS-different from the National Climate Change Secretariat formed in 2010). NCCS served as a blueprint for climate change action, profiled Singapore's efforts for local and international audiences, was part of the Singapore Green Plan 2012, and was to be reviewed every three years. NCCS 2012 aimed to create a climate for sustainable growth and to secure a livable environment for the future, employing a whole-of-nation approach. It suggested reducing emissions across sectors, building capabilities to adapt to climate change, harnessing green growth opportunities, and forging partnerships on climate change action.

Per capita carbon emissions have been stable or falling since 2000. Table 15 shows that levels of CO_2 per person (in tons) have been decreasing, perhaps reflecting the decreasing gross levels of CO_2 emissions shown in Table 14. CO_2 per S$ of GDP (kg/S$) also decreased, suggesting that economic activity in Singapore might be being decarbonized, that is carbon emissions could be growing slower than GDP, or decreasing.

Table 15.   The levels of CO_2 emissions: per person and per GDP.

Year	Per capita	Per GDP in S$2010
2000	12.17	0.27
2001	11.97	0.27
2002	11.31	0.25
2003	7.57	0.16
2004	6.83	0.13
2005	7.12	0.13
2006	7.00	0.12
2007	3.89	0.06
2008	4.06	0.07
2009	4.97	0.09
2010	2.66	0.04

Source: World Bank, World Development Indicators.

Notes: Unit for per capita CO_2 emissions is ton per person and kg per S$1. Per GDP CO_2 emissions are from the author's calculation.

5. Concluding Remarks

Decreasing energy intensity, improved energy efficiency, increased self-sufficiency in water supply, decreasing levels of carbon dioxide emissions (though not of other pollutants), and maintaining 14% green space in Singapore's land area, all suggest that Singapore's energy and environmental policies of the past 50 years have been at least partly successful. They are also linked with other public policies. Energy policy is designed to also meet the goals of national security and economic growth. Developing a new energy industry addresses the need for energy security from the supply side, while decreasing energy intensity addresses it from the demand side.

The multiplicity of goals that energy policy must meet requires careful management of potential conflicts. For example, to promote conservation both electricity and water should be priced high, yet the competitiveness motive seeks to keep the price low for electricity, and distributional concerns cause the water price to be kept low. So when the government raised the water consumption fee to curb waste and promote conservation (which would also serve national security), various grants were given to help low-income households, similar to the U-Save program for electricity, to ensure that the lowest-income households could meet their essential needs for water and electricity. Increasing water supply may also increase energy usage because of the energy needed to run desalination and NEWater plants; new energy policies such as developing solar energy might mitigate this potential conflict.

Besides their role as inputs into economic growth, energy and water usage are dependent on changes in demand resulting from business cycles and changes in economic structure — for example, a shift from manufacturing to services might lower energy use (and thus enhance national security), as in Hong Kong. Other public policies such as in housing, transportation, population and education might also have a bigger impact on energy consumption than energy policy itself. Some studies suggest that it is economic growth which causes changes in energy consumption, rather than the other way around (Chiou-Wei *et al.*, 2008; Saboori and Sulaiman, 2013), implying that Singapore can pursue energy conservation and carbon emissions reduction policies without harming its economic growth.

Looking ahead, the government sees regional and global market opportunities for Singapore's water and waste management technologies, and believes development of energy and environmental engineering research capabilities can make it a hub for exploring green technologies and a test bed for commercializing them, through private-public partnerships. For example, Budget 2015 has highlighted Smart and Sustainable Urban Solutions as a promising potential niche for the country to develop.

Acknowledgments

I would like to thank the editor of this volume, Professor Linda Lim, and Dr. Fang Zheng for their constructive comments. All errors are mine.

References

Bohi, DR and MA Toman (1996). *The Economics of Energy Security.* Boston, USA: Kluwer Academic Publishers.

British Petroleum (2014). BP Statistical Review of World Energy.

Chang, Y (2014). Energy commodity trading in Singapore. In *Energy Market Integration in East Asia: Energy Trade, Cross border Electricity, and Price Mechanism,* F Kimura and H Phoumin (eds.). Jakarta, Indonesia: Economic Research Institute for ASEAN and East Asia.

Chang, Y and A Putra (2012). The non-traditional security perspective on energy security policies in Singapore. In *Rethinking Energy Security in Asia: A Non-Traditional View of Human Security,* M Caballero-Anthony, Y Chang and NA Putra (eds.). Heidelberg, Germany: Springer.

Chang, Y and TH Tay (2006). Efficiency and deregulation of the electricity market in Singapore. *Energy Policy,* 34, 2498–2508.

Chang, Y and JF Wong (2003). Oil price fluctuations and Singapore economy. *Energy Policy,* 31, 1151–1165.

Chiou-Wei, SZ, C Chen and Z Zhu (2008). Economic growth and energy consumption revisited — Evidence from linear and nonlinear Granger causality. *Energy Economics,* 30, 3063–3076.

Dang, TQT and Y Chang (2013). Impact of vesting contracts on the efficiency of Singapore electricity market. *Proceedings of the URECA@NTU 2012–13,* Singapore.

Department of Statistics (DOS) (various years). Yearbook of Statistics Singapore.

Energy Market Authority (2014a). Review of the Vesting Contract Level for the Period 1 January 2015 to 31 December 2016, Singapore.

Energy Market Authority (2014b). Singapore Energy Statistics 2014, Singapore.

Horsnell, P (1997). *Oil in Asia: Markets, Trading, Refining and Deregulation.* U.K.: Oxford University Press.

Hyflux (2015). http://en.wikipedia.org/wiki/Hyflux, accessed on 15 April 2015.

Inter-Agency Committee on Energy Efficiency (IACEE) (1999). Report of Energy Efficiency in Singapore, Singapore.

Ministry of Trade and Industry (2002a). Singapore's Engines of Growth: A Demand-Side Perspective. Economic Survey of Singapore, February 2002, Singapore.

Ministry of Trade and Industry (2002b). Singapore's Changing Growth Engines since 1965: An Economic History of Nimble Adaptability. Economic Survey of Singapore, Second Quarter, 2002, Singapore.

Ministry of Trade and Industry (2007). Energy for Growth, National Energy Policy Report, Singapore.

Ministry of the Environment and Water Resources (MEWR) (various dates), Key Environmental Statistics, various issues, Singapore.

NParks (various dates), Annual Report, various issues, Singapore.

NUS News (2014). Singapore Nuclear Research and Safety Initiative to be hosted at NUS, 23 April 2014, National University of Singapore.

Public Utilities Board (PUB) (2013). Our Water, Our Future. Singapore.

Saboori, B and J Sulaiman (2013). CO_2 emissions, energy consumption and economic growth in Association of Southeast Asian Nations (ASEAN) countries: A cointegration approach. *Energy,* 55, 813–822.

Science Council of Singapore (1980). Environmental Protection in Singapore: A Handbook. Singapore.

Straits Times (2015. Current measures against littering in Singapore. 20 February. http://www.straitstimes.com/singapore/environment/current-measures-against-littering-in-singapore, accessed on 16 April 2015.

Singapore Infopedia (n.d). http://eresources.nlb.gov.sg/infopedia/articles/SIP_1160_2008-12-05.html, accessed on 15 April 2015.

Toman, MA (1993). The economics of energy security: Theory, evidence, policy. In *Handbook of Natural Resource and Energy Economics Kneese,* V Allen and JL Sweeney (eds.), Volume III, pp. 1167–1218. Elsevier, Amsterdam: the Netherlands.

Tuas Power (2015). http://www.tuaspower.com.sg/our-business/tembusu_complex.html, accessed on 15 April 2015. World Bank.

World Development Indicators, various issues.

About the Contributors

Tilak ABEYSINGHE has served the Department of Economics, National University of Singapore (NUS) since 1988. He obtained his PhD in Economics/Econometrics from the University of Manitoba and worked for the United States Agency for International Development (Colombo) before joining NUS. His research interests lie in a range of theoretical and applied econometric topics that include the Singapore economy, housing affordability, social epidemiology and quantitative health research. He has published in various reputable international journals like *Journal of Econometrics* and the NBER paper series. A major line of his research has been the econometric modeling of the Singapore economy, forecasting and policy analyses. As the coordinator of the Econometric Studies Unit since 1992 he has built a number of econometric models, one of which appears in the Routledge book, *The Singapore Economy: An Econometric Perspective* that he co-authored with Choy Keen Meng. Policy analyses based on these models have appeared in news media frequently. He has held various important administrative responsibilities at NUS. He is currently the Director of the Singapore Centre for Applied and Policy Economics, EXCO member of the Department of Economics, and a Senior Fellow at the Asia Competitiveness Institute, NUS.

Mukul G. ASHER is a Professorial Fellow at the Lee Kuan Yew School of Public Policy at the National University of Singapore, and a Councilor at Takshashila Institution, a public policy think-tank based in Bangalore. He studied in India and the United States. His research focuses on public financial management, social security reforms in Asia, and geo-economics issues, particularly India's external relations with the rest of Asia. He has published extensively in national and international journals; and has authored or edited more than twelve books. His most recent book is Mukul G Asher and Fukunari Kimura (eds.), *Strengthening Social Protection in East Asia*, Routledge, 2015. He has been a consultant to several Governments in Asia on tax policy and pension reforms; and to multi-lateral institutions including the Asian Development Bank, ERIA (Economic Research Institute for ASEAN and East Asia), and the World Bank.

Azad Singh BALI is a Research Fellow and Lecturer in Governance at the School of Management & Governance, Murdoch University, Australia. His research interests include comparative social policy; political economy of economic reforms; comparative public financial management. Bali's research has been published in international journals including *Social Policy and Administration, Public Administration and Development* and *Asian Economic Policy Review* amongst others.

Manu BHASKARAN is a Partner of the Centennial Group, a strategic advisory firm headquartered in Washington DC and, as Founding CEO of its Singapore subsidiary Centennial Asia Advisors, he coordinates the Asian business of the Group. Mr. Bhaskaran is also Adjunct Senior Research Fellow at the Institute of Policy Studies in Singapore where his main interests are in analyzing macroeconomic policy frameworks in Singapore. He was recently appointed as a Member of the Regional Advisory Board for Asia of the International Monetary Fund. He was educated at Magdalene College, Cambridge University where he earned an MA (Cantab) and at the John F. Kennedy School of Government at Harvard University where he obtained a Master in Public Administration. He is also a Chartered Financial Analyst.

Youngho CHANG is an Assistant Professor of Economics at the Division of Economics, Nanyang Technological University, Singapore. Apart from the academic affiliation, he is a member of the Technical Committee for Clean Development Mechanism (CDM) of the Designated National Authority (DNA), National Environment Agency, Singapore. Dr. Chang specializes in the economics of climate change, energy and security, oil and macroeconomy, and the economics of electricity market deregulation. His current research interests are oil price fluctuations and macroeconomic performance, the economics of energy security, energy use and climate change, human capital and economic growth, and education for sustainability (EfS). He has published his research output in internationally refereed academic journals such as *Energy Economics, Energy Policy, Econometric Theory* and *Economics Letters*, among others. He was a degree fellow at the East-West Center, Hawaii and received his PhD in Economics (Environmental and Resource Economics) from the University of Hawaii at Manoa, US.

Ngee-Choon CHIA is an Associate Professor in the Department of Economics at the National University of Singapore (NUS). She is the Co-editor of the *Singapore Economic Review* and the Co-director of the Next Age Institute at NUS. Her current research interests include pension economics, health economics and the fiscal impacts of aging. Her works have appeared in internationally referred journals such as the *Journal of Money, Credit and Banking, Journal of Health Economics, Journal of Policy Modeling,* and *Journal of Pension Economics and Finance.* She served as a consultant to several international organizations, for example, ADB, ADBI, ERIA, IDRC and the World Bank; and to Civil Service College and Central Provident Fund (CPF) Board. In 2012, she was commissioned by the Singapore Ministry of Manpower to study the retirement adequacy of social security in Singapore for young entrant workers using administrative data.

CHIA Siow Yue was formerly Director, Chief Executive and Professor of the Institute of Southeast Asian Studies (1996–2002); Director of the Singapore APEC Study Centre (1998–2002); founding Regional Coordinator of the East Asian Development Network (1998–2004); and Professor of Economics at the National University of Singapore (1967–1996). She obtained her BA (Honours) in Economics from the University of Malaya, Singapore and PhD in Economics from McGill University, Canada, specializing in development economics and international economics. Dr. Chia has been active in research, publication, international consultancy and training on trade and regional economic integration, international labor mobility and foreign direct investment with a focus on Singapore, ASEAN, East Asia and the Asia Pacific. Her recent publications in 2015 include: *ASEAN Economic Cooperation and* Integration (co-authored with Michael G. Plummer), Cambridge University Press; "Emerging Mega-FTAs: Rationale, Challenges and Implications" in *Asian Economic Papers*, vol. 14, no. 1; "Narrowing the Development Gap in the ASEAN Economic Community" in Mely Caballero-Anthony and Richard Barichello (eds.), *Balancing Growth for an Inclusive and Equitable ASEAN Community*. Singapore: RSIS-NTU.

Christopher GEE is Research Fellow at the Institute of Policy Studies, Lee Kuan Yew School of Public Policy, National University of Singapore where he works in the Demography and Family cluster. His research interests are focused on population-related issues, in particular housing, retirement and healthcare matters. Prior to joining IPS in April 2012, Mr. Gee worked in investment banking, analyzing the real estate sector (developers and REITs) in various markets in the Asia region from 1994 to 2012. He was rated the top Singapore analyst in the Institutional Investor surveys from 2005 to 2010. He is an independent non-executive director of CapitaLand Retail China Trust, the manager of Singapore's first and only China shopping mall REIT.

Chang Yee KWAN was with the Lee Kuan Yew School of Public Policy, National University of Singapore, where he conducted research on exchange rate management rules and regional integration in China. His research focus is largely in studying and understanding the impact of public policies, with particular interest in tax and subsidy policies, with the use of tractable economic models under monopolistic competition.

He has published on macroeconomics, international trade and public finance in several international peer-reviewed journals including the *Bulletin of Economic Research*, *Metroeconomica* and the *World Economy*. He holds a PhD and MSc in Economics respectively from the Universities of Dundee and Edinburgh, UK, and a Bachelor's degree in Business from the Nanyang Technological University, Singapore.

LEE Soo Ann is a former professor of economics and business policy in the National University of Singapore (NUS). He is the author of *Singapore: From Place to Nation* (Singapore: Pearson/Prentice-Hall, 2007) and over forty articles and chapters in various books on Singapore and development economics. Dr. Lee was the director of various business companies and seconded to the Ministry of Finance, Singapore in the late 1960s. He was a visiting scholar at Harvard and Stanford Universities. He is also the former dean of accountancy and business administration in the National University of Singapore. In November 2015, he received the Distinguished Alumni Service Award from NUS.

Linda Yuen-Ching LIM is Professor of Strategy at the Stephen M Ross School of Business at the University of Michigan, where she founded the Center for International Business Education in 1989, and directed the Center for Southeast Asian Studies from 2005–2009. Prof. Lim obtained her degrees in economics from the universities of Cambridge (BA), Yale (MA) and Michigan (PhD), and has authored, co-authored or edited four books and published over 100 other monographs, journal articles and book chapters on economic development, trade, investment, industrial policy, labor, multinational and local business in Southeast Asia. She has written extensively on the Singapore economy since 1976, with her most recent academic articles (besides those in this volume) appearing in 2014 and 2015. She has also consulted for corporations, think tanks and international development agencies, and has served on the boards of two US public companies in the tech manufacturing sector with extensive operations in Asia.

Irene Y. H. NG is an Associate Professor of Social Work and Director of the Social Service Research Centre in the National University of Singapore. She holds a joint PhD in Social Work and Economics from the University of Michigan. Her research areas include poverty and inequality, intergenerational mobility, youth crime, and social welfare policy. She is Principal Investigator of an evaluation of a national Work Support programme and Co-Principal Investigator of National Youth Surveys 2010 and 2013. She is active in the community, for instance serving in committees in the Youth Guidance Outreach Services, the Chinese Development Assistance Council, Ministry of Social and Family Development, National Council of Social Service and Ministry of Manpower. Her teaching areas include poverty, policy, youth work, and program planning.

PANG Eng Fong is Practice Professor of Strategic Management, Lee Kong Chian School of Business, Singapore Management University (SMU). Before joining SMU, he taught at the Business School in the National University of Singapore. He has been a visiting professor at the University of Michigan and Columbia. He has served also as Singapore's Ambassador/High Commissioner in Seoul, Brussels and London. Books he has written or edited include *Foreign Direct Investment and Industrialization in Malaysia, Singapore, Taiwan and Thailand* (with LYC Lim, OECD, 1991), *Regionalization and Labour Flows in Pacific Asia* (OECD, 1993), *Competing for Global Talent* (co-editor Christiane Kuptsch, ILO, 2006) and *(Almost) Uniquely Singapore: 18 Objects* (Wee Kim Wee Centre, SMU, 2013).

Sock-Yong PHANG is Vice Provost (Faculty Matters) and Professor of Economics at the Singapore Management University (SMU). She also holds the Celia Moh Professorial Chair at SMU. Professor Phang researches in the areas of housing and transport economics, focusing on the justification for and impacts of government policies on these sectors. She is the author of the recently published book *Housing Finance Systems: Market Failures and Government Failures* (Palgrave Macmillan, 2013) as well as *Housing Markets and Urban Transportation* (McGraw Hill, 1992). She has also published numerous articles on housing, transport, and public private partnerships in books and academic journals which have been widely cited. Professor Phang also serves as Commission Member of the Competition Commission of Singapore, board member of the Energy Market Authority and is also a member of the Board of Trustees of ISEAS-Yusof Ishak Institute.

TAN Kim Song is currently a faculty member at the School of Economics, Singapore Management University. Prior to joining SMU, Prof. Tan has worked in the investment banking industry, primarily in the fixed income market, and as a senior correspondent in *The Straits Times*. Prof. Tan is also involved in various businesses in the region and sits on the board of a number of companies in Singapore and in the region. He has written on various policy issues related to the development of the region. He holds a PhD in Economics from Yale University and a Bachelor of Economics (first class honours) from Adelaide University.

Peter WILSON is a former Associate Professor in Economics at the National University of Singapore where he taught from 1989 to 2007, having previously taught on Secondment in Malaysia, and Full-Time at the Universities of Warwick, Sussex, Bradford and Hull in the UK. He has been a Visiting Professor at the Faculty of Economics, Chulalongkorn University, Bangkok since 2008 and currently teaches graduate and undergraduate courses as an Adjunct at Singapore Management University. He has co-authored two books on Singapore and an Asian Edition of Mankiw's Principles of Economics (with Euston Quah) and has published in a number of scholarly journals. Since 2012 he has been a Consultant to the ASEAN+3 Macroeconomic Research Office and since 2004 to the Economic Policy Group at the Monetary Authority of Singapore where, amongst other things, he edits their bi-annual *Macroeconomic Review*. He is also a Trainer in Monetary Policy and Macroeconomic Policy at the MAS Academy.

YAP Mui Teng is Principal Research Fellow at the Institute of Policy Studies where she leads the Demography and Family Research Cluster. She is also an Associate of the Changing Family in Asia Cluster at the Asia Research Institute at the National University of Singapore. Her research interests are focused on policy responses to low fertility, migration policies, and health and social policies in aging societies. Dr. Yap has formerly worked as a statistician in the Population Planning Unit, Ministry of Health and the then Singapore Family Planning and Population Board.

Printed in the United States
By Bookmasters